Work and Cancer Su.

Michael Feuerstein

Work and Cancer Survivors

Michael Feuerstein
Uniformed Services University
 of the Health Sciences
Bethesda, MD, USA
mfeuerstein@usuhs.edu

ISBN 978-0-387-72040-1 (Hardcover)   e-ISBN 978-0-387-72041-8
ISBN 978-1-4419-8155-4 (Softcover)
DOI 10.1007/978-0-387-72041-8

Library of Congress Control Number: 2008939901

© Springer Science+Business Media, LLC 2009, First softcover printing 2011
All rights reserved. This work may not be translated or copied in whole or in part without the written permission of the publisher (Springer Science+Business Media, LLC, 233 Spring Street, New York, NY 10013, USA), except for brief excerpts for brief excerpts in connection with reviews or scholarly analysis. Use in connection with any form of information storage and retrieval, electronic adaptation, computer software, or by similar or dissimilar methodology now known or hereafter developed is forbidden.
The use in this publication of trade names, trademarks, service marks, and similar terms, even if they are not identified as such, is not to be taken as an expression of opinion as to whether or not they are subject to proprietary rights.

Printed on acid-free paper

springer.com

Work we know is both a burden and a need, both a curse and a blessing. But work is an extension of personality. It is an achievement. It is one of the ways a person defines himself or herself, measures his work and his humanity.

–Peter Drucker

Foreword

During the past decade, there has been a dramatic shift in the focus of cancer outcomes research. Five-year survival rates are no longer the gold standard; many cancers have become like other chronic diseases, where prolonged survival is common, even with repeated relapses. Success is more appropriately measured in terms of quality of life, not mortality. For most adults, work is an essential component of daily life in the developed world, a key facet of participation in society. Thus, the focus of this book is timely, and crucial, as providers and patients begin to think more broadly about life after treatment.

What can cancer researchers learn from those of us who have been studying return to work and disability prevention in musculoskeletal disorders? We bring a long tradition of theoretical and scientific development. Purely biomedical models have given way to a broader biopsychosocial view. Specific diagnoses and purely clinical measures fail to explain much of the variance in return to work outcomes. Disability is a separate condition, where motivation, skills, attitudes and outlook, employer-employee communication, accommodations, and other psychosocial factors are the primary outcome determinants. Medical interventions, at least at this point, appear to have relatively little impact compared to approaches that pursue a multidisciplinary and integrated approach, focused on case-specific barriers to return to work.

There is good evidence for efforts to improve employer responses, address patient fears and concerns, support employer-employee problem-solving about work modification, and facilitate provider-employer communication. Current investigations are now seeking to measure and predict future work capacity, avoid disability recurrence and exacerbation of symptoms by work demands and exposures, and support more effective accommodations in the workplace. These perspectives appear common to both cancer and musculoskeletal disorders. This book provides cancer researchers and practitioners with a concise, focused overview of theoretical developments and research results in our field, as well as excellent suggestions about how these results can be adapted to improve outcomes for cancer survivors.

The second half of the book addresses several challenges that may be more unique to cancer survivors. Childhood cancer treatment disrupts normal early work experiences and often leaves survivors with one or more chronic illnesses.

Without extra support, childhood cancer can result in the inability to progress in vocational development. Residual cognitive and emotional limitations, especially in persons surviving Central Nervous System tumors but other cancers as well, may not be readily obvious, but can profoundly impact work ability. Decision-making about post-treatment return to work may be challenging as well, depending on the specific cultural, legislative, benefits, and vocational milieu. Cancer-specific fears and prejudices, and reluctance of supervisors and employees to discuss the work implications of cancer, can create barriers to problem-solving. Cancer is also an illness that involves the entire family, and thus can have a significant impact on the work ability of more than just the survivor. Although rehabilitation and work reintegration services have been specifically developed for individuals with musculoskeletal, psychiatric and cardiac conditions, similar services are just now emerging for cancer survivors. Many disability compensation systems still operate on an antiquated assumption that a cancer diagnosis is equivalent to permanent and total disability.

It is in this context that this book makes a particularly important contribution. Dr. Feuerstein has done a superb job in bringing together leading researchers in cancer survivorship to present the current state of knowledge about factors affecting return to work, how return to work outcomes can be measured, and new approaches that are being developed in order to help survivors achieve their maximum potential. It represents the next logical step in the development of this field following the Institute of Medicine report. The material is authoritative, challenging, forward-looking, and well-referenced. Hopefully, this book will stimulate a new generation of researchers and will motivate practitioners to think more carefully about how they can not only treat, and often cure cancer, but also make a significant contribution to the quality of life in their patients. Significant progress in return to work in the area of work-related musculoskeletal disorders in the last few decades is very encouraging, and suggests that similar progress is just around the corner in cancer research.

Worcester, MA   Glenn Pransky

Preface

Why this book?

I am now a six year survivor of a malignant brain tumor. Just a few years ago, this would be unthinkable. Due to the very skillful management of this brain tumor by many, I am able to work. I actively manage symptoms and stay on top of my health, but this tumor can reoccur at any time. I do not take this second chance at life lightly.

I am grateful to be alive and for the wherewithal to pull this book together. The MRIs of my brain that I receive, now twice a year, indicate that the area in my cerebellum where the tumor was remains relatively tumor free, except for some dormant abnormal cells at the margins of the radiation field. Despite or because of this outcome, I am left with problems that I did not have before... episodic fatigue, "subtle" cognitive problems, blurred vision, hearing loss, and prolonged reactions to stress to name but a few. I know full well that I am a survivor of a major brain tumor. I know that brain radiation is related to residual neurosensory and cognitive problems. I am acutely aware that age can interact with these changes or even account for many of them, but all my problems as they relate to work occurred during or after treatment of my tumor. It is very clear that these symptoms impact my ability to work the way I had prior to my diagnosis and treatment.

I am also well aware there are many "survivors" that are much worse off and many who did not survive. I have had excellent heath care, great advice, and I have read almost everything that might even be remotely helpful. I have also tried many "workarounds" and accommodations and attempted to maintain a sense of "realistic optimism" needed for such resilience [1]. This is not a simple process. Despite all this information and support, I must work long hours to stay on top of work that would have taken me half the time to complete before my cancer. Clearly, this is my choice. I could have retired or slowed down, but I am now focused on a new mission in life... to help other cancer survivors.

There are many cancer survivors who similarly work at jobs with residual problems from cancer or its treatment. Also, there are many survivors of cancer who are not aware of or who cannot gain access to the opportunities that are available to optimize their ability to work. As more of us diagnosed with cancer live through the primary treatment of cancer (definition of survivor in this book), returning to as "normal" a life as possible becomes an important goal.

Work becomes a priority. The information in this book was written to help make this outcome a reality despite the symptom burden and societal barriers we may face. However, when it comes to this aspect of recovery, we must recognize that work is not always a realistic outcome. It is critical to consider each survivor's specific health, economic, and social situation in relation to work.

Returning to work is one of those aspects of life that many consider to signal a degree of normalcy and control during a period when most things are chaotic. As mentioned above, not all cancer patients can or desire to return to work during or following the diagnosis of and treatment for cancer. Some decide that it is now time to pursue another course in one's life that does not involve work. If financially feasible, some decide it is now time to retire from work altogether. Still others believe that although they want or need to work for fulfillment and/or income, they just can't make it through a full day given low energy levels, confusion, pain, or some other residual effect of the cancer and/or its treatment. Others are uncomfortable or fearful with the way they might be perceived, either appearance-wise or functionally. Some older cancer survivors who were working prior to diagnosis may desire or financially need to return to work following the bulk of treatment if possible. This group will grow in significant numbers over the next few decades as the cohort of baby boomers move into the ranks of older adults [2] and the retirement age continues to inch upward [3]. There are also those survivors who are at their peak working age [3] who desire and need to work in order to continue to provide a viable income for themselves and their family or, in the US, to make certain health care coverage is available.

Even over the past decade, much has changed regarding how we handle cancer in the workplace. Our cultural expectations have shifted along with the specificity and reduced intrusiveness of various treatments. Knowledge regarding factors related to work disability in general, and innovative approaches to assisting those with chronic illness and functional limitations, return and remain at work, have also greatly evolved over the past decade or so. Perhaps most importantly in terms of defining cancer survivorship as a public health concern is the escalation in the prevalence of survivors of many types of cancers [4]. These trends clearly justify the need for a compendium that provides a comprehensive consideration of work in cancer survivorship. This volume provides the reader with an integrated review of work in cancer survivors from research, practice, and policy perspectives. The widely publicized contribution by the Institute of Medicine [5] sensitized many to the concern of employment among cancer survivors and raised our awareness of this problem. The present volume expands that effort and addresses in more detail the epidemiology, current thinking regarding work and work disability, factors that can impact work in cancer survivors, and intervention options. Legal and policy related matters are also addressed and a global perspective is provided.

The focus we took

Topics covered in the chapters of this book were chosen to provide the reader with a perspective on work and the cancer survivor that has not been

Preface

available in the past. In section I, chapters help define several dimensions of work and cancer. Chapter 1 covers the emerging findings of relevance to the epidemiology of cancer survivorship and work to help set the stage for addressing the many dimensions of the problem covered in subsequent chapters. In chapter 2, economists known for their work on the economics of work disability related to musculoskeletal disorders provide a detailed analysis of the economic burden of cancer survivorship and work in the US. As these authors conclude, the economic burden related to cancer survivorship and work (inability to work and lost productivity) in the US alone is staggering. Work and cancer survivorship appears to be one of those world-wide public health problems that has simply been under the radar for years. While the number of cancer survivors has increased considerably [6], the economic impact of work and survivorship has been an almost unspoken consequence of the war on cancer [7–9]. It is hoped that such analyses as found in Chapter 2 will fuel efforts to better understand the many facets of this problem, improve interventions, as well as facilitate the development of evidence based policy to reduce its impact on the lives of many.

Chapter 3 shifts our attention to another aspect of burden, the perceptions of both employers and employees in relation to work and returning to work. Given the concerns of both parties it is not surprising that cancer survivors in the US workforce have more disputes related to early termination and terms and conditions such as equivalent benefits and promotions than employees with other types of impairments [10]. Clearly, not all is well at work.

Section II covers some of the basic considerations that shall guide us when it comes to work and chronic illness. I thought that readers should hear the perspective of a surgeon who made a total shift in his orientation to patients when he took a critical look at the impact of his surgery on work outcomes. Chapter 4 provides a perspective on cancer and work from an orthopedic surgeon who is now focused on an interdisciplinary approach to work disability rather than tracking down the biological root of the "problem." The author presents his persistent efforts at achieving ideal surgical outcomes or the "perfect fusion" only to observe that despite this, the approach did not have much effect on the "functional outcomes" of patients he saw, which seems somehow to be related to other non-surgical matters. He describes his own experience with the purely surgical approach to back pain and work disability that motivated him to develop and investigate innovative multidisciplinary treatments that have focused on a broader approach to the management of work disability and functional restoration. This chapter is a poignant illustration as to why it is so useful to address a broader concept of work disability as we consider the optimal approach to work reentry and work optimization in cancer survivors. We cannot simply focus on physical impairments as the exclusive factor contributing to work disability. For certain, there is a need to identify and improve the management of long-term and late health effects and their contribution to work disability in cancer survivors. However, we must also consider several other factors that can influence the ability to return and/or maintain an active work life. In short, we need a comprehensive perspective on work disability. An example of this perspective, one from someone who has focused on recovery of function from purely a biomedical perspective for years, should provide readers a reminder of the importance of an integrated approach to understanding and managing the many challenges discussed in this book. Finally, while the evidence-based developments in cancer survivorship and work will inform us as to which factors and what interventions can improve outcomes in this area, many of the work disability models that have been created for other illnesses can serve as a guiding light.

Chapter 5 provides an in-depth view of what many cancer survivors experience psychologically when faced with challenges returning to or remaining in the workplace. This level of understanding provides the reader with a deeper understanding of just what work means to many cancer survivors. This perspective argues for the need to avoid superficial or generic band-aid solutions for this problem.

Section III reviews factors that can impact return to work, work retention, and work productivity. The challenges at work experienced by survivors can perhaps be better understood from the perspective of the meaning that work has for cancer survivors. Chapter 6 covers fatigue and pain and relates these symptoms to work function. The suggestion that the areas of human factors and ergonomics can inform us of the complexities involved in work, analysis techniques, and ways to improve the human-work interface as it relates to cancer survivors is also highlighted. Chapter 7 reviews what is known presently about cognitive limitations and its rehabilitation. This is a challenging concern of cancer survivors in the workplace. The special situation related to employment and adolescent/ young cancer survivors, some who are childhood cancer survivors, is comprehensively covered in Chapter 8. This age group of survivors have experienced unique challenges related to developing careers, obtaining initial employment, shifting work places, and maintaining employment. While it is apparent that much needs to be changed to provide opportunities to this group, lessons learned with existing research in this group, particularly around late effects, can also inform us regarding symptoms and work in adult cancer survivors. While efforts have been initiated to minimize and even eliminate many of the long-term and late effects [11], it is well known among cancer survivors and some clinicians that survivors experience long-term or residual symptoms for life [12]. A greater understanding of how these symptoms impact work provides a foundation for future research, development, evaluation, and implementation of innovative interventions and policy.

Section IV includes chapters related to primary and secondary prevention of work disability in cancer survivors. The approaches included in this section involve physician practices at the front line of care, rehabilitation, accommodations at the workplace, and legal and policy related efforts to improve work outcomes. As Chapter 9 indicates, while there are simple actions providers can implement to assist in the work reentry process, very little of this information is readily available and, as such, cancer survivors receive only modest help related to work. Since cancer survivors have several opportunities to interface with health care providers, a serious consideration of just how physicians can help facilitate return to work and work retention (rather than simply indicating "when you are 'ready' to return, you can go back to work") is provided in this chapter. Chapter 9 covers research and practice related to the provision of information related to work in cancer survivors that can be directly used by primary care and occupational physicians. Attention to this element of recovery doesn't often require much beyond information and can be simple to implement, but it also has the potential to greatly impact the recovery of cancer survivors.

Chapter 10 addresses rehabilitation in the context of work. The approaches discussed consider the application of common models of disability in efforts to rehabilitate cancer survivors who are experiencing pain, fatigue, physical limitations, and/or emotional distress that can interfere with work. In the U.S. and other countries, when the cancer survivor returns to work with a documented disability that is secondary to the cancer diagnosis and/or treatment, they are entitled to reasonable accommodations (U.S.: workplace with 15 or more employees). Chapter 11 covers workplace accommodation. This approach to optimizing work in affected workers is very promising. At this point, many accommodations for cancer survivors typically do not include specific approaches to mitigate many of the concerns raised in previous chapters. This chapter provides a comprehensive consideration of options that have been used in general and to some extent in cancer survivors. Chapter 12, the final chapter in this section, addresses legal concerns that are relevant to cancer survivors in the workplace and their families. These regulations were developed to help facilitate positive outcomes regarding work and illness in general, and are applicable to cancer survivors when a limitation in function necessitates some type of employer response. Of course, the spirit of the law is often as important as the law itself. Just because a regulation exists does not mean all parties adhere to it. Also different stakeholders in this process may have different goals when considering returning to work or retaining those who are survivors of cancer. Chapter 12 provides a critical review of these laws and areas where reform can be fine-tuned and policy implemented to make these types of efforts more effective as primary prevention evidenced based policy.

Section V discusses the international perspectives of cancer survivorship and work and provides a review of both the emerging international literature in this area as well as specific programs designed to aid cancer survivors in matters related to work. It is well recognized that work disability is a global public health concern [13]. Research and interventions specific to many other countries especially the lower income countries that are becoming global partners in manufacturing, agriculture, computer-related communications, and other commercial areas need to be included in this effort. This is a first attempt to document what has transpired in certain countries where information was available. Specifically, we are seeing work coming out of the UK, the Netherlands, Denmark, Sweden, Canada, Australia, and the US, but we need information as to the status of work and cancer survivors in other countries as well. This became very clear when producing this book.

In Section VI, the final section of this book, I focus on the future. Many cancer survivors return to work and experience few problems. This book is focused on the challenges faced by those who experience work related problems, aiding heath care providers responsible for caring for them, and fostering an understanding and response at both an individual and societal level. The book addresses the basic question... how do we improve the working lives of cancer survivors and meet the needs of employers? I certainly don't profess to have the answer, but after carefully considering the information in the chapters of this book, experiencing this challenge myself as a cancer survivor, and thinking about the area of work disability for 25 years, I do have some perspective on the problem. In this final section, I consider many of the challenges covered in this book from research, practice, and policy perspectives in order to help readers integrate these areas. In this final section, I also have provided an example of the process of evidence-based policy development for those who may not be familiar with it. In order to provide a perspective on this process, not often made explicit, it is hoped that those involved in cancer survivorship and work will use this information to help transfer evidence to policy.

Each chapter in this book is written by experts in specific disciplines that can impact the working lives of cancer survivors. The reader is provided with basic evidence and thoughtful reflections in the areas of epidemiology, economics, theories of work disability, and theory and practice of work disability prevention and management. This information can impact return to work and/or work optimization in cancer survivors. The topics covered in this book will be of interest to those involved in improving efforts to assist cancer survivors with problems related to work. It should also prove useful to those involved in redesigning policies or modifying existing ones based on economic, workplace, cultural forces, and new knowledge. While we must remember that not all cancer survivors experience challenges with work, for those who do it is no longer acceptable to simply ignore this important aspect of survival.

Note: Cancer survivorship and work is an emerging area. The relevant literature is not vast. As such, authors of certain chapters cited similar studies at times. During editing, every attempt was made to reduce redundancies. However, similar citations were retained in several chapters to highlight a point in that specific chapter.

Bethesda, MD   Michael Feuerstein

References

1. Feuerstein M & Findley, P. The Cancer Survivor's Guide: The Essential Handbook to Life After Cancer. 2006. New York, NY, Avalon Publishing Group.
2. Hetzel L & Smith A. The 65 years and over population: 2000. *U.S. Census Bureau*. 2001. www.census.gov/population/www/cen2000/briefs.html
3. Gendell M. Older workers: increasing their labor force participation and hours of work. *Monthly Labor Review*. January 2008:41–54.
4. Grunfeld E. Looking beyond survival: how are we looking at survivorship? *Journal of Clinical Oncology*. 2006;24:5166–5169.
5. Hewitt M, Greenfield S, Stovall E: From Cancer Patient to Cancer Survivor: Lost in Transition. 2005. Washington, DC, The National Academies Press.
6. Welch HG, Schwartz LM, Woloshin S. Are increasing 5-year survival rates evidence of success against cancer? *Journal of the American Medical Association*. 2000;283: 2975–2978.
7. Bradley CJ, Bednarek HL, Neumark D. Breast cancer survival, work, and earnings. *Journal of Health Economics*. 2002;21:757–779.
8. Short PF, Vasey JJ, Tunceli K. Employment pathways in a large cohort of adult cancer survivors. *Cancer*. 2005;103:1292–1301.
9. Syse A, Steinar T, Kravdal O. Cancer's impact on employment and earnings-a population-based study from Norway. *Journal of Cancer Survivorship*. 2008, in press.
10. Feuerstein M, Luff GM, Harrington CB, Olsen CH. Pattern of workplace disputes in cancer survivors: a population based study of ADA claims. *Journal of Cancer Survivorship*. 2007;1:185–192.
11. Yan D, Wong J, Vicini F, Michalski J, Pan C, Frazier A, Horwitz E, Martinez A. Adaptive modification of treatment planning to minimize the deleterious effects of treatment setup errors. *International Journal of Radiation, Oncology, Biology and Physics*. 1997;38:197–206.
12. Alfano CM, Rowland JH. Recovery issues in cancer survivorship: a new challenge for supportive care. *The Cancer Journal*. 2006;12:432–443.
13. Feuerstein M. Introduction: the world challenge of work disability. *Journal of Occupational Rehabilitation*. 2005;15:451–452.

Acknowledgments

Work is one of those aspects of life that can stabilize the other dimensions of one's existence even during a major crisis such as cancer. When this pillar of normalcy cracks, crumbles or even collapses, life can change for the worse. Efforts to understand the importance of work in cancer survivorship, how to manage and ideally prevent the many problems that can impact work and efforts to help cancer survivors maximize work productivity is what this book is all about.

First I want to thank the many authors of this volume. Their commitment to the deadline and their unwavering willingness to provide overviews of critical information and new insights has made working with them an absolute pleasure. This group of authors represent experts in many disciplines related to health, disability, and work. As with most complex phenomena, an interdisciplinary focus is needed to truly address the multiple factors and rehabilitation strategies that can impact cancer survivors and work. These individuals are very experienced in their respective fields and the information they provide should inform your efforts in the laboratory, clinic, workplace, and policy arenas.

My family (Shelley, Sara, Andrew, Erica, Umang, Kiren, Maya, David and my mother Shirley), my primary source of support, need to be thanked. Their love and continuous encouragement is so important to me. They do wonder about all the time I spend on the computer on my new "mission" (i.e., cancer survivorship)! Despite their warnings, their love and support inspire me to keep going. I also would like to acknowledge my long standing colleagues at USUHS who have endured my reentry into the workplace and long-term adjustment following the diagnosis of my brain tumor: Neil Grunberg, PhD, David Krantz, PhD, Tracy Sbrocco, PhD, and Corinne Simmons. Their professional and personal interactions over these trying years mean a lot to me. My relationships with them have helped me gain a much better perspective on my cancer survivorship. They have truly helped me optimize my work experience. I also wish to thank my dear friend and colleague Glenn Pransky, MD, MOccH who has been my cheerleader and personal interpreter of all the medical and work-related concerns I have shared with him since my diagnosis. Glenn, you will never know how much you have helped me over the years.

I also want to thank Jennifer Hansen who has worked with me for the last four years. Jennifer and I conducted our first cancer survivorship study together four years ago while I was recovering from cancer. Since then I have seen her grow into a mature young scientist-practitioner. We have worked on a number of projects together including the new *Journal of Cancer Survivorship: Research and Practice* that I launched in 2007. Jennifer and Gina Luff, another research assistant at USUHS, have been very helpful in terms of all the detail required to generate this volume. For this I thank you both.

I also wish to thank Bill Tucker and Janice Stern editors at Springer in New York, with whom I have developed an excellent professional relationship with over many years. Their support and trust in my abilities has really helped move many projects to completion. Through our collaborations we will impact the lives of cancer survivors globally.

Finally, I have learned much from listening to other cancer survivors who have experienced challenges at work. When they hear that I am also "in the club" they really open up. I have heard many stories that finally motivated me to pull this book together. To these and other cancer survivors I have met and discussed work with I must thank you. This volume was generated to help you get on with your work.

Contents

Section I Defining the Problem 1

1 Epidemiology 3
   David Neary

2 Economic Burden 25
   Richard J. Butler, William G. Johnson, and Timothy Gubler

3 Employers' and Survivors' Perspectives 73
   Ziv Amir, David R. Strauser, and Fong Chan

Section II Fundamentals of Work and Chronic Illness 91

4 Work Disability: It is not just the "lesion" 93
   Patrick Loisel

5 The Meaning of Work 105
   Guy Maytal and John Peteet

Section III Factors Affecting Work 121

6 Fatigue, Pain, and Physical Function 123
   Mary E. Sesto and Maureen J. Simmonds

7 Cognitive Limitations....................................... 147
   Tracy Veramonti and Christina Meyers

8 Young Survivors of Childhood Cancer 163
   Angela de Boer, Jos Verbeek, and Frank van Dijk

Section IV Primary and Secondary Prevention 189

9 Primary and Occupational Health Care Providers............... 191
   Jos Verbeek, Angela de Boer, and Taina Taskila

10 Rehabilitation.. 211
Michael J.L. Sullivan, Maureen Simmonds, David Butler,
Shirin Shalliwani, and Mahnaz Hamidzadeh

11 Workplace Accommodations 233
Fong Chan, Elizabeth da Silva Cardoso, Jana Copeland, Robin Jones,
and Robert T. Fraser

12 Individuals with Cancer in the Workforce and Their Federal Rights... 255
Peter Blanck, William N. Myhill, Janikke Solstad Vedeler,
Joanna Morales, and Paula Pearlman

Section V Global View... 277

13 International Efforts: Perspectives, Policies, and Programs........ 279
Patricia Findley and Catherine P. Wilson

Section VI Future Directions..................................... 315

14 Future Research, Practice, and Policy 317
Michael Feuerstein

Index 331

Contributors

Ziv Amir, PhD Macmillan Research Unit, School of Nursing, Midwifery & Social Work, University Place, University of Manchester, Oxford Road, Manchester M13 9PL, UK, ziv.amir@manchester.ac.uk

Peter D. Blanck, PhD, JD Chairman, Burton Blatt Institute, Syracuse University, 900 Crouse Avenue, Crouse-Hinds Hall, Suite 300, Syracuse, New York, 13244-2130, USA, pblanck@syr.edu

David Butler, BA Welfare and Barriers to Employment, MDRC, 16 E 34th Street, New York, NY 10016, USA, david.butler@mdrc.org

Richard J. Butler, PhD Department of Economics, Brigham Young University, 183 Faculty Office Building, Provo, UT 84602-2363, USA, richard-butler@byu.edu

Elizabeth da Silva Cardoso, PhD Department of Educational Foundations, Hunter College, W 1016 695 Park Ave, New York, NY 10065, USA, ecardoso@hunter.cuny.edu

Fong Chan, PhD Department of Rehabilitation Psychology and Special Education, University of Wisconsin-Madison, Room 414, 432 N Murray St, Madison, WI 53706, USA, chan@education.wisc.edu

Jana Copeland, PhD DBTAC Rocky Mountain ADA Center, Meeting the Challenge, Inc., 3630 Sinton Road, Suite 103, Colorado Springs, CO 80907, USA, jcopeland@mfc-inc.com

Angela de Boer, PhD Coronel Institute for Occupational Health, AMC/Academic Medical Centre, Meibergdreef 9/K0-105, 1105 AZ Amsterdam, The Netherlands, a.g.deboer@amc.uva.nl

Michael Feuerstein, PhD., MPH, ABPP Departments of Medical and Clinical Psychology, and Preventive Medicine and Biometrics, Uniformed Services University of the Health Sciences 4301 Jones Bridge Rd., Bethesda MD 20814-4799, USA, mfeuerstein@usuhs.edu

Patricia A. Findley, DrPH, MSW, LCSW Rutgers University, School of Social Work, 536 George Street, New Brunswick, NJ 08901, USA, pfindley@ssw.rutgers.edu

Robert T. Fraser, PhD Neurology, Neurological Surgery, & Rehabilitation Medicine, Harborview Medical Center, 325 9th Ave, Seattle, WA 98104, USA, rfraser@u.washington.edu

Timothy Gubler, PhD Department of Economics, Brigham Young University, 183 Faculty Office Building, Provo, UT 84602-2363, USA, timgub@gmail.com

Mahnaz Hamidzadeh, PT School of Physical and Occupational Therapy, McGill University, 1745 Cedar Ave. Apt 409, Montreal, Quebec, H3G1A7, Canada, mahnaz.hamidzadeh@mail.mcgill.ca

William G. Johnson, PhD Department of Biomedical Informatics, Director, Center for Health Information & Rescarch, School of Computing and Informatics, Ira A. Fulton School of Engineering, Arizona State University, P.O. Box 878809, Tempe, AZ 85287 – 8809, USA, william.g.johnson@asu.edu

Robin Jones, PhD DBTAC: Great Lakes ADA Center, Department of Disability and Human Development, University of Illinois at Chicago, 1640 W. Roosevelt Road, Chicago, IL 60608, USA, guiness@uic.edu

Patrick Loisel, MD Faculty of Medicine and Health Sciences, Université de Sherbrooke, 1111 St-Charles Ouest, Tour ouest, bureau 500, Longueuil, Québec, Canada, J4K 5G4, patrick.loisel@usherbrooke.ca

Guy Maytal, MD Staff Psychiatrist on the Palliative Care Team, Massachusetts General Hospital, Wang ACC 812, 15 Parkman Street, Boston, MA 02114, USA, gmaytal@partners.org

Christina A. Meyers, PhD., ABPP Section of Neuropsychology, Department of Neuro-Oncology, Unit 431, M.D. Anderson Cancer Center, P.O. Box 301402, Houston, TX 77230-1402, USA, cameyers@mdanderson.org

Joanna Morales, JD Cancer Legal Resource Center, a joint program of Loyola Law School and the Disability Rights Legal Center, Adjunct Professor of Law, Loyola Law School, 919 Albany St. (Founders Hall, Rm. 214), Los Angeles, CA 90015-0019, USA, Joanna.morales@lls.edu

William N. Myhill, Med, JD BBI, Adjunct Professor of Law, Syracuse University, 446 College of Law, Syracuse, New York 13244, USA, wmyhill@syr.edu

David Neary, PhD Centre for Public Health at Liverpool John Moores University, Centre for Public Health, Castle House, 4 North Street, Liverpool L3 2AY, D.Neary@ljmu.ac.uk

Contributors

Paula Pearlman, JD Disability Rights Legal Center, Associate Clinical Professor of Law, Loyola Law School, Disability Rights Legal Center, 919 Albany Street, FH214, Los Angeles, CA 90015, Paula.pearlman@lls.edu

John R. Peteet, MD, USA Harvard University Medical School, Brigham and Women's Hospital, Psychiatry, 75 Francis St, Boston, MA 02115, USA, jpeteet@partners.org

Mary Sesto, PT, PhD Orthopedics and Rehabilitation, University of Wisconsin, 4176 Medical Sciences Center, 1300 University Ave, Madison, WI 53706, USA, msesto@facstaff.ulsc.edu

Maureen Simmonds, PhD, PT School of Physical and Occupational Therapy, McGill University, Davis House, 3654 Promenade Sir William Osler, Montreal, Quebec, Canada, H3G 1Y5, maureen.simmonds@mcgill.ca

Shirin Shalliwani, BSc, PT School of Physical and Occupational Therapy, McGill University, 4581 Anderson Crescent, Pierrefonds, Quebec, Canada, H9A 2W6, shirin.shallwani@mail.mcgill.ca

David R. Strauser, PhD Department of Kinesiology and Community Health, University of Illinois, 116 Huff Hall MC-588, 1206 South Fourth Street, Champaign, IL 61820, USA, strauser@uiuc.edu

Michael Sullivan, PhD Departments of Psychology, Medicine and Neuroscience, Canada Research Chair in Behavioural Health, McGill University, 1205 Docteur Penfield, Montreal, Quebec, Canada, H3A 1B1, michael.sullivan@mcgill.ca

Taina Taskila, PhD The University of Birmingham, Department of Primary Care and General Practice, Primary Care Clinical Sciences Building, Edgbaston, Birmingham B15 2TT, UK, k.taskila@bham.ac.uk

Frank van Dijk Coronel Institute of Occupational Health, Academic Medical Center, PO Box 22700, 1100 DE Amsterdam, The Netherlands, fij.vandijk@amc.nl

Janikke Solstad Vedeler, MS Syracuse Univeristy, Research Associate, Norwegian Social Research, Munthesgate 29, 0260 Oslo, Norway, jsv@nova.no

Tracy L. Veramonti, PhD Department of Neuro-Oncology, Unit 431, University of Texas M.D. Anderson Cancer Center, P.O. Box 301402, Houston, TX 77230-1402, USA, tlveramo@mdanderson.org

Jos Verbeek MD PhD Finish Institute of Occupational Health, Center of Good Practices, Knowledge Transfer Team, Cochrane Occupational Health Field, PO 93, 70701, Kuopio, Finland, jos.verbeek@ttl.fi

Catherine P. Wilson Rutgers University, School of Social Work, 536 George Street, New Brunswick, NJ 08901, USA, cpwcasa@pegasus.rutgers.edu

Section I
Defining the Problem

Chapter 1
Epidemiology

David Neary

Introduction

The number of cancer survivors around the world is increasing due to continuing improvements in diagnosis and treatment that are allowing more people to hopefully lead full and happy lives. Both now and in the future, millions of people who would previously have died because of cancer are going to survive and a sizeable proportion of them are going to want, and be able, to return to their working lives. Cancer survivorship is a potentially broad concept [1] that can include individuals who have been diagnosed but not yet started treatment to people who have completed their treatment and have been disease-free for five or more years. For the purposes of this chapter, the focus will be on survivors after they have completed their primary treatment.

The impact of cancer on survivors and their working lives is complex and dependent on a large number of factors that provide challenges to individual survivors, their families, work organisations, and the social welfare provisions of societies around the world. We are only beginning to address and understand them. The focus of this chapter will be on paid work, indeed usually on paid employment in the market economy, but it is important to acknowledge that a cancer diagnosis will have a considerable impact on the vast amount of unpaid work that necessarily takes place in all societies. This unpaid work, such as the care giving in households that is often performed by women, is the vital aspect of societies with a market economy but has yet to be systematically researched.

This chapter sets the scene by providing a brief overview of the scale of cancer survivorship on a global and regional scale by presenting data on the incidence, mortality, and prevalence of cancer. Although there are severe limitations in the existing data, it is important to grasp the contemporary

---

D. Neary (✉)
Public Health Researcher, Centre for Public Health at Liverpool John Moores University, Centre for Public Health, Castle House, 4 North Street, Liverpool L3 2AY, UK
e-mail: D.Neary@ljmu.ac.uk

position and to consider the future trends in cancer incidence. This is followed by a brief history of research in the area of cancer survivorship and work from the pioneering work in the USA in the 1970s to an outline of two reviews published in recent years. Although there are limitations to research in this area, there follows a thematic review of the growing literature on this topic to provide a summary of the state of knowledge. Finally, the gaps in our knowledge are briefly presented to provide possible avenues for future research.

The Scale of Cancer Survivorship

At a global level, the incidence of 26 cancers in 2002 was estimated at 10.9 million new cases by the GLOBOCAN series of the International Agency for Research on Cancer. The incidence of cancer is age-related with older people, for example those over the age of 65, are far more likely to receive a cancer diagnosis than younger people. In terms of incidence by site, lung cancer was the most common with 1.35 million new cases, followed by breast cancer with 1.15 million cases and colorectal cancer with 1.02 million people diagnosed. In terms of mortality, lung cancer was also the most common cause of death with 1.18 million cases followed by cancer of the stomach with 700,000 and of the liver with 598,000 [2] (Table 1.1).

In terms of prevalence (number of people alive with cancer at a particular point in time) there is no clear agreement on how this should be defined. For statistical purposes, survival up to five years after diagnosis is a widely used benchmark because of its association with cure and long-term survivorship. According to this measure there were an estimated 24.6 million people living with cancer in 2002. The most prevalent sites were breast with just over 4.4 million survivors followed by colorectal with 2.83 million and prostate with 2.4 million (Table 1.2).

Globally, the incidence of cancer is higher in the developed world, due mainly to demographic and lifestyle factors, although the developing world is experiencing an increase in cancer incidence. Survival rates are higher in economically developed regions than in the developing world although Eastern Europe is an exception [2] and there are a large range of variations within developed areas such as Western Europe [3] and the USA [4]. It is important to recognise that the figures from GLOBOCAN are estimates that are based on a mixture of actual data, extrapolations from limited samples, and informed guesses, but they are the most reliable available information. Looking to the future, the scale of global cancer incidence is forecast to increase from approximately 10 million cases in 2000 to about 15 million in 2020 due to demography, the level of tobacco consumption, and other risk factors [5]. Looking even further ahead, it has been estimated that the incidence of cancer could approach 70 million new cases by 2050 [6].

1 Epidemiology

Table 1.1 Global incidence and mortality by gender and cancer site, 2002

	Incidence		Mortality	
	Males Cases	Females Cases	Males Cases	Females Cases
Oral cavity	175,916	98,373	80,736	46,723
Nasopharynx	55,796	24,247	34,913	15,419
Other pharynx	106,219	24,077	67,964	16,029
Esophagus	315,394	146,723	261,162	124,730
Stomach	603,419	330,518	446,052	254,297
Colon/rectum	550,465	472,687	278,446	250,532
Liver	442,119	184,043	416,882	181,439
Pancreas	124,841	107,465	119,544	107,479
Larynx	139,230	20,011	78,629	11,327
Lung	965,241	386,891	848,132	330,786
Melanoma of skin	79,043	81,134	21,952	18,829
Breast	–	1,151,298	–	410,712
Cervix uteri	–	493,243	–	273,505
Corpus uteri	–	198,783	–	50,327
Ovary	–	204,499	–	124,860
Prostate	679,023	–	221,002	–
Testis	48,613	–	8,878	–
Kidney	139,223	79,257	62,696	39,199
Bladder	273,858	82,699	108,310	36,699
Brain, nervous system	108,221	81,264	80,034	61,616
Thyroid	37,424	103,589	11,297	24,078
Non-Hodgkin lymphoma	175,123	125,448	98,865	72,955
Hodgkin disease	38,218	24,111	14,460	8,352
Multiple myeloma	46,512	39,192	32,696	29,839
Leukaemia	171,037	129,485	125,142	97,364
All sites but skin	5,801,839	5,060,657	3,795,991	2,927,896

Adapted with permission from Parkin et al., Global Cancer Statistics, 2002, Table 1

Table 1.2 Prevalence of cancer survivors by site (selected)

	Males (000s)	Females (000s)	Total (000s)
Breast	–	4,408	4,408
Colon/Rectum	1,515	1,315	2,830
Prostate	2,369	–	2,369
Stomach	951	522	1,473
Cervix uteri	–	1410	1,410
Lung	939	423	1,362
Bladder	860	250	1,110
Corpus uteri	–	775	775
Non-Hodgkin Lymphoma	427	324	751
Oral cavity	467	274	741

Adapted with permission from Parkin et al., Global Cancer Statistics, 2002, Figure 3

At a regional level in the developed world, there are slightly more reliable statistics from cancer registry data across Europe and the USA. Across 39 European states there were an estimated 3,191,600 new cases diagnosed in 2006 with breast cancer being the most common with 429,900 people, followed by colorectal (412,900) and lung cancer (386,300). In terms of mortality, lung (334,800), colorectal (207,400), breast (131,900), and stomach cancer (118,200) were the most common causes of death from cancer across Europe [3]. In the USA, an estimated 1,437,180 new cancer cases are forecast for 2008 along with 565,650 deaths as mortality rates continue to decline [4]. The overall survival rate for people under the age of 65, a proxy for working age adults, was 70.6% and was 77.2% for people under the age of 45 who could be considered to be in the prime of their working lives [7]. There are no accurate and reliable statistics published for the incidence, mortality, and prevalence of cancer among people in employment at either a global or regional level although it is apparent from the data that we currently have that returning to paid work and remaining at work is a concern for millions of cancer survivors now and their numbers are certain to increase in the future.

The Impact of Cancer on Paid Work

The American Pioneers

The impact of cancer on paid work has been an issue for research since at least 1973, when Robert McKenna in his capacity as President of the American Cancer Society, declared that enabling a cancer patient to return to work after treatment was a joint responsibility of all society [8]. Following McKenna's initial work, Frances Feldman conducted three studies in California that examined the experiences of white and blue-collar workers and young people that were published in 1976 [9], 1978 [10], and 1980 [11]. All three studies showed high rates of returning to work after cancer but highlighted two main categories of difficulties for cancer survivors. The first set of difficulties related to disease and treatment-related issues, such as fatigue and loss of strength, while the second set of difficulties revolved around the workplace and included issues with health insurance and the attitudes of co-workers and managers leading to job discrimination. This work in the USA set the template for research on this topic although these issues were shaped by a social welfare system which provided sharp incentives for cancer patients to return to work as quickly as possible due to a lack of financial protection and a pivotal relationship between employment and health insurance [12]. It is therefore vital that the position of cancer survivors in relation to paid work is seen in the wider context of the prevailing social welfare arrangements for access to health care, financial protection due to ill health through disability benefits, or retirement provision and the legal framework for protection from discrimination in the workplace. These provisions vary considerably across countries and an acknowledgement of these differences is essential if we are to more fully understand cancer survivorship and paid work.

The Literature Reviews of Studies

With improvements in diagnosis and treatment leading to higher survival rates in most of the developed world in the 1990s, there was increased interest in the issues around cancer survivors returning to paid work. This led to a review by Spelten and colleagues [13] that covered 14 studies conducted between 1985 and 1999 on this topic. Spelten and colleagues adopted a systematic approach for their review based on the World Health Organisation's disability model that categorised issues into work-related, disease- or treatment-related, and person-related factors. The results of this review indicated that a positive attitude from co-workers and having discretion over the amount of work or the number of work hours appeared to facilitate individuals returning to work. However, most work-related factors, such as physically demanding manual labour and the pace of work, were also a hindrance to returning to work. The evidence relating to disease and treatment-related factors found that only the number of months since the end of treatment was positively associated with returning to work. There were mixed results for factors such as disease stage and cancer site although survivors of testicular cancer reported relatively few difficulties compared to people with other cancer types. For person-related factors, mobilising social support appeared to help people to return to work but for other factors such as age and education the results were either mixed or negative. Overall, Spelten and colleagues were critical of the return to work research of this period both in terms of its quantity and quality. The 14 studies all suffered from methodological weaknesses such as small samples, non-standardised study-specific research instruments, cross-sectional rather than longitudinal design, and a lack of statistical testing of results. In their view, what was needed for future research was a prospective design with a distinction between work-related, disease- and treatment-related, and person-related factors. This would also require standardised measures to allow for more reliable and valid assessment of variables and the development of a model of the factors and inter-relationships that affect return to work behaviour. Finally, they called for cancer registries to record more information on the working status of patients so that the prevalence of cancer in the working population could be accurately measured.

A second review by Steiner and colleagues [14] published in 2004 used six methodological criteria to evaluate studies of the impact of cancer on paid work. The first criteria for inclusion began with enrolment of a population-based sample of cancer survivors from a cancer registry to help avoid selection bias. Second, a longitudinal assessment of a cohort of cancer survivors beginning diagnosis and initial treatment as soon as possible in order to assess both the short- and long-term impact of cancer on work would be ideal. Third, there should be scope for comparisons between cancer survivors and a cohort of people without cancer so that the impact of cancer can be distinguished from other factors such as age, other health conditions and the overall state of the labour market. The fourth criteria included a detailed assessment of work intensity, role, and content in order to measure the complex and varied nature of paid work. Simply reporting the proportion of survivors who return to some type of paid work is a single measure that tells us nothing about the amount of work or the cognitive and physical demands placed upon survivors. Fifth, moderators of work return and work function such as cancer site, treatment modalities, individual characteristics such as age, co-morbidities, family structure, and the availability of health insurance, all might be included. Finally, the sample size of any study should be sufficient to allow multivariate analysis and have a sufficient number of survivors for a range of sub-groups such as gender, cancer site or stage, and ethnicity. Steiner and colleagues identified 18 studies that were published between 1975 and 2003 that met at least one of the necessary criteria. Seven studies had been published since 1999, the end point for Spelten and colleagues' review, indicating the increasing interest in this area of research.

There was not a single study that met all of the outlined criteria and only four that satisfied even four of them, indicating the methodological limitations of knowledge in this area. Of these four studies [15–18], three were from the United States (two used data from Detroit) and one was from the Netherlands but each had relatively small sample sizes ranging from 235 to 296 survivors. The findings from these studies are difficult to summarise because they used different sets of measures but physical symptoms were important predictors of work return and work function. It was also found that functional limitations and cancer site were also consistently predictive of subsequent work outcomes. Steiner and colleagues were similarly critical of the methodological quality of the research in this area and outlined the research needs according to the six criteria. They also suggested a conceptual model to guide future research by providing a comprehensive assessment of the influences on work after cancer (Fig. 1.1).

Steiner and colleagues also called for practical work-related interventions to be developed and evaluated so that optimal work outcomes could be achieved for cancer survivors. From a wider social and economic perspective, an optimal work outcome may well involve returning to work but future research should take into account the possibility that for some individuals this will not be the case. Cancer and paid work must be assessed in the context of individual's priorities and values rather than relying on social or economic metrics.

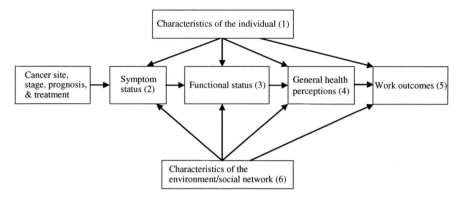

Fig. 1.1 Relationship between cancer, quality of life, and work outcomes
(1) Socio-demographic characteristics, personal goals and values, baseline physical and mental co-morbidities, and perceived importance of work.
(2) Examples include presence or absence of fatigue, pain, and dyspnea.
(3) Includes presence or absence of various physical and mental health limitations.
(4) Includes self-rating of overall health, among other self-perceptions.
(5) Includes working, work intensity, changes to job schedule and work status, work role and content including change in employer, work type, productivity, job satisfaction, value of work, and ability to change job.
(6) Includes social support, presence or absence of dependents, and need to maintain health insurance.
Source: Steiner et al., 2004.

A Thematic Review of the Literature

There should be no doubt that there are important methodological limitations in the research on cancer and paid work. However, despite these limitations there are a number of important themes that have emerged from this growing body of work. The aim here is to offer an accessible summary of the state of knowledge in this area for a wide range of readers by providing a thematic overview rather than repeating the reviewing exercises that have been outlined.

Most Cancer Survivors Are Able to Return to Work

Numerous studies conducted since the year 2000 have shown high return to work rates for cancer survivors. From the United States, Bradley and Bednarek [15] found that 67% of the 141 cancer survivors in their sample from metropolitan Detroit who were employed at the time of their diagnosis were still in full time employment some five to seven years later. Their results suggested that there was good reason to be optimistic about the ability of cancer survivors to return and thrive in the labour market. Short and colleagues' [19] study in

Pennsylvania and Maryland found that the return to work rate for 1433 survivors increased from 43% between diagnosis and five months, to 73% after six to eleven months, to 84% after thirty-six to forty-seven months. Once again, these results suggest that there are grounds to be optimistic about the ability of survivors to return to work. Bouknight and colleagues' [20] study of breast cancer survivors in Detroit also found a high rate of returning to work with only 18% not working twelve months after diagnosis which can be considered as encouraging. Sanchez and colleagues [21], in their study of colorectal survivors in Los Angeles, found that 89% returned to work and 80% of this group were still working five years later. In Quebec, Canada, Maunsell and colleagues' [22] study of breast cancer survivors found that 21% of them were not working three years after diagnosis compared to 15% of a comparable cancer-free sample of women. Once again, this provides solid evidence that most breast cancer survivors are able to return to work. Spelten and colleagues [18], in their study in the Netherlands, also found an upward trend in the proportion of survivors who were able to return to work from 25% at six months after diagnosis to 64% at 18 months. In their study in Norway, Gudbergsson and colleagues [23] found no significant differences in the labour market position of 430 breast, prostate, and testicular cancer survivors and an appropriate control group. Across numerous advanced industrial countries around the world there is every reason to be optimistic about the ability of cancer survivors to recover and return to work.

The Importance of Cancer Site to Return to Work

The term cancer describes a heterogeneous group of diagnoses with a variety of treatment regimes and a range of prognoses in terms of survival rates. So while there are good grounds to be more optimistic now than in the past about cancer survivors being able to return to work, there are significant variations by cancer site. This variation has been known to be an important factor in returning to work since the pioneering research of Feldman [9–11] in the late 1970s. The extent of the variation varies between studies, but one of the largest samples to measure this variation was Taskila-Abrandt and colleagues' [24] study of all working age cancer survivors in Finland known to be alive on December 31st 1997. Overall, they found that 50% of cancer survivors were employed compared to 55% of appropriately age and gender-matched referents. However, there was considerable variation between different sites with lung, multiple myeloma, and cancer of the nervous system survivors having a much lower likelihood of being employed. Encouragingly, the most prevalent cancer sites – breast, female and male genital organs, and urinary – had employment rates that were only slightly below the norm for the referents (Table 1.3).

It is likely that there will continue to be considerable variation in the ability of survivors to return to work because of the differing prognoses and cancer

Table 1.3 Employment of cancer survivors with age and gender matched referents

	Number	% of cancer survivors employed	% of referents employed	Relative risk
All cancer sites	46,312	50	55	0.91 (0.90–0.92)
Head & neck	1,823	43	51	0.80 (0.74–0.86)
Digestive organs	4,051	45	50	0.90 (0.85–0.94)
Female genital organs	5,105	48	52	0.93 (0.89–0.97)
Urinary & male genital organs	4,558	44	48	0.92 (0.88–0.96)
Skin	3,997	60	56	1.07 (1.03–1.11)
Sarcomas	1,122	52	59	0.87 (0.81–0.94)
Lymphomas	3,791	51	59	0.87 (0.83–0.90)
Lung	934	29	46	0.63 (0.56–0.71)
Breast	13,086	54	56	0.96 (0.94–0.98)
Nervous system	3,667	43	60	0.72 (0.69–0.75)
Thyroid gland	2,840	63	64	0.99 (0.95–1.02)
Multiple myeloma	269	32	48	0.67 (0.54–0.83)

Source: Taskila-Abrandt et al., 2005

survivorship challenges for different forms of cancer. However, for the vast majority of people who receive a cancer diagnosis during their working lives, there is still hope and evidence that they could return to work.

The Impact of Treatment and Symptom Burden Matters

Treatment for cancer varies according to the site and stage of the disease and may involve surgery, chemotherapy, radiotherapy, and hormone treatment either singly or in combination. The impact of treatment on an individual's health can be significant as it can induce fatigue and a range of other physical symptoms such as nausea and sleep disturbance. Diagnosis and treatment can also influence an individual's mental well-being by inducing anxiety or depression and there can also be effects on a person's cognitive ability and therefore their ability to function in the workplace at the same level prior to their diagnosis. The treatment regime that patients undergo and the ensuing symptoms that survivors endure play an important part in individuals feeling able to return to work.

Satariano and DeLorenze [17], in their study of women with breast cancer, found that limitations in upper body strength and fatigue were important factors that inhibited survivors' ability to return to work. Spelten and colleagues [18] explored a range of cancer/treatment-related factors, such as sleep problems and physical complaints, in their prospective study in the Netherlands and came to the view that it was difficult to disentangle the relationship between these individual factors and returning to work. The more general complaint of fatigue, a component of many cancer/treatment-related symptoms, provided a more suitable concept to address as they found that the risk of staying off work for a prolonged period was 2.5 times greater for survivors who felt very tired for most of the time after treatment when compared to those who did not experience such a level of fatigue.

Sanchez and colleagues [21] found that colorectal survivors who experienced debilitating effects from chemotherapy were more likely to require a prolonged period of sickness absence compared to those who did not have chemotherapy. Similarly, Bradley and colleagues [25] found a strong relationship between the length of absence from work and the stage of diagnosis that affected treatment regimes amongst breast and prostate cancer survivors. Those who were diagnosed at a later stage were more likely to undergo surgery, chemotherapy, and radiotherapy which lead to an average sickness absence of 68 days for breast cancer survivors and 40 days for prostate cancer survivors. Those who were diagnosed at an earlier stage in the disease were less likely to experience such invasive and prolonged treatment and consequently had much shorter periods of sickness absence. The average sickness absence of breast cancer survivors who had only surgical treatment was only 26 days while for prostate survivors who had only radiotherapy, it was only nine days of sickness absence. The negative effects of chemotherapy on survivors' ability to work were also found by Taskila and colleagues [26] in a study of 591 Finnish survivors of lymphoma, breast, prostate, and testicular cancers. They found that men and women who had chemotherapy had more than twice the risk of having impaired physical work ability than those who had undergone other treatments.

There have been significant advances in treatment regimes, particularly developments in chemotherapy, over the last 20 years that have contributed to increases in survival rates. Reducing the side effects of treatments, better screening programmes so that the disease is diagnosed at an early stage, and clear guidelines for the management of fatigue should all contribute to improving the ability of survivors to return to work.

Educational Attainment and Occupational Status also Matter

While cancer site, treatment regimes, and their associated symptom burden all influence the ability of cancer survivors to return to work, there are other factors such as educational attainment and occupation, which modify these effects. Taskila-Abrandt and colleagues [27] conducted a large-scale study in Finland that covered all 12,312 new cases of cancer diagnosed during 1987–1988 and 1992–1993 for people between the ages of 15 and 60 years who were known to be alive on December 31, 1990 and 1995 respectively. They matched this sample of cancer survivors with an appropriate control group and found that before diagnosis the employment rate for both groups was 78%. Two to three years after diagnosis, the employment rate for all cancer survivors was 64% compared to 73% for the cancer-free control group. There were variations in employment rate between cancer site with a lower probability of

Table 1.4 Employment rate and Relative Risk of being employed by cancer type 2–3 years after diagnosis with their referents

	Number	Percentage of cancer survivors employed	Percentage of referents employed	Relative risk (95% CI)
Stomach	284	38	54	0.71 (0.59–0.85)
Colon	538	53	59	0.90 (0.81–0.99)
Rectum	331	43	54	0.79 (0.68–0.93)
Cervix uteri	183	58	75	0.77 (0.67–0.90)
Corpus uteri	548	42	51	0.84 (0.74–0.95)
Ovary	534	54	65	0.83 (0.75–0.92)
Prostate	240	30	34	0.87 (0.67–1.13)
Testis	206	72	69	1.02 (0.93–1.19)
Kidney	404	50	55	0.91 (0.80–1.04)
Bladder	364	47	57	0.82 (0.72–0.95)
Melanoma of the skin	853	68	66	1.03 (0.97–1.11)
Non-melanoma of the skin	203	56	53	1.06 (0.88–1.26)
Leukaemia	222	45	64	0.70 (0.59–0.84)
Non-Hodgkin's lymphoma	411	49	66	0.75 (0.66–0.84)
Hodgkin's disease	269	64	65	0.98 (0.87–1.11)
Lung	279	19	43	0.45 (0.34–0.59)
Breast	4098	61	65	0.95 (0.92–0.98)
Nervous system	878	45	69	0.66 (0.61–0.71)
Thyroid gland	629	70	70	1.01 (0.94–1.08)

Source: Taskila-Abrandt et al., 2004

being employed for people who had been diagnosed with lung and stomach cancer. People with leukaemia and cancer of the nervous system were also less likely to be employed than their referents. Again, breast cancer survivors, the most prevalent single group, had a similar employment rate to their referents which is encouraging (Table 1.4).

As well as variation by cancer site, Taskila-Abrandt and colleagues also found that there were variations by occupation. In potentially physically demanding occupations such as agriculture, forestry, fishery, transport, communications, manufacturing, and services cancer survivors had an 18–20% lower probability of being employed than their referents. By contrast, survivors who worked in administrative, clerical, managerial, technical, humanistic, and artistic work had only a 7% lower probability of being employed. The level of educational achievement also had a modifying effect on the employment rates of survivors. Survivors who had only primary education were 19% less likely to be employed than their referents whereas those who had completed vocational or professional school were 12% less likely to be employed. Amongst survivors who had received university education, there were no statistically significant differences in employment regardless of cancer site with the exception of cancers of the nervous system.

The impact of educational attainment and occupational status on the rate of survivors returning to work has also been noted in other studies. Short and colleagues [19] found that cancer survivors who had post-graduate education were less likely to quit working than any other educational group. Bouknight and colleagues' [20] study of breast cancer survivors in Detroit found that women without a high school diploma who also had a lower annual household income were significantly less likely to return to work than women with a college degree who were employed in higher earning white collar occupations. This stark reality for survivors with lower income levels was also found by Choi and colleagues [28] in their prospective cohort study of 305 Korean men with stomach, liver, or colorectal cancer. They found that the risk of job loss, and 53% of the sample lost their job over the 24 months period of the study, was associated with older, less educated, lower income survivors in non-sedentary (physically demanding) occupations.

There are particularly severe difficulties for survivors around the world, who have a lower level of educational attainment that is often associated with a physically demanding job when it comes to returning to work. This appears to be inevitable, given that manual labour continues to be part of the operation of many work organisations, but there is often scope for accommodations and adjustments in the workplace that allow cancer survivors to remain economically active. This raises questions about the health status of cancer survivors and the extent of work limitations that they experience that need to be explored in more depth.

The Health Status and Extent of Work Limitations Among Cancer Survivors

Survivors can make a complete recovery and be able to resume their working lives without any lasting effects from their cancer or treatment. Some survivors may be unable to return to work or choose to leave the labour market for retirement as their priorities in life change. Between these two groups are those survivors who are able to return to work but experience the effects of cancer as a chronic disease that has damaged their health and inflicts work limitations upon them. It is this group who have survived their cancer but not fully recovered their health and work capacity that is the focus of this section.

Hewitt and colleagues [29] examined the health status of 4,878 survivors who had been diagnosed from less than two to more than twenty years ago compared to 90,737 people without a history of cancer. They found that nearly 30% of survivors reported being in poor or fair health compared to 10% of people without a history of cancer. Those most likely to report being in poor or fair health were survivors of lung and respiratory cancers, leukaemia, and lymphoma. Survivors had higher rates of other chronic illnesses such as asthma, diabetes, kidney, liver, and heart diseases than the cancer-free group. They calculated that having a history of cancer at least doubled the likelihood of poor health and when this was coupled with another chronic disease, the risk increased by a magnitude of five to ten times compared to the cancer-free group. In terms of work limitations, nearly 17% of survivors reported being unable to work compared to only 5% of the cancer-free group. A further 7% of survivors were able to work but with some physical or mental limitations compared to 3% of people without a history of cancer. These findings are stark but need to be treated cautiously because of the cross-sectional nature of the research that precludes simply inferring causal associations between having a history of cancer and poor health.

Yabroff and colleagues [30] used the National Heath Interview Survey in the USA to compare 1823 survivors with 5469 suitably age, gender, and educational attainment matched referents. The survivors were a diverse group in terms of cancer site and time since diagnosis with a range of less than a year to more than 11 years since their diagnosis. They found that 18% of survivors were unable to work because of health problems compared to 10% of the control group and 27% of survivors reported experiencing work limitations compared to 17% of referents. While the burden of illness was greatest for survivors in the first year after diagnosis, there were still statistically significant differences in lost productivity and health limitations among survivors who were well beyond five years of their diagnosis. Once again, these findings appear to indicate the greater difficulties that cancer survivors face in the workplace over a prolonged period but this was a cross-sectional study that provides a snapshot of the situation rather than a prospective longitudinal study that follows survivors over time following diagnosis.

Short and colleagues [19], in their study of 1433 survivors in Pennsylvania and Maryland, found that 21% of females and 16% of men who were working at the time of their diagnosis reported work limitations that they attributed to their cancer and treatment. Of this group of survivors who reported work limitations, just over half were still working but the remainder had quit. In a further study, Short and colleagues [31] compared the work disability of 647 survivors in the age range of 55–65 years old with 5988 similarly aged cancer-free people, some of whom had other chronic illnesses, from the Health and Retirement Study. The sample of survivors had been diagnosed between two and six years earlier (average 46 months) with a range of cancer sites, with breast and prostate the most common. They found that 30% of survivors reported some work disability, which was three times higher than for disease-free adults, and that just over half of this group attributed this to their cancer diagnosis and treatment. Encouragingly, the work disability rate for cancer survivors was lower than for people with other chronic diseases such as diabetes, chronic lung or heart disease, stroke, and arthritis/rheumatism. However, survivors who had a cancer recurrence or also had a co-morbid chronic condition had much higher rates of work disability.

A recent prospective longitudinal cohort study by Bradley and colleagues [32] explored the experiences of 496 female breast cancer and 294 male prostate cancer survivors over a period of 18 months from diagnosis with a control group of more than 300 people. They found that the employment rate for women was 17% lower than the control group after six months but were similar after 12 and 18 months. However, women reduced their workload by an average of seven hours per week and those women with health insurance through their spouse were more likely to reduce their working hours or to quit their job than women who did not have this form of access to health care. In terms of work limitations 12 months after diagnosis, 49% of the women whose work involved physical effort and 62% of the women whose work required heavy lifting reported experiencing difficulties. The extent of cognitive work limitations was lower with 31% reporting difficulties with concentration and 28% with analysis in the workplace. There was a similar pattern for the employment rate of the male survivors, which was 10% lower than the control group at six months but similar after 12 and 18 months. Men reduced their workload by an average of 3.3 hours per week and were more likely to retire than the women affected by breast cancer and the control group. The prevalence and rate of work limitations 12 months after diagnosis was lower for men, with 30% of men whose work involved heavy lifting experiencing difficulties. For cognitive work limitations, fewer men reported difficulties with concentration (12%) and analysis (9%) than women. The findings from this type of study show the changing dynamics for survivors in the labour market with regard to employment rate and work limitations. All of these studies have indicated the position of cancer survivors in the United States but there is also a need to explore the situation elsewhere in the world.

Gudbergsson and colleagues [23], in their study of breast, prostate, and testicular cancer survivors, have explored the position in Norway. They compared the position of 430 survivors, who were between two and six years after diagnosis, with 596 control subjects and encouragingly found no significant differences in their employment rate, working hours, living standards, or level of social participation. However, survivors reported having significantly more co-morbid diseases and significantly worse subjective health status along with higher somatic symptom levels than their controls. In terms of physical and mental work limitations, there were statistically significant differences for both male and female survivors compared to their controls. These findings suggest that survivors were able to return to work but were experiencing health difficulties and work limitations that might affect their ability to maintain their position in the labour market until the normal retirement age of 67. However, this would require a longitudinal study that would track the health status and labour market position of survivors over a period of many years.

Taskila and colleagues [26], in their study of 591 survivors and 757 referents, explored the work ability of survivors in Finland. The work ability of employed survivors with a good prognosis, which was measured by mean values, was similar to that of their referents. People with a higher level of educational attainment reported higher levels of work ability than those with less education. Older age and other illnesses lowered the work ability of both survivors and their referents. However, among the survivors, some 26% reported a physical work limitation and 19% reported a mental work limitation. For the female survivors, work limitations were associated with older age with the oldest age group (55–64 years) being nearly five times more likely to experience difficulties at work than the youngest age group (25–34 years) as a result of cancer. Among the male survivors, a lower level of educational attainment and the presence of co-morbid illnesses increased the likelihood of diminished work ability. Psycho-social factors, such as the level of commitment to the work organisation and support from co-workers, were also associated with a reduced risk of impaired work ability indicating the scope for improvements in these areas that could help survivors return to work and maintain their health and labour market status.

The research on the health status and work limitations of survivors is somewhat mixed in terms of its findings. There are grounds for concern about the long-term health status and work capacity of survivors who are able to return to work, especially when survivors also have another illness to cope with or face physical demands at work. These issues require a great deal more research, particularly longitudinal studies, in countries around the world.

Psycho-social Factors at Work Can Help Survivors to Return to Work

The pioneering research conducted in the USA in the 1970s highlighted the blatant discrimination that cancer survivors faced in the workplace from managers and co-workers. In much of the developed world, this situation has changed with legal protection for survivors and a sea change in attitudes about living with and beyond cancer. Writing about the situation in the USA, Hoffman [33] was able to look back over 'a generation of progress' for cancer survivors and to call for greater advocacy efforts to ensure legal rights were upheld and reasonable accommodations in the workplace were forthcoming. Although there undoubtedly has been considerable progress for survivors in the workplace over the last generation, there are still grounds for concern. Feuerstein and colleagues [34], in their study of claims made under the Americans with Disabilities Act, found that survivors were more likely to file claims for job loss and for differential treatment related to workplace policies than other groups with an impairment. The results suggest that while the position of survivors in the workplace has improved compared to a generation ago, there are still problems that need to be addressed.

As was mentioned earlier, psycho-social work-related factors such as support from co-workers and the level of commitment that individuals felt towards their workplace have been found to be associated with lower levels of work limitations [26]. Social support from co-workers and accommodations at work were found to be important factors in assisting work return by Main and colleagues [35] in their qualitative study of survivors in Colorado. Bouknight and colleagues [20] in their study of breast cancer survivors, found that 87% of women perceived that their employer was accommodating of their illness and need for treatment while only 7% thought that they had been discriminated against due to their cancer diagnosis. Furthermore, all of the women who returned to work went back to the same position that they had before their diagnosis whereas there was an association between perceived employer discrimination and not returning to work.

Taskila and colleagues [36] examined issues of emotional, informational, and practical support in the workplace from co-workers, occupational health professionals, and supervisors in Finland with a sample of 640 cancer survivors who had returned to work. They found that women received more support in the workplace than men and that people whose treatment had involved chemotherapy received more support than people who had other forms of treatment. People received significantly more support from their co-workers and supervisors than from occupational health professionals, although people with a higher level of educational attainment received the most support from this source. Males employed in manual occupations received less support in the workplace compared to people employed in professional occupations. The most important types of support were practical support from supervisors who took illness into account when planning and managing the workload and when occupational health professionals were providing guidance on the working conditions that a survivor would be able to cope with.

Support in the workplace from supervisors and co-workers appear to help survivors make a successful return to work although more research is needed to develop appropriate workplace guidance. There has been considerable progress over the last generation but it will need to continue in the future as the number of survivors of working age increases.

The Role of the Medical Profession

The role of the medical profession, whether they are part of the oncology care team or providers of primary care or occupational health professionals, is another factor in helping survivors to make an appropriate decision on work return. There is limited research on these issues for cancer survivors but they suggest that there is considerable scope for improvement.

Maunsell and colleagues [37], in a small qualitative study of women who had returned to work after breast cancer in Quebec, found that they had received very little advice from treating physicians about work beyond the need for a period of sick leave. Main and colleagues' [35] qualitative study of work return in Colorado also found that only a few survivors had received limited advice from clinicians about returning to work. In a qualitative study from the United Kingdom, Kennedy and colleagues [38] found a similar lack of medical advice about work.

An interesting pilot intervention study in the Netherlands conducted by Nieuwenhuijsen and colleagues [39] aimed to enhance communication about treatment type and duration between physicians in the oncology team and occupational health professionals. Alongside this strand of the intervention, cancer survivors and occupational health professionals received a leaflet detailing the steps of a rehabilitation plan based on the principles of graded activity and goal setting. The results of the intervention were difficult to interpret as there was a high degree of satisfaction with the processes involved and adherence to the leaflet among survivors, but there was no clear statistical link to the likelihood of returning to work. This type of intervention study involving the medical profession and patients in the process of reaching an appropriate decision about paid work is an important area for future research. This is particularly pertinent in the United States where the Institute of Medicine [40] has highlighted the need for the development of survivorship care plans that would include recommendations on how to maintain health and well-being, information on legal protections regarding employment, and the availability of psycho-social services in the community. This form of comprehensive approach to post-treatment care should ease the transition from cancer patient to cancer survivor and help address the many anxieties that people can feel during this process.

And Finally, Retirement

The final theme from the literature is what is known about survivors' decisions on retirement from paid work. Given the age-related incidence of cancer, there is an increased likelihood that diagnosis will take place as a person approaches retirement age and the option of early retirement may be available to them and be preferable to returning to work. The decision about whether to retire will depend on a range of factors including the survivor's health and work status, their age relative to the normal retirement age, their financial circumstances, the prevailing arrangements for early retirement, and the cultural norms of the society.

Taskila-Abrandt and colleagues [24], in their study of all working age cancer survivors in Finland, found that 34% had retired compared to 27% of age and gender-matched referents. There was a greater likelihood of retirement across all cancer sites with the exception of melanoma of the skin and the greatest risk of retirement was for survivors of leukaemia and cancer of the nervous system that can be attributed the generally poor prognosis of these highly disabling cancers. Bednarek and Bradley [41], in their study of cancer survivors in Detroit, found that just over a third of the 89 survivors who retired in a one- to seven-year period after their diagnosis reported that they felt they had been forced to retire. However, just under a third of survivors who retired prior to their diagnosis also reported that they felt they had been forced to retire. The most common reasons given for retirement were poor health, did not need to work for financial reasons, and wanting to do other things. Interestingly, on a range of measures, including the level of satisfaction with retirement, survivors who retired after diagnosis reported similar findings to that reported by those who retired before their diagnosis, suggesting that individuals shared similar concerns about the retirement decision regardless of cancer.

A recent study on the take up of early retirement pension (a benefit provided by the state regardless of socio-economic position) in Denmark by Carlsen and colleagues [42] compared the relative risk of claiming this benefit of 40,884 survivors diagnosed between 1981 and 2000 and 196,109 cancer-free controls. They found that there was a 55–60% higher relative risk of claiming an early retirement pension for cancer survivors compared to the control group. The risk factors associated with take up of an early retirement pension were sickness leave in the year before claiming the benefit, older age (mean age for men to start claiming was 54.4 years and 53.3 years for women), co-morbidity, and a lower level of education and income. The relative risk of claiming an early retirement pension was greatest for survivors with leukaemia, ovarian, and prostate cancer and lowest for survivors of melanoma, testicular, and uterine cancers. The most prevalent group, the 24,711 breast cancer survivors, had a particularly interesting trajectory with a relative risk of claiming an early retirement pension in the first year after diagnosis that was lower than the control group but this was followed by an increased risk in the one- to three-year period following diagnosis. The greater risk of claiming an early retirement pension also persisted for 12 years for breast cancer survivors suggesting that the effects of breast cancer persist for years after diagnosis and treatment. However, it should be noted that this study could not distinguish between those who voluntarily chose to claim an early retirement pension and those who were forced to retire prematurely because of health reasons.

There is, as yet, relatively little research on the retirement decisions of cancer survivors but it is probably reasonable to assume that they are likely to be broadly similar to people with other chronic diseases. There is also likely to be variation in the work-retirement decisions of survivors that is dependent on the institutional structure of pension provision in particular nations. Following the life course of survivors of working age into retirement to assess their health and well-being over time is a further area for research.

Gaps in Our Knowledge

There is a great need for more accurate data on the prevalence of cancer among the working populations of the world. It is seemingly inevitable that the number of working age cancer survivors will increase in the future, but policy makers, service providers, and researchers all need to have better information for decision making, planning, and investigation. Until there is more accurate data available there will be reliance on the incomplete data currently available, estimates from limited samples, and informed guesses that cannot fully serve the best interests of survivors or wider society.

It is commonplace for academics to call for more research on issues of interest and this chapter has been littered with the limitations of our current knowledge and suggestions of possible avenues for further work. The World Health Organisation's model of disability that categorises issues in work-related, disease- or treatment-related, and person-related factors provides a framework for the rigorous research that will be needed in the future. The methodological criteria set out by Steiner and colleagues [14] should also serve to guide future research in this area. What is also required in the future is a greater appreciation of the wider social welfare context that cancer survivors experience. The pivotal relationship between employment and health insurance in the United States is not shared by most other countries in the developed world, so it is reasonable to assume that the work decisions of individual survivors will be different and will be shaped by institutional context of social welfare provision for health and social care and cash benefits.

There is clearly a need for better guidance for clinicians, survivors, and work organisations about how to manage cancer in the workplace. Improving support for survivors at work may take many forms but is likely to require more information on the late effects of treatment, possible work limitations, and suitable accommodations that could allow a survivor to be economically active if that is what they choose to do. Improving the evidence base for such guidance and evaluating the effectiveness of interventions is essential if millions of survivors, now and in the future, are to lead full and happy lives.

Acknowledgments This review was conducted whilst David Neary was employed as Macmillan Research Fellow at the Macmillan Research Unit, University of Manchester (UK). Thanks to Macmillan Cancer Support (UK) for supporting and funding this research programme.

References

1. Feuerstein M. Defining cancer survivorship. J Cancer Survivorship. 2007;1(1):5–7.
2. Parkin DM, Bray F, Ferlay J, Pisani P. Global cancer statistics, 2002. CA Cancer J Clin. 2005 Mar-Apr;55(2):74–108.
3. Ferlay J, Autier P, Boniol M, Heanue M, Colombet M, Boyle P. Estimates of the cancer incidence and mortality in Europe in 2006. Ann Oncol. 2007 Mar;18(3):581–92.
4. Jemal A, Siegel R, Ward E, Hao Y, Xu J, Murray T, et al. Cancer statistics, 2008. CA Cancer J Clin. 2008 Mar-Apr;58(2):71–96.
5. Stewart BW, Kleihues P, (eds). World Cancer Report. Lyon: IARCPress 2003.
6. World Cancer Research Fund, American Institute for Cancer Research. Food, Nuitrition, Physical Activity, and the Prevention of Cancer: A Global Perspective. Washington, DC: AICR 2007.
7. Surveillance, Epidemiology and End Results (SEER) Cancer Statistics Review 1975–2004. Survival rates by race, sex, diagnosis year and age. [cited 2008 February 22]; Available from: http://seer.cancer.gov/csr/1975_2004/results_single/sect_02_table.05.pdf.

8. Reemployment Problems of the Recovered Cancer Patient. A report by the Ad Hoc Sub committee on Employability Problems of the Recovered Cancer Patient. San Francisco: American Cancer Society, Calformia Division 1973.
9. Feldman FL. Work and Cancer Health Histories: A Study of the Experiences of Recovered Patients. Oakland, CA: American Cancer Society, California Division 1976.
10. Feldman FL. Work and Cancer Histories: A Study of the Experiences of Recovered Blue-Collar Workers. San Francisco, CA: American Cancer Society, California Division 1978.
11. Feldman FL. Work and Cancer Health Histories: Work Expectations and Experiences of Youth with Cancer Histories. Oakland, CA: American Cancer Society, California Division 1980.
12. Verbeek J, Spelten E. Work. In: Feuerstein M, (ed.), *Handbook of Cancer Survivorship*. New York, NY: Springer 2007:381–96.
13. Spelten ER, Sprangers MA, Verbeek JH. Factors reported to influence the return to work of cancer survivors: a literature review. Psychooncology. 2002 Mar-Apr;11(2):124–31.
14. Steiner JF, Cavender TA, Main DS, Bradley CJ. Assessing the impact of cancer on work outcomes: what are the research needs? Cancer. 2004 Oct 15;101(8):1703–11.
15. Bradley CJ, Bednarek HL. Employment patterns of long-term cancer survivors. Psychooncology. 2002 May-Jun;11(3):188–98.
16. Greenwald HP, Dirks SJ, Borgatta EF, McCorkle R, Nevitt MC, H YE. Work disability among cancer patients. Soc Sci Med. 1989;29:1253–9.
17. Satariano WA, DeLorenze GN. The likelihood of returning to work after breast cancer. Public Health Rep. 1996 May-Jun;111(3):236–41.
18. Spelten ER, Verbeek JH, Uitterhoeve AL, Ansink AC, van der Lelie J, de Reijke TM, et al. Cancer, fatigue and the return of patients to work-a prospective cohort study. Eur J Cancer. 2003 Jul;39(11):1562–7.
19. Short PF, Vasey JJ, Tunceli K. Employment pathways in a large cohort of adult cancer survivors. Cancer. 2005 Mar 15;103(6):1292–301.
20. Bouknight RR, Bradley CJ, Luo Z. Correlates of return to work for breast cancer survivors. J Clin Oncol. 2006 Jan 20;24(3):345–53.
21. Sanchez KM, Richardson JL, Mason HR. The return to work experiences of colorectal cancer survivors. AAOHN J. 2004 Dec;52(12):500–10.
22. Maunsell E, Drolet M, Brisson J, Brisson C, Masse B, Deschenes L. Work situation after breast cancer: results from a population-based study. J Natl Cancer Inst. 2004 Dec 15;96(24):1813–22.
23. Gudbergsson SB, Fossa SD, Borgeraas E, Dahl AA. A comparative study of living conditions in cancer patients who have returned to work after curative treatment. Support Care Cancer. 2006 Oct;14(10):1020–9.
24. Taskila-Abrandt T, Pukkala E, Martikainen R, Karjalainen A, Hietanen P. Employment status of Finnish cancer patients in 1997. Psychooncol. 2005 Mar;14(3):221–6.
25. Bradley CJ, Oberst K, Schenk M. Absenteeism from work: the experience of employed breast and prostate cancer patients in the months following diagnosis. Psychooncol. 2006 Aug;15(8):739–47.
26. Taskila T, Martikainen R, Hietanen P, Lindbohm ML. Comparative study of work ability between cancer survivors and their referents. Eur J Cancer. 2007 Mar;43(5):914–20.
27. Taskila-Brandt T, Martikainen R, Virtanen SV, Pukkala E, Hietanen P, Lindbohm ML. The impact of education and occupation on the employment status of cancer survivors. Eur J Cancer. 2004 Nov;40(16):2488–93.
28. Choi KS, Kim EJ, Lim JH, Kim SG, Lim MK, Park JG, et al. Job loss and reemployment after a cancer diagnosis in Koreans – a prospective cohort study. Psychooncol. 2007 Mar;16(3):205–13.

29. Hewitt M, Rowland JH, Yancik R. Cancer survivors in the United States: age, health, and disability. J Gerontol A Biol Sci Med Sci. 2003 Jan;58(1):82–91.
30. Yabroff KR, Lawrence WF, Clauser S, Davis WW, Brown ML. Burden of illness in cancer survivors: findings from a population-based national sample. J Natl Cancer Inst. 2004 Sep 1;96(17):1322–30.
31. Short PF, Vasey JJ, Belue R. Work disability associated with cancer survivorship and other chronic conditions. Psychooncology. 2008 Jan;17(1):91–7.
32. Bradley CJ, Neumark D, Luo Z, Schenk M. Employment and cancer: findings from a longitudinal study of breast and prostate cancer survivors. Cancer Invest. 2007 Feb;25(1):47–54.
33. Hoffman B. Cancer survivors at work: a generation of progress. CA Cancer J Clin. 2005 Sep–Oct;55(5):271–80.
34. Feuerstein M, Luff GM, Harrington CB, Olsen CH. Patterns of workplace disputes in cancer survivors: A population study of ADA claims. Journal of Cancer Survivorship. 2007;1:185–92.
35. Main DS, Nowels CT, Cavender TA, Etschmaier M, Steiner JF. A qualitative study of work and work return in cancer survivors. Psychooncology. 2005 Nov;14(11):992–1004.
36. Taskila T, Lindbohm ML, Martikainen R, Lehto US, Hakanen J, Hietanen P. Cancer survivors' received and needed social support from their work place and the occupational health services. Support Care Cancer. 2006 May;14(5):427–35.
37. Maunsell E, Brisson C, Dubois L, Lauzier S, Fraser A. Work problems after breast cancer: an exploratory qualitative study. Psychooncology. 1999 Nov–Dec;8(6):467–73.
38. Kennedy F, Haslam C, Munir F, Pryce J. Returning to work following cancer: a qualitative exploratory study into the experience of returning to work following cancer. Eur J Cancer Care (Engl). 2007 Jan;16(1):17–25.
39. Nieuwenhuijsen K, Bos-Ransdorp B, Uitterhoeve LL, Sprangers MA, Verbeek JH. Enhanced provider communication and patient education regarding return to work in cancer survivors following curative treatment: a pilot study. J Occup Rehabil. 2006 Dec;16(4):647–57.
40. Hewitt M, Greenfield S, Stoval E. From Cancer Patient to Cancer Survivor: Lost in Transition. Washington, DC: Institute of Medicine and National Research Council 2005.
41. Bednarek HL, Bradley C. Work and retirement after cancer diagnosis. Res Nursing and Health. 2005;2:126–35.
42. Carlsen K, Oksbjerg-Dalton S, Frederiksen F, Dideriksen F, Jahansen C. Cancer and the risk for taking early retirement pension: A Danish cohort study. Scand J Public Health. 2008;36:117–25.

Chapter 2
Economic Burden

Richard J. Butler, William G. Johnson, and Timothy Gubler

Introduction

Within the last generation, cancer survivors' quality of life has improved significantly. As recently as 25 years ago, less than one half of those diagnosed with cancer survived more than five years [1]. Treatments were less precise and more disabling. Misunderstandings about cancer risks and options were common. As a result, cancer survivors experienced substantial problems obtaining and retaining employment [2–4].

Currently, more than 1 million people per year are diagnosed with cancer in the United States [1]. This number is expected to double by the year 2050, reflecting an aging population and an increase in population size [5, 6]. In addition, improvements in early diagnosis and treatment have led to improved survival following diagnosis for many tumor sites [1, 7, 8]. These factors are likely to increase the number of cancer survivors over the next several decades, including many who will want to continue to work. These survivors will include individuals cured of their disease and no longer undergoing active treatments, as well as individuals with recurrences or treatment resistant chronic conditions that will require ongoing management. Regardless of disease status, survivors can experience lasting effects of treatment, which may affect ability to remain active in the labor force. The net effect of recent legal and medical treatment advancements on the labor force participation of cancer survivors is ambiguous. To the extent that treatment improves ability to work for those with a given cancer severity, it should be generally expected to increase employment rates. However, to the extent that treatment maintains the lives of those who would otherwise have died, and who are too sick to work, it may decrease employment rates among cancer survivors.

Until recently, most "costs of cancer" studies have been taken from samples defined by tumor sites or specific treatments [9–11], or from specific regions of the country or from samples of patients from specific institutions [2, 9]. These

---

R.J. Butler (✉)
Martha Jane Knowlton Coray University Professor, Brigham Young University, 183 FOB, Provo, UT 84602, USA
e-mail: richard-butler@byu.edu

studies usually included only cancer patients, without data on similar individuals without cancer [2]. More recently, there have been a few population-based estimates of employment among cancer victims and productivity costs of cancer in the U.S., particularly the research of Hewitt, Rowland, and Yancik [3] and Yabroff et al. [4]. We build upon those population-based estimates by utilizing data from a large national survey, the Integrated Health Interview Survey (IHIS) [12], to estimate lost productivity due to morbidity. These data, combined with estimates of mortality risk from other data sources, allows us to estimate the productivity costs of cancer by cancer type.

In this chapter, we use the 1997–2005 waves of the IHIS to quantitatively examine the employment experience of those with a prior diagnosis of cancer, comparing employment experience across cancer types with those in the population who have never been diagnosed with cancer. Employment outcomes vary significantly across type of cancer, with employment rates for cancer survivors generally less than half the rate of those in the non-cancer population. Those cancer types with the lowest employment rates, after controlling for other demographic factors such as age, educational attainment, gender, and race, include cancers of the blood, bone, brain, esophagus, leukemia, liver, lung, mouth, pancreas, throat, and rectum. Cancers resulting in employment outcomes not significantly different from the general population include melanoma, testicular, and thyroid cancers. For cancer survivors, while the likelihood of employment increases as the duration from initial diagnosis increases, there is no evidence that this duration/employment relationship has improved in recent years (1997–2005).

The overall effect of cancer on work is the product of mortality (which unambiguously decreases the likelihood of working) and morbidity (which may increase or decrease working probabilities among cancer survivors). Given our interest in cancer survivors, we primarily focus on trends in the morbidity effects of cancer on employment, as well as the overall trends in employment following diagnosis (Table 2.7). We find morbidity effects initially outweigh mortality effects and that employment generally increases during the first three or four years after a cancer diagnosis. After this, the mortality effects (Table 2.9) and morbidity effects both work to decrease employment likelihood thereafter.

Cancer Morbidity and Employment: A Descriptive Overview by Cancer Status

Cancer affects employment outcomes in two ways. Cancer deaths lower mortality (increases the likelihood of an earlier death), and therefore, it lowers employment controlling for age. Cancer can also lower employment through a morbidity effect—even if an individual doesn't die from the cancer, the effects of living with and treating the cancer can lower employment to some degree.

The mortality effect of cancer on employment is irreversible: once you die, you can never work again. But unlike this mortality effect, the morbidity effect of cancer may at first worsen and then improve as survivors health improves sufficiently to return to work. In Tables 2.1 and 2.2, we combine descriptive

Table 2.1 Demographic characteristics by cancer status

	No cancer diagnosis			Bladder			Blood			Bone			Brain			Breast		
	N	Mean (or %)	std d	N	mean (or %)	std d	N	mean (or %)	std d	N	mean (or %)	std d	N	mean (or %)	std d	N	mean (or %)	std d
Age	859 K	34.02	21.80	370	69.43	11.72	45	59.49	17.26	93	56.35	18.51	104	49.01	15.33	3129	66.06	13.57
Married	658 K	0.54	0.49	370	0.56	0.50	45	0.29	0.46	93	0.40	0.49	102	0.43	0.50	3123	0.40	0.49
Male	859 K	0.48	0.49	370	0.68	0.47	45	0.40	0.50	93	0.48	0.50	104	0.49	0.50	3129	0.01	0.10
U.S. Citizen	749 K	0.90	0.28	329	0.99	0.11	42	0.93	0.26	80	0.98	0.16	88	0.95	0.21	2750	0.98	0.14
Born in U.S.	854 K	0.84	0.36	370	0.94	0.25	45	0.87	0.34	93	0.86	0.35	104	0.84	0.37	3127	0.91	0.28
White	859 K	0.59	0.49	370	0.72	0.45	45	0.67	0.48	93	0.57	0.50	104	0.58	0.50	3129	0.68	0.47
Black	859 K	0.10	0.31	370	0.04	0.20	45	0.11	0.32	93	0.13	0.34	104	0.08	0.27	3129	0.07	0.26
Asian	859 K	0.02	0.16	370	0.01	0.07	45	0.00	0.00	93	0.02	0.15	104	0.03	0.17	3129	0.01	0.11
Hispanic	859 K	0.22	0.42	370	0.05	0.21	45	0.11	0.32	93	0.12	0.32	104	0.11	0.31	3129	0.07	0.26
Family Size	859 K	3.47	1.76	370	1.83	0.95	45	2.20	1.59	93	1.92	1.19	104	2.21	1.30	3129	1.78	1.04
BMI	257 K	26.77	5.56	370	28.54	11.71	45	25.89	6.40	93	29.56	15.80	104	28.61	13.44	3129	29.75	15.77
Weight (lbs.)	243 K	168.00	35.81	350	176.10	36.01	44	159.90	36.73	85	166.60	32.51	96	167.30	39.17	2842	154.00	30.30
Height (inches)	249 K	66.62	3.85	351	67.72	3.67	44	66.57	4.09	85	66.67	3.84	98	66.54	4.06	2915	63.93	2.51
Cancer Duration (yr)	–	–	–	365	7.94	8.74	44	10.02	12.82	93	10.13	11.20	103	9.30	11.80	3096	10.11	10.81
Education																		
No high school	297 K	38.86		86	23.50		14	31.11		28	30.43		19	18.81		663	21.35	
High school	291 K	38.07		191	52.19		17	37.78		39	42.39		43	42.57		1556	50.10	
Associates Degree	49 K	6.50		22	6.01		5	11.11		10	10.87		8	7.92		268	8.63	
Bachelors Degree	84 K	11.04		41	11.20		5	11.11		11	11.96		20	19.80		386	12.43	
Masters/Prof.	37 K	4.87		22	6.01		3	6.67		3	3.26		10	9.90		214	6.89	
Doctorate Degree	5 K	0.66		4	1.09		1	2.22		1	1.09		1	0.99		19	0.61	
Family Income																		
$01–$4999	19 K	3.10		8	3.02		2	5.71		6	8.33		5	6.41		63	2.82	
$5000–$9999	32 K	5.20		14	5.28		6	17.14		9	12.50		10	12.82		275	12.32	
$10000–$14999	40 K	6.56		27	10.19		4	11.43		9	12.50		12	15.38		263	11.78	
$15000–$19999	39 K	6.39		25	9.43		3	8.57		5	6.94		4	5.13		239	10.71	
$20,000–$24,999	45 K	7.42		36	13.58		8	22.86		9	12.50		5	6.41		196	8.78	
$25,000–$34,999	79 K	12.84		39	14.72		3	8.57		9	12.50		6	7.69		293	13.13	
$35,000–$44,999	68 K	11.10		31	11.70		2	5.71		7	9.72		4	5.13		214	9.59	
$45,000–$54,999	61 K	9.96		16	6.04		1	2.86		1	1.39		7	8.97		152	6.81	
$55,000–$64,999	49 K	8.02		14	5.28		0	0.00		3	4.17		8	10.26		88	3.94	
$65,000–$74,999	40 K	6.53		11	4.15		0	0.00		0	0.00		3	3.85		93	4.17	
$75,000 and over	141 K	22.88		44	16.60		6	17.14		14	19.44		14	17.95		356	15.95	

Table 2.1 (continued)

	Cervical			Colon			Esophagus			Gallbladder			Kidney			Larynx		
	N	mean (or%)	std d	N	mean (or%)	std d	N	mean (or%)	std d	N	mean (or%)	std d	N	mean (or%)	std d	N	mean (or%)	std d
Age	1558	45.04	16.12	1284	70.60	12.44	60	62.82	15.72	17	62.00	15.74	260	66.43	13.56	64	65.98	11.26
Married	1554	0.40	0.49	1279	0.43	0.49	60	0.60	0.49	17	0.53	0.51	260	0.47	0.50	64	0.55	0.50
Male	1558	0.00	0.00	1284	0.42	0.49	60	0.70	0.46	17	0.24	0.44	260	0.55	0.50	64	0.70	0.46
U.S. Citizen	1348	0.98	0.15	1137	0.99	0.12	53	1.00	0.00	17	0.94	0.24	224	1.00	0.07	58	0.97	0.18
Born in U.S.	1557	0.94	0.23	1283	0.92	0.27	60	0.92	0.28	17	0.76	0.44	260	0.93	0.25	64	0.91	0.29
White	1558	0.66	0.47	1284	0.66	0.47	60	0.62	0.49	17	0.76	0.44	260	0.68	0.47	64	0.69	0.47
Black	1558	0.06	0.23	1284	0.09	0.28	60	0.08	0.28	17	0.12	0.33	260	0.05	0.23	64	0.13	0.33
Asian	1558	0.00	0.07	1284	0.01	0.10	60	0.00	0.00	17	0.00	0.00	260	0.01	0.11	64	0.00	0.00
Hispanic	1558	0.08	0.27	1284	0.06	0.24	60	0.12	0.32	17	0.24	0.44	260	0.07	0.26	64	0.11	0.31
Family Size	1558	2.52	1.38	1284	1.73	0.94	60	1.85	0.92	17	2.24	1.20	260	1.80	0.99	64	1.77	0.90
BMI	1558	29.41	15.01	1284	29.20	14.55	60	27.18	7.78	17	30.69	19.28	260	30.13	13.03	64	27.90	11.05
Weight (lbs.)	1417	156.40	33.59	1146	165.90	35.67	51	168.40	31.42	14	156.00	37.42	244	179.10	36.89	58	165.80	30.56
Height (inches)	1460	64.46	2.56	1172	66.03	3.81	51	67.55	3.61	14	64.86	3.08	246	67.24	4.13	58	67.52	4.12
Cancer Duration (yr)	1550	13.28	11.36	1274	8.55	10.00	60	6.33	10.89	17	7.59	8.49	260	8.20	9.24	64	10.52	10.69
Education																		
No high school	287	18.48		379	30.03		23	40.35		6	35.29		64	24.81		21	32.81	
High school	861	55.44		608	48.18		20	35.09		8	47.06		121	46.90		31	48.44	
Associates Degree	180	11.59		82	6.50		6	10.53		0	0.00		13	5.04		3	4.69	
Bachelors Degree	158	10.17		116	9.19		5	8.77		3	17.65		33	12.79		4	6.25	
Masters/Prof.	61	3.93		59	4.68		2	3.51		0	0.00		24	9.30		4	6.25	
Doctorate Degree	6	0.39		18	1.43		1	1.75		0	0.00		3	1.16		1	1.56	
Family Income																		
$01–4999	59	4.56		24	2.63		3	5.88		1	7.69		6	2.96		2	4.65	
$5000–9999	165	12.75		138	15.15		10	19.61		0	0.00		25	12.32		6	13.95	
$10000–14999	114	8.81		144	15.81		3	5.88		2	15.38		21	10.34		8	18.60	
$15000–19999	115	8.89		107	11.75		3	5.88		2	15.38		15	7.39		8	18.60	
$20,000–24,999	107	8.27		93	10.21		6	11.76		1	7.69		23	11.33		5	11.63	
$25,000–34,999	199	15.38		112	12.29		9	17.65		0	0.00		29	14.29		3	6.98	
$35,000–44,999	132	10.20		82	9.00		8	15.69		4	30.77		25	12.32		6	13.95	
$45,000–54,999	109	8.42		60	6.59		1	1.96		1	7.69		15	7.39		3	6.98	
$55,000–64,999	77	5.95		35	3.84		1	1.96		1	7.69		11	5.42		1	2.33	
$65,000–74,999	45	3.48		27	2.96		3	5.88		0	0.00		6	2.96		0	0.00	
$75,000 and over	172	13.29		89	9.77		4	7.84		1	7.69		27	13.30		1	2.33	

2 Economic Burden

Table 2.1 (continued)

	Leukemia			Liver			Lung			Lymphoma			Melanoma			Mouth		
	N	mean (or%)	std d	N	mean (or%)	std d	N	mean (or%)	std d	N	Mean (or%)	std d	N	mean (or%)	std d	N	mean (or%)	std d
Age	208	56.34	19.83	90	63.42	15.11	548	67.18	11.24	459	58.70	15.92	950	60.17	15.32	105	65.37	13.92
Married	206	0.44	0.50	90	0.47	0.50	547	0.47	0.50	457	0.55	0.50	948	0.58	0.49	105	0.46	0.50
Male	208	0.42	0.50	90	0.62	0.49	548	0.51	0.50	459	0.46	0.50	950	0.48	0.50	105	0.51	0.50
U.S. Citizen	187	0.99	0.10	84	0.98	0.15	481	0.98	0.14	415	0.98	0.15	853	0.99	0.11	90	1.00	0.00
Born in U.S.	208	0.96	0.20	90	0.82	0.38	547	0.93	0.26	458	0.92	0.27	950	0.95	0.21	105	0.95	0.21
White	208	0.70	0.46	90	0.66	0.48	548	0.69	0.46	459	0.72	0.45	950	0.79	0.41	105	0.67	0.47
Black	208	0.05	0.22	90	0.08	0.27	548	0.09	0.28	459	0.04	0.20	950	0.01	0.10	105	0.06	0.23
Asian	208	0.00	0.00	90	0.04	0.21	548	0.01	0.07	459	0.01	0.09	950	0.00	0.00	105	0.01	0.10
Hispanic	208	0.08	0.27	90	0.18	0.38	548	0.06	0.23	459	0.08	0.27	950	0.02	0.14	105	0.07	0.25
Family Size	208	2.11	1.24	90	1.98	1.41	548	1.77	0.97	459	2.12	1.14	950	2.04	1.08	105	1.75	0.86
BMI	208	28.12	11.42	90	28.67	12.33	548	27.48	13.22	459	28.61	13.22	950	29.54	14.60	105	27.81	12.06
Weight (lbs.)	196	170.50	36.44	85	172.50	35.92	503	164.90	36.15	426	169.00	36.67	879	172.40	37.09	94	167.00	39.11
Height (inches)	198	66.76	3.76	86	66.97	3.60	515	67.00	3.96	431	66.76	3.96	898	67.20	3.93	94	66.90	3.63
Cancer Duration (yr)	206	10.68	13.71	87	6.36	12.37	542	6.51	10.69	457	9.25	10.80	946	9.89	10.74	104	8.68	10.25
Education																		
No high school	35	16.99		23	25.84		182	33.39		86	18.82		136	14.35		31	29.81	
High school	113	54.85		45	50.56		255	46.79		207	45.30		419	44.20		50	48.08	
Associates Degree	20	9.71		6	6.74		29	5.32		59	12.91		113	11.92		6	5.77	
Bachelors Degree	28	13.59		10	11.24		47	8.62		74	16.19		175	18.46		9	8.65	
Masters/Prof.	10	4.85		4	4.49		27	4.95		24	5.25		85	8.97		7	6.73	
Doctorate Degree	0	0.00		1	1.12		5	0.92		7	1.53		20	2.11		1	0.96	
Family Income																		
$01–4999	4	2.56		0	0.00		12	2.89		6	1.72		15	2.01		1	1.16	
$5000–9999	22	14.10		13	20.00		57	13.73		26	7.47		47	6.28		10	11.63	
$10000–14999	18	11.54		8	12.31		55	13.25		30	8.62		39	5.21		9	10.47	
$15000–19999	10	6.41		8	12.31		40	9.64		28	8.05		57	7.62		11	12.79	
$20,000–24,999	17	10.90		6	9.23		49	11.81		31	8.91		55	7.35		9	10.47	
$25,000–34,999	22	14.10		5	7.69		66	15.90		41	11.78		97	12.97		17	19.77	
$35,000–44,999	16	10.26		7	10.77		44	10.60		42	12.07		76	10.16		5	5.81	
$45,000–54,999	14	8.97		4	6.15		31	7.47		36	10.34		70	9.36		7	8.14	
$55,000–64,999	10	6.41		3	4.62		18	4.34		27	7.76		48	6.42		7	8.14	
$65,000–74,999	4	2.56		3	4.62		9	2.17		20	5.75		43	5.75		2	2.33	
$75,000 and over	19	12.18		8	12.31		34	8.19		61	17.53		201	26.87		8	9.30	

Table 2.1 (continued)

	Other			Ovarian			Pancreatic			Prostate			Rectal			Soft Tissue		
	N	mean (or%)	std d	N	mean (or%)	std d	N	mean (or%)	std d	N	mean (or%)	std d	N	mean (or%)	std d	N	mean (or%)	std d
Age	824	56.88	17.30	530	55.61	18.01	69	65.38	13.47	1878	72.37	8.76	96	69.89	12.40	83	56.12	17.43
Married	820	0.49	0.50	525	0.40	0.49	69	0.49	0.50	1876	0.62	0.48	96	0.35	0.48	83	0.40	0.49
Male	824	0.39	0.49	530	0.00	0.00	69	0.49	0.50	1878	1.00	0.00	96	0.49	0.50	83	0.45	0.50
U.S. Citizen	714	0.98	0.13	473	0.95	0.22	65	0.98	0.12	1669	0.99	0.12	84	0.98	0.15	78	0.99	0.11
Born in U.S.	824	0.92	0.26	530	0.92	0.28	69	0.87	0.34	1878	0.93	0.26	96	0.91	0.29	83	0.94	0.24
White	824	0.67	0.47	530	0.68	0.47	69	0.72	0.45	1878	0.65	0.48	96	0.71	0.46	83	0.72	0.45
Black	824	0.05	0.22	530	0.06	0.25	69	0.10	0.30	1878	0.12	0.33	96	0.07	0.26	83	0.07	0.26
Asian	824	0.01	0.10	530	0.01	0.11	69	0.03	0.17	1878	0.01	0.07	96	0.00	0.00	83	0.01	0.11
Hispanic	824	0.07	0.26	530	0.11	0.32	69	0.04	0.21	1878	0.06	0.23	96	0.05	0.22	83	0.11	0.31
Family Size	824	2.08	1.18	530	2.13	1.34	69	1.84	1.02	1878	1.81	0.82	96	1.53	0.70	83	2.05	1.14
BMI	824	29.65	14.48	530	29.95	14.76	69	27.52	16.27	1878	28.05	9.36	96	29.05	13.90	83	29.82	14.75
Weight (lbs.)	742	168.80	36.76	476	157.50	33.62	56	156.30	34.81	1781	185.80	30.74	87	172.10	33.60	76	171.10	34.21
Height (inches)	760	66.41	3.88	482	64.14	2.61	58	66.69	4.31	1784	69.44	2.61	90	66.81	3.96	79	66.84	3.87
Cancer Duration (yr)	814	11.19	11.67	525	13.15	12.70	69	7.90	13.03	1859	6.71	9.85	95	9.12	9.05	83	9.64	11.46
Education																		
No high school	156	19.07		123	23.47		13	18.84		542	29.23		25	26.04		13	15.66	
High school	397	48.53		262	50.00		36	52.17		763	41.15		52	54.17		41	49.40	
Associates Degree	61	7.46		58	11.07		5	7.25		103	5.56		10	10.42		6	7.23	
Bachelors Degree	121	14.79		57	10.88		7	10.14		245	13.21		7	7.29		14	16.87	
Masters/Prof.	71	8.68		22	4.20		5	7.25		173	9.33		2	2.08		8	9.64	
Doctorate Degree	12	1.47		2	0.38		3	4.35		28	1.51		0	0.00		1	1.20	
Family Income																		
$01–4999	32	5.04		18	4.47		3	6.52		29	2.13		3	4.17		2	3.08	
$5000–9999	68	10.71		60	14.89		5	10.87		105	7.70		9	12.50		8	12.31	
$10000–14999	56	8.82		59	14.64		3	6.52		139	10.19		16	22.22		6	9.23	
$15000–19999	44	6.93		43	10.67		1	2.17		139	10.19		7	9.72		5	7.69	
$20,000–24,999	51	8.03		38	9.43		6	13.04		158	11.58		8	11.11		4	6.15	
$25,000–34,999	81	12.76		44	10.92		7	15.22		241	17.67		9	12.50		9	13.85	
$35,000–44,999	56	8.82		36	8.93		4	8.70		139	10.19		7	9.72		4	6.15	
$45,000–54,999	65	10.24		34	8.44		2	4.35		112	8.21		4	5.56		5	7.69	
$55,000–64,999	43	6.77		15	3.72		4	8.70		75	5.50		3	4.17		7	10.77	
$65,000–74,999	37	5.83		16	3.97		3	6.52		48	3.52		1	1.39		5	7.69	
$75,000 and over	102	16.06		40	9.93		8	17.39		179	13.12		5	6.94		10	15.38	

2 Economic Burden

Table 2.1 (continued)

	Stomach			Testicular			Throat			Thyroid			Uterine			NM Skin Cancer		
	N	mean (or%)	std d	N	mean (or%)	std d	N	mean (or%)	std d	N	mean (or%)	std d	N	mean (or%)	std d	N	mean (or%)	std d
Age	192	65.49	16.33	150	45.25	13.71	222	64.45	13.65	357	54.54	15.81	1278	58.75	16.22	3228	63.70	13.82
Married	192	0.33	0.47	150	0.55	0.50	222	0.45	0.50	357	0.54	0.50	1276	0.37	0.48	3224	0.58	0.49
Male	192	0.47	0.50	150	1.00	0.00	222	0.68	0.47	357	0.22	0.42	1278	0.00	0.00	3228	0.49	0.50
U.S. Citizen	166	0.93	0.25	132	0.98	0.15	191	0.97	0.16	320	0.98	0.14	1100	0.98	0.15	2863	1.00	0.07
Born in U.S.	192	0.85	0.36	150	0.95	0.23	222	0.94	0.24	357	0.93	0.26	1277	0.93	0.26	3228	0.97	0.18
White	192	0.58	0.49	150	0.77	0.42	222	0.64	0.48	357	0.70	0.46	1278	0.65	0.48	3228	0.77	0.42
Black	192	0.14	0.34	150	0.00	0.00	222	0.07	0.26	357	0.05	0.22	1278	0.07	0.25	3228	0.00	0.06
Asian	192	0.03	0.16	150	0.01	0.08	222	0.00	0.07	357	0.02	0.13	1278	0.00	0.06	3228	0.00	0.06
Hispanic	192	0.15	0.36	150	0.09	0.28	222	0.07	0.26	357	0.06	0.25	1278	0.10	0.29	3228	0.02	0.12
Family Size	192	1.83	1.07	150	2.37	1.36	222	1.83	1.09	357	2.30	1.38	1278	1.97	1.22	3228	1.95	1.00
BMI	192	29.29	16.62	150	27.45	4.63	222	25.64	7.53	357	31.55	17.03	1278	31.11	15.75	3228	27.77	11.15
Weight (lbs.)	168	163.80	35.85	144	191.50	30.56	199	171.20	39.29	311	168.20	35.31	1094	159.20	33.56	3059	169.20	34.49
Height (inches)	172	66.12	3.99	144	70.33	2.82	200	68.11	3.90	326	65.88	3.42	1136	63.91	2.51	3101	67.12	3.86
Cancer Duration (yr)	184	9.56	11.60	150	12.85	11.39	222	10.28	13.42	355	13.37	11.68	1273	16.46	13.03	3191	10.24	11.36
Education																		
No high school	70	36.84		16	10.74		75	33.94		51	14.29		359	28.18		370	11.49	
High school	84	44.21		59	39.60		91	41.18		175	49.02		658	51.65		1406	43.68	
Associates Degree	12	6.32		22	14.77		16	7.24		36	10.08		102	8.01		302	9.38	
Bachelors Degree	18	9.47		37	24.83		24	10.86		50	14.01		100	7.85		634	19.70	
Masters/Prof.	6	3.16		13	8.72		12	5.43		37	10.36		51	4.00		433	13.45	
Doctorate Degree	0	0.00		2	1.34		3	1.36		8	2.24		4	0.31		74	2.30	
Family Income																		
$01-4999	9	6.16		2	1.53		3	1.75		2	0.72		49	4.83		36	1.42	
$5000-9999	32	21.92		4	3.05		28	16.37		22	7.94		174	17.16		133	5.25	
$10000-14999	19	13.01		6	4.58		29	16.96		23	8.30		148	14.60		166	6.56	
$15000-19999	14	9.59		7	5.34		14	8.19		14	5.05		92	9.07		154.0	6.08	
$20,000-24,999	15	10.27		9	6.87		17	9.94		23	8.30		106	10.45		199	7.86	
$25,000-34,999	10	6.85		22	16.79		27	15.79		22	7.94		124	12.23		347	13.71	
$35,000-44,999	16	10.96		16	12.21		10	5.85		32	11.55		98	9.66		276	10.90	
$45,000-54,999	6	4.11		11	8.40		11	6.43		32	11.55		55	5.42		245	9.68	
$55,000-64,999	5	3.42		11	8.40		8	4.68		16	5.78		42	4.14		171	6.76	
$65,000-74,999	6	4.11		6	4.58		3	1.75		16	5.78		38	3.75		160	6.32	
$75,000 and over	14	9.59		37	28.24		21	12.28		75	27.08		88	8.68		644	25.44	

Table 2.1 (continued)

	Unknown Skin Cancer		
	N	mean (or %)	std d
Age	1843	65.86	14.67
Married	1839	0.50	0.50
Male	1843	0.50	0.50
U.S. Citizen	1623	0.99	0.08
Born in U.S.	1842	0.95	0.21
White	1843	0.77	0.42
Black	1843	0.01	0.08
Asian	1843	0.00	0.05
Hispanic	1843	0.02	0.14
Family Size	1843	1.84	0.99
BMI	1843	28.64	13.29
Weight (lbs.)	1710	169.5	36.04
Height (inches)	1738	66.95	3.90
Cancer Duration (yr)	1806	10.06	12.07
Education			
No high school	391	21.35	
High school	864	47.19	
Associates Degree	136	7.43	
Bachelors Degree	257	14.04	
Masters/Prof.	161	8.79	
Doctorate Degree	22	1.20	
Family Income			
$01–$4999	27	2.00	
$5000–$9999	139	10.27	
$10000–$14999	152	11.23	
$15000–$19999	129	9.53	
$20,000–$24,999	115	8.50	
$25,000–$34,999	181	13.38	
$35,000–$44,999	152	11.23	
$45,000–$54,999	114	8.43	
$55,000–$64,999	67	4.95	
$65,000–$74,999	59	4.36	
$75,000 and over	218	16.11	

Source: The Health Interview Surveys, 1997–2005.

information from all waves of the IHIS, and present it presuming that cancer employment experience has not appreciably changed over time (we empirically examine this assumption below). An examination of the descriptive statistics show that while the average age of the general population is 34 years of age, cancer survivors are older: 69 years old is the average age for those with bladder cancer, 59 the average of those with cancer of the blood, etc. Cancer survivors are not only more likely to be older, they also are more likely to have smaller families, and are less likely to be Hispanic (except, notably, for cancer of the gall bladder) than the general population. Otherwise, cancer survivors have similar sociodemographic values to those without cancer, as indicated in the top half of Table 2.1. In particular, body mass index (BMI), marital status, and educational attainment of cancer survivors mirrors that of the general population. Interestingly, however, cancer seems to be related to income. With the notable exceptions of melanoma, pancreatic, skin, testicular, and thyroid cancer, those with cancer diagnoses have considerably less family income than the general population. For example, 37% of the general (non-cancer) population has family income greater than $55,000, but, as is typical of most cancers, only 26% of those with bladder cancer have family income greater than $55,000. On the other end of the spectrum, 39% of those with melanoma have family incomes in excess of $55,000.

The "outcome" variables in Table 2.2 suggest that actual employment outcomes tracked perceived health and perceived ability to work fairly well. About 63% without a cancer diagnosis were working over our sample period, about twice the rate of any of those with a cancer diagnosis except cervical (55%), testicular (73% – higher than the general population rate because it is a male disease and males work more than females), and thyroid (49%) cancer. In multivariate regressions below, those with these three cancers are not statistically different in their employment outcomes than those with no prior cancer diagnosis.

Likewise, while two-thirds of the general population describes their health as very good or excellent (36.44 + 30.70%, from the far right hand column), generally only one-third of those with cancer describe their health as very good or excellent. For example, people with bladder, blood, or bone cancers report that they were in very good or excellent health only about 30% of the time or less at the time of the survey. On the other hand, those with the three cancers who had roughly the same employment experience as the general population reported their health was much better than those with other cancers; 48% of those with cervical cancer, 59% of those with testicular cancer, and 43% of those with thyroid cancer report being in very good or excellent health.

Of the seven Likert-scaled variables measuring health and general mental state of being (self-described "health", "everything an effort", "left hopeless", "felt nervous", "felt restless", "felt sad", "felt worthless"), listed at the bottom of Table 2.2, self-described health has a stronger (both statistically and in magnitude) positive correlation with employment outcomes than any of the mental state of health variables. While all the mental state of health variances are highly significant and of the expected sign in explaining "employment" and "limited in work due to health" when included in multivariate logistic regressions, such as those in Tables 2.3, 2.4

Table 2.2 Outcomes by cancer status

	No cancer diagnosis			Bladder			Blood			Bone		
	N	mean (or%)	std d	N	mean (or%)	std d	N	mean (or%)	std d	N	mean (or%)	std d
Working	604 K	0.63	0.48	370	0.24	0.43	45	0.22	0.42	93	0.27	0.45
Limited in Work from Health	608 K	0.10	0.30	370	0.28	0.45	45	0.38	0.49	93	0.40	0.49
Work loss days past 12 months	188 K	4.32	18.51	115	8.01	31.95	14	12.79	39.62	41	34.41	69.15
Bed disability days past 12 months	264 K	4.49	24.20	362	9.70	43.51	44	19.07	42.34	89	21.09	62.09
# nights in hospital past 12 months	857 K	0.50	4.23	368	1.75	4.61	45	6.40	19.60	92	8.11	31.08
Frequently depressed past 12 months	28 K	0.16	0.37	35	0.20	0.41	4	0.25	0.50	8	0.25	0.46
Had insomnia past 12 months	28 K	0.17	0.38	35	0.17	0.38	4	0.00	0.00	9	0.44	0.53
Had severe headaches past 3 mos.	269 K	0.15	0.36	368	0.07	0.26	45	0.22	0.42	93	0.17	0.38
Days had 5 + drinks, past year	156 K	13.05	45.46	187	16.57	60.91	20	7.25	23.76	46	14.09	56.22
# cigarettes in past 30 days	11 K	13.12	8.77	13	18.00	10.20	2	9.50	6.36	4	12.50	2.89
Smoked 100 + cigarettes in life	266 K	0.43	0.49	365	0.81	0.40	45	0.53	0.50	91	0.47	0.50
Unable to work due to health	611 K	0.06	0.24	369	0.18	0.38	45	0.29	0.46	93	0.31	0.47
Has any activity limitation	855 K	0.11	0.32	370	0.34	0.47	45	0.56	0.50	93	0.57	0.50
Act. limited by difficulty remembering	858 K	0.01	0.13	370	0.07	0.26	45	0.09	0.29	93	0.14	0.35
Self-described health												
Excellent	311 K	36.44		29	7.86		5	11.11		11	11.83	
Very Good	262 K	30.70		88	23.85		6	13.33		15	16.13	
Good	203 K	23.85		130	35.23		14	31.11		33	35.48	
Fair	58 K	6.84		76	20.60		10	22.22		18	19.35	
Poor	18 K	2.17		46	12.47		10	22.22		16	17.20	
Felt everything an effort, past 30 days												
None of the time	202 K	76.25		275	75.34		28	63.64		56	60.22	
A little of the time	26 K	10.02		31	8.49		8	18.18		15	16.13	
Some of the time	21 K	8.21		38	10.41		6	13.64		12	12.90	
Most of the time	8 K	3.25		15	4.11		2	4.55		7	7.53	
All of the time	6 K	2.27		6	1.64		0	0.00		3	3.23	
How often felt hopeless, past 30 days												
None of the time	232 K	87.60		319	87.40		38	86.36		72	77.42	
A little of the time	14 K	5.63		20	5.48		2	4.55		9	9.68	
Some of the time	11 K	4.41		16	4.38		4	9.09		6	6.45	
Most of the time	4 K	1.55		9	2.47		0	0.00		3	3.23	
All of the time	2 K	0.81		1	0.27		0	0.00		3	3.23	

2 Economic Burden

Table 2.2 (continued)

	No cancer diagnosis			Bladder			Blood			Bone		
	N	mean (or%)	std d	N	mean (or%)	std d	N	mean (or%)	std d	N	mean (or%)	std d
How often felt nervous, past 30 days												
None of the time	173 K	65.32		249	68.03		27	61.36		49	52.69	
A little of the time	48 K	18.14		59	16.12		10	22.73		22	23.66	
Some of the time	31 K	11.95		38	10.38		5	11.36		14	15.05	
Most of the time	7 K	2.95		14	3.83		1	2.27		6	6.45	
All of the time	4 K	1.64		6	1.64		1	2.27		2	2.15	
How often felt restless, past 30 days												
None of the time	177 K	67.08		244	66.67		26	59.09		46	50.00	
A little of the time	41 K	15.55		59	16.12		9	20.45		22	23.91	
Some of the time	31 K	11.92		38	10.38		6	13.64		16	17.39	
Most of the time	9 K	3.40		16	4.37		0	0.00		5	5.43	
All of the time	5 K	2.06		9	2.46		3	6.82		3	3.26	
How often felt sad, past 30 days												
None of the time	196 K	73.94		251	68.58		31	70.45		49	53.26	
A little of the time	35 K	13.32		56	15.30		7	15.91		24	26.09	
Some of the time	23 K	9.03		42	11.48		4	9.09		10	10.87	
Most of the time	6 K	2.64		14	3.83		2	4.55		5	5.43	
All of the time	2 K	1.07		3	0.82		0	0.00		4	4.35	
How often felt worthless, past 30 days												
None of the time	239 K	90.41		326	89.32		42	95.45		77	82.80	
A little of the time	11 K	4.18		17	4.66		0	0.00		8	8.60	
Some of the time	8 K	3.36		12	3.29		2	4.55		3	3.23	
Most of the time	3 K	1.29		8	2.19		0	0.00		2	2.15	
All of the time	2 K	0.76		2	0.55		0	0.00		3	3.23	

Table 2.2 (continued)

	Brain			Breast			Cervical			Colon		
	N	mean (or %)	std d	N	mean (or %)	std d	N	mean (or %)	std d	N	mean (or %)	std d
Working	104	0.31	0.46	3128	0.27	0.45	1555	0.55	0.50	1284	0.20	0.40
Limited in Work from Health	104	0.54	0.50	3116	0.29	0.45	1556	0.22	0.42	1278	0.31	0.46
Work loss days past 12 months	45	25.29	58.07	1085	12.55	34.34	1043	9.39	25.99	323	17.28	43.76
Bed disability days past 12 months	101	24.14	59.54	3051	8.77	35.38	1533	12.18	39.17	1239	11.52	42.88
# nights in hospital past 12 months	104	3.22	7.99	3122	1.50	5.63	1555	1.28	7.24	1276	3.38	11.03
Frequently depressed past 12 months	8	0.25	0.46	325	0.21	0.41	175	0.42	0.49	136	0.24	0.43
Had insomnia past 12 months	8	0.38	0.52	326	0.31	0.46	175	0.47	0.50	135	0.24	0.43
Had severe headaches past 3 mos.	104	0.34	0.47	3123	0.13	0.34	1557	0.39	0.49	1282	0.10	0.30
Days had 5+ drinks, past year	41	35.00	91.20	1382	2.55	19.61	975	9.23	38.83	535	11.52	52.74
# cigarettes in past 30 days	7	9.14	9.30	84	13.36	9.19	84	14.13	8.45	30	17.07	9.64
Smoked 100+ cigarettes in life	103	0.51	0.50	3101	0.42	0.49	1552	0.64	0.48	1275	0.52	0.50
Unable to work due to health	104	0.45	0.50	3122	0.17	0.38	1557	0.15	0.36	1281	0.20	0.40
Has any activity limitation	104	0.63	0.49	3123	0.37	0.48	1558	0.27	0.44	1283	0.43	0.50
Act. limited by diffic. remembering	104	0.33	0.47	3125	0.06	0.24	1558	0.05	0.22	1283	0.07	0.26
Self-described health												
Excellent	13	12.50		417	13.34		274	17.62		118	9.23	
Very Good	15	14.42		756	24.19		439	28.23		259	20.27	
Good	27	25.96		1101	35.23		484	31.13		480	37.56	
Fair	25	24.04		620	19.84		250	16.08		278	21.75	
Poor	24	23.08		231	7.39		108	6.95		143	11.19	
Felt everything an effort, past 30 days												
None of the time	56	54.37		2242	72.70		905	58.42		930	74.28	
A little of the time	15	14.56		323	10.47		220	14.20		116	9.27	
Some of the time	12	11.65		314	10.18		227	14.65		119	9.50	
Most of the time	12	11.65		119	3.86		113	7.30		45	3.59	
All of the time	8	7.77		86	2.79		84	5.42		42	3.35	
How often felt hopeless, past 30 days												
None of the time	72	69.90		2650	86.04		1163	75.03		1087	86.75	
A little of the time	9	8.74		185	6.01		115	7.42		72	5.75	
Some of the time	11	10.68		168	5.45		175	11.29		52	4.15	
Most of the time	6	5.83		38	1.23		72	4.65		21	1.68	
All of the time	5	4.85		39	1.27		25	1.61		21	1.68	

Table 2.2 (continued)

	Brain			Breast			Cervical			Colon		
	N	mean (or%)	std d	N	mean (or%)	std d	N	mean (or%)	std d	N	mean (or%)	std d
How often felt nervous, past 30 days												
None of the time	49	47.57		1842	59.61		719	46.36		828	66.03	
A little of the time	19	18.45		617	19.97		325	20.95		213	16.99	
Some of the time	22	21.36		445	14.40		312	20.12		138	11.00	
Most of the time	11	10.68		111	3.59		121	7.80		48	3.83	
All of the time	2	1.94		75	2.43		74	4.77		27	2.15	
How often felt restless, past 30 days												
None of the time	50	48.54		2020	65.44		739	47.65		820	65.60	
A little of the time	15	14.56		469	15.19		269	17.34		204	16.32	
Some of the time	19	18.45		424	13.74		311	20.05		146	11.68	
Most of the time	15	14.56		103	3.34		135	8.70		44	3.52	
All of the time	4	3.88		71	2.30		97	6.25		36	2.88	
How often felt sad, past 30 days												
None of the time	52	50.49		2074	67.27		872	56.22		874	69.48	
A little of the time	18	17.48		498	16.15		280	18.05		179	14.23	
Some of the time	23	22.33		380	12.33		258	16.63		138	10.97	
Most of the time	8	7.77		92	2.98		105	6.77		45	3.58	
All of the time	2	1.94		39	1.27		36	2.32		22	1.75	
How often felt worthless, past 30 days												
None of the time	72	69.90		2728	88.51		1234	79.66		1118	89.23	
A little of the time	7	6.80		150	4.87		103	6.65		51	4.07	
Some of the time	11	10.68		138	4.48		136	8.78		43	3.43	
Most of the time	9	8.74		37	1.20		50	3.23		22	1.76	
All of the time	4	3.88		29	0.94		26	1.68		19	1.52	

Table 2.2 (continued)

	Esophagus			Gallbladder			Kidney			Larynx		
	N	mean (or%)	std d	N	mean (or%)	std d	N	mean (or%)	std d	N	mean (or%)	std d
Working	60	0.22	0.42	17	0.23	0.44	259	0.28	0.45	64	0.23	0.43
Limited in Work from Health	60	0.50	0.50	17	0.41	0.51	260	0.37	0.48	64	0.48	0.50
Work loss days past 12 months	17	8.24	16.34	7	6.00	8.74	90	13.04	30.78	23	20.48	49.06
Bed disability days past 12 months	59	26.53	63.61	16	10.19	16.41	257	8.75	25.54	61	12.10	54.07
# nights in hospital past 12 months	60	7.45	22.88	17	3.06	5.83	260	3.38	7.90	63	3.06	11.86
Frequently depressed past 12 months	4	0.75	0.50	1	1.00	.	33	0.30	0.47	12	0.33	0.49
Had insomnia past 12 months	5	0.40	0.55	1	1.00	.	33	0.30	0.47	12	0.25	0.45
Had severe headaches past 3 mos.	60	0.18	0.39	17	0.06	0.24	260	0.14	0.35	64	0.16	0.37
Days had 5+ drinks, past year	20	21.25	78.80	7	0.00	0.00	119	6.10	31.80	33	13.09	63.66
# cigarettes in past 30 days	1	21.00	.	0	.	.	4	16.50	10.47	0	.	.
Smoked 100+ cigarettes in life	60	0.60	0.49	16	0.56	0.51	259	0.59	0.49	64	0.84	0.37
Unable to work due to health	60	0.40	0.49	17	0.24	0.44	260	0.23	0.42	64	0.38	0.49
Has any activity limitation	60	0.60	0.49	17	0.41	0.51	260	0.45	0.50	64	0.56	0.50
Act. limited by difficulty remembering	60	0.13	0.34	17	0.00	0.00	260	0.05	0.23	64	0.06	0.24
Self-described health												
Excellent	2	3.39		1	5.88		22	8.53		2	3.13	
Very Good	10	16.95		2	11.76		54	20.93		13	20.31	
Good	17	28.81		6	35.29		91	35.27		15	23.44	
Fair	17	28.81		5	29.41		61	23.64		23	35.94	
Poor	13	22.03		3	17.65		30	11.63		11	17.19	
Felt everything an effort, past 30 days												
None of the time	35	59.32		9	52.94		175	67.57		43	69.35	
A little of the time	9	15.25		2	11.76		24	9.27		2	3.23	
Some of the time	10	16.95		2	11.76		30	11.58		12	19.35	
Most of the time	3	5.08		4	23.53		15	5.79		2	3.23	
All of the time	2	3.39		0	0.00		15	5.79		3	4.84	
How often felt hopeless, past 30 days												
None of the time	49	83.05		9	52.94		215	83.01		53	84.13	
A little of the time	5	8.47		5	29.41		11	4.25		2	3.17	
Some of the time	3	5.08		0	0.00		21	8.11		6	9.52	
Most of the time	1	1.69		2	11.76		6	2.32		0	0.00	
All of the time	1	1.69		1	5.88		6	2.32		2	3.17	
How often felt nervous, past 30 days												
None of the time	35	59.32		9	52.94		162	62.55		40	63.49	
A little of the time	9	15.25		3	17.65		43	16.60		9	14.29	

2 Economic Burden

Table 2.2 (continued)

	Esophagus			Gallbladder			Kidney			Larynx		
	N	mean (or%)	std d	N	mean (or%)	std d	N	mean (or%)	std d	N	mean (or%)	std d
Some of the time	9	15.25		4	23.53		33	12.74		9	14.29	
Most of the time	4	6.78		1	5.88		10	3.86		1	1.59	
All of the time	2	3.39		0	0.00		11	4.25		4	6.35	
How often felt restless, past 30 days												
None of the time	33	55.93		8	47.06		157	60.62		35	55.56	
A little of the time	11	18.64		6	35.29		40	15.44		5	7.94	
Some of the time	8	13.56		1	5.88		40	15.44		18	28.57	
Most of the time	4	6.78		2	11.76		12	4.63		4	6.35	
All of the time	3	5.08		0	0.00		10	3.86		1	1.59	
How often felt sad, past 30 days												
None of the time	36	61.02		9	52.94		171	66.02		40	62.50	
A little of the time	10	16.95		3	17.65		41	15.83		7	10.94	
Some of the time	7	11.86		3	17.65		33	12.74		12	18.75	
Most of the time	3	5.08		2	11.76		7	2.70		4	6.25	
All of the time	3	5.08		0	0.00		7	2.70		1	1.56	
How often felt worthless, past 30 days												
None of the time	51	86.44		13	76.47		224	86.82		55	87.30	
A little of the time	4	6.78		1	5.88		10	3.88		4	6.35	
Some of the time	3	5.08		0	0.00		15	5.81		2	3.17	
Most of the time	1	1.69		3	17.65		3	1.16		0	0.00	
All of the time	0	0.00		0	0.00		6	2.33		2	3.17	

Table 2.2 (continued)

	Leukemia			Liver			Lung			Lymphoma		
	N	mean (or%)	std d	N	mean (or%)	std d	N	mean (or%)	std d	N	mean (or%)	std d
Working	208	0.28	0.45	90	0.22	0.42	548	0.15	0.35	459	0.38	0.49
Limited in Work from Health	207	0.42	0.49	90	0.58	0.50	548	0.53	0.50	457	0.32	0.47
Work loss days past 12 months	79	18.23	58.36	26	26.04	66.59	129	24.80	63.70	205	17.34	42.72
Bed disability days past 12 months	201	21.00	57.32	85	45.28	87.74	530	23.69	60.81	451	16.49	49.90
# nights in hospital past 12 months	207	5.09	14.63	90	6.51	12.24	547	5.21	10.89	458	3.89	16.65
Frequently depressed past 12 months	22	0.36	0.49	6	0.50	0.55	66	0.41	0.50	54	0.31	0.47
Had insomnia past 12 months	22	0.27	0.46	6	0.17	0.41	66	0.29	0.46	54	0.31	0.47
Had severe headaches past 3 mos.	208	0.23	0.42	89	0.18	0.39	545	0.11	0.31	459	0.14	0.34
Days had 5+ drinks, past year	88	8.88	41.60	32	3.94	12.87	226	25.52	86.52	228	7.97	42.36
# cigarettes in past 30 days	6	17.50	11.73	1	5.00		21	18.33	10.23	10	12.60	8.82
Smoked 100+ cigarettes in life	208	0.49	0.50	89	0.64	0.48	544	0.86	0.35	457	0.54	0.50
Unable to work due to health	207	0.29	0.45	90	0.39	0.49	547	0.38	0.49	457	0.21	0.41
Has any activity limitation	207	0.50	0.50	90	0.67	0.47	548	0.63	0.48	457	0.40	0.49
Act. limited by difficulty remembering	208	0.08	0.27	89	0.16	0.37	548	0.11	0.31	458	0.07	0.25
Self-described health												
Excellent	18	8.70		3	3.37		26	4.79		51	11.11	
Very Good	36	17.39		7	7.87		63	11.60		89	19.39	
Good	63	30.43		22	24.72		157	28.91		148	32.24	
Fair	55	26.57		31	34.83		162	29.83		108	23.53	
Poor	35	16.91		26	29.21		135	24.86		63	13.73	
Felt everything an effort, past 30 days												
None of the time	128	64.00		45	51.72		338	63.41		319	70.11	
A little of the time	24	12.00		10	11.49		54	10.13		50	10.99	
Some of the time	30	15.00		15	17.24		77	14.45		47	10.33	
Most of the time	8	4.00		6	6.90		35	6.57		20	4.40	
All of the time	10	5.00		11	12.64		29	5.44		19	4.18	
How often felt hopeless, past 30 days												
None of the time	162	81.00		61	70.11		421	78.84		375	82.60	
A little of the time	15	7.50		6	6.90		32	5.99		37	8.15	
Some of the time	14	7.00		12	13.79		51	9.55		23	5.07	
Most of the time	4	2.00		4	4.60		16	3.00		12	2.64	
All of the time	5	2.50		4	4.60		14	2.62		7	1.54	
How often felt nervous, past 30 days												
None of the time	101	50.25		47	54.02		312	58.32		252	55.38	
A little of the time	41	20.40		11	12.64		77	14.39		97	21.32	

2 Economic Burden

Table 2.2 (continued)

	Leukemia			Liver			Lung			Lymphoma		
	N	mean (or%)	std d	N	mean (or%)	std d	N	mean (or%)	std d	N	mean (or%)	std d
Some of the time	49	24.38		18	20.69		97	18.13		74	16.26	
Most of the time	5	2.49		7	8.05		26	4.86		19	4.18	
All of the time	5	2.49		4	4.60		23	4.30		13	2.86	
How often felt restless, past 30 days												
None of the time	111	55.50		43	49.43		310	58.05		254	55.95	
A little of the time	32	16.00		14	16.09		78	14.61		92	20.26	
Some of the time	35	17.50		17	19.54		93	17.42		78	17.18	
Most of the time	15	7.50		6	6.90		28	5.24		17	3.74	
All of the time	7	3.50		7	8.05		25	4.68		13	2.86	
How often felt sad, past 30 days												
None of the time	123	61.50		42	48.84		333	62.24		304	66.81	
A little of the time	35	17.50		15	17.44		75	14.02		64	14.07	
Some of the time	30	15.00		15	17.44		89	16.64		58	12.75	
Most of the time	7	3.50		10	11.63		21	3.93		22	4.84	
All of the time	5	2.50		4	4.65		17	3.18		7	1.54	
How often felt worthless, past 30 days												
None of the time	170	85.00		68	78.16		441	82.58		396	87.22	
A little of the time	6	3.00		5	5.75		28	5.24		26	5.73	
Some of the time	15	7.50		3	3.45		41	7.68		16	3.52	
Most of the time	4	2.00		2	2.30		9	1.69		12	2.64	
All of the time	5	2.50		9	10.34		15	2.81		4	0.88	

Table 2.2 (continued)

	Melanoma			Mouth			Other			Ovarian		
	N	mean (or%)	std d	N	mean (or%)	std d	N	mean (or%)	std d	N	mean (or%)	std d
Working	950	0.43	0.47	105	0.23	0.42	824	0.41	0.49	530	0.37	0.48
Limited in Work from Health	948	0.22	0.41	104	0.33	0.47	821	0.32	0.47	529	0.32	0.47
Work loss days past 12 months	477	6.99	23.97	28	7.57	20.29	410	11.31	32.35	241	11.06	30.91
Bed disability days past 12 months	940	7.92	36.48	100	18.10	61.39	803	12.69	40.61	515	15.03	46.33
# nights in hospital past 12 months	945	1.61	7.78	105	2.80	9.69	820	2.20	7.07	527	3.25	12.97
Frequently depressed past 12 months	106	0.18	0.39	8	0.13	0.35	75	0.33	0.47	51	0.43	0.50
Had insomnia past 12 months	107	0.20	0.40	9	0.22	0.44	75	0.28	0.45	51	0.45	0.50
Had severe headaches past 3 mos.	949	0.14	0.35	105	0.04	0.19	824	0.19	0.39	528	0.26	0.44
Days had 5 + drinks, past year	549	8.62	41.38	44	12.73	55.99	470	8.27	39.32	254	7.29	31.12
# cigarettes in past 30 days	28	14.64	9.98	4	6.00	4.62	25	12.52	9.66	29	15.10	7.51
Smoked 100+ cigarettes in life	945	0.53	0.50	104	0.71	0.46	821	0.53	0.50	528	0.52	0.50
Unable to work due to health	950	0.12	0.32	105	0.25	0.43	824	0.20	0.40	528	0.21	0.41
Has any activity limitation	949	0.29	0.45	104	0.43	0.50	824	0.40	0.49	527	0.40	0.49
Act. limited by difficulty remembering	950	0.03	0.17	105	0.10	0.31	824	0.08	0.27	529	0.08	0.27
Self-described health												
Excellent	194	20.44		8	7.62		107	13.00		58	11.03	
Very Good	300	31.61		30	28.57		212	25.76		125	23.76	
Good	258	27.19		24	22.86		240	29.16		162	30.80	
Fair	136	14.33		33	31.43		179	21.75		125	23.76	
Poor	61	6.43		10	9.52		85	10.33		56	10.65	
Felt everything an effort, past 30 days												
None of the time	703	74.79		73	70.87		531	65.15		305	57.77	
A little of the time	106	11.28		9	8.74		104	12.76		68	12.88	
Some of the time	84	8.94		12	11.65		108	13.25		83	15.72	
Most of the time	33	3.51		6	5.83		44	5.40		45	8.52	
All of the time	14	1.49		3	2.91		28	3.44		27	5.11	
How often felt hopeless, past 30 days												
None of the time	829	88.19		89	86.41		648	79.61		399	75.71	
A little of the time	55	5.85		4	3.88		71	8.72		48	9.11	
Some of the time	39	4.15		6	5.83		66	8.11		46	8.73	
Most of the time	9	0.96		3	2.91		20	2.46		22	4.17	
All of the time	8	0.85		1	0.97		9	1.11		12	2.28	

2 Economic Burden

Table 2.2 (continued)

	Melanoma			Mouth			Other			Ovarian		
	N	mean (or%)	std d	N	mean (or%)	std d	N	mean (or%)	std d	N	mean (or%)	std d
How often felt nervous, past 30 days												
None of the time	594	63.39		68	66.02		451	55.41		269	51.14	
A little of the time	182	19.42		17	16.50		173	21.25		98	18.63	
Some of the time	105	11.21		14	13.59		132	16.22		90	17.11	
Most of the time	31	3.31		2	1.94		37	4.55		43	8.17	
All of the time	25	2.67		2	1.94		21	2.58		26	4.94	
How often felt restless, past 30 days												
None of the time	588	62.62		69	66.99		445	54.60		276	52.37	
A little of the time	171	18.21		13	12.62		155	19.02		91	17.27	
Some of the time	122	12.99		17	16.50		146	17.91		95	18.03	
Most of the time	37	3.94		2	1.94		44	5.40		45	8.54	
All of the time	21	2.24		2	1.94		25	3.07		20	3.80	
How often felt sad, past 30 days												
None of the time	700	74.31		74	71.84		521	63.77		306	57.95	
A little of the time	149	15.82		15	14.56		135	16.52		82	15.53	
Some of the time	74	7.86		11	10.68		122	14.93		90	17.05	
Most of the time	9	0.96		2	1.94		32	3.92		36	6.82	
All of the time	10	1.06		1	0.97		7	0.86		14	2.65	
How often felt worthless, past 30 days												
None of the time	838	89.24		88	85.44		678	83.50		419	79.36	
A little of the time	41	4.37		7	6.80		62	7.64		39	7.39	
Some of the time	42	4.47		5	4.85		50	6.16		41	7.77	
Most of the time	8	0.85		2	1.94		13	1.60		16	3.03	
All of the time	10	1.06		1	0.97		9	1.11		13	2.46	

Table 2.2 (continued)

	Pancreatic			Prostate			Rectal			Soft Tissue		
	N	mean (or%)	std d	N	mean (or%)	std d	N	mean (or%)	std d	N	mean (or%)	std d
Working	69	0.23	0.43	1877	0.19	0.40	96	0.15	0.35	83	0.36	0.48
Limited in Work from Health	69	0.51	0.50	1877	0.28	0.45	96	0.47	0.50	82	0.34	0.48
Work loss days past 12 months	24	31.50	73.90	478	9.68	31.98	17	7.94	28.91	41	25.10	67.83
Bed disability days past 12 months	69	15.14	0.00	1841	8.41	38.63	93	18.26	56.03	82	21.22	63.13
# nights in hospital past 12 months	69	5.48	28.70	1869	2.24	8.44	95	3.11	9.01	83	3.69	11.30
Frequently depressed past 12 months	9	0.33	5.00	211	0.15	0.36	12	0.25	0.45	11	0.27	0.47
Had insomnia past 12 months	9	0.22	9.01	212	0.17	0.38	12	0.33	0.49	11	0.00	0.00
Had severe headaches past 3 mos.	69	0.23	0.50	1876	0.06	0.23	96	0.13	0.33	83	0.17	0.38
Days had 5 + drinks, past year	32	15.00	0.44	929	11.97	55.40	46	8.13	34.58	46	4.39	11.43
# cigarettes in past 30 days	0	.	0.43	30	14.40	9.84	3	18.33	7.64	5	5.80	6.46
Smoked 100+ cigarettes in life	69	0.51	65.00	1866	0.66	0.47	96	0.63	0.49	83	0.58	0.50
Unable to work due to health	69	0.38	5.00	1874	0.16	0.37	96	0.33	0.47	82	0.24	0.43
Has any activity limitation	69	0.54		1877	0.39	0.49	96	0.55	0.50	83	0.41	0.49
Act. limited by difficulty remembering	69	0.10	0.30	1877	0.08	0.26	95	0.09	0.29	83	0.08	0.28
Self-described health												
Excellent	5	7.25	0.50	208	11.10		9	9.38		13	15.66	
Very Good	15	21.74	0.49	387	20.65		13	13.54		18	21.69	
Good	15	21.74	0.50	655	34.95		34	35.42		22	26.51	
Fair	16	23.19		464	24.76		25	26.04		23	27.71	
Poor	18	26.09		160	8.54		15	15.63		7	8.43	
Felt everything an effort, past 30 days												
None of the time	40	58.82		1438	78.62		63	67.02		46	56.79	
A little of the time	8	11.76		172	9.40		9	9.57		17	20.99	
Some of the time	10	14.71		129	7.05		13	13.83		6	7.41	
Most of the time	6	8.82		55	3.01		5	5.32		6	7.41	
All of the time	4	5.88		35	1.91		4	4.26		6	7.41	
How often felt hopeless, past 30 days												
None of the time	48	70.59		1633	89.23		82	87.23		60	74.07	
A little of the time	8	11.76		95	5.19		5	5.32		13	16.05	
Some of the time	5	7.35		60	3.28		4	4.26		6	7.41	
Most of the time	5	7.35		27	1.48		1	1.06		1	1.23	
All of the time	2	2.94		15	0.82		2	2.13		1	1.23	
How often felt nervous, past 30 days												
None of the time	36	52.94		1326	72.54		59	62.77		45	55.56	
A little of the time	12	17.65		283	15.48		17	18.09		19	23.46	

2 Economic Burden

Table 2.2 (continued)

	Pancreatic			Prostate			Rectal			Soft Tissue		
	N	mean (or%)	std d	N	mean (or%)	std d	N	mean (or%)	std d	N	mean (or%)	std d
Some of the time	13	19.12		141	7.71		13	13.83		10	12.35	
Most of the time	4	5.88		41	2.24		4	4.26		7	8.64	
All of the time	3	4.41		37	2.02		1	1.06		0	0.00	
How often felt restless, past 30 days												
None of the time	39	57.35		1273	69.56		56	59.57		43	53.09	
A little of the time	7	10.29		281	15.36		13	13.83		19	23.46	
Some of the time	15	22.06		182	9.95		16	17.02		14	17.28	
Most of the time	5	7.35		59	3.22		6	6.38		4	4.94	
All of the time	2	2.94		35	1.91		3	3.19		1	1.23	
How often felt sad, past 30 days												
None of the time	34	50.00		1394	76.26		59	62.77		42	51.85	
A little of the time	11	16.18		202	11.05		20	21.28		26	32.10	
Some of the time	17	25.00		158	8.64		11	11.70		8	9.88	
Most of the time	4	5.88		47	2.57		3	3.19		3	3.70	
All of the time	2	2.94		27	1.48		1	1.06		2	2.47	
How often felt worthless, past 30 days												
None of the time	54	79.41		1657	90.55		83	88.30		68	83.95	
A little of the time	5	7.35		75	4.10		4	4.26		9	11.11	
Some of the time	3	4.41		61	3.33		4	4.26		1	1.23	
Most of the time	4	5.88		23	1.26		1	1.06		3	3.70	
All of the time	2	2.94		14	0.77		2	2.13		0	0.00	

Table 2.2 (continued)

	Stomach			Testicular			Throat			Thyroid		
	N	mean (or%)	std d	N	mean (or%)	std d	N	mean (or%)	std d	N	mean (or%)	std d
Working	191	0.23	0.42	150	0.73	0.45	222	0.25	0.43	356	0.49	0.50
Limited in Work from Health	192	0.46	0.50	149	0.17	0.38	222	0.45	0.50	357	0.20	0.40
Work loss days past 12 months	58	12.98	36.44	125	8.70	29.27	68	15.15	33.73	204	12.88	46.86
Bed disability days past 12 months	185	25.12	73.49	149	8.74	36.03	214	21.17	61.71	353	8.09	30.21
# nights in hospital past 12 months	190	3.77	10.78	150	1.58	7.41	220	5.44	22.12	356	1.94	9.97
Frequently depressed past 12 months	25	0.16	0.37	13	0.08	0.28	30	0.27	0.45	47	0.23	0.43
Had insomnia past 12 months	25	0.36	0.49	13	0.08	0.28	30	0.27	0.45	47	0.34	0.48
Had severe headaches past 3 mos.	191	0.25	0.43	150	0.13	0.34	222	0.15	0.36	357	0.19	0.39
Days had 5 + drinks, past year	65	18.48	68.02	109	18.50	56.70	119	31.82	85.99	195	6.68	36.62
# cigarettes in past 30 days	9	15.78	7.41	13	10.69	6.79	10	16.40	9.74	8	16.75	11.47
Smoked 100+ cigarettes in life	190	0.54	0.50	150	0.51	0.50	221	0.79	0.41	356	0.46	0.50
Unable to work due to health	192	0.32	0.47	150	0.12	0.33	222	0.36	0.48	356	0.12	0.33
Has any activity limitation	192	0.54	0.50	149	0.21	0.41	222	0.60	0.49	357	0.25	0.44
Act. limited by difficulty remembering	192	0.11	0.32	150	0.01	0.12	222	0.11	0.32	356	0.03	0.17
Self-described health												
Excellent	12	6.25		41	27.33		17	7.69		45	12.61	
Very Good	32	16.67		47	31.33		32	14.48		110	30.81	
Good	47	24.48		42	28.00		68	30.77		114	31.93	
Fair	61	31.77		13	8.67		60	27.15		62	17.37	
Poor	40	20.83		7	4.67		44	19.91		26	7.28	
Felt everything an effort, past 30 days												
None of the time	121	65.76		114	76.00		134	62.04		262	74.01	
A little of the time	16	8.70		21	14.00		31	14.35		36	10.17	
Some of the time	17	9.24		9	6.00		20	9.26		31	8.76	
Most of the time	21	11.41		1	0.67		16	7.41		13	3.67	
All of the time	9	4.89		5	3.33		15	6.94		12	3.39	
How often felt hopeless, past 30 days												
None of the time	136	73.91		140	93.33		158	73.15		311	87.85	
A little of the time	20	10.87		5	3.33		25	11.57		18	5.08	
Some of the time	13	7.07		2	1.33		15	6.94		13	3.67	
Most of the time	9	4.89		2	1.33		11	5.09		9	2.54	
All of the time	6	3.26		1	0.67		7	3.24		3	0.85	
How often felt nervous, past 30 days												
None of the time	99	53.80		95	63.33		112	51.38		223	62.99	
A little of the time	29	15.76		32	21.33		47	21.56		63	17.80	

Table 2.2 (continued)

	Stomach			Testicular			Throat			Thyroid		
	N	mean (or%)	std d	N	mean (or%)	std d	N	mean (or%)	std d	N	mean (or%)	std d
Some of the time	37	20.11		16	10.67		35	16.06		49	13.84	
Most of the time	13	7.07		5	3.33		10	4.59		9	2.54	
All of the time	6	3.26		2	1.33		14	6.42		10	2.82	
How often felt restless, past 30 days												
None of the time	107	58.47		93	62.00		112	51.38		210	59.32	
A little of the time	22	12.02		30	20.00		43	19.72		71	20.06	
Some of the time	30	16.39		17	11.33		41	18.81		51	14.41	
Most of the time	12	6.56		6	4.00		12	5.50		14	3.95	
All of the time	12	6.56		4	2.67		10	4.59		8	2.26	
How often felt sad, past 30 days												
None of the time	102	55.14		120	80.00		125	57.60		258	73.09	
A little of the time	25	13.51		18	12.00		32	14.75		52	14.73	
Some of the time	35	18.92		8	5.33		35	16.13		29	8.22	
Most of the time	16	8.65		3	2.00		19	8.76		10	2.83	
All of the time	7	3.78		1	0.67		6	2.76		4	1.13	
How often felt worthless, past 30 days												
None of the time	143	78.14		141	94.00		177	81.57		317	90.06	
A little of the time	15	8.20		3	2.00		8	3.69		14	3.98	
Some of the time	11	6.01		4	2.67		13	5.99		13	3.69	
Most of the time	8	4.37		0	0.00		10	4.61		4	1.14	
All of the time	6	3.28		2	1.33		9	4.15		4	1.14	

Table 2.2 (continued)

	Uterine			NM Skin Cancer			Unknown Skin Cancer		
	N	mean (or%)	std d	N	mean (or%)	std d	N	mean (or%)	std d
Working	1278	0.33	0.47	3228	0.38	0.48	1838	0.30	0.46
Limited in Work from Health	1275	0.36	0.48	3220	0.20	0.40	1841	0.31	0.46
Work loss days past 12 months	520	8.75	26.07	1485	4.72	20.26	668	5.49	23.65
Bed disability days past 12 months	1246	13.30	42.77	3207	5.35	25.55	1797	9.05	38.62
# nights in hospital past 12 months	1275	1.87	7.13	3227	0.91	4.75	1840	1.43	6.16
Frequently depressed past 12 months	135	0.41	0.49	392	0.21	0.41	224	0.25	0.44
Had insomnia past 12 months	135	0.43	0.50	392	0.26	0.44	226	0.31	0.46
Had severe headaches past 3 mos.	1276	0.29	0.46	3223	0.13	0.34	1838	0.14	0.34
Days had 5 + drinks, past year	568	5.84	30.76	2007	6.09	34.82	930	7.13	36.15
# cigarettes in past 30 days	50	15.64	9.74	72	12.56	8.60	35	13.43	10.25
Smoked 100+ cigarettes in life	1274	0.55	0.50	3216	0.54	0.50	1832	0.56	0.50
Unable to work due to health	1276	0.24	0.43	3225	0.11	0.31	1841	0.19	0.39
Has any activity limitation	1278	0.44	0.50	3224	0.28	0.45	1840	0.40	0.49
Act. limited by difficulty remembering	1276	0.09	0.29	3225	0.04	0.20	1841	0.07	0.26
Self-described health									
Excellent	152	11.92		727	22.56		310	16.85	
Very Good	275	21.57		999	31.00		459	24.95	
Good	408	32.00		980	30.41		568	30.87	
Fair	309	24.24		382	11.85		342	18.59	
Poor	131	10.27		135	4.19		161	8.75	
Felt everything an effort, past 30 days									
None of the time	768	60.90		2421	75.73		1293	71.52	
A little of the time	136	10.79		363	11.35		206	11.39	
Some of the time	185	14.67		269	8.41		174	9.62	
Most of the time	99	7.85		93	2.91		73	4.04	
All of the time	73	5.79		51	1.60		62	3.43	
How often felt hopeless, past 30 days									
None of the time	967	76.69		2868	89.71		1550	85.64	
A little of the time	104	8.25		166	5.19		98	5.41	
Some of the time	121	9.60		107	3.35		99	5.47	
Most of the time	35	2.78		39	1.22		40	2.21	
All of the time	34	2.70		17	0.53		23	1.27	
How often felt nervous, past 30 days									
None of the time	623	49.41		1998	62.46		1092	60.36	
A little of the time	235	18.64		722	22.57		351	19.40	
Some of the time	239	18.95		354	11.07		238	13.16	

Table 2.2 (continued)

	Uterine			NM Skin Cancer			Unknown Skin Cancer		
	N	mean (or%)	std d	N	mean (or%)	std d	N	mean (or%)	std d
Most of the time	85	6.74		89	2.78		93	5.14	
All of the time	79	6.26		36	1.13		35	1.93	
How often felt restless, past 30 days									
None of the time	648	51.27		2034	63.60		1116	61.79	
A little of the time	189	14.95		629	19.67		318	17.61	
Some of the time	247	19.54		394	12.32		233	12.90	
Most of the time	107	8.47		96	3.00		81	4.49	
All of the time	73	5.78		45	1.41		58	3.21	
How often felt sad, past 30 days									
None of the time	699	55.34		2480	77.60		1291	71.52	
A little of the time	214	16.94		411	12.86		239	13.24	
Some of the time	223	17.66		218	6.82		189	10.47	
Most of the time	79	6.25		69	2.16		60	3.32	
All of the time	48	3.80		18	0.56		26	1.44	
How often felt worthless, past 30 days									
None of the time	1010	79.97		2903	90.75		1566	86.52	
A little of the time	71	5.62		146	4.56		91	5.03	
Some of the time	100	7.92		96	3.00		90	4.97	
Most of the time	44	3.48		32	1.00		43	2.38	
All of the time	38	3.01		22	0.69		20	1.10	

Source: The Health Interview Surveys, 1997–2005.

and 2.7, the causal connection between employment and health/mental health variables are complex. As it is surely the case that depression can affect job interviews and job performances (and hence employment probability), it is also the case that when people lose a job it is a depressing experience. Causality is likely to go in both directions, which makes inclusion of these health variables in an employment regression potentially problematic. We exclude them in the analysis below, and interpret our results as the overall reduced effect of the socioeconomic variables included on the right hand side. That is, the coefficient for the age variable will represent both the direct effect of age on employment and the indirect effect of age on health status times the effect of health status on employment.

Cancer Survivors: Has There Been a Shift in Morbidity Employment Experience as Taken from the Case of Breast Cancer?

Improvements in the treatment and earlier detection of cancer have increased the number of cancer survivors [13]. As a large proportion of younger and middle-aged survivors will be part of the potential work force after their diagnosis, understanding the work outlook for them has important behavioral as well as policy implications. In order to address these issues, we employ nine years of data (from nine separate surveys, integrated by the Minnesota Population Center) to construct employment experiences of cancer survivors after diagnosis. We do this by creating synthetic cohorts—that is, taking the 3100 breast cancer survivors (using as one example) and treating them as if they were one statistical breast cancer survivor whose average experience reveals the "typical" breast cancer survivor's employment outcomes following diagnosis.

The validity of a breast cancer employment pattern from such a synthetic cohort analysis depends on whether the employment pattern assorted with cancer morbidity has been stable given recent medical advances. In the face of changing technology for treatments, employment following diagnosis may have changed for several reasons. Early detection and better treatment options with less permanent residual damage would increase the average health capital of survivors and increase employment likelihood following diagnosis. On the other hand, to the extent that treatments preserve the lives of the sickest individuals, it might well lower the health capital of the pool of survivors (by including more sick individuals, the pool looks less healthy on average because of a selection effect), and appear to decrease employment likelihood of the pool following diagnosis. The question of shifts in employment following diagnosis is then an empirical issue which can be readily tested.

To examine whether there have been shifts in cancer survivor's employment following diagnosis (without specifying the nature of the shift, just whether there has been a change in survivors' employment patterns), let $y = 1$ if the survivor worked at the time of interview:

Table 2.3 Changes in employment trends for cancer survivors

	Likelihood of working				Limited in work due to health			
	Trend change specification		Dummy variables change specification		Trend change specification		Dummy variables change specification	
	Coefficient	Prob. signif.	Coefficient	Prob. signif.	Coefficient	Prob. signif.	Coefficient	Prob. signif.
yr dummy = 1997	−0.1602	0.0931	−0.2070	0.0549	0.1627	0.0451	0.2011	0.0280
yr dummy = 1998	−0.1450	0.1300	−0.1387	0.2073	0.0843	0.3071	0.1796	0.0549
yr dummy = 1999	−0.1258	0.1950	−0.0755	0.4940	−0.0394	0.6373	−0.0844	0.3731
yr dummy = 2000	−0.1364	0.1635	−0.1819	0.0988	0.0147	0.8607	0.0425	0.6526
yr dummy = 2001	0.0105	0.9125	−0.0504	0.6357	−0.0059	0.9438	0.0394	0.6700
yr dummy = 2002	0.0089	0.9236	−0.0243	0.8217	0.0835	0.2958	0.1835	0.0444
yr dummy = 2003	−0.1397	0.1149	−0.0675	0.5421	0.0074	0.9233	−0.0338	0.7205
yr dummy = 2004	−0.0535	0.5085	−0.1256	0.2449	−0.0301	0.6711	0.0917	0.3195
can. duration	0.0217	0.0096	0.0101	0.1491	0.0019	0.7468	−0.0021	0.6835
can. duration sq.	−0.00031	0.0082	−0.0003	0.0085	0.0001	0.0580	0.0001	0.0551
can. dur*trend	−0.00211	0.5208			−0.0026	0.2788		
can. dur*trend sq.	0.000112	0.7242			0.0002	0.3975		
can_dur*dum = 1997			0.0128	0.1022			0.0016	0.7794
can_dur*dum = 1998			0.0054	0.4981			−0.0058	0.3140
can_dur*dum = 1999			−0.0009	0.9079			0.0059	0.3142
can_dur*dum = 2000			0.0080	0.3128			−0.0022	0.7065
can_dur*dum = 2001			0.0084	0.2665			−0.0047	0.3998
can_dur*dum = 2002			0.0047	0.5405			−0.0106	0.0638
can_dur*dum = 2003			−0.0072	0.3770			0.0026	0.6510
can_dur*dum = 2004			0.0077	0.9880			−0.0121	0.0346
Sample size	19753		19753		19721		19721	
−2*loglikelihood	17428.292		17421.506		22181.266		22166.435	
Test: duration vars	<.0102		0.0303		0.0698		0.0967	
Test: shift in dur.	0.3801		0.3743		0.3540		0.0325	

Notes: Included in the specification, but not reported here, are all the other socio-demographic variables in Tables 2.3 and 2.4, including dummy variables for each cancer type.

Table 2.4 The determinants of working, logistic regressions using 1997–2005 health interview survey

	Full sample		Cancer sample, without duration variables		Cancer only sample, with duration var.	
	Coefficient	Prob. sign.	Coefficient	Prob. sign.	Coefficient	Prob. sign.
Intercept	−3.2324	<.0001	−2.2502	<.0001	−2.1938	<.0001
male	0.8128	<.0001	0.3974	<.0001	0.4014	<.0001
age	0.1940	<.0001	0.1489	<.0001	0.1457	<.0001
age square	−0.0026	<.0001	−0.00204	<.0001	−0.00202	<.0001
age 65+ dummy	−0.4588	<.0001	−0.4254	<.0001	−0.4274	<.0001
educational attainment	0.2770	<.0001	0.2837	<.0001	0.2819	<.0001
Black	−0.1894	<.0001	−0.3632	<.0001	−0.3406	<.0001
Hispanic	−0.1298	<.0001	−0.2435	0.0015	−0.2430	0.0017
Asian	−0.2845	<.0001	0.1363	0.5301	0.2078	0.3440
Cancer duration					0.0148	0.0018
Cancer duration squared					−0.0003	0.0071
Bladder	−0.2710	0.0469	−0.2002	0.1592	−0.2059	0.1512
Blood	−1.0908	0.0032	−0.9586	0.0087	−0.9330	0.0119
Bone	−1.3560	<.0001	−1.1877	<.0001	−1.2272	<.0001
Brain	−1.8467	<.0001	−1.6663	<.0001	−1.7426	<.0001
Breast	−0.1153	0.0162	−0.2367	0.0022	−0.2550	0.0013
Cervical	−0.1219	0.0258	−0.1696	0.0405	−0.2281	0.0078
Colon	−0.2161	0.0097	−0.2122	0.0290	−0.2239	0.0236
Esophagus	−1.3208	0.0002	−1.1032	0.0017	−1.0913	0.0020
Gallbladder	−0.9836	0.1113	−1.0164	0.0977	−1.0255	0.0949
Kidney	−0.4785	0.0043	−0.3768	0.0266	−0.3850	0.0241
Larynx	−0.6113	0.0537	−0.4745	0.1276	−0.5060	0.1060
Leukemia	−0.9673	<.0001	−0.8827	<.0001	−0.9431	<.0001
Liver	−1.2525	<.0001	−1.0916	<.0001	−1.1599	<.0001
Lung	−1.1947	<.0001	−1.0805	<.0001	−1.0621	<.0001
Lymphoma	−0.4189	0.0002	−0.3296	0.0074	−0.3524	0.0047
Melanoma	−0.1529	0.0520	−0.1042	0.2683	−0.1256	0.1898
Mouth	−1.0301	<.0001	−0.8713	0.0008	−0.8852	0.0007
Other	−0.4574	<.0001	−0.3862	<.0001	−0.4178	<.0001
Ovarian	−0.3899	0.0001	−0.4353	0.0001	−0.4729	<.0001
Pancreatic	−0.8660	0.0135	−0.7809	0.0233	−0.7859	0.0231
Prostate	−0.3555	<.0001	−0.2191	0.0209	−0.2055	0.1346
Rectum	−1.0489	0.0024	−0.9290	0.0058	−0.9155	0.0067
Skin Unknown	−0.3366	<.0001	−0.2825	0.0009	−0.3026	0.0005
Skin Non-melanoma	−0.2195	<.0001	−0.1796	0.0175	−0.2017	0.0094
Soft Tissue Stomach	−0.7884	0.0032	−0.6960	0.0083	−0.7229	0.0064
Testicular	−0.5980	0.0068	−0.4958	0.0230	−0.4994	0.0233
Throat	−0.1894	0.3872	0.1580	0.4814	0.0992	0.6611
Thyroid	−0.9385	<.0001	−0.7516	<.0001	−0.7734	<.0001
Uterus	−0.0665	0.6112	−0.0670	0.6295	−0.1002	0.4778
1997 year	−0.3367	<.0001	−0.3825	<.0001	−0.4314	<.0001
1998 year	−0.0701	<.0001	−0.0838	0.2759	0.0854	0.2702

Table 2.4 (continued)

	Full sample		Cancer sample, without duration variables		Cancer only sample, with duration var.	
	Coefficient	Prob. sign.	Coefficient	Prob. sign.	Coefficient	Prob. sign.
1999 year	−0.0587	<.0001	−0.0963	0.2210	−0.0855	0.2813
2000 year	0.0075	0.5732	−0.0863	0.2753	−0.0812	0.3080
2001 year	0.0114	0.3834	−0.1055	0.1812	−0.1043	0.1893
2002 year	0.0191	0.1453	0.0319	0.6745	0.0321	0.6745
2003 year	−0.0419	0.0016	0.0131	0.8657	0.0226	0.7716
2004 year	−0.0615	<.0001	−0.1202	0.1253	−0.1325	0.0941
	−0.0358	0.0068	−0.0607	0.4288	−0.0503	0.5158
Sample size	607284		20065		19753	
−2*Log likelihood	621327.25		17681.579		17430.219	

$$\text{Prob}(y_i = 1) = G(C_i\varphi + X_i\alpha + t_i\beta_t + (\tau_i * t_i)\delta_\tau) \tag{2.1}$$

where t = years since diagnosis (this is "cancer duration"), and τ is a secular trend variable taking a value of one in 1997 and equal to the survey year minus 1996 (so that it is a linear trend of the year in which the survey was taken, so for survey year 1997, $\tau = 1$, for survey year 1998, $\tau = 2$, for survey year 1999, $\tau = 3$, etc.). This employment relationship will be estimated by a logistic regression model, where the X vector includes dummy variables for the year of the survey, gender, race, current age, age-squared, educational attainment, and marital status. The C-vector includes dummy variables for each cancer type. Hence, the δ_τ represents the secular shift in the employment/cancer duration relationship. If this parameter is estimated to be zero, there has been no shift in employment patterns following diagnosis during the sample period—they are the same in one year as in any other year.

We let "cancer duration's impact on the employment rate" change over time by allowing the duration/employment rates to increase or decrease over time, such that the parameters β_t and δ_τ become:

$$\beta_t = \lambda_0 + \lambda_1 t \quad \text{and} \quad \delta_\tau = \phi_0 + \phi_1 \tau \tag{2.2}$$

Substitute equation (2.2) into equation (2.1) to get

$$\begin{aligned}\text{Prob}(y_i = 1) &= G(C_i\varphi + X_i\alpha + t_i * (\lambda_0 + \lambda_1 t_i) + \phi_0(t_i\tau_i) + \phi_1(t_i\tau_i^2)) \\ &= G(X_i\alpha + \lambda_0 t_i + \lambda_1 t_i^2 + \phi_0(t_i\tau_i) + \phi_1(t_i\tau_i^2))\end{aligned} \tag{2.3}$$

As an alternative test, we further generalize and allow the shift to be unspecified by including dummy variables for each year (corresponding to a non-parametric secular, τ_i-type effect). This allows us to test for shifts in the employment relationship following diagnosis by including dummy variables for each year interacted with cancer duration (time since diagnosis).

These results, partially presented in Table 2.3, indicate there is no shift during our sample period in the employment pattern following diagnosis. In the likelihood of working regressions, neither the "cancer duration*trend" nor the "cancer duration*trend square" variables in the far left hand column, which measure shifts in employment probability based on cancer duration, turn out not to be statistically significant (nor quantitatively important) as individual coefficients. Moreover, they are jointly insignificant as indicated by probability significance level given in the last row. The non-significant result applies despite the very large sample of cancer survivors (N = 20,000).

The non-significance of these variables simply indicates that there is no CHANGE in the cancer duration*employment relationship during the period; it does NOT mean that cancer duration is unimportant to employment. The "cancer duration" and "cancer duration squared" variables are statistically significant and relatively large in their effect, though they are not reported in Table 2.3 (but are included and reported for the other tables below). Table 2.3 indicates that the relationship between time since diagnosis and employment probability did not SHIFT over the sample period. That is also true for logistic regression of being limited in work due to health (results given in the right hand columns of Table 2.3).

The absence of a shift gives more credence to our synthetic cohort analysis below and suggests that it may not be much of a distortion to compare cancer survivors across different survey panels. More substantially, it also means that there is no evidence that recent changes in the treatment of cancer have changed *net* employment outcomes during the past decade (perhaps because of potentially offsetting morbidity and sample selection effects due to mortality changes).

Employment Among Cancer Survivors: Morbidity Effects

There are three dimensions of work available in the IHIS that we analyzed in this study: the likelihood of being employed at the time the sample was taken (Table 2.4), the likelihood of being limited in hours of work because of health (Table 2.5), and the likelihood of being unable to work because of health (Table 2.6). In all three, the demographic variables have their expected impact: males work more (and are less likely to miss work because of health), older people work less, and the more educated work more. This is true both for cancer survivors (in the right four columns) and for the population in general (the two left hand columns include both cancer and non-cancer populations).

The year dummy variables at the bottom of these specifications indicate that employment has been cyclical, peaking in 2001 for both the non-cancer and

Table 2.5 Limited in work because of health, logistic regressions using 1997–2005 health interview survey

	Full sample		Cancer only sample, w/ duration variables	
	Coefficient	Prob. sign.	Coefficient	Prob. sign.
Intercept	−3.8526	<.0001	−2.4300	<.0001
male	−0.0536	<.0001	−0.0326	0.4640
age	0.0636	<.0001	0.0373	<.0001
age square	−0.0001	<.0001	−0.0001	0.4523
age 65 + dummy	−0.4448	<.0001	−0.5517	<.0001
educational attainment	−0.4135	<.0001	−0.3116	<.0001
Black	0.2403	<.0001	0.4379	<.0001
Hispanic	−0.4213	<.0001	0.0272	0.6986
Asian	−0.6820	<.0001	−0.3511	0.1176
Cancer duration			−0.0045	0.1787
Cancer duration square			0.0001	0.0749
Bladder	0.2013	0.0518	0.1381	0.2047
Blood	0.8562	0.0030	0.5261	0.0649
Bone	1.1938	<.0001	0.9669	<.0001
Brain	2.2867	<.0001	1.7115	<.0001
Breast	0.3648	<.0001	0.2120	0.0005
Cervical	0.7870	<.0001	0.2882	0.0002
Colon	0.3518	<.0001	0.2800	<.0001
Esophagus	1.1062	<.0001	0.8720	0.0004
Gallbladder	1.1345	0.0098	0.9173	0.0297
Kidney	0.8130	<.0001	0.6458	<.0001
Larynx	1.2025	<.0001	0.9993	<.0001
Leukemia	1.3258	<.0001	0.9777	<.0001
Liver	1.5900	<.0001	1.2737	<.0001
Lung	1.2416	<.0001	1.1014	<.0001
Lymphoma	0.8005	<.0001	0.5128	<.0001
Melanoma	0.3157	<.0001	0.1142	0.1724
Mouth	0.5495	0.0063	0.3709	0.0646
Other	0.8775	<.0001	0.5683	<.0001
Ovarian	0.8035	<.0001	0.5077	<.0001
Pancreatic	1.3700	<.0001	1.1315	<.0001
Prostate	0.1816	0.0006	0.0747	0.3149
Rectum	0.8620	<.0001	0.7770	0.0002
Skin Unknown	0.5048	<.0001	0.3498	<.0001
Skin Non-melanoma	0.1509	0.0010	−0.0293	0.6454
Soft Tissue	1.0974	<.0001	0.7542	0.0015
Stomach	1.0048	<.0001	0.7253	<.0001
Testicular	0.6344	0.0072	0.0741	0.7503
Throat	1.1086	<.0001	0.8802	<.0001
Thyroid	0.1979	0.1642	−0.1051	0.4600
Uterus	0.8262	<.0001	0.5516	<.0001
1997 year	0.1573	<.0001	0.2157	0.0013
1998 year	0.1038	<.0001	0.1167	0.0943
1999 year	0.0194	0.2868	−0.0245	0.7261
2000 year	−0.0317	0.0819	0.0170	0.8066
2001 year	0.0022	0.9016	−0.0128	0.8511
2002 year	0.0188	0.3065	0.0729	0.2856

Table 2.5 (continued)

	Full sample		Cancer only sample, w/ duration variables	
	Coefficient	Prob. sign.	Coefficient	Prob. sign.
2003 year	0.0020	0.9141	−0.0048	0.9448
2004 year	−0.0007	0.9682	−0.0380	0.5785
Sample size	607356		19721	
-2*Log likelihood	374488.11		22183.343	

Table 2.6 Unable to work because of health, logistic regressions using 1997–2005 health interview survey

	Full sample		Cancer only sample, w/ duration variables	
	Coefficient	Prob. sign.	Coefficient	Prob. sign.
Intercept	−4.5352	<.0001	−3.1168	<.0001
male	−0.0666	<.0001	−0.0538	0.3033
age	0.0769	<.0001	0.0564	<.0001
age square	−0.0002	<.0001	−0.0002	0.0054
age 65 + dummy	−0.7175	<.0001	−0.7693	<.0001
educational attainment	−0.5386	<.0001	−0.4016	<.0001
Black	0.4164	<.0001	0.5696	<.0001
Hispanic	−0.3067	<.0001	0.0181	0.8208
Asian	−0.6634	<.0001	−0.5999	0.0463
Cancer duration			−0.0109	0.0049
Cancer duration square			0.0002	0.0016
Bladder	0.3245	0.0061	0.2601	0.0359
Blood	1.0771	0.0004	0.6896	0.0252
Bone	1.4270	<.0001	1.1862	<.0001
Brain	2.5125	<.0001	1.8953	<.0001
Breast	0.3228	<.0001	0.1397	0.0460
Cervical	0.8036	<.0001	0.2721	0.0023
Colon	0.3883	<.0001	0.2888	0.0003
Esophagus	1.2109	<.0001	0.9431	0.0003
Gallbladder	1.0236	0.0243	0.8190	0.0614
Kidney	0.6955	<.0001	0.5215	0.0004
Larynx	1.3793	<.0001	1.1444	<.0001
Leukemia	1.3643	<.0001	0.9753	<.0001
Liver	1.3279	<.0001	1.0708	<.0001
Lung	1.2275	<.0001	1.0501	<.0001
Lymphoma	0.7812	<.0001	0.4528	0.0002
Melanoma	0.1299	0.1755	−0.1104	0.2911
Mouth	0.6664	0.0023	0.4499	0.0423
Other	0.7994	<.0001	0.4756	<.0001
Ovarian	0.7113	<.0001	0.4124	0.0002
Pancreatic	1.3839	<.0001	1.1080	<.0001
Prostate	0.0970	0.1333	−0.0307	0.7282
Rectum	0.8637	<.0001	0.8088	0.0002

Table 2.6 (continued)

	Full sample		Cancer only sample, w/ duration variables	
	Coefficient	Prob. sign.	Coefficient	Prob. sign.
Skin Unknown	0.4821	<.0001	0.2941	0.0002
Skin Non-melanoma	0.0340	0.5649	0.1918	0.0132
Soft Tissue	1.2485	<.0001	0.8672	0.0008
Stomach	0.9306	<.0001	0.6824	<.0001
Testicular	0.7779	0.0047	0.1530	0.5743
Throat	1.2959	<.0001	1.0353	<.0001
Thyroid	0.1646	0.3370	−0.1619	0.3499
Uterus	0.8269	<.0001	0.5287	<.0001
1997 year	0.1115	<.0001	0.1733	0.0275
1998 year	0.0681	0.0023	0.1187	0.1468
1999 year	0.0360	0.1087	−0.0906	0.2761
2000 year	0.0464	0.0378	0.0411	0.6142
2001 year	0.0105	0.6363	−0.0304	0.7069
2002 year	0.0195	0.3855	0.0113	0.8891
2003 year	0.0232	0.3039	0.0558	0.4935
2004 year	0.0308	0.1719	−0.0228	0.7774
Sample size	609581		19736	
-2*Log likelihood	268259.24		17275.182	

cancer samples (Table 2.4). However, self-reported work limitations (Table 2.5) or inability to work (Table 2.6) are not so cyclical: the dummy variables in these specifications are generally statistically insignificant and quantitatively small. This is not surprising as the actual employment (given in Table 2.4) depends not only on the ability to work (supply of labor, including sufficient health capital to work) but also on the demand for labor (which varied over the recent business upturn). The outcomes "limited in work" (Table 2.5) and "unable to work" (Table 2.6) really concern mostly the supply of labor, which is less sensitive to cyclical variations in demand.

Cancer survivors, on average, are older, often past retirement age, though the onset of cancer is most often before retirement (see Table 2.10 and text below). To separate the effect of retirement opportunities from the onset of cancer at older ages, we not only included age and age squared as control variables in all specifications, we also included a dummy variable if the respondent was 65 years or older, to partially control for retirement incentives. As expected, in all models of working likelihood, the coefficient on the 65 plus dummy variable was negative and large in magnitude, and always statistically significant.

The variables of most interest in these logistic regressions are the cancer duration variables (given in the specification on the far right hand side columns in Tables 2.4, 2.5, and 2.6) and the dummy variables for individual cancer types. The full sample specification in Table 2.4 estimates the likelihood of working at the time of interview, and the dummy variables for various cancer types indicates the likelihood of working at date of interview relative to those without cancer. Again, these are morbidity only estimates, not accounting for those who have already died because of the cancer. Hence the three statistically insignificant cancer dummy variables (melanoma, testicular, and thyroid cancer) indicate that morbidity employment effect for these three cancer groups, controlling for socio-demographic variables, is not statistically different than employment for the general population.

All other cancer types exhibit a significantly lower likelihood of being employed, the coefficients indicating the relative magnitudes of the effects. Brain cancer has the lowest relative employment probability, with an estimated coefficient of −1.8467 (in Table 2.4). This translates into about a 43 percentage point reduction in the probability of working, or about a 66% reduction in working (from the general population average of 63 percentage points down by 43 percentage points). The pancreatic cancer effect of "−0.866" translates into about a 20 percentage point reduction, or a decrease in the likelihood of working of about 32% (0.20/0.63) in Table 2.4. Cancers that have the greatest reductions in employment include those reported in Syse, Kravdal, and Tretli [14] for prime-age Norwegian males: brain, bone, leukemia, and lung. Our analysis includes both adult males and females of all ages, however, and we find large employment reductions in addition for those with cancers of the blood, esophagus, liver, mouth, pancreas, rectum, and throat. Short, Vasey, and Tunceli [2] also found the largest employment reductions for those with cancers of the brain, blood, and lymph systems.

Work Limitations and Inability to Work

In contrast, Tables 2.5 and 2.6 measure the likelihood of being limited in work (Table 2.5) and unable to work (Table 2.6). These are both important outcomes by themselves, but they also provide a robustness check for our employment results. We expect to find coefficients with signs just the opposite to those of the employment model but of roughly similar relative magnitudes. This turns out to be exactly what we find. In all specifications, brain cancer has the lowest employment likelihood while those with thyroid cancer continue to have outcomes not statistically different from the general non-cancer population. These tables provided data for all the major variants of cancer.

Employment Changes Post Diagnosis

In order to gauge how the likelihood of employment changes after an initial cancer diagnosis, we define cancer duration as the number of years since a first diagnosis of cancer and see how employment changes following diagnosis. We already know from the cancer dummy variables that the probability of being employed drops substantially at first. An interesting empirical issue is whether, and to what extent, cancer survivors recover to their pre-cancer levels of employment. Hence, by including cancer duration and the square of cancer duration in the logistic probability model, we are able to examine the changes in each survivor's employment probabilities as they age. The coefficients for the cancer duration and cancer duration square variables in Table 2.4 indicate that, with respect to the morbidity effect of cancer on employment, employment increases after the initial diagnosis at a decreasing rate, up to a cancer duration of 24 years and thereafter decreases. This makes up about 7 percentage points in the probability of being employed over the first two and a half decades after diagnosis, on average, which for most cancers only makes up about a third of the initial loss in the likelihood of working. That is, even accounting for subsequent employment gains due to morbidity improvements, cancer survivors on average never fully recover to their pre-cancer levels of employment.

Similar implied cancer duration trends are exhibited in Tables 2.5 and 2.6. In Table 2.5, cancer survivors continue to gain in ability to work (the likelihood of work limitations falls) until 20 years after initial diagnosis. In Table 2.6, cancer survivors continue to gain in ability to work (the likelihood of being unable work due to health falls) until 24 years after initial diagnosis.

In Table 2.7, we simultaneously examine the life cycle and business cycle differences associated with cancer status for cancer survivors. The joint tests for shifts in life cycle effects (when employment rates are highest with respect to age) and business cycle effects (when employment rates are highest with respect to the business cycle), given in the bottom rows of Table 2.7, indicate that cancer survivors are statistically different from the non-cancer population. Whereas the age and age-squared coefficients for the general population indicates that employment rates, from the left hand columns in Table 2.7, are highest at 38 years of age, the cancer survivors' employment probabilities peak slightly earlier at 36 years of age because of morbidity associated with the cancer. Results from the "likelihood of being limited in work" regression show a qualitatively similar impact of age on work limitations: the likelihood of being limited in work increases at a decreasing rate and is minimized at about 39 of age for both the general population and for cancer survivors.

For the population in general, employment peaked in the relative prosperous 1999–2001 period, as those years exhibited positive coefficients relative to the omitted 2005 comparison year (which is implicitly zero). Interestingly, cancer survivors are also subject to these same cyclical forces, but don't exhibit any additional cyclical changes beyond the regular population. Tests of equality of the "cancer-yes*year dummy" interactions (the last nine variables in Table 2.7) fail to reject the null hypothesis of equality across all years, indicating a uniform shift in employment probabilities for cancer survivors relative to the general population.

In summary, employment experiences following the diagnosis vary considerably by type of cancer. Those with melanoma, testicular, or thyroid cancers have employment rates not significantly different from the non-cancer population, though for other types of cancer, there is a drop in employment probability

Table 2.7 Work trends compared—cancer survivors and no cancer population

	Likelihood of working		Limited in work because of health	
	Coefficient	Probability significance	Coefficient	Probability significance
Intercept	−3.2587	<.0001	−3.8197	<.0001
male	0.8134	<.0001	−0.0511	<.0001
age	0.1955	<.0001	0.0610	<.0001
age square	−0.0026	<.0001	−0.0001	<.0001
age 65+ dummy	−0.4684	<.0001	−0.4355	<.0001
cancer*age	−0.0472	<.0001	−0.0240	0.0025
cancer*age square	0.0005	<.0001	0.00004	0.5204
cancer*age 65+ dummy	0.0332	0.6746	−0.1365	0.0399
educational attainment	0.2768	<.0001	−0.4130	<.0001
black	−0.1897	<.0001	0.2412	<.0001
Hispanic	−0.1306	<.0001	−0.4171	<.0001
Asian	−0.2851	<.0001	−0.6790	<.0001
Bladder	−0.3133	0.0278	0.1062	0.3247
Blood	−1.0325	0.0051	0.5878	0.0374
Bone	−1.2723	<.0001	0.9505	<.0001
Brain	−1.7244	<.0001	1.7056	<.0001
Breast	−0.0772	0.3045	0.1789	0.0020
Cervical	−0.0287	0.7232	0.2139	0.0041
Colon	−0.2551	0.0092	0.2520	0.0003
Esophagus	−1.2694	0.0003	0.8617	0.0005
Gallbladder	−0.9534	0.1183	0.9100	0.0329
Kidney	−0.4642	0.0069	0.6249	<.0001
Larynx	−0.6044	0.0543	0.9850	<.0001
Leukemia	−0.9238	<.0001	0.9545	<.0001
Liver	−1.1756	<.0001	1.3570	<.0001
Lung	−1.1594	<.0001	1.0682	<.0001
Lymphoma	−0.3674	0.0030	0.4915	<.0001
Melanoma	−0.1190	0.2058	0.0599	0.4715
Mouth	−0.9644	0.0002	0.3508	0.0794
Other	−0.3866	<.0001	0.5476	<.0001
Ovarian	−0.3150	0.0048	0.4741	<.0001
Pancreatic	−0.8138	0.0189	1.1194	<.0001
Prostate	−0.4550	<.0001	0.0884	0.1972
Rectum	−1.0194	0.0027	0.7537	0.0003
Skin Unknown	−0.3200	0.0002	0.3083	<.0001
Skin Non-melanoma	−0.1972	0.0086	−0.0757	0.2245
Soft Tissue	−0.7143	0.0074	0.7584	0.0015
Stomach	−0.5630	0.0106	0.8045	<.0001
Testicular	−0.0836	0.7082	0.0504	0.8279
Throat	−0.8721	<.0001	0.8494	<.0001
Thyroid	0.0104	0.9405	−0.1356	0.3381
Uterus	−0.2483	0.0048	0.5011	<.0001
dummy year = 1997	−0.0701	<.0001	0.1566	<.0001
dummy year = 1998	−0.0579	<.0001	0.1052	<.0001
dummy year = 1999	0.0103	0.4433	0.0245	0.1943
dummy year = 2000	0.0144	0.2783	−0.0334	0.0778

Table 2.7 (continued)

	Likelihood of working		Limited in work because of health	
	Coefficient	Probability significance	Coefficient	Probability significance
dummy year = 2001	0.0191	0.1517	0.0027	0.8875
dummy year = 2002	−0.0435	0.0013	0.0163	0.3953
dummy year = 2003	−0.0597	<.0001	0.0031	0.8718
dummy year = 2004	−0.0350	0.0091	0.0032	0.8654
cancer*dummy year = 1997	0.8851	0.0005	1.7723	<.0001
cancer*dummy year = 1998	0.8631	0.0007	1.7265	<.0001
cancer*dummy year = 1999	0.7819	0.0021	1.6857	<.0001
cancer*dummy year = 2000	0.7719	0.0023	1.7895	<.0001
cancer*dummy year = 2001	0.8964	0.0004	1.7353	<.0001
cancer*dummy year = 2002	0.9432	0.0002	1.7962	<.0001
cancer*dummy year = 2003	0.8260	0.0012	1.7481	<.0001
cancer*dummy year = 2004	0.8622	0.0007	1.7135	<.0001
cancer*dummy year = 2005	0.8927	0.0004	1.7668	<.0001
Sample Size		607284		607356
-2*log-likelihood		621246.61		374113.26
Joint significance: age, age-sq, 65+		<.0001		<.0001
Joint sign.: cancer age, age-sq, 65+		<.0001		<.0001
Joint significance: year effects		<.0001		<.0001
Joint significance: cancer year effects		0.0154		<.0001

of about 33% for cancer survivors that reach more than 50% for some cancers. The initial drop in employment due to morbidity is subsequently partially recovered as morbidity employment experience (symptom burden) improves after diagnosis. And cancer survivors are subject to the same cyclical pressures across the business cycle as the general population. In the next section we show that this morbidity effect outweighs the mortality effect for the first three or four years after diagnosis, then the mortality effect dominates and employment rate steadily decline.

Cancer and Employment Rates: The Combined Impact of Mortality and Morbidity

As surveys generally don't question the families of survivors about the characteristics of other family members who have died, and as interviewing cancer mortality victims is impossible, the only information on the mortality effects of cancer come from the Vital Statistics files. Computer ready, detailed versions of these records (including socio-demographic factors) are publicly available only after a lengthy period, and hence, we cannot replicate anything like our multivariate analysis in Tables 2.1, 2.2, 2.3, 2.4, 2.5, 2.6, and 2.7 for mortality trends. However, the National Cancer Institute does publish mortality survival rates by cancer duration, which we reproduce in Table 2.8 by cancer type.

The survivor rates in many ways mirror the results for morbidity: cervical, testicular, and thyroid cancers—which had morbidity employment rates similar to the general non-cancer population—also have relatively high survival rates. In particular, cancer of the thyroid has the highest survival rate after the first few years except for prostate cancer (only breast cancer, melanoma, and testicular cancers have higher survival rates in the first year). After the third year, cancer of the thyroid has the highest survival rate of all cancer types, including a 95.2% survival rate at the end of ten years after diagnosis. Cancers with low survival rates, which are also cancers with low morbidity employment rates, include pancreatic cancer, and cancers of the brain, esophagus, gallbladder, liver, and lung. However, morbidity and mortality rates do not always track each other well: prostate and rectum cancers, which had relatively low morbidity employment rates, have relatively good mortality survival rates.

Those cancers with the relatively greatest declines in mortality ten years after initial diagnosis include cancers of the blood (from 73.5 to 15.1%), esophagus (from 42.4 to 10.2%), gallbladder (from 34.4 to12.6%), liver (from 26.8 to 6.3%), lung (from 41.3 to 10.5%), pancreas (from 21.3 to 3.4%), and stomach (from 47.5 to 18.7%). Hence, these ought to also exhibit the largest net decline in employment rates (=mortality effect*morbidity effect), when the effects of mortality and morbidity are combined. The net results for blood and esophagus cancers in Table 2.9 indicate that this tends to be the case. The decline in mortality for these other cancers exhibiting a sharp decline is so rapid that the sample size often becomes too small for reliable estimates. This is the case with gallbladder, liver, and pancreatic cancer. For most of the rest of cancers in Table 2.9, there is a clear trend of increasing employment rates for the first few years following the diagnosis—where the morbidity effects outweigh the mortality effects, and thereafter decreasing employment rates as the cancer duration lengthens.

As examples, those cancers with employment rates peaking in the second year after diagnosis include cervical, kidney, melanoma, prostate, and testicular

2 Economic Burden

Table 2.8 Morbidity by years since diagnosis

	Survival rate									
	Years after diagnosis									
	1(%)	2(%)	3(%)	4(%)	5(%)	6(%)	7(%)	8(%)	9(%)	10(%)
Bladder	90.9	86.4	84.0	82.3	80.9	79.6	78.3	77.3	76.4	75.5
Blood	73.5	59.9	48.4	39.3	32.0	26.7	22.2	19.0	16.9	15.1
Bone	88.6	79.5	74.8	71.3	68.9	67.3	65.8	64.3	63.6	63.5
Brain	55.2	40.8	36.9	34.8	33.5	32.5	31.7	31.1	30.7	30.3
Breast	97.4	94.6	91.8	89.4	87.3	85.5	83.8	82.5	81.1	79.9
Cervical	88.6	80.7	76.5	73.9	72.5	71.3	70.5	69.7	69.0	68.5
Colon	82.0	74.1	69.1	65.5	63.0	61.3	59.8	58.7	57.9	57.0
Esophagus	42.4	24.7	18.8	15.8	14.3	13.1	12.4	11.8	11.0	10.2
Gallbladder	34.4	22.6	18.2	15.8	14.6	14.3	13.9	13.2	12.7	12.6
Kidney	78.1	71.3	67.9	65.3	63.5	61.9	60.4	59.4	58.5	57.0
Larynx	87.3	77.7	72.2	67.9	64.6	61.4	59.2	56.5	53.9	51.6
Leukemia	67.7	58.9	54.5	50.9	48.3	46.0	43.9	42.1	40.7	39.5
Liver	26.8	16.6	12.2	10.0	8.4	7.6	7.0	6.7	6.5	6.3
Lung	41.3	25.1	19.4	16.6	14.9	13.7	12.7	11.9	11.2	10.5
Lymphoma	83.8	78.4	75.4	73.1	71.2	69.5	67.8	66.5	65.5	64.6
Melanoma	97.3	94.8	93.0	91.7	90.8	90.1	89.7	89.2	89.1	88.9
Mouth	82.9	71.1	64.9	60.8	58.0	55.5	53.3	51.3	49.2	47.5
Other	–	–	–	–	–	–	–	–	–	–
Ovarian	74.4	61.9	53.1	47.6	43.9	41.4	40.1	39.2	38.5	38.1
Pancreatic	21.3	9.6	6.4	5.2	4.6	4.3	4.0	3.8	3.6	3.4
Prostate	99.3	98.3	97.3	96.3	95.3	94.2	92.9	91.6	90.1	88.4
Rectum	82.0	74.1	69.1	65.5	63.0	61.3	59.8	58.7	57.9	57.0
UN Skin	–	–	–	–	–	–	–	–	–	–
NM Skin	–	–	–	–	–	–	–	–	–	–
Soft Tissue	85.6	76.6	71.5	68.8	66.8	65.3	64.0	63.2	62.3	61.8
Stomach	47.5	33.2	27.2	24.3	22.8	21.4	20.6	19.9	19.4	18.7
Testicular	98.0	96.6	96.0	95.9	95.8	95.7	95.6	95.3	95.2	95.2
Throat	82.9	71.1	64.9	60.8	58.0	55.5	53.3	51.3	49.2	47.5
Thyroid	97.0	96.8	96.6	96.4	96.3	96.1	96.1	96.1	96.1	96.1
Uterus	92.9	88.8	86.4	85.1	84.3	83.5	83.2	82.6	82.4	82.0

Source: SEER Cancer Statistics. National Cancer Institute. Bethesda, MD, http://seer.cancer.gov/faststats. Accessed on November 13, 2007. No Mortality rates available for other or skin cancers. The Lymphoma cancer rates are simple averages of Non-Hodgkins and Hodgkins Lymphoma. Throat and Mouth were grouped together on the SEER site.

cancers. Those with employment rates peaking in the third year after diagnosis include brain, breast, colon, and lung cancers. Others peak even later on. In general, then, employment rates initially rise for most cancer types as morbidity effects outweigh mortality effects. Thereafter, they begin to fall as mortality effects dominate, and as mortality and morbidity effects both start to contribute to a decline in employment rates.

Table 2.9 Net fraction working, combining morality and morbidity trends: By year after diagnosis and cancer type

	0–1 years after	1–2 years after	2–3 years after	3–4 years after	4–5 years after	5–6 year after	6–7 year after	7–8 years after	8–9 years after	9–10 years after
	% Working	% Working	% Working	% Working	% Working	% Working	% Working	% Working	% Working	% Working
Bladder	05.4	14.6	21.0	15.6	21.8	34.2	45.4	19.3	09.9	3.1
Blood	27.9	10.1	06.7	–	–	17.6	10.6	–	–	–
Bone	16.8	22.2	20.1	–	35.1	14.8	05.9	–	–	2.0
Brain	12.6	07.7	16.2	07.6	06.3	08.1	19.0	08.0	07.0	1.5
Breast	24.3	32.1	32.1	31.2	24.4	28.2	26.8	21.4	21.0	2.6
Cervical	50.5	53.2	48.9	50.9	45.6	42.0	41.5	45.3	39.3	4.7
Colon	10.6	18.5	20.7	14.4	17.6	09.8	12.5	09.9	16.2	1.1
Esophagus	21.2	07.4	05.6	01.4	00.0	04.3	04.5	–	–	–
Gallbladder	–	–	–	07.1	–	–	–	–	–	–
Kidney	26.5	29.9	24.4	11.7	15.2	21.6	12.6	20.1	04.0	06.0
Larynx	37.5	.	21.6	34.6	–	13.5	–	–	–	–
Leukemia	05.4	20.0	19.6	16.2	09.1	00.0	15.3	19.3	14.6	0.5
Liver	00.0	01.8	03.6	–	01.2	–	01.6	–	–	–
Lung	03.3	03.2	03.4	02.1	02.6	04.2	01.7	01.3	01.5	0.1
Lymphoma	33.5	29.0	30.1	35.8	37.7	15.2	31.1	25.9	17.6	4.5
Melanoma	36.9	48.3	43.7	33.0	39.9	47.7	34.0	28.5	36.5	4.8
Mouth	04.9	00.0	18.1	36.4	27.2	17.7	04.7	–	00.0	1.9
Ovarian	13.3	24.1	23.3	25.2	23.2	10.3	14.8	26.2	21.9	21.7
Pancreatic	02.5	02.7	00.7	03.8	02.9	00.0	.	00.0	–	–
Prostate	15.8	29.4	28.2	19.2	20.9	17.8	20.4	12.8	09.0	22.9
Rectum	00.0	25.1	00.0	15.7	26.4	11.6	00.0	17.0	–	–
Soft Tissue	41.9	17.6	10.7	37.1	–	00.0	30.7	37.9	–	61.8
Stomach	09.5	11.9	05.1	10.4	03.4	02.3	09.8	06.7	00.0	11.4
Testicular	69.5	96.6	55.6	72.8	95.8	54.5	84.1	95.3	89.4	65.6
Throat	16.5	14.9	15.5	21.8	09.2	32.7	07.9	14.8	26.0	26.1
Thyroid	45.5	54.2	50.2	36.6	52.0	60.5	41.3	79.7	33.6	40.3
Uterus	24.1	31.9	31.9	35.7	46.0	33.4	41.6	28.9	18.1	31.2

Based upon weighted averages for labor force participation from calculations from the IHIS and Table 2.6 statistics. Missing values for cells with 3 or fewer observations.

The Cost of Cancer-Related Productivity

We found no evidence that cancer employment following diagnosis shifted at all during our period: those working for a given number of "X" years after diagnosis in 1997, were equally likely to be working X years after a diagnosis in 2005. While changes in treatment modalities may have had differential impacts on survivability, or on quality of life, recent changes seem to have had no impact on the employability of cancer survivors.

But cancer outcomes are not uniform by cancer type. There are some cancers (melanoma, testicular, and thyroid) whose impact on employment outcomes seems to be statistically indistinguishable from the general non-cancer population. For most other cancers, employment rates fall by one-third to one-half after the initial diagnosis, although there is some recovery in employability—usually that peaks two to four years after diagnosis—in which improvements in cancer morbidity offsets the effects of cancer mortality on employment rates.

Being able to return to work and to stay at work following a cancer diagnosis is important both to the individual cancer patient and to society. While the data available for our analysis does not allow us to address cancer survivors' gain in quality of life (or, their "utility" in the economic sense), we can get some rough idea about productivity losses due to cancer. While our sample sizes for many of the cancer types examined here are probably too small to draw any overarching conclusions, we can choose one cancer to illustrate the likely importance of productivity loss associated with employment, and then use this index to gauge the relative importance of each cancer type in the estimation of productivity losses due to cancer.

The Case of Colon Cancer

We choose to examine colon cancer for three reasons. First, colon cancer can be significantly reduced through periodic screenings for those at risk. Hence, real productivity gains are possible through increased screenings. Second, we have nearly 1300 individuals in our sample with a diagnosis of colon cancer (see Tables 2.1 and 2.2), which increases the reliability (decreases the sample variance) of our estimators. Third, the real wages of those with colon cancer are virtually identical to those of the general non-cancer populations. This equivalence is given in Figs. 2.1 and 2.2, where box-plots giving the quartiles of the distribution (and means with the little embedded " + " signs) are presented for the population without a cancer diagnosis ("abs" for "absence a cancer diagnosis" in the far left hand side box plot of the first figure) and those with colon cancer in the box plot labeled "col." Note however, that for those who work, regardless of cancer type, the wages are surprisingly similar to those in the general non-cancer population. This is not surprising, as cancer is widespread

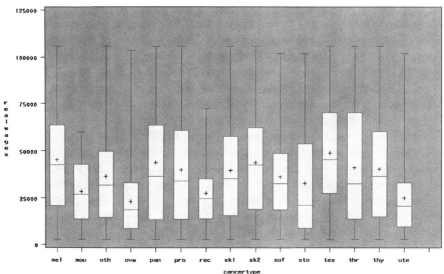

Fig. 2.1 Real (2005) wage quartiles of cancer survivors, with "+" indicating average annual wage

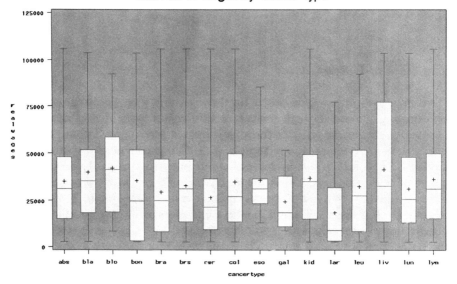

Fig. 2.2 Real (2005) wage quartiles of cancer survivors, with "+" indicating average annual wage

across the demographic distribution. Consequently, the colon cancer losses per capita are likely to be more or less true for other types of cancers (after adjusting for the substantial differences in employment rates across cancer types).

For example, the annual average real wage for those with colon cancer (in 2005 dollars) is $34,700 in our sample, compared to $34,997 for those in the non-cancer population. Rounding up to $35,000 per year, and using the data from the IHIS tapes on age specific employment rates by, we can get an estimate of the productivity cost of cancer in the first ten years after diagnosis. The average age of those with colon cancer is 70 years of age, and the average duration is 8.55 years. The average across all cancers is about ten years. This type of duration statistic is known as an "interrupted spell" (by the survey) duration, and may be more than or less than the mean of the true completed spell duration, depending on the shape of the distribution. This is discussed extensively in Butler and McDonald [15]. Drawing on their results, we assume that the average age that the cancer started is ten years before the currently observed average age, taken in the midst of the cancer treatment. So for colon cancer, we assume the average start age is 70–10 = 60 years of age, and then consider the employment rates from the non-cancer population for the next 10 years (age 60 to age 59 for colon cancer, as indicated in the second column from the left in Table 2.10). From age specific calculations for males and females in our sample from 60 years of age to 69 years of age, we find the average employment rate is 33.2% for those without cancer. We then take this average rate for those without cancer and compare it with the average rate of those with colon cancer in Table 2.9, as a measure of the number of lost working years per 100 workers. This can be scaled up by the wages (as a measure of worker productivity) to get an estimate of the cost of colon cancer per "typical" colon cancer victim.

For example, from Table 2.9, the average employment rate for the first ten years after diagnosis with colon cancer is 13.1%. Since, normally, 33.2% work during those ages in their life cycle (from age 65 to 74 years of age), the average productivity loss per 100 workers is (33.2–13.1)*$35,000*10 years or $7 million per hundred individuals with colon cancer, or about $70,350 per individual for the first ten years after diagnosis.

With 112,340 new cases of colon cancer each year (see Table 2.10), this suggests that the productivity losses for each new cohort (each annual new crop of colon cancer victims) of colon cancer patients is $70,350 * 112,340 = $7.9 billion. This will be an underestimate to the extent that they might have had a working life longer than ten additional years; an overestimate to the extent that their working life would have been shorter. Since the average age of those reporting cancer is about 60 years of age, and this average cohort has generally had cancer for six to 13 years (see age and cancer duration averages from Table 2.1), the ten additional years of work estimate is probably a reasonable average for the cancer cohort, if they had not had cancer. Moreover, we only examine whether someone reported working during the survey period, but we do not consider that many will count themselves working, but at reduced hours

Table 2.10 Estimated productivity losses by cancer type

	10 year age comparison period	First 10 year lost per cancer ($)	Number of new cancer cases in 2007	Estimated Productivity Losses for Each New Cohort of Cancer Victims (i.e., for those diagnoses of cancer in 2007) ($)
Bladder	59–68	64,225	67,160	4.3 billion
Blood	49–58		NA	NA
Bone	46–55	204,715	2,370	0.5 billion
Brain	39–48	242,760	20,500	5.0 billion
Breast	56–65	64,645	180,510	11.7 billion
Cervical	35–44	99,260	11,150	1.1 billion
Colon	60–69	70,350	112,340	7.9 billion
Esophagus	52–61	202,955	15,560	3.2 billion
Gallbladder	52–61	NA	9,250	NA
Kidney	56–65	117,460	51,190	6.0 billion
Larynx	55–64	126,572	11,300	1.4 billion
Leukemia	46–55	221,165	44,240	9.8 billion
Liver	53–62	208,390	19,160	3.4 billion
Lung	57–66	152,040	213,380	32.4 billion
Lymphoma	48–57	162,155	71,380	11.6 billion
Melanoma	50–59	117,915	59,940	7.1 billion
Mouth	55–64	145,977	10,660	1.6 billion
Ovarian	45–54	167,755	22,430	3.8 billion
Pancreatic	55–64	182,805	37,170	6.8 billion
Prostate	63–72	39,760	218,890	8.7 billion
Rectum	59–68	88,918	41,420	3.7 billion
Soft Tissue	50–59	163,546	9,220	1.5 billion
Stomach	55–64	164,430	21,260	3.5 billion
Testicular	35–44	33,285	7,920	0.3 billion
Throat	54–63	137,305	11,800	1.6 billion
Thyroid	44–53	96,320	33,550	3.2 billion
Uterus	48–57	116,025	39,080	4.5 billion
Total				144.6 billion (partial sum)

Based upon an average real 2005 salary of $35,000 (the non-cancer mean salary), and adjusted for missing years to be put on the same 10 year basis. The healthy comparison groups for breast, cervical, ovarian, and uterus cancer losses were calculated using age specific female working rates from the female no-cancer population; prostate and testicular cancers, using male specific working rates from the male no-cancer population. The healthy, no-cancer rates were calculated using the integer value of the mean age of the cancer specific age less 10 years as the start age (as the average duration of interrupted spells is about 10 years or slightly higher), then computing the age specific working rates for the proceeding next ten years. These comparison ages are given in the second column from the left. The data in the second column from the right come from the National Cancer Institute for 2007 new cancer cases, downloaded 16 February 2008 from the following website: http://www.seer.cancer.gov/csr/1975_2004/results_single/sect_01_table.01.pd7

because of the cancer. Syse, Kravdal and Tretli [14] estimate such a decline in wages for working cancer survivors, relative to those without a cancer diagnosis with the same socio-demographic profiles. This effect will bias our estimates of productivity loss downward (so that on this basis, the Table 2.10 numbers are underestimated).

Table 2.10 provides estimates of productivity losses for the other cancer types which met some minimal sample size. These productivity losses are in real 2005 dollars, for each new cohort. These productivity losses count only losses in the market place: they do not consider changes in non-market production (work at home or volunteer work), although these sorts of productive activities may also have decreased after a cancer diagnosis (or, perhaps for some cancers, increased if the individual perhaps took an early retirement to do volunteer work that would have been much more extensive than otherwise). While the direction and magnitude of changes in these non-market productive activities is ambiguous, we suspect that on net these also decreased, making our productivity loss estimates again too small.

Productivity losses are the product of wage loss for the specific cancer type and number of new cases of that cancer type. Hence, it is not surprising that lung cancer is far and away the most expensive cancer type in terms of productivity losses, with a large wage loss per individual and a large number of new cases each year. Hence, each year, lung cancer generates about $32.4 billion in new market productivity losses. A distinct second and third are breast cancer ($11.7 billion) and lymphoma ($11.6 billion), followed by leukemia ($9.8 billion), prostate cancer ($8.7 billion), and colon cancer ($7.9 billion). These six cancers, the most expensive in terms of productivity losses, account for 57% of all productivity losses in Table 2.10.

For the cancers for which we are able to make our calculations, we estimate the productivity, opportunity costs of cancer to be about $145 billion (bottom of Table 2.10) per year. This would need to be added to the direct costs for cancer treatment. The National Cancer Institute estimated in 2005 that about 74 billion dollars were spent for direct cancer treatment [7]. Our estimated opportunity cost of cancer (in terms of lost productivity) is two times greater than these direct, treatment costs.

Our findings here are generally consistent with the literature. Short, Vasey, and Tunceli [2] found that 20% of cancer survivors report cancer-related work limitations during the one to five years following cancer treatment. They report that 50% of cancer survivors quit working in the first year, 25% of them permanently. Even at four years after diagnosis still 13% of all previously employed cancer survivors are not working. Hewitt, Rowland, and Yancik [3], using the National Health Interview Survey, found that 17% of workers with a history of cancer report that they are unable to return to work for health related reasons, compared to 5% of those with no past history of cancer. Yabroff et al. [4] estimated that 18% of cancer survivors were unable to work due to health problems, compared to 10.3% of non-cancer controls. Bradley et al. [9] found that men diagnosed with prostate cancer (the most common cancer in men) were 10% less likely to remain employed than control subjects. The National Cancer Institute [7] estimates productivity losses around 135.9 billion dollars—bringing their estimate of total economic cancer burden in 2005 to 209.9 billion. Our estimate of the productivity losses (at $145 billion) is rather close to their estimate of $135.9 billion.

Further research will be able to improve upon these estimates by adding more information from additional waves of the Health Interview Survey (and other similar data sets), and by systematically exploiting mortality information (controlling for socio-demographic variables) as well as morbidity information. However these estimates are generated, and improved upon, it will still be the case that the costs of cancer represent a considerable burden on the U.S. economy in the foreseeable future and efforts to reduce this impact are justified from humanitarian and economic perspectives.

References

1. American Cancer Society. Cancer Facts and Figures 200. Atlanta, GA: American Cancer Society 2007.
2. Short PF, Vasey JJ, Tunceli K. Employment pathways in a large cohort of adult cancer survivors. Cancer. 2005;103(6):1292–301.
3. Hewitt M, Rowland JH, Yancik R. Cancer survivors in the United States: Age, health, and disability. The Journals of Gerenotology: Series A Biological Sciences and Medical Sciences. 2003;58(1):82–91.
4. Yabroff KR, Lawrence WF, Clauser S, Davis WW, Brown ML. Burden of illness in cancer survivors: Findings from a population-based national sample. Journal of the National Cancer Institute. 2004;96(17):1322–30.
5. Edwards BK, Howe HL, Ries LAG, Thun MJ, Rosenberg HM, Yancik R, et al. Annual report of the nation on the status of cancer, 1973–1999, featuring implications of age and aging on US cancer burden. Cancer. 2002;94(10):2766–92.
6. Yancik R. Epidemiology for cancer in the elderly: Current stats and projections for the future. RAYS. 1997;22(Suppl 1):3–9.
7. National Cancer Institute. 2006 Fact Book. cited 2008 May 8.; Available from: http://obf.cancer.gov/financial/attachments/06Factbk.pdf
8. Howe HL, Wu X, Ries LA, Cokkinides V, Ahmed F, Jemal A, et al. Annual report to the nation on the status of cancer, 195–2003, featuring cancer among US Hispanic/Latino populations. Cancer. 2006;107(8):1711–42.
9. Bradley CJ, Neumark D, Luo Z, Bednarek H, Schenk M. Employment outcomes of men treated for prostate cancer. Journal of the National Cancer Institute. 2005;97(13):958–65.
10. Drolet M, Maunsell E, Brisson J, Brisson C, Masse B, Beschenes L. Not working three years after breast cancer: Predictors in a population-based study. Journal of Clinical Oncology. 2005;23(33):8305–12.
11. Barlow WE, Taplin SH, Yoshida CK, Buist DS, Seger D, Brown ML. A cost comparison of mastectomy versus breast conserving therapy for early-stage breast cancer. Journal of the National Cancer Institute. 2001;93(6):447–55.
12. Minnesota Population Center and State Health Access Data Assistance Center. Integrated Health Interview Survey: Version 1.0. University of Minnesota, Saint Paul, MN, USA.
13. Coebergh JWW, Janssen-Heijnen MLG, van der Heijnen LH, Masseling HGMB, Razenberg PPA. Comorbidity in newly diagnosed patients with cancer. In: Coebergh JWW, van der Heijnen LH, Janssen-Heijnen MLG, (eds.), *Cancer Incidence and Survival in the*

Southeast of the Netherlands. Eindhoven: Comprehensive Cancer Center South 1995:107–8.
14. Syse A, Kravdal O, Tretli S. Cancer's impact on employment and earnings: A population-based study from Norway. Journal of Cancer Survivorship: Research and Practice. 2008;2:149–158.
15. Butler RJ, McDonald JB. Trends in unemployment duration data. Review of Economics and Statistics. 1986;68(4):545–57.

Chapter 3
Employers' and Survivors' Perspectives

Ziv Amir, David R. Strauser, and Fong Chan

Introduction

Despite the passage of the Americans with Disabilities Act (ADA), a recent National Council on Disability report [1] indicated that only 35% of working-age people with chronic illness and disability are employed comparing to 78% of those without disabilities. Two-thirds of the unemployed persons with chronic illness and disability indicated that they would like to work but could not find jobs. Disturbingly, the employment rate of people with disabilities has been hovering around 35% for the past two decades [2]. While these data are not specific to cancer survivors, at this point, there is no reason to assume that this group differs. In fact, while cancer survivors make up a small percentage of these cases [3], this may be a general observation in those with various types of chronic illness. To date, most of the focus on rehabilitation for those with disabilities has been on the "supply-side" approach (i.e., the individual with disability) and less on the demand characteristics (i.e., the employer) of the labor economy. The typical vocational rehabilitation process is to first comprehensively evaluate functional limitations, abilities, and career interests of individuals with chronic illness and disability to help them develop appropriate vocational goals; then, provide them with physical and mental restoration interventions (if necessary) and education/training and support services; and when they completed physical rehabilitation and vocational training, provide job placement assistance to help them find a job in the labor economy. This approach and its underlying rationale ignores variables related to employer demand (and the interaction of employer demand/supply and the environment) as predictors of employment outcomes for people with chronic illness and disability.

Recently, attention to the use of demand-side employment models to help provide a more complete picture of the problem and thus improve work outcomes has been proposed. According to the National Institute on Disability and

---

Z. Amir (✉)
Macmillan Research Unit, School of Nursing, Midwifery & Social Work, University Place, University of Manchester, Oxford Road, Manchester M13 9PL, UK
e-mail: ziv.amir@manchester.ac.uk

Rehabilitation Research (NIDRR, [4]), the focus of demand-side employment models is on the employer and work environment (i.e., occupational shifts and industrial change). The United States Department of Labor's Office of Disability Employment Policy (ODEP) indicate demand-driven employment strategies must emphasize the preparation of persons with chronic illness and disability for jobs that employers need to fill [5]. To increase demand, research must be able to identify demand occupations and develop and evaluate effective job modifications and accommodations and develop approaches to identify qualified persons with disabilities to fill these difficult to fill positions. In order for this to become a reality, we must have a thorough understanding of the real concerns of employers about hiring persons with disabilities and be able to address their concerns and needs as well. By focusing on the needs of employers and demand occupations, demand-side employment and job placement models have potential to significantly improve the employment rates of people with disabilities.

However, this demand-side driven approach assumes that employers with positions that are difficult to fill will be receptive to hiring "qualified" persons with chronic illness and disability as long as they receive active support and consultation from a competent demand-side employment and placement specialist. This assumption is not supported by a recent ODEP study [5]. The ODEP's Employer Assistance Recruiting Network (EARN) conducted focus group studies in 13 major metropolitan areas with 26 groups of private sector executive-level managers and human resources professionals, representing a variety of industries, company sizes, and both for-profit and not-for-profit organizations [5]. The purpose of the focus group study was to find out from employers what they consider as the most important issue affecting the poor hiring and job retention climate for people with chronic illness and disability. The most common answer given was that employers need more accurate and practical information to dispel preconceptions and concerns about hiring and retaining people with chronic illness and disability. ODEP concluded that before demand-side employment can become a reality, research into employer perceptions and attitudes toward hiring and retaining persons with chronic illness and disability is needed to complement the current supply-side employment research.

It is anticipated that demand-side employment models have better potential than the traditional supply-side approaches to significantly improve the employment rates of people with chronic illness and disability including cancer survivors. However, before the demand-side employment and job placement approach can be successful, we need to conduct research to better understand employer perceptions and attitudes toward hiring and retaining persons with chronic illness and disability. Information about employer attitudes will help cancer survivors become better prepared to work effectively with their employers to make a successful transition back to gainful employment and ideally remain at work for years. This chapter provides a review of the results of several general and cancer survivor-specific employer surveys and focus groups to discern attitudinal and other barriers facing cancer survivors who plan to return to work and pursue a meaningful career. In our efforts to obtain a more complete picture of the challenges faced by employer, we must not forget the perceptions of cancer survivors. This chapter also provides an overview of these concerns.

Employers' Attitudes Regarding People with Chronic Illness and Disability

Demand-side employment research is emerging as an important line of employment and disability research. One emphasis of this line of research is to examine the perceptions of chronic health and disability from the employer perspective. This research is important if effective interventions are going to be developed to facilitate the return to work, job retention, and career development of cancer survivors. Effective interventions need to be comprehensive in nature and focus on the interaction of the individual, cancer, and work related factors (Fig. 3.1). The section below provides an overview of this emerging line of research related to employer perspectives. Although the research presented is based on people with disabilities, cancer survivors experience issues related to symptom burden that may result in similar attitudes and perceptions regarding physical, cognitive, and emotional functioning and the impact on productivity and barriers presented in hiring and job retention.

To date very little research has been conducted that has examined issues related to the return to work of cancer survivors from the employer perspective. To further complicate the picture, very little research has been done that has

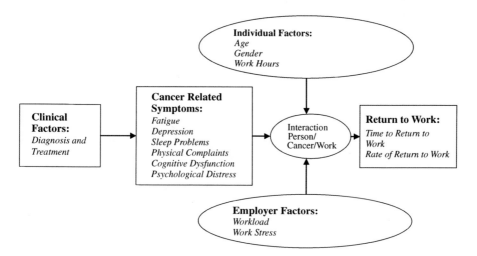

Fig. 3.1 Factors impacting return to work

examined the employer perspective related to chronic health related conditions and disability. The limited research that has been completed has indicated that employers have three major areas of concern related to employment and return to work of individuals with disabilities and chronic health conditions. First, employers have expressed concern related to the individual's ability to meet productivity standards developed by the company. Second, employers indicate that they do not have the adequate knowledge and understanding of how to hire and retain qualified individuals with chronic health conditions. Third, employers have expressed interest in receiving assistance and support that can help identify appropriate workplace supports and accommodations and vocational services that would be helpful in facilitating job retention and return to work [6, 7].

To fully understand the employer's perspective related to the employment of cancer survivors, it is important to understand how employers define productivity and its relationship to the global business model. This is important because businesses are pressed to participate in the global economy; research has suggested that employers are becoming less concerned with their human capital and focusing more on conserving and maximizing their financial capital [6, 8, 9]. In a recent study, Strauser and Chan [7] conducted a focus group study with human resources managers and hiring project managers from 20 national and international employers. The participants in their study defined a productive employee as an individual who is able to generate the required *quantity* (volume) and *quality* (low error) of work for the position as specified by the particular goals of the company. In addition, coming in under cost, having positive social relationships with team members and co-workers, and coming in under budget were all factors that were identified as being related or contributing to and individual's productivity. The Strauser and Chan study provided significant information regarding how employers perceive individuals with chronic health conditions in terms of productivity, barriers to hiring and job retention, perceived benefits, and their perceptions of the types of services and resources needed to increase the retention and placement of people with chronic illness. While Strauser and Chan focused on employers' attitudes toward hiring and retaining chronic illness and disability in general, their findings could have implications for understanding employers' perspective related to return-to-work issues facing cancer survivors in the workplace.

In general, employers indicated that there were negative perceptions related to people with disabilities that adversely impact the employment and retention of individuals with chronic health conditions. Commonly held negative perceptions include that, individuals with chronic illness and disabilities: (1) lack maturity, (2) have poor social skills, (3) have poor mental health, and (4) take things too personally. Because of these concerns, employers feel integrating these individuals into the employment setting is difficult and may create negative feelings and low moral among co-workers. In addition, employers expressed specific concerns regarding productivity, identified barriers to hiring, and identified strategies that they perceive would be helpful in increasing employment and retention of individuals with disabilities and chronic health conditions.

Productivity Concerns

Employers indicated that they felt that many times individuals with chronic illness and disability may need "special treatment" such as job accommodations, job restructuring, and potentially more supervision. Providing these services may create resentment among the other employees causing the morale of the work environment to decrease. Employers also indicated that they were concerned about the individual's ability to meet productivity demands in terms of *quality* and *quantity* due to their medical condition and associated symptom burden. Concerns regarding physical stamina and low cognitive functioning were frequently mentioned. Low skill sets related to both technical and applied social skills were cited as barriers to productivity (Table 3.1).

Based on these perceptions, employers indicated their concern that they would have to lower productivity standards and spend more time training or retraining employees. Again, the perception of special or additional treatment was perceived as a problem due to the negative impact on the morale this might have. Several employers indicated their concern that the individuals with disabilities and chronic health conditions would not be accepted into the work environment, and that co-workers would not feel comfortable communicating with individuals who have disabilities or chronic health conditions. They also indicated that co-workers and supervisors have a tendency to "mother" co-workers with disabilities and health related issues and lack the ability to develop positive and productive social relationships with these individuals. The need for additional supervision and the lack of qualified employees were also cited as factors that negatively impact productivity. Overall, issues related to physical stamina and the need for additional services and supports were cited as being critical factors impacting the employment and job retention of individuals with chronic illness and disability.

Table 3.1 Productivity concerns
- The need for special treatment on the job and in the workplace
- Inability to meet the employer quality and quantity standards
- Low physical stamina and poor cognitive functioning
- The need to lower the company's production standards
- Negative impact on the morale of the company
- More supervision to ensure quality work

Barriers to Hiring and Retention

The overall lack of familiarity with disability related matters was identified as a major issue impacting the employment and job retention of individuals with disabilities and other health related conditions. Specifically, the lack of knowledge on how to interview individuals with disabilities and chronic health conditions was identified as a significant barrier to employment. Related to this problem, employers indicated that they did not have good knowledge regarding disability legislation and how to integrate legal information into the job hiring and retention process. This is surprising as Americans with Disabilities Act (ADA) training was considered important with high priority immediately after the passage of the ADA in 1990. The overall lack of exposure to people with disabilities, under developed skills to communicate effectively with people with disabilities, and a lack of employment success stories were cited as factors that contribute to human resource personnel and front line managers' lack of enthusiasm for hiring individuals with disabilities (Table 3.2).

Employers expressed an overall aversion to the risk of interviewing and hiring individuals with disabilities and chronic health conditions. One of their major concerns is that it may be difficult and time consuming (in terms of documentation) to fire people with chronic illness and disability for poor job performance. Lacking the knowledge of how to effectively communicate with this group and not knowing how to ask and discuss disability and health related issues were identified as major factors. Hiring managers also indicated that disability and health related conditions are not included as part of the diversity training that they received. As a result, they do not feel adequately equipped to address the disability and health related issues in the workplace.

Employer Strategies

Employers identified several strategies that they felt would be important in improving the employment and job retention of individuals with disabilities and chronic health related conditions. One of the strategies that employers felt

Table 3.2 Barriers to hiring and retention
- Not familiar with disability and chronic health issues
- Lack of knowledge on how to effectively interview individuals with disability and health care issues
- Lack of knowledge regarding disability legislation
- Lack of exposure to people with disability and chronic health conditions in the work environment
- Lack of knowledge of how to communicate with individuals with disability or chronic health conditions

would be beneficial would be to use internships and temporary employment. The use of temporary employment and internships allows the individual an opportunity to become familiar with the work environment, demonstrate competence, and display appropriate social skills in the work setting. It also provides the individual an opportunity to integrate into the employer's corporate culture and become accepted by co-workers. Demonstrating the ability to perform the job and integrate into corporate culture was identified by employers as a method for building small but meaningful success stories that provide the employer appropriate opportunity to develop the necessary communication skills (Table 3.3).

Employers also expressed the need for employer consultation services by job placement agencies and other employment professionals. Developing a relationship with state vocational rehabilitation agencies (the US has them in all states) was identified as a positive and needed relationship. Employers indicated that any assistance vocational counsellors could give in terms of providing better assessment of skill and potential job match would be extremely helpful. External vocational and disability consultants may also be very beneficial in helping companies develop effective and positive relationships with community-based groups that are involved in disability and health care related issues. Finally, employers indicated that they would be very interested in working with disability and vocational consultants in helping better prepare individuals with disabilities and chronic health conditions for participation in the labor force and being better able to meet the demands of the labor market.

Employers also indicated a significant need to change the corporate culture so that it is more accessible and accepting of individuals with disabilities and chronic health conditions. Providing better training to human resource and front line managers was identified as a critical need. Employers indicated that disability and health issues needed to be included as part of their diversity training and included in the company's diversity plan. The need to develop clear and pro-active strategies for hiring and retaining individuals with disabilities and chronic health conditions was identified as important issue for employers to address. Employers felt that developing a recruitment and retention strategy would send a very positive message to the employees and help facilitate a positive workplace culture that was inclusive of disability and health care issues.

Table 3.3 Employer strategies

- Effective use of temporary employment and internships
- Utilize disability and vocational consultants
    - Liaison with community disability and healthcare organizations
    - Enhance skill match on the job
- Incorporate disability as part of the companies diversity plan
- Develop a strategy to recruit and retain individuals with disability and chronic health conditions

As a follow-up to their focus group studies, Chan and Strauser [10] developed a 71-item employer survey and conducted a large-scale survey study to examine hiring managers' attitudes toward hiring and retaining people with chronic illness and disability. Preliminary results based on the responses of 80 hiring managers indicated that their companies support diversity in the workplace. However, the focus on diversity is directed at gender and race; disability is not a major part of the company's diversity plan and hiring people with disabilities is not emphasized. There is no incentive or quotas to hire or retain people with disabilities at the departmental or unit levels. Hiring managers are not trained in diversity management related to individuals with disability. They also reported that the resources for recruiting people with chronic illness and disability are limited and disability sensitivity training for line managers is less than adequate. Nevertheless, the hiring managers indicate that they will not have problem hiring and retaining people with chronic illness and disability in their department. They feel that people with chronic illness and disability have workplace socialization skills, are reliable, can perform essential tasks, and meet productivity standards. They seemed to agree that hiring people with chronic illness and disability help promote an inclusive workplace and provide another opportunity to help employees learn to work with people from diverse groups. They also indicated that their companies have resources in-house to help them with ADA issues and they have access to government supported technical assistance resources (e.g., regional Disability and Business Technical Assistance Centers) in the community. Although they have in-house resources to deal with ADA issues, they also indicated that there is no in-house job accommodation expert available for consultation and that they are not as knowledgeable about the ADA as they should. These findings triangulate the results of their focus group studies.

Because employers are not as well trained in ADA as when this legislation was first passed in the early 1990s, employers may not be knowledgeable about the conditions under which cancer survivors are considered as having a disability and are protected by ADA. Employers may not be familiar with their obligations to cancer survivors with documented disabilities related to completing essential job demands in the workplace especially in the area of job accommodations. The lack of experience in accommodating employees who are cancer survivors may result in lack of specific needs and sensitivity to the needs of cancer survivors and inability to provide effective accommodations for cancer survivors in the workplace. This concern does need to be placed in the context that the scientific and clinical knowledge for cost effective accommodations for specific limitations in certain types of cancer survivors are still unknown. However, generic and some cancer specific approaches have been well worked out.

The healthcare and other accommodation needs of cancer survivors over a protracted period of time may create resentment among co-workers. The condescending attitudes of supervisors and co-workers could also be a source of stress and frustration for cancer survivors in the workplace. Although hiring managers express a non-judgmental attitude toward hiring people with chronic illness and disability, there is no incentive for them to hire or retain cancer survivors in the workplace. Some cancer survivors may prefer to make a career change that is compatible with their current health functioning and cognitive status. It is unclear whether or not employers are willing to provide them with career counselling and help them find alternative employment within the company. Some cancer survivors felt that company sick leave policy may prematurely push them back to work, which affects their performance. It appears that transitional employment programs designed for individuals with work injuries could be an effective return-to-work strategy for cancer survivors. Cancer survivors must become familiar with disability management programs within their companies.

The effects of organization level variables (e.g., types of job, types of business/industry, company size, diversity climate, geographical region, etc.) on the return-to-work experience of cancer survivors are relatively unknown. Future research with a focus on the effect of factors such as line-managers and organization variables and the interaction effect between line-manager variables and organizational variables on employment and workplace support for cancer survivors using appropriate research design and statistics such as multi-level analysis appears to be warranted. This kind of research will help rehabilitation professionals design effective return-to-work and work retention interventions for cancer survivors in their journey back to and their ability to remain involved in financially rewarding and meaningful employment.

Finally, it is clear from the findings of these employer perspective research is focused on human resources and line managers who tend to be ambivalent about hiring and retaining people with chronic illness and disability. This ambivalence may have significant implications for cancer survivors who want to return to work to either with the same employer or a different employer. It will be very important to study cancer survivors specifically in relation to the concerns raised above. In the following section, we will provide a review of cancer-specific studies to contrast and compare similarities and differences in employer perceptions about cancer survivors with certain functional limitations and individuals with other chronic illness and disability.

Cancer Survivors' Perspectives

Factors Influencing Individual Decisions to Work After a Cancer Diagnosis

Returning to paid work is a milestone for many employees with a cancer diagnosis, and could be seen as an important part of the transition from patient to survivor. Research suggests that a wide variety of factors are involved when people make decisions about work after a cancer diagnosis. These include:

- Demographic characteristics
- Financial circumstances
- Physical conditions
- Individual accomplishment

Demographic Characteristics

A study from the USA by Foley and colleagues [11] found that age at diagnosis was a major influence on how people managed their cancer experience. Younger people were more likely to view the diagnosis as a life-changing event, to have a greater sense of urgency in wanting to return to 'normal life,' and to report greater levels of psychological co-morbidity. In contrast, older people were more likely to regard a diagnosis as part of the ageing process and generally felt more able to cope with the life events associated with a cancer diagnosis and treatment. Cancer survivors of older working age were more likely to be able to retire, had they wished to do so, but older workers who chose to return to work experienced higher levels of co-morbidity making it considerably more difficult for them to maintain employment until normal retirement age.

The greater impact of a cancer diagnosis and treatment on overall lifestyle and paid work of younger women following breast cancer was also reported in a small scale study from Australia [12]. A population survey in the North West of England pointed out a strong correlation between the lengths of absenteeism and returning to work; a shorter period of absence predicted better continuity, in terms of returning to the same employer and working the same hours as before cancer diagnosis. Achieving this milestone was viewed positively by the participants. Gender and socio-economic status were found to be associated with the length of absenteeism; despite the fact that males were more likely than females to take no sick leave at all, they were also more likely to take longer periods of absence (18 months and over). Furthermore, economic deprivation was associated with the length of sick leave, with those in the lowest economic deprivation levels being slightly more likely to take no leave at all, which may be explained by strong financial needs to make immediate return to paid employment [13].

Financial Circumstances

In a study of return to work in the USA, Main and colleagues [14] found a complex range of motivations around returning to work but identified financial and health insurance pressures as important economic influences. A study of breast cancer survivors from the UK reported financial pressures as the primary motivation for returning to work in nearly half of the studied population [15].

Another UK qualitative study reported numerous acknowledgements of financial pressures to return to work: A speech therapist in her fifties with colon cancer who had just under six months sick leave on full pay was typical of many participants who felt an acute financial pressure to return to work when asked why they returned at the time they did:

> Purely financial. I did not feel quite ready physically and I still felt a bit wobbly mentally and emotionally but I was coming to the end of my full pay and I just couldn't afford to go onto half pay... If financial things hadn't been a factor I would have perhaps wanted another month and then gone back [16].

Physical Conditions

Recent research from the USA examined the impact of cancer compared to other chronic diseases on the prevalence of disability among a sample of older people [17]. Rates of disability of 647 cancer survivors from Pennsylvania and Maryland nearing the end of their working lives, most of whom were in employment at diagnosis, were compared with a group of 5988 similarly aged cancer-free people from the national Health and Retirement Survey. Approximately 30% of cancer survivors reported being disabled, defined as having impairments or health problems that limited the kind or amount of paid work they could perform, following their diagnosis and treatment. This was a lower incidence of disability compared to other chronic diseases but a co-existent cancer diagnosis or another chronic disease greatly increased the odds of reporting a disability compared to an otherwise disease-free cancer survivor.

Spelten and colleagues [18] in the Netherlands found that the level of reported fatigue was the most important factor in cancer survivors' decisions on return to work and was a reliable indicator at six months after diagnosis of the duration of sickness absence. A range of other factors including diagnosis, treatment, and age were also related to the time taken to return to work. Amir and colleagues in the UK [13] found that the type of treatment modality was a statistically significant factor in return to work, with the highest proportion of returnees among those who received surgery alone (93%) and lowest in those who received other modalities other than surgery (71%).

Individual Accomplishment

Returning to work was also considered to be an individual accomplishment that demonstrated a sense of worth. A desire to return to normality and a sense of loyalty to their employer were also important factors [14, 15]. The overriding importance of work to people after their cancer diagnosis and during their treatment was the strongest theme which emerged from qualitative data in a UK study. This was the case both post-diagnosis but pre-treatment, when a large majority stayed at work or returned to work after a short period of sick leave. At this difficult time, work provided a structured routine to people's lives, valuable social support from colleagues, and was of a therapeutic value.

you know whilst being at work you sort of push it aside for a little while ...

This strong commitment to work extended to the minority of people who continued to work during their treatment. This group reported being able to cope with at least some of the physical and mental demands of their jobs. Furthermore, returning to work soon after the completion of treatment was a major goal for many participants.

I wanted to get back to work as soon as possible ... work was the normal life I had before and that's why I focused on it

Many employees affected by cancer also felt a profound sense of boredom and isolation during their period of sick leave and several subjects acknowledged that they had been diagnosed with depression [16].

The Main Obstacles to Returning to Paid Work

Returning to paid work after treatment for certain cancer survivors is not easy or straightforward given the likelihood of a prolonged period of absence and the long-term effects of radiotherapy and chemotherapy leading to fatigue and potential limitations in the workplace. Evidence highlights two main obstacles:

- The role of employers in the return to work process
- A lack of medical advice about returning to work

Workplace Accommodations

Steiner and colleagues [19] highlighted the need for research on workplace accommodations by employers in their review of the literature. They noted that little is known about either adaptations in the physical workplace or the content of work that may ease the return of cancer survivors or about the downstream impact of returning cancer survivors on the employer. Workplace accommodations have only been sporadically mentioned in the literature. However, Bouknight and colleagues' [20] study of female breast cancer survivors in Detroit is notable for exploring the role that employers' accommodations and adjustments play in facilitating a return to work after breast cancer. They found that just over 80% of women in their sample returned to work over an 18-month period and all returned to the same position in the labor market. Some 87% reported that they felt that their employer had been accommodating during their cancer journey while only 7% perceived that they had experienced employment discrimination. The role of the employer, specifically, whether they were accommodating or discriminatory, was found to be a statistically significant factor in determining whether or not the women returned to work.

Taskila and colleagues' [21] study of social support is unusual in focussing on the workplace with an examination of the role of co-workers, supervisors, and occupational health services in the return to work process. They found that women received more support than men and that those who underwent chemotherapy also received more support than those who had other forms of treatment. Practical support from supervisors, notably by taking illness and fatigue into consideration when planning and managing work tasks, was particularly important to cancer survivors.

Evidence from the UK about the role played by employers is minimal although a survey of telephone calls to the Disability Rights Commission's advice line suggests that there are still concerns about discrimination against cancer survivors despite the introduction of new rights in the workplace under the Disability Discrimination Act 1995 [22].

Other research from the UK has shown a lack of awareness among employers about cancer in their workforce and a generally inadequate level of information and support for employees. On an encouraging note, it was shown that when employers are faced with employees affected by cancer they generally respond positively (in the view of personnel and human resources practitioners who completed the survey) by providing flexible working, work adjustments and phased return to work [23].

Physician or Health Care Provider Input on Matters Related to Work

Maunsell and colleagues reported that Canadian women in Quebec with breast cancer qualitatively reported a distinct lack of medical advice about work during and after their treatment. There was also a high level of apprehension about returning to work due to lost confidence about job competency and fear of disappointing co-workers because their ability to be productive might have declined [24]. Work by Main and colleagues [14] in the US and Verbeek and colleagues [25] similarly reported that there was considerable scope for improvement with regard to medical advice related to returning to work for cancer survivors (refer to chapter by Verbeek et al. in this volume).

Kennedy and colleagues [15] from the UK also reported that health professionals provided very little medical advice about work for most people through their cancer journey. Importantly, for future efforts at improving this situation, a third of respondents reported experiencing difficulties when they had returned to the workplace. Another British study supporting this evidence used qualitative in-depth interviews and showed that few people reported that they received any worthwhile medical advice from their cancer care team or from their own general practitioners about returning to work:

> I was very pleased with the treatment that I received from both my consultant and breast care nurses. I was given lots of information about breast cancer and its effects but I wasn't given any information about what I should do about work [16].

What this overview indicates is that at present, medical involvement in the return to work process and work process in general is limited in many countries.

Indeed this area appears to be present in a number of countries and not very surprising given the relative importance of health versus work and the lack of knowledge in this area and limited dissemination to health care providers as to evidence-based answers to many questions that survivors have when available.

Role of Employer Attitudes and Actions

There is a significant gap in the literature when it comes to examining the role of employers, supervisors/managers, and co-workers in the return to work process. There is evidence to suggest that a supportive work environment assists returning to work but the reality is that little is known about this area. The lack of medical advice about work is a concern in a number of countries but fortunately it is a factor that is potentially amenable to change. Although the organization of medical practitioners between hospital specialists, general practitioners in the community, and occupational health physicians is different in the Netherlands compared to the UK, it is almost certain that there is scope for an intervention in this area to ensure that people with a cancer diagnosis receive the optimal level of advice about cancer treatment and work.

Cancer Survivors' Relationship with Their Employer

A major influence on returning to work after cancer is the relationship that employees have with their employers, particularly their line managers and colleagues. These employment relationships have been built up over many years and it appears that the duration of service rather than occupational status (professional or non-professional) is an important factor in people successfully returning to work after cancer. This may be due to the development over a longer period of time of an implicit psychological contract between the employer and the employee relating to what constitutes fair and reasonable behaviour.

A British study [16] indicated that nearly every employee disclosed their cancer diagnosis to their employer shortly after they had received it and the vast majority initially received a broadly sympathetic and supportive response from their manager and work colleagues. In several instances, a line manager's response was particularly supportive and highly valued by interviewees for putting their mind at ease about job security and sick pay arrangements, at what was an already difficult time. A large majority of employees with cancer diagnoses are keeping in touch with work colleagues either through visits to the workplace or co-workers visiting them at home and a continuing level of support from colleagues during their sick leave is appreciated by a large number of interviewees. For example, a local government officer in her mid-thirties with rectal cancer who was off work for nearly a year was effusive in her praise for the support she received from her manager and colleagues throughout her cancer journey.

> I couldn't have done it without them. It was absolutely fantastic and then when I had my second operation they were just as supportive, they were brilliant. And when I wanted to come back to work I came back on a very slow return and they looked after me every step of the way.

While the level of support in this instance was particularly notable, work colleagues organized a rotation so that she was always accompanied to medical appointments and arranged transport for her immediate family when she was in hospital recovering from surgery. In another case, a factory worker in her late thirties whose breast cancer spread after her initial course of treatment and had exhausted her sick pay entitlement due to a second prolonged period of absence was very grateful for colleagues keeping in touch for social occasions and for organizing collections in work to help her with her debts. Interestingly, those people whose work colleagues did not keep in touch experienced some difficulties when they returned to work and seemed to resent this neglect by their co-workers. An interviewee in her early fifties with a brain tumour who was on sick leave from nursing fervently expressed this view:

> My work colleagues only came to see me once in all that time. They brought flowers and stuff which is very nice but it was only once in seven months... I suppose I sort of felt if they were in my position I would have visited them more often really, you know. Once in seven months isn't very much.

In general, staying in contact with work and colleagues was regarded positively although there were a few instances when people felt a greater pressure to return to work because they were well enough to drop into work or go out to lunch with colleagues. Given the anxiety that many people feel when they are on sick leave it was widely felt that it was important for employers to manage appropriately both the amount and the tone of the contact during a person's time off work. People wanted to feel that they were still wanted by their employer and to be generally supported, but several respondents acknowledged that they were sensitive to contact from their employer at this time.

Conclusion

In this chapter we have considered the evidence related to the challenges that employers and employees with chronic illness and disability face in general as well as cancer survivor specific information related to returning and remaining at work. The research reviewed in this chapter suggests that work outcomes can be influenced by a complex interaction among employer, employee or prospective employee, and the work environment. Research related to employer perspectives of those with chronic illness and disability in general has provided valuable insight into how employers are conceptualizing and attempting to manage disability and health related issues in the work environment.

Individual factors including demographics, personal economics, physical status, and the individual's accomplishments pre-illness have been found to be significantly related to employment and job retention. These relationships probably vary somewhat by type of cancer; however, this has not been extensively addressed in research in this area as yet. The research discussed also suggests that cancer survivors who maintain contact with their employer, co-workers, and work environment may fair better in terms of work outcomes. When addressing employment and job retention it is important to consider both the individual and employer and how both interact. The involvement of health care providers in this process is something survivors are looking for as well. Future research is needed to better understand how the characteristics of the individual (both modifiable and non-modifiable), work environment, and cancer related symptoms interact to impact work outcomes in specific types of cancer survivors with specific relationships with symptom burden and work [26, 27]. Investigations of cancer survivorship and work that generate findings across many types of cancer survivors are also important so we can apply certain generalizations with some sense of certainty. Employers can benefit from such generic information. Effective, innovative, and cost conscious approaches to employment, long-term work retention, and work optimization in cancer survivors depends on this evidence base.

Acknowledgments Preparation of this chapter is supported in part by funding from SPR, Inc., an Information Technology services film, located in Chicago, Illinois, USA. We would like to thank Mr. Patrick Maher, manager of the *n*Ablement Division of the SPR, Inc., for his extraordinary efforts and contributions to the success of the employer perceptions project funded by SPR, Inc. Furthermore, we would like to thank Macmillan Cancer Support (UK) for supporting and funding this research conducted in the United Kingdom.

References

1. National Council on Disability. Empowerment for Americans with Disabilities: Breaking Barriers to Careers and Full Employment. 2007.
2. Chan F, Cheing G, Chan JYC, Rosenthal DA, Chronister JA. Predicting employment outcomes of rehabilitation clients with orthopedic disabilities: A CHAID analysis. Disability and Rehabilitation. 2006;28:257–70.
3. Chan F, Strauser D, Cardoso EdS, Zheng LX, Chan JYC, Feuerstein M. State vocational services and employment in cancer survivors. Journal of Cancer Survivorship. 2008;2:169–78.
4. National Institute on Disability and Rehabilitation Research. Long-range plan for fiscal year 2005–2009. 2006.
5. Grizzard WR. Meeting demand-side expectations and needs. APA 15th Anniversary Seminar; 2005; Washington, DC; 2005.
6. Stensrud R. Developing relationships with employers' means, considering the competitive business environment and the risks it produces. Rehabilitation Counselling Bulletin. 2007;50:226–37.
7. Strauser D, Chan F. Demand side employment factors affecting job placement and job retention among people with disabilities. *Cancer Survivorship and Work Seminar*. Goldsmith College, London 2007.

8. Greider W. One World, Ready or Not: The Manic Logic of Global Capitalism. New York: Simon & Shuester 1997.
9. Murry M. After long boom, workers confront downward mobility. The Wall Street Journal. 2003;Sect. A1, A6.
10. Strauser D, Chan F. Employer perceptions of productivity and barriers to hiring individuals with disabilities. *Abilitylinks Annual Training Conference*. Chicago, IL 2008.
11. Foley KL, Farmer DF, Petronis VM, Smith RG, McGraw S, Smith K, et al. A qualitative exploration of the cancer experience among long-term survivors: Comparisons by cancer type, ethnicity, gender, and age. Psycho-Oncology. 2006;15(3):248–58.
12. Thewes B, Butow P, Girgis A, Pendlebury S. The psychosocial needs of breast cancer survivors: A qualitative study of the shared and unique needs of younger versus older survivors. Psycho-Oncology. 2004;13:177–89.
13. Amir Z, Moran A, Walsh L, Iddenten R, Luker K. Return to paid work – The British experience. Journal of Cancer Survivorship. 2007;1:129–36.
14. Main DS, Nowels CT, Cavender TA, Etschmaier M, Steiner JF. A qualititative study of work and work return in cancer survivors. Psycho-Oncology. 2005;14:992–1004.
15. Kennedy F, Haslam C, Munir F, Pryce J. Returning to work following cancer: A qualitative exploratory study into the experience of returning to work. European Journal of Cancer Care. 2007;16:17–25.
16. Amir Z, Neary D, Luker K. Cancer survivors' view of work 3 years post diagnosis: A UK perspective. European Journal of Oncology Nursing. 2008;12:190–7.
17. Farley Short P, Vasey JJ, BeLue R. Work disability associated with cancer survivorship and other chronic conditions. Psycho-Oncology. 2007;17:91–7.
18. Spelten E, Verbeek J, Uitterhoeve A, Ansink A, vand der Lelie J, de Reijke T, et al. Cancer, fatigue, and the return of patients to work: A prospective cohort study. European Journal of Cancer. 2003;39:1562–7.
19. Steiner JF, Cavender TA, Main DS, Bradley C. Assessing the impact of cancer on work outcomes: What are the research needs? Cancer. 2004;101(8):1703–10.
20. Bouknight R, Bradley C, Luo Z. Correlates of return to work for breast cancer survivors. Journal of Clinical Oncology. 2006;24(3):345–52.
21. Taskila T, Lindbohm M, Martikainen R, Lehto U, Hakanen J, Hietanen P. Cancer survivors' received and needed social support from their work place and the occupational health service. Support Care in Cancer. 2006;14:427–35.
22. Directgov. Definition of 'disability' under the Disability Discrimination Act (DDA). 2006 cited 2006 June 21.; Available from: http://www.direct.gov.uk/en/DisabledPeople/RightsAndObligations/DisabilityRights/DG_4001069
23. Cancer Backup. Work and Cancer: How Cancer Affects Working Lives. London: Cancer Backup 2006.
24. Maunsell M, Brisson C, Dubois L, Lauzier S, Fraser A. Work problems after breast cancer: An exploratory qualitative study. Psycho-Oncology. 1999;8:467–73.
25. Verbeek J, Spelten E, Kammeijer M, Sprangers M. Return to work of cancer survivors: A prospective cohort study in the quality of rehabilitation by occupational physicians. Journal of Occupational and Environmental Medicine. 2003;6:353–7.
26. Feuerstein M, Hansen JA, Calvio LC, Johnson L, Ronquillo J. Work productivity in brain turmo survivors. Journal of Occupational and Environmental Medicine. 2007;2007(49).
27. Hansen JA, Feuerstein M, Olsen CH, Calvio LC. Breast cancer survivors at work. Journal of Occupational and Environmental Medicine. 2008;50(7):777–84.

Section II
Fundamentals of Work and Chronic Illness

Chapter 4
Work Disability: It is not just the "lesion"

Patrick Loisel

First I prepared myself for dying – now I have to re-orientate myself to work life ...
A cancer survivor (Cited from [1])

Introduction

I used to be an orthopedic surgeon. When I was an undergraduate medical student, I was fascinated by the brain, as it looked to me the most mysterious part of the body and I registered for my first rotation in neurosurgery at a famous neurological hospital in Paris. Unfortunately at this time, neurosurgery was far less advanced than now and most patients had severe trauma or advanced tumors. The wards were filled with comatose patients and in the Operating Room, the concussed brain was suctioned ... My next rotation was orthopedic surgery. I found the fundamentals and action of rebuilding what was sick and broken, leading to functional recovery very appealing. The spine combines bones and nerves in a complex interesting way and I became a spine surgeon. Twenty years and many spine fusions later, I had accumulated excellent fusion rates with splendid X-Rays. Alas, I followed up with many patients who were experiencing pain as before or worse, were disabled, and unable to return to work. Many of these patients were even crying at follow up due to their distress. I progressively realized that the book chapters and clinical papers that I was reading and applying in practice might not always tell the truth or the whole story regarding the treatment of spinal osteoarthritis or other sources of "mechanical spinal pain." Also, filling Workers Compensation Board (WCB) or other insurance forms out for patients, I realized that the more I fused, the more the disability was being created in the forensic attribution of compensation, as every new fusion was considered to add disability instead of improving the patient's status. Some colleagues having obviously similar results were

---

P. Loisel (✉)
Faculty of Medicine and Health Sciences, Université de Sherbrooke, 1111 St-Charles Ouest, Tour ouest, bureau 500, Longueuil, Québec, Canada, J4K 5G4
e-mail: patrick.loisel@usherbrooke.ca

telling me that many patients were just "too lazy to return to work" and happy to combine surgery with benefits. I could not accept that. I could not accept that my "successful surgical procedure" led to overall failures in the lives of my patients. One day, the dean of my School of Medicine asked me: Dr. Loisel, your colleagues, the neurosurgeons, tell me that they send you patients with failures of disc surgery and that you refuse to operate on them. Why? I answered: because, most of the time, I know now that I cause more harm than good: I cure the lesion but I increase the disability. My colleagues as well will recognize this in ten years from now. I was committed to provide the proof.

I began reading the literature on spinal disorders, such as the Quebec task force report [2] and Alf Nachemson's paper "Work for all, for those with Back Pain as well" [3] and decided to build an interdisciplinary team in order to investigate different ways to help patients with back pain resume activity and return to work. It was a completely new experience for me. I hired a psychologist who was treating cancer patients at an advanced stage. I told her: "this should be a great change for you to treat low back pain patients." She answered: "not that different: when cancer patients have accepted their disease and outcome, their pain subsides. It looks the same for back pain patients." I progressively learned the close body-mind relationship and the influence of the environment. I developed, with an occupational physician, a different way of thinking about how to manage back pain (the Sherbrooke model) and tested its effectiveness in a population of workers with subacute back pain with the collaboration of colleagues from McGill University [4]. I learned that an occupational intervention was effective for returning these patients to work while the clinical intervention was not. I found that combining both in a work rehabilitation process was the winner. I was pleased that our approach relieved the disability often related to back pain rather than augmenting it. We now had to follow up with our patients by phone as they were too busy at work to lose time by attending the clinic. Exclusive focus on the "lesion" did not seen to be the answer.

We must always remember that our patients are first and foremost human beings. They have fears and anxiety when they feel pain or hear a frightening diagnosis that can take their lives. This may make them withdraw from many types of activity losing confidence in these ability to work, thus enhancing the likelihood of disability associated with the disorder. A decision to no longer work after attempting to remain in the workplace for several years, cancer survivors become disabled in the same sense as the patients I saw following my surgeries. We as clinicians must now think about how to manage the disability along with the long-term and late physical effects of the cancer and its treatment. We must help them not only address their medical concerns, we also need to help them cope with the fact that they have a chronic illness but in most cases can work if they wish to. We need to address work disability with other stakeholders, and help bring them back to the workplace.

You Say: "Disability"?

Work disability has been the focus of research and clinical activity for the past 20 years. It may be defined as a declared work incapacity linked to a health problem [5]. In order to avoid the negative financial consequences of work disability for workers, public and private insurance systems have been developed that are generally financed by employers or policyholders. Tradition in insurance has been to link the risk of work absence directly related to a disease or the health consequences of an accident and to ascertain the link between the specified disease or accident and the work absence. This has been referred to as the "forensic model" of disability [6]. In order to avoid possible "abuse" of this compensation system by workers, insurers have developed control systems that typically require repeated ascertainment, generally from physicians or other health care providers (HCP), that the incapacity to work is and continues to be directly related to a medical diagnosis. From an historical perspective, numerous symptoms presented by workers and leading to work disability have been difficult to understand. This has led physicians to create "supposed" diagnoses in order to explain symptoms difficult to understand in the framework of conventional disorders and help convince insurers of a persistent pathology rather that suspected "malingering." This began with the so-called "railway spine" in the nineteenth century (unexplainable symptoms following railway accidents) to the recent "whiplash syndrome" [7]. At first glance, difficulty to return to work for a cancer survivor looks as though it is a totally different story in a completely different context and a relatively recent problem issuing from recent advances in the treatment of cancer. However, the past twenty years of research, in particular on disability issuing from spinal and other musculoskeletal disorders, have identified unexpected causes that may be relevant to cancer survivors and predictors of work disability [8]. Experience from this field helps generate hypotheses on the true causes of difficulties in resuming or maintaining work experienced by some cancer survivors.

Work Disability as a Specific Paradigm

Work is invaluable and provides financial autonomy, self-respect, dignity, quality of life, and self-worth [9]. However, every year, a large number of workers are unable to work because of disability arising from various disorders, primarily musculoskeletal disorders (MSDs) and mental health disorders (MHDs), which together account for more than half of all short- and long-term disability [10]. Not all workers with back pain are work disabled, which is fortunate as low back pain is estimated to have an 80% lifetime prevalence and that about 25% of workers have an annual prevalence of back pain limiting activities [11]. Spitzer et al. [2], in a landmark study published in 1987, have shown that only 7% of workers having one day or more of absence from work remained work disabled for more than six months but this minority accounted for 75% of the direct costs paid by the Quebec Workers' Compensation Board WCB. Thus, the vast majority of workers having back pain return to work quickly even if they have a residual amount of pain. Also, the 1998 Quebec Health Survey found an 83% yearly prevalence of pain in one or more body parts in Quebec workers (37% having pain from time to time and 46% quite often or all the time). Interestingly, though, while 51% of these workers attributed their pain to their job, only 11% reported missing time from work because of their pain, and no more than 1.5% were absent for more than three months [11]. This indicates that pain in the workplace is so frequent that it may appear as a "fact of life", but that work absence from pain is fortunately infrequent. While the exact temporal characteristics of work disability differ in cancer survivors (see Chapters 2 and 10), framing our understanding of work disability to the history of work disability in cancer survivors may prove to be a very useful heuristic.

Waddell et al. [12] found, based on numerous studies, that pain (symptom burden) explained only 5% of the cases of work disability in back pain, even though pain is usually evoked as the reason for not returning to work. Pain is a complex phenomenon which is characterized by "an unpleasant sensory and emotional experience associated with actual or potential tissue damage, or described in terms of such damage" [13]. It may persist, through several mechanisms, even if the disorder responsible for the initial pain has resolved. These mechanisms include a lowered threshold of interconnecting spinal neural cells and a release of inflammatory substances depending not only on nociceptive peripheral impulses but also on centrally mediated impulses from past and present cognitions and emotions [14]. These biological phenomena may explain the persistence of pain in some patients that can lead to kinesophobia (fear of movement) and disability [15]. Movement and function have been shown not only to be beneficial in terms of quick recovery but also to be part of the means by which pain perception can be reformulated [16].

This scientific data might look like a "mystery" to most involved in "hightech" health care, insurance coverage. Many workers who have been accused of "abusing the system," preferring to continue to be compensated and not working. However, through years of research we have identified a vast number of predictors of work disability in those with back pain that are not directly linked to the disorder in the back. On the contrary, most of the imaging findings showing anatomical disorders have been unable to be linked to the occurrence of disability. Similar findings have been shown for other musculoskeletal disorders leading to disability in some cases, as upper extremity disorders. While there is always a possibility that our measurement tools are currently too crude, it has become clearer and clearer that work disability is a multidimensional problem, and recent evidence makes a plea for considering a disability paradigm that differs from the usual biomedical paradigm [8]. The biomedical paradigm is of limited relevance to work disability since various factors other than the initial biological pathology are involved, exacerbate the symptom complex and make returning to work a difficult and frightening experience. In fact, the disability paradigm indicates that return to work (RTW) or work retention depends on the complex interaction of biological (e.g., medical status, physical capacity), psychological (e.g., fear, distress), and social (e.g., work environment, family) factors. Evidence also indicates that disability results from the complex interplay involving several stakeholders (employer, insurer, healthcare providers) interacting with the patient/worker in the disability process [17]. Work disability may be the result of complex set of workplace factors often including organizational factors, the worker's fears of returning to a perceived or actual difficult environment, or the healthcare system favoring rest rather than activity resumption. It is reasonable that work disability associated with cancer survivorship as a chronic illness possesses many of the same characteristics as we have found in back pain.

Modeling Work Disability

Various models explaining work disability have been proposed and recently reviewed by Schultz et al. [6]. Biomedical models directly linking the disease to the disability have been found inappropriate as mentioned above. The forensic models that use the medical model to explain the disability in relation to benefits received by the patient during the disability process may lead to inappropriate actions when there is a perception from the insurer of a discrepancy between the nature or severity of the disorder and the disability process. As the actual factors that explain the disability are not often identified or understood, benefits may be cut because the disorder appears of benign nature. Conversely, return to work may not be encouraged due to stakeholders' perception of severity.

Biopsychosocial models appear to be of greater value for explaining the disability process as they correspond to the many factors that have been found to explain work absence in many studies. The biopsychosocial model first described by Engel [18] has been applied to disability from back pain by Waddell and Main [19] and from variations in medical status associated with various medical conditions by Feuerstein [5]. It emphasizes that psychological factors (e.g., fears, anxiety, depression, distress), social factors (e.g., work perceived demands, perceptions of co-workers) and the discrepancy between demands of the work and capabilities of the worker explain the prolonged work absence and that these points have to be addressed rather than exclusive focus on the disease itself (once it is healed or stabilized). Also, these models emphasize the temporal nature of the return to work process that requires readiness for change from a disabled to a more active working status, as an application of Prochaska's readiness for change model [20]. In this model, the patient progresses through the stages of pre-contemplation, contemplation, preparation for action, action, and maintenance. If too early in the process, the return to work is unlikely. Also, Vlaeyen et al. [15] have developed a model showing the disability process as a "vicious cycle", where fears lead to activity restriction that lead to physical and psychological deconditioning with disuse and depression, reinforcing the pain perception and activity restriction. The major interest of the biopsychosocial models is to help develop interventions that will stop the focus on the original medical disorder and address factors to reverse the disability process and facilitate return to work and work retention.

More recently, ecological case management models have emphasized not only the multifactorial origin of work disability but also its multipartite nature involving many stakeholders that may influence the disability process [21]. These models recognize that the return to work process may be viewed differently by various stakeholders involved in the process and that the patient/worker is placed at the center of a multidimensional social system and also participates to this system. Interactions among the worker and other stakeholders from the workplace, the insurance, and the healthcare systems will influence the motivation and the process for return to work. The potential of this model, in the arena of work disability (Fig. 4.1), is in its ability to help identify multiple "players" in order to facilitate dialogue and agreement on the

Fig. 4.1 The arena in work disability prevention (figure adapted with permission from Loisel, P., Buchbinder, R., Hazard, R., Keller, R., Scheel, I., van Tulder, M., & Webster, B., 2005, "Prevention of work disability due to musculoskeletal disorders: The challenge of implementing evidence" *Journal of Occupational Rehabilitation,* 15(4), p. 509)

return to work process [17]. This can assist in overcoming the differences in interests and language of various stakeholders that may have a different understanding of the nature of the work disability. Also legal and cultural issues surround all these stakeholders and may help explain why a solution that may be appropriate in a specific culture or country may not directly apply to another.

Various Diseases and Work Disability

As mentioned, the most frequently researched disorder linked to work disability has been low back pain. This has been due to its prevalence in industry and the efforts of Nachemson [3], and others with direct links to major industries such as an automotive manufacturer. Nachemson claimed in the early 1980s that workers having back pain should have the right and opportunity to work as well as others. His argument was that psychosocial factors have been shown to predict more of the disability than the spinal structures. So, from a spinal health perspective why can't these individuals work? Also, the role of the multiple stakeholders in the disability process [22] and the positive effect on overall function of progressively more demanding duties [23] have been demonstrated over the years. This has also been shown for upper extremity disorders [24]. Interventions have been developed and tested in the 1990s taking into account these perspectives and have been successful in improving the return to work and disability outcomes [4, 24] and they have even been shown to be cost effective [25]. Recently, mental health disorders have expanded in workplaces in a quasi epidemic fashion, leading to prolonged work disability for many workers. Again organizational workplace factors have been found as a contributor to much of this work disability [26]. Recently, Briand et al. [27] have advocated for extending knowledge developed from musculoskeletal disorders and the disability paradigm perspective to work disability related to mental health disorders. They demonstrated how the disability diagnostic interview developed for workers with MSDs may be adapted to mental disorders and how return to work centralized in the workplace may be also of value for disability originating from mental health disorders. Authors have also shown that for cardiovascular disorders, subsequent work disability was not related to the severity of the disease but to psychosocial factors [28]. This confirms that when someone is absent from work for a prolonged time, the main reason may not be the actual medical disorder alone but different factors related to the person and his/her environment perhaps triggered by the medical disorder.

The Case of Cancer Survivors

Cancer is a disease that appears as very different from musculoskeletal disorders or mental health disorders. It is generally life threatening and in some cancers the mortality rate remains high. However, as presented in earlier chapters recent advances in early diagnosis and more effective treatment has allowed recovery or prolonged survival, far beyond previous figures, for many types of cancer [29]. These new figures have led to a greater focus on return to normal activity, including work, of these patients particularly those for which this is a goal. Depending on the type of cancer and its treatment, residual anatomical or physiological status and functional limitations may be very different, ranging from none to major residual impairment. Physical defects, residual pain, and fatigue often explain a proportion of the work disability. However, other factors contributing to work disability might be considered, especially in the light of the work disability paradigm, as developed above. Cancer, as a life-threatening disease, may add considerable stress to the physical disease element and result in high levels of distress. However, high levels of distress have been as well considered in MSD patients [30] with prolonged work disability. Also, interpersonal relationships might be altered with relatives, coworkers and employer. Also, disclosing the diagnosis might be a problem, similar to mental health with the fear of subsequent discrimination [31].

Recent literature in the field of cancer survivorship and work shows interesting findings, especially when interpreted in relation to disability from MSD disorders. First, return to work rates of cancer has demonstrated large variation among studies from 44 to 100% [1]. However, overall survivors' return to work appears high in most studies and the difference between cancer survivors and matched controls remains between 5 and 9% [32]. Some authors may have deduced that the problem is in fact trivial. However, these figures are similar to those of back pain shown for many years [2]. This may induce the hypothesis that the relation between the cancer and employment as with back pain and other chronic illnesses is not a direct one but mediated through other variables.

A recent qualitative study has explored the patients' perceptions of the factors aiding or hindering return to work after a cancer diagnosis [29]. Factors perceived as aiding were job flexibility, co-worker support, and healthcare provider support. Factors perceived as hindering were ignorance about cancer in the workplace, lack of emotional support, and physical effects of cancer. Workplace factors look as important for return to work of cancer survivors as they are in models developed for MSDs. Verbeek et al. [1] have shown that when occupational physicians apply return to work guidelines developed for back pain or MSDs to cancer patients, they facilitate their return to work.

Taskila [32] has recently examined, in a large cohort of Finnish cancer patients and matched controls, factors associated with employment, work ability, and social support. She found that "early departure from work life, as well as impaired work ability and the lack of social support are the most common problems encountered by many cancer survivors." Work ability had been measured as a *perceived* work ability assessed with a validated questionnaire, the Work Ability Index [33]. Social support of co-workers and from occupational health services looks to be of primary importance for easing return to work. She presents a model where socio-demographic and disease-related factors influence work resumption through the mediation of the

4 Work Disability: It is not just the "lesion"

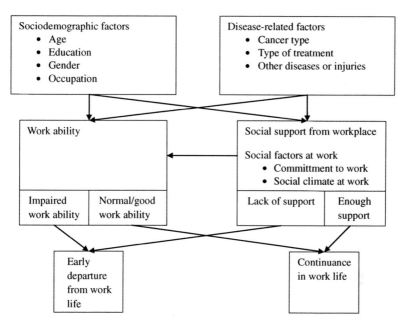

Fig. 4.2 Factors associated with work ability, employement, and social support of cancer survivors (figure adapted with permission from Cancer Survivors at Work: Work-Related Problems and Factors Associated with their employment, Work Ability and Social Support from the Work Community, 2007, Finnish Institute of Occupational Health)

perceived work ability and social support from the workplace (Fig. 4.2). Again occupational factors influence return to work similar to other models but with an emphasis on the disorder itself.

Conclusion

It appears from a limited number of recent studies that work disability may present many similarities among very different disorders. This appears to be the case with cancer survivors despite the paucity of studies to date. The fact that cancer related studies of work disability are relatively rare is not unexpected. This also occurred in the early days of back pain research. Real progress on explaining predictors of prolonged disability or return to work happened when the vast field of possible causes was explored (Fig. 4.1). In particular, it is likely that insurance modalities and cultural views on cancer can also lead to different return to work outcomes. In the scope of a growing cancer lifetime prevalence, estimated to be 40% for females and 45% for men in Canada [34], a relatively small percentage of survivors not returning to work or leaving work represents a significant number of citizens who may be denied a place in the workforce.

Work disability in cancer survivors can have an impact not only on there well being and sense of accomplishment, but also on loss of expertise for workplaces and as indicated in an earlier chapter significant economical social costs for society. The disability paradigm and the arena of work disability should be considered in future epidemiologic and intervention studies in order to identify pertinent variables and stakeholders, thus allowing further steps in helping cancers survivors as well to resume a normal and rewarding work life [35]. All of us invloved in the health and well being of our patients must never forget our patients are not just the "lesion".

References

1. Verbeek J, Spelten E, Kammeijer M, Sprangers M. Return to work of cancer survivors: a prospective cohort study into the quality of rehabilitation by occupational physicians. Occupational & Environmental Medicine. 2003;60(5):352–7.
2. Spitzer WO, LeBlanc FE, Dupuis M. Scientific approach to the assessment and management of activity-related spinal disorders. A monograph for clinicians. Report of the Quebec Task Force on Spinal Disorders. Spine. 1987;12(7 Suppl):S1–59.
3. Nachemson A. Work for all. For those with low back pain as well. Clinical Orthopaedics & Related Research. 1983(179):77–85.
4. Loisel P, Abenhaim L, Durand P, Esdaile JM, Suissa S, Gosselin L, et al. A population-based, randomized clinical trial on back pain management. Spine. 1997;22(24):2911–8.
5. Feuerstein M. A multidisciplinary approach to the prevention, evaluation, and management of work disability. Journal of Occupational Rehabilitation. 1991;1(1):5–12.
6. Schultz IZ, Stowell AW, Feuerstein M, Gatchel RJ. Models of return to work for musculoskeletal disorders. Journal of occupational rehabilitation. 2007 Jun;17(2):327–52.
7. Thomas CS. Psychological consequences of traumatic injury. British Journal of Psychiatry. 2002;180:392–3.
8. Loisel P, Durand MJ, Berthelette D, Vézina N, Baril R, Gagnon D, et al. Disability prevention – New paradigm for the management of occupational back pain. Disease Management & Health Outcomes. 2001;9(7):351–60.
9. Limoges J, Lemaire R, Dodier F. Trouver son travail. Montréal: Éditions Fides 1987.
10. Watson Wyatt. Staying@Work: Making the connection to a healthy organization. Report: Watson Wyatt Worldwide; 2005. Report No.: W-806.
11. Institut de la statistique du Québec. Enquête social et de santé 1998. 2nd ed. Sainte-Foy, Québec: Les Publications du Québec 2001.
12. Waddell G, Burton AK, Main CJ. Screening to identify people at risk of long-term incapacity for work. London UK: Royal Society of Medicine Press 2003.
13. Merskey H, Bogduk N. Classification of chronic pain: Description of chronic pain syndromes and definitions of pain terms. 2nd ed. Seattle: IASP Press 1994.
14. Coderre TJ, Katz J, Vaccarino AL, Melzack R. Contribution of central neuroplasticity to pathological pain: review of clinical and experimental evidence. Pain. 1993;52(3):259–85.
15. Vlaeyen JW, Kole-Snijders AM, Boeren RG, van Eek H. Fear of movement/(re)injury in chronic low back pain and its relation to behavioral performance. Pain. 1995;62(3):363–72.
16. Fordyce WE. Back pain in the workplace. Management of disability in non-specific conditions. Seattle: IASP Press 1994.
17. Feuerstein M, Huang GD, Ortiz JM, Shaw WS, Miller VI, Wood PM. Integrated case management for work-related upper-extremity disorders: Impact of patient satisfaction on health and work status. Journal of Occupational and Environmental Medicine. 2003;45(8):803–12.

18. Engel GL. The need for a new medical model: a challenge for biomedicine. Science. 1977;196(4286):129–36.
19. Waddell G, Main C. A new clinical model of low back pain and disability. In: Waddell G, ed. *The back pain revolution*. Toronto: Churchill Livingstone 1998:223–40.
20. Prochaska JO, DiClemente CC, Norcross JC. In search of how people change. Applications to addictive behaviors. American Psychologist. 1992;47(9):1102–14.
21. Loisel P, Buchbinder R, Hazard R, Keller R, Scheel I, van Tulder M, et al. Prevention of work disability due to musculoskeletal disorders: The challenge of implementing evidence. Journal of Occupational Rehabilitation. 2005;15(4):507–24.
22. Frank J, Sinclair S, Hogg-Johnson S, Shannon H, Bombardier C, Beaton D, et al. Preventing disability from work-related low-back pain. New evidence gives new hope if we can just get all the players onside. CMAJ Canadian Medical Association Journal. 1998;158(12):1625–31.
23. Krause N, Dasinger LK, Neuhauser F. Modified work and return to work: a review of the literature. Journal of Occupational Rehabilitation. 1998;8(2):113–39.
24. Feuerstein M, Callan-Harris S, Hickey P, Dyer D, Armbruster W, Carosella AM. Multidisciplinary rehabilitation of chronic work-related upper extremity disorders. Long-term effects. Journal of Occupational Medicine. 1993;35(4):396–403.
25. Loisel P, Lemaire J, Poitras S, Durand MJ, Champagne F, Stock S, et al. Cost-benefit and cost-effectiveness analysis of a disability prevention model for back pain management: a six-year follow up study. Occupational and Environmental Medicine. 2002;59:807–15.
26. Funk M. Mental health policies and programs in the workplace. Geneva, Switzerland: World Health Organization 2005.
27. Briand C, Durand MJ, St-Arnaud L, Corbière M. Work and mental health: Learning from Return-to-Work Rehabilitation Programs designed for workers with musculoskeletal disorders. The International Journal of Law and Psychiatry. 2007;30:444–57.
28. Mittag O, Kolenda KD, Nordman KJ, Bernien J, Maurischat C. Return to work after myocardial infarction/coronary artery bypass grafting: patients' and physicians' initial viewpoints and outcome 12 months later. Social Science & Medicine. 2001;52(9):1441–50.
29. Nachreiner NM, Dagher RK, McGovern PM, Baker BA, Alexander BH, Gerberich SG. Successful return to work for cancer survivors. AAOHN Journal. 2007;55(7):290–5.
30. Coutu M, Durand M, Loisel P, Goulet C, Gauthier N. Level of distress among workers undergoing work rehabilitation for musculoskeletal disorders. Journal of Occupational Rehabilitation. 2007;17(2):289–303.
31. Feuerstein M. Defining cancer survivorship. Journal of Cancer Survivorship. 2007;1(1):5–7.
32. Taskila T. Cancer survivors at work. Work-related problems and factors associated with their employment, work ability and social support from the work community. Helsinki, Finland: Finnish Institute of Occupational Health 2007.
33. Tuomi K, Ilmarinen J, Jahkola A, Katajarinne L, Tulkki A. Work Ability Index. Helsinki, Finland: Finnish Institute of Occupational Health 1998.
34. Canadian Cancer Society/National Cancer Institute of Canada. Canadian cancer statistics 2008. 2008 cited; Available from: http://www.cancer.ca/vgn/images/portal/cit_86751114/10/34/614137951cw_library_WYNTK_Bladder_Punjabi2005.pdf
35. Feuerstein M. Cancer Survivorship and Work. Journal of Occupational Rehabilitation. 2005;15(1):1–2.

Chapter 5
The Meaning of Work

Guy Maytal and John Peteet

Introduction

Work is one of the central organizing structures of adult life. The significance of a cancer diagnosis to work life has been radically altered during the past half-century. Driven by innovations in diagnosis and treatment, individuals diagnosed with cancer are living longer, better-quality lives. For example, in 1960, 25% of adults diagnosed with cancer survived five years, while in 2007, 65% of cancer patients lived for five years [1]. In the majority of cases, the notion of a cancer diagnosis has evolved from an almost certain death sentence to either a persistent/chronic condition or even a curable disease with some long-term sequellae. Furthermore, not only are more adults surviving cancer, but the generation of children treated for cancer in the 1970s and 1980s are now entering the workforce [1]. Both the fact that one has had cancer and the long-term psychological sequellae of the diagnosis and the treatment often lead individuals to renegotiate their relationship to work life. Therefore, the meaning that work has in the life of a cancer survivor has begun to take on increased salience for the estimated 3.8 million working age adults (ages 20 to 64) with a history of cancer [1]. The nature and scope of the challenges faced by cancer survivors as they continue in or renegotiate work are discussed elsewhere in this book. This chapter focuses instead on the meaning of work for those who survive cancer and how the psychological burden of cancer survivorship affects them.

We will begin by discussing the unique meaning that cancer has in our culture and then briefly review the significance that work holds for self-concept and life roles. We will also review the literature on the meaning and emotional issues surrounding work in cancer patients and survivors. Next, we will review the impact of cancer on patients from a developmental perspective (e.g., how cancer survival affects one's relationship to work at the various stages of the life cycle).

G. Maytal (✉)
Staff Psychiatrist on the Palliative Care Team, Massachusetts General Hospital, Wang ACC 812, 15 Parkman Street, Boston, MA 02114, USA
e-mail: gmaytal@partners.org

We will discuss disease-specific concerns related to the meaning of work. And finally, we will review therapeutic interventions from a psychiatric or psychological perspective to help cancer survivors return to and remain in the workforce. Lastly, we propose directions for future research.

The Meaning of Surviving Cancer

Perhaps more than any other illness, the metaphors and cultural meanings that surround cancer and its treatment define the ways in which patients (and clinicians who treat them) relate to the illness and to themselves both during and after treatment. The meanings, language, and metaphors that patients use to discuss cancer can be detrimental to their well-being and ability to cope with current and future challenges. For example, despite a widespread consensus that cancer is most often an enduring condition characterized by multiple trajectories and ongoing physical and psychosocial concerns, most cancer patients (and many of those who treat them) continue to discuss it as a single event with a particular end (e.g., life or death). Many cancer survivors experience a dissonance between their expectations (e.g., full remission with return to pre-morbid level of functioning) and their experience of life after treatment (e.g., a variety of physical and psychological concerns). As a result, many cancer survivors develop post-cancer distress – at least 30% according to one study [2]. Another important meaning that many cancer survivors ascribe to their illness is its inexorable link with death. During diagnosis and treatment, patients must struggle with the fact of their own mortality and find some way to accommodate to it. After treatment is complete, these same individuals eventually realize that although they may not have died from their cancer, they will certainly die at some point in the future [2]. Consequently, many cancer survivors find new meaning and vitality in their lives, taking on new roles at home and at work, or recommitting themselves to old roles with renewed vigor. However, others become paralyzed by fear and a sense of futility about living their lives, and find it difficult to regain momentum in their life paths [3].

Simply stated, individuals ascribe meaning to life events in order to understand them and give them a context. Ultimately, the ways in which individuals, after cancer treatment, construct meaning about life in general, and about work in particular, depend on a variety of factors. These include the disease course before, during, and after acute treatment. For example, an otherwise healthy woman in her 30s diagnosed with localized breast cancer and treated only with surgery and radiation will have a very different conceptualization of her illness than a life-long smoker in his 60s diagnosed with metastatic lung cancer. The individual's social roles and support systems also influence the meanings he or she constructs about their illness after treatment. A religious man in his 40s who is fully employed and has a family to support will have a very different experience of surviving cancer than a widow in her 60s with no children. Finally, how patients have coped with and made meaning of difficult events in the past also helps determine how they will make sense of having survived cancer. Past traumas and the experiences of friends and relatives with major medical illnesses, as well as past resilience in the face of adversity can all influence the experience of the cancer patient.

Underlying all of these individually constructed meanings are broader cultural metaphors about cancer that have evolved over the past 150 years. Throughout this process, society and the individual have attempted to cope with a disease that is seen to inexorably lead to death and whose etiology is unclear. In the early 20th century, illness was viewed as an expression of character, and therefore it was often surmised that one's character was at the heart of illness. As Karl Menninger, the prominent psychiatrist wrote, "Illness is in part what the world has done to a victim, but in a larger part it is what the victim has done with his world, and with himself." More specifically, cancer was conceived as caused by a repression of emotion and an overall impotence in life. This all-or-nothing message laid the blame of the illness squarely at the feet of the patient [4].

However, by the mid-20th century the United States government and medical establishment decided to take a different approach to cancer and the fear it engenders. Armed with a sense of optimism and indefatigability, along with faith in medical science, the United States declared the "war on cancer." Influenced by the Vietnam War, where chemical weapons (e.g., Agent Orange and napalm) were frequently used, and nuclear weapons (e.g., the atomic bomb) were on everyone's mind, the war on cancer quickly transformed the vocabulary used to describe cancer and its treatment – a new vocabulary of military metaphor quickly emerged. Today we have inherited this vocabulary and its underlying worldview. The illness is described as "invasive" and the body's "defenses" are deemed inadequate against the invader. Even the way in which the illness is characterized assesses its threat level in military terms (e.g., "malignant" vs. "benign"). These words have become so prevalent in talking about cancer that they seem to be perfectly ordinary and their militaristic undertones usually go unnoticed. However, it is the military nature of language describing cancer that frames the medical "response" to it. It is common practice to justify nearly all damage to healthy tissue in order to "save a life." As part of the treatment we "bombard" the tumor with "toxic rays" or use "toxic chemicals" against it (the first chemotherapy was derived from nitrogen mustard gas). Cancer is an all-or-nothing phenomenon that must be destroyed at all costs, regardless of the impact of these interventions on the physical or psychological well-being of the patient [4].

In popular conversation, this rigid thinking extends to cancer survivors as well. Just as some war veterans thrive after returning home (John McCain and John Kerry are two prominent examples), some survivors are heralded as exemplars for their ability to return to full functioning after treatment (e.g., Lance Armstrong as the most famous cancer survivor). However, just as many war veterans struggle to function in life, many individuals who complete cancer treatment have a variety of long-term physical and/or psychological sequelae from their illness and treatment that precludes them from returning to their prior mode of functioning. What the military metaphor fails to recognize is that cancer is not simply a singular event with a particular end. Cancer consists of a variety of enduring conditions characterized by multiple trajectories and ongoing physical and psychosocial concerns.

In other words, there is no complete "cure." Even those individuals whose cancer enters remission worry about disease recurrence. And so, the common understanding of what a cancer survivor is supposed to be like (i.e., returning to normal function as if the cancer never happened) is not only unattainable for most, but leaves many cancer survivors confused and concerned after remission. It is in this context of uncertainty, worry, and ongoing physical and psychological difficulties that adult survivors of cancer approach their relationship to work.

Having discussed some of the complexities surrounding cancer survivorship, we now turn to a brief discussion of the meaning of work in our culture.

The Meaning of Work

Sociologists have long understood the importance of work to self-concept, self-esteem, and satisfaction [5–8]. As cancer treatments have improved, increased attention has been given to the meaning of work for cancer survivors. In this section, we present a brief discussion of the meaning of work in our society in general and for patients with cancer in particular.

Work is important to self-esteem and the self-concept of a large proportion of the population. As one patient stated, "what you do is what you are" [9]. Work allows individuals to express and to realize core values – such as contributing to society and providing for oneself or one's loved ones. To identify with a particular profession or trade is an important component of many individuals' social role. And the financial freedom of a salary not only contributes to self-esteem, but often influences power dynamics in family structures. On the negative side, work can also serve as an arena for competition and control, as well as an outlet for self-defeating compulsivity and as a means of avoiding intimacy (e.g., workaholism).

The literature on the meaning of work to cancer survivors is quite limited. However, there is a growing literature on work-related issues for patients with disabilities that can be extrapolated (with some caveats) to cancer patients. Furthermore, more is now known about the factors influencing cancer patients' ability to return to work and their satisfaction with it.

Freedman and Fesko [9] studied the meaning that work has for individuals with severe disabilities and their families. They organized a series of focus groups and asked a series of detailed questions about job satisfaction and job obstacles, interviewing a total of 23 individuals with disabilities and their families (ages ranging from 24 to 68 years). Both, family members and the disabled individuals stated that feeling productive and keeping busy were at the core of meaningful work. All rated self-esteem as a critical outcome of having a job. These concerns are echoed in the conversations of cancer survivors about work.

In their study, Freedman and Fesko [9] also examined job obstacles for the disabled. Many of these individuals had difficulty in getting or keeping jobs (which they related to their disabilities). A key concern was whether to disclose "hidden" disabilities (e.g., mental illness or traumatic brain injury). This concern was complicated by certain individuals' needs for accommodation of their disabilities. This concern is particularly salient for cancer survivors, many of whom have cognitive or physical limitations that they may or may not want to reveal to potential employers. The major themes noted by Freedman and Fesko [9] as being discussed in the focus groups they conducted are presented in Table 5.1.

Table 5.1 Key themes in consumer and family focus croups (table adapted with permission from Freedman, R.I., & Fesko, S.L. 1996, "The Meaning of Work in the Lives of People with Significant Disabilities: Consumer and Family Perspectives" Journal of Rehabilitation, 62(3), p. 52)

Key Themes in Consumer and Family Focus Groups		
Key Themes	Consumers	Families
Job Outcomes/ Satisfaction	Activity/productivity Self-esteem/well-being Compensation/benefits	Activity/productivity Self-esteem/well-being Socialization opportunities
Relationships at Work	Feelings of belonging/acceptance Some co-workers patronizing Praise from employers and customers	Social isolation Social vulnerability
Support at Work	Security/reinforcement from program staff Support/backup from job coaches Encouragement/flexibility from employers	Security/reinforcement from Program staff Support/backup from job coaches Job coaches also support families
Job Obstacles	Stigma/discrimination re: • gaps in job history • disclosure of disabilities • job accommodations • health insurance • job promotion Lack of support from state rehabilitation agency Lack of information on rights	Lack of appropriate job matches "Dead end" mental work Negative expectations of staff/ public Lack of transportation
Job Expectations	Content with current job Desire to upgrade skills/find new job Further schooling/training Personal goal setting	Limited potential for advancement Lack of job security for future

One way to evaluate the relevance of the literature on disability and work for cancer survivors would be to quantify the amount of work disability attributable to cancer. Short and coworkers [10] studied the increase in work disability due to cancer in a cohort of survivors and compared it to other chronic conditions. They examined a sample of 647 survivors (ages 55–65) and compared them to 5988 cancer-free age-matched individuals. In this study, the rate of disability in cancer-free survivors was significantly higher as compared to adults without chronic conditions. However, there were no significant differences between disability rates for cancer and other chronic health conditions. Short et al. argue that cancer survivorship should be viewed as a chronic condition requiring longitudinal care. In a separate study looking at employment pathways after cancer treatment, Short and colleagues [11] interviewed 1433 cancer survivors (ranging from one to five years after diagnosis) by phone. They found that 20% of those surveyed reported cancer-related disabilities, but half of those individuals were working. Overall, 13% of cancer survivors had quit working for cancer-related reasons. Those individuals with central nervous system, head and neck, and stage IV hematologic cancers had the highest rates of disability or quitting work.

Several researchers have examined the influence of psychosocial factors on work characteristics and patterns after cancer treatment. In a prospective study of 235 cancer survivors, Spelten and colleagues [12] evaluated the impact of fatigue and other cancer-related symptoms on the return to work of cancer survivors at 6, 12, and 18 months. They found that fatigue, female gender, depression, and increased workload were all associated with increased time taken to return to work. In a separate publication, Spelten and associates [13] reviewed the literature on factors affecting the return to work for cancer survivors. They found that across the 14 studies reviewed, the mean rate of return to work was 62%. The following factors were negatively associated with returning to work: non-supportive work environment, manual labor, and having had head and neck cancer. Steiner et al. [14] surveyed 100 cancer survivors to evaluate the influence of psychosocial concerns and physical symptoms on changes in their work. They found that fatigue, feeling bored or useless, and feeling depressed were significantly associated with a reduction in work hours or change in occupational role.

To better understand the impact of cancer on the survivor's quality of life, Main and colleagues [15] carried out a qualitative study of the work experiences of a group of 28 cancer survivors. They performed extensive interviews of these individuals and found that their work experiences after cancer were quite diverse and did not follow any particular pattern. They also found that cancer survivors had received little guidance from their physicians about work. Overall, it seems that fatigue, physical symptom burden, severity and type of illness, and depression are all associated with longer return to work, increased rates of disability, and less satisfaction at work. Furthermore, the area of work-related concerns is often neglected by physicians.

Developmental Aspects

What work means to each individual can differ at each life stage. Therefore, the ways in which work is disrupted by cancer and cancer survivorship also differs at various stages of the adult lifecycle. In this section, we borrow from the work of Erik Erikson [16] to address the impact of being a cancer survivor at the three developmental stages of adult life: early adulthood, middle adulthood, and late adulthood Table 5.2. In early adulthood (approximately ages 18–35), the challenge is to create intimacy and solidarity in order to construct a satisfying life, and to avoid isolation and distance. The main themes of this stage are affiliation and love. In this stage, individuals complete their education and begin to work and/or build a career. When it comes to work, patients who survive cancer as children or young adults overall have similar rates of graduation from high school, employment rates, and levels of psychological distress as the general population. Many of these individuals use the defense of denial to function, while others attribute significant personal growth and maturity to their cancer experience. A 28-year-old woman with a history of childhood lymphoma and adult-onset thyroid cancer was in full remission from both. She joined a cancer survivor group because of problems in intimate relationships, but was quite successful at her computer programming job. She said that her past cancers had not influenced her work-life at all and, in fact, no one at work knew about her past cancers. During the course of the group, she was genuinely surprised to learn that many cancer survivors socialize with each other. After the group's end, she continued to choose to not reveal her medical history to her employer because she did not feel it affected her work performance.

However, selected sub-groups of childhood cancer survivors have lower socio-economic status, lower employment rates, and more psychological distress [17–19]. These individuals are more likely to have had intracranial tumors or cranial radiation, greater amounts of chemotherapy or radiation, and are "poor copers." These patients are more likely to be struggling with cognitive difficulties or fatigue from their illness and treatment. They may also have chronic medical problems as a result of their illnesses. Consider Ms. M., an attractive 23-year-old woman who had been cured of renal cancer as an adolescent, but subsequently developed recurrent urinary tract infections that were

Table 5.2 Developmental aspects of the meaning of work

Stage	Life challenge	Meaning of work	Task for the cancer patient
Early adulthood	Intimacy	Identity	Preservation of the self in relationships
Middle adulthood	Generativity	Productivity	Preservation of provider role
Late adulthood	Integrity	Fulfillment	Achievement of wisdom and balance

resistant to oral antibiotics. The infections caused severe abdominal pain and necessitated frequent hospitalizations. Although she appeared physically well, she was unable to hold a job because of her frequent absences. Circumstances like these are likely to keep some cancer survivors out of the workforce, or prevent them from pursuing the career of their choosing. Individuals in these circumstances may be more likely to choose isolation over solidarity in the development process. However, many also find ways to compensate for their limitations at work either by modifying their work expectations or by finding satisfaction and identity in other aspects of their lives (e.g., family affiliations, friendships, or volunteer work). For example, Ms. M. chose to work for her mother's printing business. Her mother was able to accommodate her work expectations to Ms. M.'s need for frequent medical care. Furthermore, Ms. M.'s close relationship to her mother and boyfriend, as well as the opportunity to contribute to her family's business, gave her a sense of solidarity within both the work and personal aspects of her life along with an opportunity to express love and affinity in the world.

During the stage of middle adulthood (approximately ages 35–65) the challenge is to be generative and avoid stagnation or self-absorption. Prominent themes in this stage are productivity and care. During this prime of adult life, the key tasks are becoming occupied with meaningful work and family issues, as adults take on being caregivers and contributing to the betterment of others. Surviving cancer in this stage can disrupt long-held patterns of meaning surrounding work and its relative importance to an individual, creating a crisis that can lead to self-absorbed despair or new avenues of personal growth. Consider the case of Mr. H., a 40-year-old unmarried partner in a prominent law firm who regularly worked long hours. After developing and completing treatment for a thymoma he noticed that "work means nothing to me." He used the fact of his cancer as an opportunity to reevaluate his life priorities and chose to work less and concentrate on other aspects of his life after treatment. Another example is Mr. N., a 37-year-old man who was treated for lymphoma, during which time he left his job as a production manager for a large corporation. After treatment, he sought out individual and group therapy to discuss returning to his previous line of work (which he now thought of as safe and boring) versus pursuing his lifelong passion of being a commercial airline pilot. After extensive conversations, Mr. N. decided that his prior line of work was more financially stable and that he was more concerned about restoring his financial integrity than flying planes. He decided to return to his previous line of work and found a higher paying job. In both of these cases, the individuals chose generativity (of different types) as solutions to their existential dilemmas.

These questions of meaning and generativity take on particular salience for individuals who need to work to support their loved ones. For example, Mrs. B., a 52-year-old married woman who was the primary breadwinner for her family, refused to work less despite ongoing fatigue. She was worried that her family was dependent on her salary and health insurance. Ultimately, Mrs. B.'s immediate and extended family rallied around her in support, which allowed her to cut back on her work hours and be more connected with her children. Paradoxically, Mrs. B.'s narrow focus on having to work left her in a state of stagnation and self-absorption. Only by allowing herself to be cared for, could she actually contribute to others.

During late adulthood (approximately age 65 to death) the challenge is one of generating integrity or falling into despair. By integrity, Erikson meant generating a sense of fulfillment about lives and the decisions we have made. He also referred to developing a concern for the entirety of life, and ultimately accepting death as its completion. In this stage, the prominent theme is developing wisdom. Individuals who survive cancer at this stage often need to grieve the loss of everything that work means for them. For older individuals who are completely reliant on work for their identity, having to stop working can precipitate a state of despair and even suicidal ideation. Some individuals find connection and meaning in other areas of life, such as long-neglected hobbies or spending time with friends and family, that ultimately give them great joy, satisfaction, and peace.

Spectrum of Severity of Work Problems

Cancer can interfere with work to various degrees, with differing emotional impact. Many individuals continue to work during cancer treatment, despite symptoms such as fatigue and impaired concentration. While some do so for financial reasons or to maintain health insurance, many value the intrinsic rewards, social benefits, and sense of normality or identity that their work provides [20]. Hence, worsening symptoms that force the individual to consider a sick leave can precipitate an emotional crisis. For those in some degree of denial, the need to take a leave from work may be the first real indication that they have a serious illness.

The way that employers and co-workers respond to a request for a medical leave for surgery or chemotherapy can be very encouraging, as in the case of a boss who calls to say "Do what you need to take care of yourself, you have a job when you're ready to come back", or of the fellow employees who donate vacation time to a sick bank. It can, on the other hand, be devaluing and distressing for a boss to simply refer the request to Human Resources to deal with administratively, and demoralizing for co-workers to neither call nor write.

Leaves of absence that extend beyond paid sick time can generate realistic anxiety over being able to keep one's family housed and provided for. The need to consider asking for assistance from extended family members can sometimes reactivate old concerns about being dependent and a burden. How warmly members respond when asked for help is crucial in determining whether the patient feels respected and supported.

Many patients try to return to work after treatment, if only on a part-time basis. Flexibility in the type of work (e.g., work that can be done at a computer at home, with loose deadlines) can be crucial. On the other hand, inflexibility on the part of an employer (whether out of fear of cancer or expectation of future time off) can contribute to anxiety, depression, and fears of discrimination. As an example, a chef who completed radiation and chemotherapy for head and neck cancer was refused permission to return to work because he could not yet safely lift 50 pound loads. He wondered if he was being extruded from the workplace for reasons related to his cancer, his prior criminal record, or his position as the union's shop steward. Eventually, his resulting legal struggles and financial hardship led him to feel the workplace was so hostile that he could not return to it. Taskila and colleagues [21] examined the amount of practical and emotional support that a group of 6400 cancer survivors needed and actually received from their coworkers, supervisors, and the occupational health personnel at their place of employment. The survivors reported receiving the most support from their co-workers and needed more support from occupational health. Furthermore, Pryce and coworkers [22] studied the role of work adjustments and cancer disclosure to supervisors and co-workers on working during treatment and on return to work after treatment. They surveyed 328 cancer survivors to assess for a variety of work and cancer-related variables. Several factors were associated with continuing to work during treatment. These included opportunities for flexible work, disclosure to colleagues, and paid time off to attend medical appointments. Furthermore, a return to work meeting with an employer was associated with a faster return to work.

Even with a flexible and supportive work environment, patients may have difficulty deciding when they should give up disability income and how much responsibility to take back. For example, a 55-year-old research coordinator felt unable to return to work due to fatigue several months after adjuvant treatment for breast cancer. Despite pressure from her disability provider to take on at least part-time duties, she feared that as a manager who tended to be overly conscientious she would take on too much and be unable to continue. Other individuals fear re-entry into the workplace because of perceived or actual stigma, or anticipate that they will be rejected because of their changed appearance, or lost capacity (for example, diminished physical function).

Some individuals with significant, chronic morbidity or fear of recurrence conclude that they need to either change careers (for example, to a less physical, or public one), or retire. This can be stressful if their financial future is not secure, or if their spouse does not agree. It can be easier for younger patients with energy to look for meaningful volunteer activities. As an example, a 30-year-old biologist who completed his Ph.D. dissertation about the same time that he completed radiation for an astrocytoma decided to work with youth in a camp rather than continue a laboratory or teaching career. He explained that he hoped to have the kind of impact on others that he experienced from his own mentors as an adolescent.

Disease-Specific Work Problems

In addition to the ways that cancer generally can influence work life, particular cancers present specific problems for patients that complicate their adjustment:

Chemotherapy for hematologic malignancies often causes immunosuppression that necessitates avoidance of crowds and indoor workplaces. Bone marrow transplant recipients may be isolated and effectively disabled from months to several years that their jobs are gone when they are able to return.

Disfigurement due to cancers of the skin, head or neck, as well as chemotherapy related baldness understandably interfere with jobs that depend on how individuals present themselves before. However, patients with breast altering surgery or colostomies may also fear returning to public view, particularly in warmer weather.

Patients who lose their voice due to a laryngectomy now may rely as much on email as on artificial speech, and so be able to continue some kinds of work, but their difficulty communicating by phone is typically very frustrating. The need to depend indefinitely on others for help can impose considerable strain on even close relationships.

Impaired mental acuity related to treatment (so called "chemo brain" [23, 24]) are distressing for many individuals whose work requires a high degree of concentration. Cognitive and behavioral deficits due to brain tumors or metastases are especially "painful" when they signal a loss of who the individual was, that it is time to permanently retire, or that the course of illness is now irreversibly downhill. Mr. R. was a 44-year-old software engineer who had completed treatment for AML (including a bone marrow transplant). His cancer went into remission but he noticed ongoing cognitive limitations. Although he was able to continue working, it was at a less sophisticated level. He stopped getting promoted and found it increasingly difficult to make friends and connect with his co-workers. His response to this situation was one of anger and loss: "Cancer treatment was like a warm, safe tunnel...and when it ends, you get spit out into nothingness." At times, the loss is too threatening to face, and others must force retirement. Consider the example of a successful veterinarian who threatened suicide after his increasingly impulsive behavior led his partner to insist that he leave the practice.

Psychiatric complications of cancer and its treatment such as depression, demoralization, medication dependence, post traumatic anxiety, and fears of recurrence limit the ability of many survivors to regain their previous functional status and return to the workplace. Symptoms can be difficult to distinguish from constitutional symptoms of cancer or side effects of treatment such as fatigue, anorexia, and insomnia, all of which can contribute to discouragement in their own right [25, 26].

Fatigue deserves particular emphasis as a frustrating, poorly understood, often chronic consequence of treatment that can interfere with any work requiring effort [27]. Older individuals facing the decision whether to retire may wonder if age is responsible for the fatigue, or if they can hope for their fatigue to improve with time.

Therapeutic Approaches

Fortunately, with growing attention to survivorship, there are more ways to address these challenges related to work. Other chapters in this volume consider systemic (policy and education) related approaches to reducing discrimination, ensuring insurability, and increasing public awareness as well as individually focused rehabilitation and changes in work accommodation and the nature of work, all of which have additional psychological benefits. We consider here the options available directly targeting psychological dimensions.

Individual counseling and psychotherapy, available through most cancer treatment centers, includes a number of potentially helpful approaches. Psychodynamically oriented therapy can help individuals to better understand why a work related problem has been so devastating, to work through conflict or ambivalence about trying to return, and to grieve necessary losses [28–30]. Supportive therapy can help individuals feel understood which is sustained during a period of multiple losses and uncertainty [31]. Cognitive behavioral approaches can help survivors recognize and modify irrational and unhelpful assumptions about themselves in relation to work (for example, that they are only worthwhile as long as they can perform). Interpersonal therapy can help individuals overcome relationships with bosses or family members that continue to impede progress. When inability to work affects the whole family, and a spouse or other family member may be a source of pressure on the cancer survivor, it can be helpful to include the family in some form of family therapy as well [32–34].

A variety of supportive, psycho-educational, and psychotherapeutic group approaches exist that address many of the same objectives. Groups comprised of individuals who share similar treatment and/or survival status can offer one another uniquely powerful support in struggling with whether or not to return to and stay with their old work [35–37]. For example, one of us (GM) has led a time-limited group for survivors called "What Now?" that focused on having cancer survivors make an effective transition out of the patient role and back to full functioning in their lives.

Cancer and the interruption of work it causes often raise existential questions [38], force a reassessment of priorities, and can stimulate post-traumatic growth [3]. As a result, existential and spiritual approaches can play an important role in helping individuals find meaning and purpose in whatever course they eventually choose to take. Hospital chaplains, spiritual directors, religious communities, meaning centered groups [39], and even spiritually oriented psychotherapists [40] can be useful resources.

Medication is an important adjunct for individuals with distressing or disabling symptoms of anxiety or depression. Stimulants such as methylphenidate can be dramatically helpful in treating fatigue [41]. Psychiatric consultation can also be helpful in clarifying whether psychotropic medications such as benzodiazepines, antihistamines, hypnotics, and opiates accumulated in the course of the individual's symptom management have outlived their usefulness, and are responsible for unwanted fatigue, sedation, or dependence [42].

Finally, advocacy can be both concretely and psychologically important to individuals struggling to deal with perceived or actual discrimination in the workplace or in obtaining disability income. Social workers can help individuals obtain legal and sometimes financial assistance, and primary clinicians can provide timely documentation of patient deficits.

Directions for Future Research

Research has begun to focus on both the overall quality of life and the work related concerns of cancer survivors. More study is needed regarding the most important causes of disability in cancer patients and approaches both at societal and individual levels that are most helpful in dealing with them. How important are psychological symptoms in the ability to return to work? What is most helpful to patients when they are unable to return? What workplace practices that encourage flexibility and connection are effective and feasible? What minimal psychosocial and advocacy services should be available through cancer centers? What is the demonstrated effectiveness of interventions for work-related distress and disability?

While the meaning of work is often implicit in large scale epidemiological efforts to better understand work disability associated with cancer, this chapter provides a more in-depth consideration of the psychology of work and disability in cancer survivors. Cultural, developmental, disease specific, and individual factors each play a role. An understanding of their influence can serve to both guide therapeutic approaches and inform future research.

References

1. Hewitt M, Greenfield S, Stovall E. From Cancer Patient to Cancer Survivor: Lost in Transition. Washington, DC: The National Acadamies Press 2006.
2. Little M, Sayers EJ. The skull beneath the skin: Cancer survival and awareness of death. Psycho-Oncology. 2004;13(3):190–8.
3. Cordova MJ, Andrykowski MA. Responses to cancer diagnosis and treatment: Posttraumatic stress and posttraumatic growth. Seminars in Clinical Neuropsychiatry. 2003;8(4):286–96.
4. Sontag S. Illness as Metaphor and AIDS and its Metaphors. New York, NY: Picador USA 1978.
5. Baruch GK, Barnett RC. If the study of midlife had begun with women. *Annual Scientific Meeting of the Gerontological Society*: National Science Foundation Clearinghouse 1979.

6. Dell Orto AE. The Psychological and Social Impact of Illness and Disability. New York, NY: Springer Publishing Company 2007.
7. Gerstein M, Papen-Daniel M. Understanding Adulthood: A Review and Analysis of the Works of Three Leading Authorities on the Stages and Crises in Adult Development: California Personnel and Guidance Association Monograph Number 15 1981.
8. Holohan CK, Holohan CJ, Wonacott NL. Selfappraisal, life satisfaction, and retrospective life choices across one and three decades. Psychology and Aging. 1999;14:238–44.
9. Freedman RI, Fesko SL. The meaning of work in the lives of people with significant disabilities: Consumer and family perspectives. The Journal of Rehabilitation. 1996;62(3):49–55.
10. Short PF, Vasey JJ, Belue R. Work disability associated with cancer survivorship and other chronic conditions. Psycho-Oncology. 2008;17(1):91–7.
11. Short PF, Vasey JJ, Tunceli K. Employment pathways in a large cohort of adult cancer survivors. Cancer. 2005;103(6):1292–301.
12. Spelten ER, Verbeek JH, Uitterhoeve AL, Ansink AC, van der Lelie J, de Reijke TM, et al. Cancer, fatigue, and the return of patients to work: A prospective cohort study. European Journal of Cancer. 2003;39(11):1562–7.
13. Spelten ER, Sprangers MA, Verbeek JH. Factors reported to influence the return to work of cancer survivors: A literature review. Psycho-Oncology. 2002;11(2):124–31.
14. Steiner JF, Cavender TA, Nowels CT, Beaty BL, Bradley CJ, Fairclough DL, et al. The impact of physical and psychosocial factors on work characteristics after cancer. Psycho-Oncology. 2008;17(2):138–47.
15. Main DS, Nowels CT, Cavender TA, Etschmaier M, Steiner JF. A qualitative study of work and work return in cancer survivors. Psycho-Oncology. 2005;14(11):992–1004.
16. Erikcson E. Identity and the Life Cycle. New York, NY: International Universities Press, Inc 1959.
17. Boman KK, Bodegard G. Life after cancer in childhood: Social adjustment and educational and vocational status of young-adult survivors. Journal of Pediatric Hematology/Oncology. 2004;26(6):354–62.
18. Gerhardt CA, Dixon M, Miller K, Vannatta K, Valerius KS, Correll J, et al. Educational and occupational outcomes among survivors of childhood cancer during the transition to emerging adulthood. Journal of Developmental and Behavioral Pediatrics. 2007;28(6):448–55.
19. Servitzoglou M, Papadatou D, Tsiantis I, Vasilatou-Kosmidis H. Psychosocial functioning of young adolescent and adult survivors of childhood cancer. Supportive Care in Cancer. 2008;16(1):29–36.
20. Peteet JT. Cancer and the meaning of work. General Hospital Psychiatry. 2003;22(3):200–5.
21. Taskila T, Lindbohm ML, Martikainen R, Lehto US, Hakanen J, Hietanen P. Cancer survivors' received and needed social support from their work place and the occupational health services. Supportive Care in Cancer. 2006;14(5):427–35.
22. Pryce J, Munir F, Haslam C. Cancer survivorship and work: Symptoms, supervisor response, co-worker disclosure, and work adjustment. Journal of Occupational Rehabilitation. 2007;17(1):83–92.
23. Tannock IF, Ahles TA, Ganz PA, Van Dam FS. Cognitive impairment associated with chemotherapy for cancer: Report of a workshop. Journal of Clinical Oncology. 2004;22(11):2233–9.
24. Vardy J, Rourke S, Tannock IF. Evaluation of cognitive function associated with chemotherapy: A review of published studies and recommendations for future research. Journal of Clinical Oncology. 2007;25(17):2455–63.
25. Block SD. Assessing and managing depression in the terminally ill patient. Annals of Internal Medicine. 2000;132(3):209–18.
26. Carr D, Goudas L, Lawrence D, Pirl W, Lau J, DeVine D, et al. Management of cancer symptoms: Pain, depression, and fatigue. Evidence Report/Technology Assessment (Summary). 2002(61):1–5.

27. Braun IM, Greenberg DB, Pirl WF. Evidence-based report on the occurrence of fatigue in long-term cancer survivors. Journal of the National Comprehensive Cancer Network. 2008;6(4):349–54.
28. Postone N. Psychotherapy with cancer patients. American Journal of Psychotherapy. 1998;52(4):412–24.
29. Akechi T, Okuyama T, Onishi J, Morita T, Furukawa T. Psychotherapy for depression among incurable cancer patients. Cochrane Database of Systematic Reviews. 2008(2).
30. Stanton AL. Psychosocial concerns and interventions for cancer survivors. Journal of Clinical Oncology. 2006;24(32):5132–7.
31. Speigel D. Health caring. Psychosocial support for patients with cancer. Cancer. 1994;74(4 Suppl):1453–7.
32. Alfano CM, Rowland JH. Recovery issues in cancer survivorship: A new challenge for supportive care. Cancer. 2006;12(5):432–43.
33. Edwards AG, Hailey S, Maxwell M. Psychological interventions for women with metastic breast cancer. Cochrane Database of Systematic Reviews. 2004(2).
34. Ronson A. Psychiatric disorders in oncology: Recent therapeutic advances and new conceptual frameworks. Current Opinion in Oncology. 2004;16(4):318–23.
35. Classen C, Butler LD, Koopman C, Miller E, DiMiceli S, Giese-Davis J, et al. Supportive-expressive group therapy and distress in patients with metastatic breast cancer: A randomized clinical intervention trial. Archives of General Psychiatry. 2001;58(5):494–501.
36. Taylor KL, Lamdan RM, Siegel JE, Shelby R, Moran-Klimi K, Hrywna M. Psychological adjustment among African American breast cancer patients: One-year follow-up results of a randomized psychoeducational group intervention. Health Psychology. 2003;22(3):316–23.
37. Vos PJ, Visser AP, Garssen B, Duivenvoorden HJ, de Haes HC. Effectiveness of group psychotherapy compared to social support groups in patients with primary, non-metastatic breast cancer. Journal of Psychosocial Oncology. 2007;25(4):37–60.
38. Peteet JT. Putting suffering into perspective: Implications of the patient's world view. Journal of Psychotherapy Practice and Research. 2001;10(3):187–92.
39. Breitbart W. Spirituality and meaning in supportive care: Spirituality- and meaning-centered group psychotherapy interventions in advanced cancer. Supportive Care in Cancer. 2002;10(4):272–80.
40. Sperry L, Shafranske EP. Spiritually Oriented Psychotherapy. Washington, DC: American Psychological Association 2005.
41. Minton M, Stone P, Richardson A, Sharpe M, Hotopf M. Drug therapy for the management of cancer related fatigue. Cochrane Database of Systematic Reviews. 2008(1).
42. Miovic M, Block S. Psychiatric disorders in advanced cancer. Cancer. 2007;110(8):1665–76.

Section III
Factors Affecting Work

Chapter 6
Fatigue, Pain, and Physical Function

Mary E. Sesto and Maureen J. Simmonds

Introduction

It is now generally recognized that cancer is a chronic condition. Like many other chronic conditions, once issues of immediate survival or acute exacerbations are resolved, quality as well as quantity of life assumes greater relevance. This is true for the patient, their family, and the treatment team as they contend with the present and plan for the future. Quality of life is not a tangible concept. It is multidimensional and comprised of physical, psychological and social components. The specific factors that contribute to an individual's quality of life vary. Quality of life is influenced by symptoms such as pain or fatigue, psychological state such as depressed mood or anxieties, physical dysfunction, and occupational and recreational difficulties or opportunities. For individuals with cancer, work is an important aspect of the quality of life [1, 2]. Work becomes even more important as long-term survivorship becomes a reality for many.

The scope of occupational difficulties among cancer survivors is not well understood and much of the thinking is based on untested assumptions and generalizations of impact from other conditions. Cancer-related fatigue, pain and physical limitations are known to persist in certain cancer survivors and have an impact on overall function [3–20]. The interpretation of cancer-related symptoms is an inextricable aspect of the cancer survivorship experience and can be a lifelong process that can influence how individuals view their meaning and purpose in life. Ultimately, existential concerns related to questions about the order and purpose of one's life may shape or be shaped by perceptions of symptoms and their impact on functional capacity and ability to work. However, despite the persistence of similar cancer-related symptoms, some survivors report a meaningful return to daily life and functioning while others experience more difficulty. The persistence of these symptoms and ongoing or recurrent medical interventions are expected to impact

M.E. Sesto (✉)
Orthopedics and Rehabilitation, University of Wisconsin, 4176 Medical Sciences Center, 1300 University Ave, Madison, WI 53706, USA
e-mail: msesto@facstaff.ulsc.edu

work. This chapter will focus on characterizing the potential role of fatigue, pain and physical limitations on employment outcomes among cancer survivors.

Symptom Burden in Cancer Survivors

The effect cancer-related fatigue, pain, and physical limitations have on work outcomes is receiving increased attention [4, 21, 22]. Cancer survivors report fatigue as one of the most common and debilitating side effects of treatment [5]. Cancer-related fatigue appears to differ from normal fatigue due to lack of rest or overexertion as it involves more severe and lasting cognitive and physical effects [6]. Cancer-related pain is also commonly reported among survivors, often persisting after the active treatment phase is complete [7]. Physical limitations were found to be 1.5 times more prevalent among cancer survivors than those with no history of cancer [23]. Collectively, cancer-related fatigue, pain, and physical dysfunction may persist, often for years following treatment, and comprise a major symptom burden reported by cancer survivors.

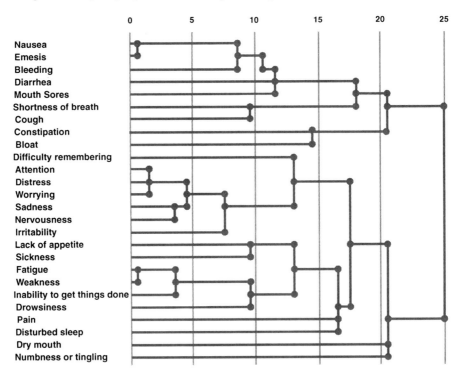

Fig. 6.1 Relative distance among symptoms associated with cancer and cancer treatment. Symptoms that cluster earlier in the analysis (toward the *left side*) are identified by patients as occurring together. Cancer. 2000;89:1634–1646. ©2000 American Cancer Society. Reprinted by permission of Wiley-Liss, Inc., a subsidiary of John Wiley & Sons, Inc [24, 25]

Uncertainty persists in terms of the specific effects of concurrent symptoms or symptom clusters on function and quality of life. At present, the impact of interventions on these outcomes is unclear. In terms of the co-occurrence of symptoms, Cleeland et al. [24] found certain groups of symptoms tended to cluster together (Fig. 6.1). For example, cognitive (e.g., difficulty remembering, attention) and affective symptoms (e.g., worrying, distress) often co-occurred [24]. The fatigue-related symptoms were closely related to cognitive and affective symptoms and less so to gastrointestinal and respiratory symptoms [24]. This pattern of symptom burden often persists years after diagnosis and may impair function related to occupation.

Cancer-Related Fatigue

Research shows that fatigue is often a significant aspect of residual symptoms following the treatment of cancer [5]. In fact, fatigue has been discussed as one of the most debilitating symptoms of cancer treatment, often interfering with social, recreational, and occupational activities [4, 5, 26–29]. Symptoms of fatigue often persist beyond the treatment period and can continue to interfere with functioning for months or years. Surveys suggest that 60–90% of cancer survivors who undergo treatment with chemotherapy, radiotherapy, or both may experience the symptoms of fatigue [26, 30, 31]. Furthermore, the interference of fatigue on activity levels may prevent social and recreational activities from serving as a buffer to certain stressors experienced as a cancer survivor [28]. Given that the task of coping with cancer can be resource demanding, the cancer survivor with significant symptoms of fatigue might be particularly vulnerable to the adverse effects of other residual symptoms or life stresses associated with cancer [32].

Cancer-related fatigue appears to differ from normal fatigue related to lack of rest or overexertion as it can involve more severe, prolonged and disabling symptoms [6]. In a study of long-term breast cancer survivors (10 years after cancer diagnosis) approximately one-quarter to one-third reported persistent fatigue [8, 9]. Factors contributing to cancer-related fatigue appear to be multifactorial, including both psychological and physiological factors. Types of cancer-related fatigue include: general fatigue, physical fatigue, emotional fatigue, and mental fatigue [33–41]. Since there is no commonly agreed upon definition of cancer-related fatigue, assessment, measurement, and description of fatigue can be difficult [42].

Several reviews have been published summarizing the likely mechanisms contributing to cancer-related fatigue [33, 35, 37, 40, 41]. Although the mechanisms associated with the development of cancer-related fatigue are not well understood, fatigue appears to be a consequence of cancer and its treatments. Several factors including the production of cytokines, presence of anemia, muscle fatigue and wasting are associated with the development, exacerbation, or maintenance of fatigue [25, 43–45]. Additional factors include depression, insomnia, and a decrease in physical activity [33, 37].

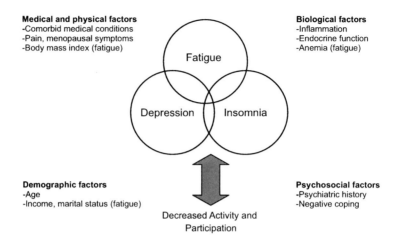

Fig. 6.2 Medical and physical, biological, demographic and psychosocial factors are associated with symptoms of fatigue, depression and insomnia. Collectively these symptoms may result in decreased activity and participation in recreational, social and occupational pursuits. (Adapted from Bower [33])

A recent review of behavioral symptoms in breast cancer survivors found symptoms of depression and insomnia frequently co-occur with fatigue (Fig. 6.2) [33]. These symptoms have been found to persist up to ten years after the breast cancer diagnosis [8]. The pertinent factors that likely affect these symptoms are broken into four domains – medical and physical, demographic, psychosocial, and biological. Collectively, these symptoms are associated with decreased ability and participation in recreational, social, and occupational pursuits [38].

Cancer-Related Pain

The residual symptoms that have been reported most frequently by cancer survivors include pain, fatigue, and depression [4]. The persistence of these symptoms in cancer survivors is central to issues of occupational rehabilitation since symptoms of pain, fatigue, and distress have been shown to be significant determinants of work disability across various debilitating health conditions [46, 47].

Pain symptoms in cancer survivors can arise from multiple causes including adverse effects of cancer treatment, infection, and musculoskeletal problems [48–51]. Research suggests that 30–60% of individuals with cancer continue to experience pain symptoms that persist in the post-treatment period, with several studies reporting symptoms persisting more than two years after treatment [10–13, 52–56]. Neuropathic and somatic pain conditions are the most common pain diagnoses in cancer survivors [25, 57, 58].

The prevalence and type of pain syndrome varies depending on cancer and treatment type. For example, cancer-related pain is frequently reported in

Table 6.1 Summary of pain syndromes secondary to cancer treatment

Treatment Type		Pain Syndrome
Surgery	Amputation	Phantom limb pain
		Residual limb pain
	Head/Neck surgery	Neck pain
		Myofacial pain
		Shoulder pain
		Accessory nerve injury
		Cervical plexus injury
	Mastectomy/Lumpectomy	Phantom breast pain
		Intercostobrachial neuralgia
		Neuroma (scar) pain
		Nerve injury
		Shoulder pain
	Thoracotomy	Intercostal nerve injury
		Chest wall pain
Radiation		Brachial plexopathy
		Lumbosacral plexopathy
		Connective tissue fibrosis
		Myelopathy
Chemotherapy		Peripheral neuropathy
	with corticosteroids	Osteonecrosis

survivors of central nervous system, head and neck, and hematologic cancers. In conjunction with fatigue, these symptoms result in poorer employment outcomes [59, 60]. In a study of 384 head and neck cancer survivors, more than half reported being unable to work four to five years after treatment and those with high pain scores had increased odds of being unable to work [59]. The Head and Neck Quality of Life Pain Scale (0–100; lower score indicates increased symptoms) [61] was used to evaluate pain. For each 10-point decrease, which indicates worsening pain symptoms, there was a 20% increase in the odds of being unable to work [59]. A summary of pain syndromes secondary to cancer treatment is listed in Table 6.1.

Physical Function

Impairment in physical function compromises the ability to perform activities of daily living, recreational, and occupational activities [18–20, 23, 62–64]. Quantitative assessment of physical function is often inferred from standard clinical tests of physical impairment (e.g., pain, joint range of motion, and muscle strength), but function may be influenced by other factors including psychological, cognitive, social, and environmental factors [47]. Therefore, traditional impairment measures may not adequately characterize functional status.

Additionally, the type of physical impairment varies depending upon the type of cancer and cancer treatment. Potential cancer-related impairments that may affect physical function in the workplace are listed in Table 6.2 [14, 16–20, 38, 62, 65, 66].

Table 6.2 Cancer and treatment-related impairments

Impairments	Cancer Type	Treatment
Decreased grip strength	Breast	Surgery
	Prostate	Androgen deprivation therapy
Decreased strength or range of motion	Breast	Surgery
	Head/Neck	Surgery
	Prostate	Androgen deprivation therapy
Lymphedema	Breast	Surgery; Radiotherapy
Numbness/Tingling in extremities		Chemotherapy
Reduced sense of touch		Chemotherapy
Reduced proprioception		Chemotherapy
Loss of deep tendon reflexes		Chemotherapy
Voice or hearing loss	Head/Neck	Radiotherapy; Surgery; Chemotherapy
Balance	Head/Neck	Radiotherapy
	Breast	Chemotherapy

Physical impairments due to peripheral neuropathy caused by chemotherapy can be especially problematic. Chemo-induced peripheral neuropathy may result in sensory, motor, and autonomic deficits with symptoms of pain, numbness, tingling, burning, reduced vibratory sense and proprioception, orthostatic hypotension, ataxia, dizziness or syncope, and polyneuropathies [14, 16–20, 38, 62, 65, 66]. These impairments may persist for several years after treatment has been completed [18]. Upper extremity neuropathy may impair occupational activities that require upper limb strength or fine motor skills. Lower extremity impairments may affect occupational activities that require prolonged walking or balance.

Grip strength, which has been used to characterize physical function, may also be affected in cancer survivors [67]. Research has shown that the simple measurement of grip strength can be used to characterize overall body muscle strength deficiencies [67]. A strong association between handgrip strength and manual dexterity, and therefore upper extremity functional status, was described by Hyatt et al. [68] Multiple studies have found decreased grip strength to be a predictor of future disability in both healthy older men and women [69, 70].

With these relationships in mind, the effects of treatments for various types of cancer on grip strength have been investigated. For instance, the relationship between grip strength on the affected side and grip strength on the contralateral side has been repeatedly examined in breast cancer survivors. Several studies found greater than a 10% difference in grip strength between affected and non-affected sides in 16–40% of individuals [15, 71, 72]. A few studies have compared grip force changes in the same hand preoperatively to as much as 2 years postoperatively. At 6 months postoperatively, 26% demonstrated weakness; at 12 months, 16% of women had 20% or greater decrease in grip strength compared to the original measurement [73]. In a study examining the effects

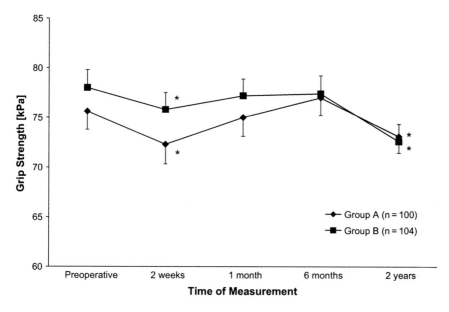

Fig. 6.3 Grip strength (kPa) for Group A (early shoulder exercises) and Group B (delayed shoulder exercises). Bars represent Standard Error and Asterisks indicate significant differences from preoperative levels (p<0.05). (Data are from Bendz et al. [74])

of shoulder exercise on recovery from breast cancer surgery, the results indicated that grip strength significantly decreased 2 weeks after surgery, recovered at 1 month and 6 months, and then was significantly lower again at 2 years postoperatively. This decrease in strength at two years was present regardless of when participants began shoulder exercises for rehabilitation (Fig. 6.3) [74]. It is unclear if the strength declines at 2 years are a result of the cancer, the treatment, pain, fatigue, deconditioning, or some other unknown factor.

Concerning prostate cancer, it has been found that the leading treatment method, androgen deprivation therapy, significantly lowers grip strength for cancer survivors as compared to age-matched controls [62]. Similar results were found in long-term survivors of pediatric sarcomas where over half of the participants had grip strengths more than one standard deviation below normal [75]. Although not all studies agree, grip strength has been found to decrease after diagnosis and treatment of certain types of cancer. As an indicator of total body muscle strength and upper extremity function, this measure may be an important index of a cancer survivor's current and future functional status.

Collectively, symptom burden can affect function. Compromised function is usually multifactorial and can result from the disease, the treatment, and/or from prolonged inactivity [5, 14, 17, 19, 63, 76–78]. Regardless of its genesis, rehabilitation and management of function, and its impact on work, needs to be investigated as an option for recovery of function, post-primary treatment. This may involve very simple short-term efforts with self-management over the long term [79]. In addition to the functional changes that can impact work, there are a number of work-related factors which need to be considered as potentially interacting with the physical limitations.

Work and Symptom Burden

Cancer-related fatigue, pain, and physical limitations may affect survivors' ability to return to work or continue in the workplace [27, 59, 60]. For example, a decrease in work productivity and an increase in absenteeism have been reported among survivors [34, 80, 81]. Cancer survivors had the highest reported prevalence of work impairment and the greatest absenteeism as compared to other chronic conditions such as arthritis, respiratory, cardiovascular, and anxiety disorders [80]. Results from the National Health Interview Survey (2000) found decreased employment outcomes for cancer survivors (time since diagnosis ranged from one year to more than 11 years) compared to age-, gender-, and education-matched controls [82]. Whereas, when using a shorter time-frame since diagnosis (12 and 18 months), significant differences in employment between controls and breast or prostate survivors were not found [83].

Fatigue appears to have a negative effect on work impairment, absenteeism, and return to work [80]. Higher levels of physical fatigue were associated with work limitations in breast cancer survivors in contrast to the non-cancer comparison group [34]. Spelten et al. [27] found that fatigue levels predicted return to work, although the effect of fatigue was not independent of the other cancer-related symptoms of depression and physical complaints. These findings are not surprising since as mentioned previously fatigue, pain, and other cancer symptoms may co-occur. While it is difficult to ascertain the individual contributions of fatigue, pain, or physical limitations on employment, a recent study by Hansen et al. [84] indicated that, when investigating multiple dimensions of symptom burden, fatigue was identified to be independently related to work limitations in breast cancer survivors (average four years post-diagnosis) to a greater degree than in a non-cancer comparison group of workers [84].

Estimates of cancer-related work disability vary substantially, with a recent review reporting return to work rates ranging from 41 to 84% [85]. While most survivors return to work, approximately 20% of survivors report cancer-related limitations that affect employment 1–5 years post diagnosis, and at least one-half of these individuals could not work due to these limitations [64]. The presence of limitations was ascertained by asking survivors whether they had any impairments or health problems that were related to their cancer and limited the type or amount of work they could do [64]. These results are similar to those of another study that found approximately 17% of working-age cancer survivors report an inability to work, with an additional 7.4% being limited in their ability to work due to physical, mental, or emotional difficulties [86]. It is clear that there are numerous challenges presented by the growing population of survivors, with return to work and work limitations among them.

Work-Related Factors

Cancer Survivors

The effect of work-related factors on survivors and employment outcomes is a relatively recent area of research. One area that appears to be problematic for cancer survivors is completing workplace tasks that have high physical demands [27, 87–91]. In a study of breast, lung, colon, and prostate cancer survivors, physical tasks such as lifting heavy loads and awkward postures (stooping, kneeling and crouching) were identified as being problematic, with cancer-related limitations affecting ability to perform such tasks [90]. Those with physically demanding jobs show higher work disability rates than those with sedentary jobs [91]. Work-related factors negatively associated with return to work include heavy lifting and other physically demanding tasks [27, 87–89]. Furthermore, workers with physically demanding jobs leave the workforce at a greater rate than those who had jobs that were less physically demanding [89]. It is important to note that employees without illness also report that these elements of work are problematic and often associated with increases in symptoms of fatigue and pain [92].

Other Chronic Illnesses

Of course, cancer survivors can experience other health problems as well as the cancer. In general, results from cancer survivor return to work research are similar to those from studies investigating other chronic illnesses (e.g., rheumatoid arthritis, diabetes, respiratory illness). Burton et al. [46] completed a systematic review of productivity loss due to rheumatoid arthritis (RA). An overall decrease in RA-related work disability was reported. This decrease was related to an overall decrease in the number of physically demanding work tasks, rather than to demographic or self-report levels of disability. In comparison, for individuals with RA who continue to perform manual work, a decrease in RA-related work disability was not evident. Physically demanding work, older age, and severity of RA were predictive of increased work disability [46]. While pain was a factor in the previous study, not all cancer survivors report pain. In a study of individuals with chronic respiratory illnesses (e.g., asthma, chronic obstructive pulmonary disease) where pain is unlikely, similar findings for return to work were observed [93]. Increased work disability was found in these individuals with respiratory illnesses where blue collar workers took longer to return to work than office workers [93]. Furthermore, increased job loss was reported for less educated workers and for those working for smaller companies [93]. In another systematic review of work disability in RA, physical job demands, low functional capacity, older age, and low education predict work disability [94]. Therefore, in addition to the common findings of age and education related to work disability, the mismatch between the physical demands of a job and the functional capacity of the individual with many types of chronic illnesses is an important feature of work disability. Factors that can impact functional capacity include strength, endurance, fatigue, and pain.

Occupational Injuries

While the majority of research addressing work disability has focused on occupational injuries and illnesses primarily related to the musculoskeletal system, the application of this information to other chronic conditions including cancer, and the effects of such conditions on work disability may be useful for our understanding of cancer, physical limitations, pain, and work [95]. Optimizing work outcomes among cancer survivors may be achieved through the application of the theories, methodologies, and perspectives from areas such as human factors, occupational ergonomics and occupational rehabilitation. These fields have a long history of success in mitigating workplace risks to optimize an individual's performance at work.

Numerous studies have reported an association between certain risk factors and increased risk of injury or illness, symptoms, or the exacerbation and maintenance of such outcomes. Although the evidence clearly delineating a dose-response relationship is limited [92], much can be learned from this area of research and application. Occupational risk factors that are potentially causative for musculoskeletal injuries or disorders include forceful hand and arm exertions, repetitive activity of various body parts, posture extremes, static postures, lifting, heavy physical work, and vibration [92]. A summary of common risk factors for bodily discomfort are listed in Table 6.3. It is unknown specifically whether exposure to elevated levels of these factors is associated with difficulty returning or continuing in the workplace for cancer survivors. However, efforts to attenuate these exposures are associated with a more successful return to work for musculoskeletal injuries [96–99]. Also, there is research to indicate that, if unattended to, these factors can exacerbate and/or maintain decrements in workplace productivity [100–105].

Conceptual Model of Physical Load, Physical Capacity, Pain and Work Disability

A conceptual model (Fig. 6.4) developed by the National Research Council and Institute of Medicine [107] illustrates the roles various factors have in the development of work-related injuries and functional difficulties in completing work tasks, primarily at a physical level. This model can perhaps elucidate the relationship between work-related demands and functional outcome in survivors. Two categories are included in the model: (1) workplace factors and (2)

Table 6.3 Risk factors by body part (Adapted from Chengalur et al. [106])

Body part	Risk factors for discomfort
Eyes	Glare or reflections on a display Lower contrast on screen of hard copy Repetitive eye movements between screen, document, keyboard, etc. Visual distances too great or too close Everything at same focal distance Competing visual targets or contrasts Brightness contrast between visual work and background is too great
Head, neck, and upper back	Head forward Head turned or tilted Neck extended Upper trunk bent forward Shoulders rounded forward
Shoulders	Shoulders elevated Arm raised to a higher work surface Static loading on shoulders Working overhead Extended reaches forward or to the side Reaching behind trunk Work above shoulder height Unsupported arms while working at elbow height
Upper arm and elbow	Extended reaches High forces exerted while rotating forearm Elbow behind trunk Hands below elbow during repetitive work Pressure on elbow Unsupported arms Wide grips
Forearm, wrist, hand, and fingers	Shoulder tension Pressure on wrist Non-neutral wrist postures Wide or narrow grips Pinch grips High forces High repetition rates Wrist rotation
Lower back, trunk, and chest	Bending forward Leaning Trunk twisted Asymmetric sitting Slouched in chair Asymmetric lifting or carrying Feet unsupported while seated Legs turned to one side or crossed when seated Static loading during sitting

Body part	Risk factors for discomfort
	Table 6.3 (continued)
Hip, leg, and knee	Pressure on back of thighs when seated Inadequate leg/thigh clearance
	Twisting on one leg
	One leg higher than the other when seated
	Walking more than 3.5 miles per shift
	Constant standing or sitting while stooping
Ankle, foot, and toes	Standing on tiptoes
	Repetitive foot pedal use
	Forceful pedal activation
	Slippery surfaces
	Standing or walking on uneven or loose surfaces

individual characteristics. Workplace factors include external loads (in addition to organizational and social context variables). External loads are produced in the physical work environment and create internal loads on tissues and anatomical structures. Body position, exertions, forces and motions, as well as individual factors such as age, strength, agility, and dexterity mediate the transmission of external loads to internal loads on tissues and anatomical

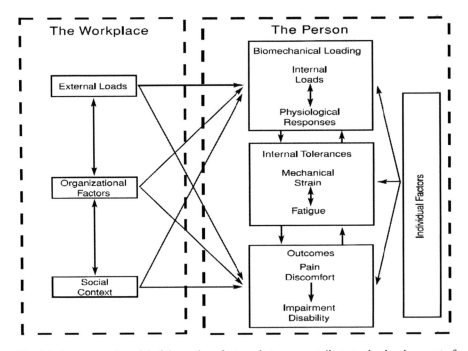

Fig. 6.4 A conceptual model of the various factors that may contribute to the development of musculoskeletal disorders. (Adapted from "Musculoskeletal Disorder and the Workplace," IOM [107])

structures. Tissue damage may occur when the imposing loads exceed the internal tolerance of the tissue. This overloading results in discomfort, pain, impairment, or disability.

Fatigue and pain, common symptoms in certain cancer survivors, can influence this system and also, in turn, can be influenced by this process. Research needs to better describe and explain how the elements of this model or specific modifications impact work optimization in various types of cancer survivors. The physical limitations due to actual strength deficits or symptom burden such as prolonged fatigue or pain can impact the biomechanical pathways described, altering work function. This model suggests the need to consider the work demands from a biomechanical perspective in order to influence work and health outcomes. This model implies that altering the workplace as well as the worker (increase strength, aerobic capacity) can change the dynamics associated with work disability. The focus however is on changing or engineering the work thus reducing or eliminating risk from the job. This is more of a public health approach to reducing risk rather than a traditional medical approach which generally involved rehabilitating the person. Both are most likely necessary.

Organizational and social factors can also influence loading and affect tissue tolerance, as well as the risk of developing a disorder or symptoms. Examples of organizational factors include work pace, work involvement, and organization of work tasks. Examples of social factors include support systems and relationships with supervisors and co-workers.

Specifically, the model proposes that injuries or symptoms may develop from the accumulated effect of workplace factors that, in isolation, are insufficient to exceed internal tolerances of tissues [107]. Internal tolerance of tissues may be exceeded when accumulation of loading occurs due to repeated exposures, or exposures of long duration.

This expanded biomechanical model may be applicable to cancer survivors who must complete a set of physical tasks as part of their work such as lifting, working on a computer for long periods of time or even sitting at a work station in a static posture for long periods of time. The ability of survivors to continue to work or to recover the function necessary to optimally complete such tasks may be negatively affected if the demands of the workplace exceed the abilities of the survivors. For example, individual characteristics of pain and fatigue may decrease overall tolerance to physical stresses in the workplace. If the internal tolerance of tissues to resist mechanical strain or fatigue is exceeded, this may lead to an increase in symptoms (fatigue or pain) and a decrease in work productivity. Therefore, efforts should be made to increase the capacity of the individual through exercise, rehabilitation, or medications. Concurrently, the demands of the workplace should be reduced through redesign or ergonomic intervention. Collectively, these changes could improve the imbalance, or mismatch, between capacity and demands and thus optimize the workers' abilities.

Interventions

The research to date suggests that cancer survivors experience greater levels of job loss, lower productivity, and more difficulty in return to work and maintenance of work after return than individuals without cancer [80, 82]. Although the exact reasons for such outcomes remain unclear and need to be further investigated, factors contributing to work disability in general appear to be multifactorial, including medical, individual, occupational, and legal [99, 108]. Similar to other chronic conditions with co-morbidities and functional limitations, return to work and work retention challenges for the cancer survivor persist. Challenges to employment exist not only in the short-term during active treatment, but also for a longer duration with survivors experiencing functional limitations years after treatment has ended. As survivors progress through treatment and recovery, a variety of barriers may be encountered as they attempt to return to work or continue in the workplace (see chapters in this book). Despite more working-aged adults being diagnosed with cancer, little is known about effective interventions for improving employment outcomes.

The symptom burden associated with cancer type and treatment is an important predictor of employment outcomes. Therefore, medical, clinical, and supportive services aimed at prevention or better management of symptoms are needed. In addition, the effect of functional limitations due to the symptom burden may be mitigated through rehabilitation. Of further interest is that the care of cancer survivors appears to present similar ongoing challenges as that of individuals with other chronic conditions [21]. Therefore, this is an area to evaluate for interventions. However, unlike other chronic diseases where the functional limitations are typically caused by the disease itself, with cancer, the functional limitations are often secondary to the treatment.

Work System Interventions: Potential Application of Ergonomics

Work system interventions may serve to reduce the consequences of cancer-related symptoms at work by reducing the occupational demands incurred by survivors. To date, the models and methods of work system interventions and their application to cancer survivors is limited. Work system interventions, in conjunction with individual rehabilitation interventions, may increase the opportunities for survivors to return to, and continue in, the workplace.

Although there are similarities in work disability between cancer survivors and individuals with occupational injuries, the associated return to work methodologies and determinants may be quite different [95]. For example, the occupational health and work systems often interact to facilitate return to work for individuals with occupational injuries. This is based on a long history of cooperation. This interaction may not occur with cancer survivors, leaving survivors to navigate between these systems without assistance. Vocational rehabilitation and other workplace specialists (e.g., ergonomists, physical therapists and occupational therapists) can help make this a reality.

Ergonomics, the study of humans at work, seeks to understand the complex relationships among people, machines, technology, tools, job demands, tasks, and work methods. Using the knowledge of human abilities and limitations, ergonomics can be used to improve the design of systems, organizations, jobs, machines, and tools for safe, efficient, and comfortable use. Employment outcomes for individuals with occupational injuries or illnesses have been improved through ergonomic interventions such as organizational changes, improved technology and product design, workplace and work task redesign, and training [99, 109, 110]. As of yet, the application of this information to other medical conditions has been limited.

One theory from the area of ergonomics that may be particularly useful in designing interventions to improve employment outcomes for cancer survivors is the Balance Theory of Job Design [111]. According to this theory, the work system consists of five elements—the individual, tasks, tools and technologies, physical environment, and the organization. Collectively, the elements of the work system interact to produce a load on the individual. Similar to the conceptual model discussed previously, this load can challenge one's resources. The individual's responses to the applied load are influenced by the individual's physical capacity, health status, and motivation. If the stress load is sustained over time and depends on the individual characteristics, it can produce adverse effects, such as health and safety problems and decreased performance (Fig. 6.4) [111, 112]. A systems approach is emphasized with the Balance Theory [112]. Therefore, all elements of the work system should be considered in order to improve performance, health, and safety (Fig. 6.5).

All work, regardless of its type or nature, places both physical and cognitive loads on the worker. If the loads are excessive, undesirable outcomes may

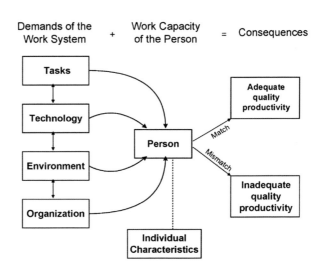

Fig. 6.5 Relationship of work system and work capacity of the person. (Modified from Smith and Carayon [111] and Kumar [113])

occur. The application of ergonomic principles facilitates fitting of workplace conditions and job demands to the capabilities of the working population. Effective and successful "fit" assures high productivity, avoidance of illness and injury risks, and increased satisfaction among the workforce.

In order to design the work system to match the characteristics of the user, it is important to understand the capabilities and limitations of the user [113]. Given the aging of the population, accompanied by more individuals working with chronic diseases and illnesses, the characteristics of the population are not homogeneous. Rather, they are diverse with varying capabilities. Work system interventions may be able to minimize the effects of fatigue, pain, and physical limitations through workplace and task design. The capabilities and limitations of the individual should be assessed with an overall objective to design the workplace to fit the person, instead of forcing the person to fit the workplace. For example, demands of some jobs (especially jobs with high physical or cognitive demands) may be problematic, but can be somewhat alleviated by work system design. Table 6.4 includes a list of factors which result in increased load on the individual. As applied to cancer survivors, there is little research on the effectiveness of currently available ergonomic modifications or accommodations for reducing work-related productivity loss except for the use of administrative accommodations such as a reduction in work hours or flexible schedules [89].

A systematic review to evaluate the effectiveness of workplace-based interventions found strong evidence that work accommodations and contact between the healthcare provider and workplace significantly reduced work disability duration associated with musculoskeletal or other pain conditions [99]. Work accommodation offers include: reduced hours or flexible work hours [114], a lighter job [114], and ergonomic interventions [96] to reduce physical and psychosocial stressors. Furthermore, moderate evidence was found to support interventions including early contact with the worker by the workplace, ergonomic work site visits, and presence of a return to work coordinator [99]. Since these interventions have been shown to work with individuals with musculoskeletal injuries, it is imperative to identify whether similar interventions work in the cancer survivor population to improve return to work outcomes and work retention.

Table 6.4 Factors Resulting in Increased Workload on Individual (Adapted from Chengalur et al. [106])

Sustained awkward working postures
Low operator control over work
Very repetitive hand/foot work with force
Environmental stressors (heat, glare, noise, vibration)
Heavy manual handling
High forces
High external pacing
Complex tasks
Multiple tasks done simultaneously

Often, the topic of design for functional limitations and human disability is thought of as a special application of ergonomics. Researchers interested in the design for human disability and aging have stressed the need for more accessible and flexible design of the work system [115]. Though not targeted at cancer survivors specifically, these design recommendations are focused on accommodating functional limitations in general. These accommodations and recommendations can cover limitations resulting from the full range of congenital and acquired conditions, injuries, illnesses, and age-related changes. By better understanding how cancer-related pain, fatigue, and physical dysfunction (cognitive function not a focus of this chapter) affect function and work productivity, we can improve and better apply these standard and design accommodation strategies to improve performance. The goal would be to ensure these guidelines and principles address cancer survivors as well as other groups with functional limitations and disabilities.

Through ergonomic and work system interventions, gains can be made in designing work systems for diverse populations. Difficulties due to functional limitations can be reduced or overcome by proper work system design [115]. These changes will not only benefit individuals with functional limitations due to chronic conditions, but also older workers (who are becoming a large portion of the work force). These changes may include tool design and selection, arrangement of work procedures and task, and administrative changes such as flexible work schedules and work breaks. Examples would include work station design by ensuring appropriate work height, and reducing physically demanding activities, such as prolonged and awkward postures and lifting activities. For technology-related activities, appropriate software and task design can reduce the cognitive load. These approaches will need to be evaluated in employed cancer survivors with various functional limitations due to residual or late effects of the cancer and its management in order to develop a set of evidence-based interventions to maximize return to work, retention, and optimization.

Conclusions

This chapter provides an overview of fatigue, pain, and physical limitations experienced by some cancer survivors and their potential impact on work. A summary of the potential influence of fatigue, pain, and physical limitations on work, primarily in non-cancer workers was provided and when possible, specific information relevant to cancer survivors was covered. At this point very little cancer-specific research is available upon which to make cancer-specific conclusions, but this area is emerging. It is expected that as we revise this chapter in the future we will be able to provide more information regarding cancer-specific physical limitations and effect on work demands. While the area of cancer survivorship and work will develop many of its own methodologies and concepts, the research in other areas, such as occupational musculoskeletal disorders can serve as a foundation for research that is specific to the mechanisms and management of cancer-related symptom burden and work function.

Acknowledgments The authors thank Dr. Curt B Irwin and Ms. Danielle K Ebben for their comments and contributions.

References

1. Main DS, Nowels CT, Cavender TA, Etschmaier M, Steiner JF. A qualitative study of work and work return in cancer survivors. Psychooncology. 2005;14(11):992–1004.
2. Peteet JR. Cancer and the meaning of work. Gen Hosp Psychiatry. 2000;22(3):200–5.
3. Ness KK, Bhatia S, Baker KS, Francisco L, Carter A, Forman SJ, et al. Performance limitations and participation restrictions among childhood cancer survivors treated with hematopoietic stem cell transplantation: the bone marrow transplant survivor study. Arch Pediatr Adolesc Med. 2005;159(8):706–13.
4. Beck SL, Dudley WN, Barsevick A. Pain, sleep disturbance, and fatigue in patients with cancer: using a mediation model to test a symptom cluster. Oncol Nurs Forum. 2005;32(3):542.
5. Curt GA. Fatigue in cancer. BMJ. 2001;322(7302):1560.
6. Bower JE. Prevalence and causes of fatigue after cancer treatment: the next generation of research. J Clin Oncol. 2005;23(33):8280–2.
7. Burton AW, Fanciullo GJ, Beasley RD, Fisch MJ. Chronic pain in the cancer survivor: a new frontier. Pain Med. 2007;8(2):189–98.
8. Bower JE, Ganz PA, Desmond KA, Bernaards C, Rowland JH, Meyerowitz BE, et al. Fatigue in long-term breast carcinoma survivors: a longitudinal investigation. Cancer. 2006;106(4):751–8.
9. Servaes P, Gielissen MF, Verhagen S, Bleijenberg G. The course of severe fatigue in disease-free breast cancer patients: a longitudinal study. Psychooncology. 2007;16(9):787–95.
10. Bjordal K, Mastekaasa A, Kaasa S. Self-reported satisfaction with life and physical health in long-term cancer survivors and a matched control group. Eur J Cancer B Oral Oncol. 1995;31B(5):340–5.
11. Cleeland CS. The impact of pain on the patient with cancer. Cancer. 1984;54(11 Suppl):2635–41.
12. Macdonald L, Bruce J, Scott NW, Smith WC, Chambers WA. Long-term follow-up of breast cancer survivors with post-mastectomy pain syndrome. Br J Cancer. 2005;92(2):225–30.
13. Mao JJ, Armstrong K, Bowman MA, Xie SX, Kadakia R, Farrar JT. Symptom burden among cancer survivors: impact of age and comorbidity. J Am Board Fam Med. 2007;20(5):434–43.
14. Clay CA, Perera S, Wagner JM, Miller ME, Nelson JB, Greenspan SL. Physical function in men with prostate cancer on androgen deprivation therapy. Phys Ther. 2007;87 (10):1325–33.
15. Rietman JS, Dijkstra PU, Debreczeni R, Geertzen JH, Robinson DP, De Vries J. Impairments, disabilities and health related quality of life after treatment for breast cancer: a follow-up study 2.7 years after surgery. Disabil Rehabil. 2004;26(2):78–84.
16. Rietman JS, Geertzen JH, Hoekstra HJ, Baas P, Dolsma WV, de Vries J, et al. Long-term treatment related upper limb morbidity and quality of life after sentinel lymph node biopsy for stage I or II breast cancer. Eur J Surg Oncol. 2006;32(2):148–52.

17. Hayes S, Battistutta D, Newman B. Objective and subjective upper body function six months following diagnosis of breast cancer. Breast Cancer Res Treat. 2005;94(1):1–10.
18. Bakitas MA. Background noise: the experience of chemotherapy-induced peripheral neuropathy. Nurs Res. 2007;56(5):323–31.
19. Levy ME, Perera S, van Londen GJ, Nelson JB, Clay CA, Greenspan SL. Physical function changes in prostate cancer patients on androgen deprivation therapy: a 2-year prospective study. Urology. 2008;71(4):735–9.
20. Fialka-Moser V, Crevenna R, Korpan M, Quittan M. Cancer rehabilitation: particularly with aspects on physical impairments. J Rehabil Med. 2003;35(4):153–62.
21. Hewitt M. Greefield S. Stovall E. From Cancer Patient to Cancer Survivor: Lost in Translation. The National Academies Press: Washington, DC, 2006.
22. Steiner JF, Cavender TA, Main DS, Bradley CJ. Assessing the impact of cancer on work outcomes: what are the research needs? Cancer. 2004;101(8):1703–11.
23. Ness KK, Wall MM, Oakes JM, Robison LL, Gurney JG. Physical performance limitations and participation restrictions among cancer survivors: a population-based study. Ann Epidemiol. 2006;16(3):197–205.
24. Cleeland CS, Mendoza TR, Wang XS, Chou C, Harle MT, Morrissey M, et al. Assessing symptom distress in cancer patients: the M.D. Anderson Symptom Inventory. Cancer. 2000;89(7):1634–46.
25. Cleeland CS, Bennett GJ, Dantzer R, Dougherty PM, Dunn AJ, Meyers CA, et al. Are the symptoms of cancer and cancer treatment due to a shared biologic mechanism? A cytokine-immunologic model of cancer symptoms. Cancer. 2003;97(11):2919–25.
26. Vogelzang NJ, Breitbart W, Cella D, Curt GA, Groopman JE, Horning SJ, et al. Patient, caregiver, and oncologist perceptions of cancer-related fatigue: results of a tripart assessment survey. The Fatigue Coalition. Semin Hematol. 1997;34(3 Suppl 2):4–12.
27. Spelten ER, Verbeek JH, Uitterhoeve AL, Ansink AC, van der Lelie J, de Reijke TM, et al. Cancer, fatigue and the return of patients to work-a prospective cohort study. Eur J Cancer. 2003;39(11):1562–7.
28. Pryce J, Munir F, Haslam C. Cancer survivorship and work: symptoms, supervisor response, co-worker disclosure and work adjustment. J Occup Rehabil. 2007;17(1):83–92.
29. Morrow GR, Shelke AR, Roscoe JA, Hickok JT, Mustian K. Management of cancer-related fatigue. Cancer Investigation. 2005;23(3):229–39.
30. Curt GA, Breitbart W, Cella D, Groopman JE, Horning SJ, Itri LM, et al. Impact of cancer-related fatigue on the lives of patients: new findings from the Fatigue Coalition. Oncologist. 2000;5(5):353–60.
31. Irvine D, Vincent L, Graydon JE, Bubela N, Thompson L. The prevalence and correlates of fatigue in patients receiving treatment with chemotherapy and radiotherapy. A comparison with the fatigue experienced by healthy individuals. Cancer Nurs. 1994;17(5): 367–78.
32. van Weert E, Hoekstra-Weebers J, Otter R, Postema K, Sanderman R, van der Schans C. Cancer-related fatigue: predictors and effects of rehabilitation. Oncologist. 2006; 11(2):184–96.
33. Bower JE. Behavioral symptoms in patients with breast cancer and survivors. J Clin Oncol. 2008;26(5):768–77.
34. Feuerstein M, Hansen JA, Calvio LC, Johnson L, Ronquillo JG. Work productivity in brain tumor survivors. J Occup Environ Med. 2007 Jul;49(7):803–11.
35. Gutstein HB. The biologic basis of fatigue. Cancer. 2001;92(6 Suppl):1678–83.
36. Dodd M. Cancer-related fatigue. Cancer Invest. 2000;18(1):97.
37. Bower JE. Cancer-related fatigue: links with inflammation in cancer patients and survivors. Brain Behav Immun. 2007; 21(7):863–71.
38. Luctkar-Flude MF, Groll DL, Tranmer JE, Woodend K. Fatigue and physical activity in older adults with cancer: a systematic review of the literature. Cancer Nurs. 2007;30(5): E35–45.

39. Mallinson T, Cella D, Cashy J, Holzner B. Giving meaning to measure: linking self-reported fatigue and function to performance of everyday activities. J Pain Symptom Manage. 2006;31(3):229–41.
40. Ryan JL, Carroll JK, Ryan EP, Mustian KM, Fiscella K, Morrow GR. Mechanisms of cancer-related fatigue. Oncologist. 2007;12(Suppl 1):22–34.
41. Stone PC, Minton O. Cancer-related fatigue. Eur J Cancer. 2008;44(8):1097–104.
42. Jacobsen PB. Assessment of fatigue in cancer patients. J Natl Cancer Inst Monogr. 2004(32):93–7.
43. Valentine AD, Meyers CA. Cognitive and mood disturbance as causes and symptoms of fatigue in cancer patients. Cancer. 2001 Sep 15;92(6 Suppl):1694–8.
44. Collado-Hidalgo A, Bower JE, Ganz PA, Cole SW, Irwin MR. Inflammatory biomarkers for persistent fatigue in breast cancer survivors. Clin Cancer Res. 2006;12(9):2759–66.
45. Morrow GR, Andrews PL, Hickok JT, Roscoe JA, Matteson S. Fatigue associated with cancer and its treatment. Support Care Cancer. 2002;10(5):389–98.
46. Burton W, Morrison A, Maclean R, Ruderman E. Systematic review of studies of productivity loss due to rheumatoid arthritis. Occup Med (Lond). 2006;56(1):18–27.
47. Simmonds MJ, Novy D, Sandoval R. The differential influence of pain and fatigue on physical performance and health status in ambulatory patients with human immunodeficiency virus. Clin J Pain. 2005;21(3):200–6.
48. Grond S, Zech D, Diefenbach C, Radbruch L, Lehmann KA. Assessment of cancer pain: a prospective evaluation in 2266 cancer patients referred to a pain service. Pain. 1996;64(1):107–14.
49. Caraceni A, Portenoy RK. An international survey of cancer pain characteristics and syndromes. IASP Task Force on Cancer Pain. International Association for the Study of Pain. 1999;82(3):263–74.
50. Peters CM, Ghilardi JR, Keyser CP, Kubota K, Lindsay TH, Luger NM, et al. Tumor-induced injury of primary afferent sensory nerve fibers in bone cancer pain. Exp Neurol. 2005;193(1):85–100.
51. Pronneke R, Jablonowski H. [Pain therapy in cancer patients]. MMW Fortschr Med. 2005;147(22):27–30.
52. Dow KH, Ferrell BR, Leigh S, Ly J, Gulasekaram P. An evaluation of the quality of life among long-term survivors of breast cancer. Breast Cancer Res Treat. 1996;39(3):261–73.
53. Portenoy RK. Cancer pain management. Clin Adv Hematol Oncol. 2005;3(1):30–2.
54. Berglund G, Bolund C, Fornander T, Rutqvist LE, Sjoden PO. Late effects of adjuvant chemotherapy and postoperative radiotherapy on quality of life among breast cancer patients. Eur J Cancer. 1991;27(9):1075–81.
55. Carpenter JS, Andrykowski MA, Sloan P, Cunningham L, Cordova MJ, Studts JL, et al. Postmastectomy/postlumpectomy pain in breast cancer survivors. J Clin Epidemiol. 1998;51(12):1285–92.
56. Chaplin JM, Morton RP. A prospective, longitudinal study of pain in head and neck cancer patients. Head Neck. 1999;21(6):531–7.
57. Jung BF, Herrmann D, Griggs J, Oaklander AL, Dworkin RH. Neuropathic pain associated with non-surgical treatment of breast cancer. Pain. 2005;118(1-2):10–4.
58. Foley KM. Advances in cancer pain management in 2005. Gynecol Oncol. 2005;99(3 Suppl 1):S126.
59. Taylor JC, Terrell JE, Ronis DL, Fowler KE, Bishop C, Lambert MT, et al. Disability in patients with head and neck cancer. Arch Otolaryngol Head Neck Surg. 2004;130(6):764–9.
60. Buckwalter AE, Karnell LH, Smith RB, Christensen AJ, Funk GF. Patient-reported factors associated with discontinuing employment following head and neck cancer treatment. Arch Otolaryngol Head Neck Surg. 2007;133(5):464–70.
61. Terrell JE, Nanavati KA, Esclamado RM, Bishop JK, Bradford CR, Wolf GT. Head and neck cancer-specific quality of life: instrument validation. Arch Otolaryngol Head Neck Surg. 1997;123 (10):1125–32.

62. Soyupek F, Soyupek S, Perk H, Ozorak A. Androgen deprivation therapy for prostate cancer: Effects on hand function. Urol Oncol. 2008;26(2):141–6.
63. Hayes SC, Battistutta D, Parker AW, Hirst C, Newman B. Assessing task "burden" of daily activities requiring upper body function among women following breast cancer treatment. Supportive Care in Cancer. 2005;13(4):255–65.
64. Short PF, Vasey JJ, Tunceli K. Employment pathways in a large cohort of adult cancer survivors. Cancer. 2005;103(6):1292–301.
65. de Boer AG, Verbeek JH, van Dijk FJ. Adult survivors of childhood cancer and unemployment: A metaanalysis. Cancer. 2006;107(1):1–11.
66. Oldenburg J, Fossa SD, Dahl AA. Scale for chemotherapy-induced long-term neurotoxicity (SCIN): psychometrics, validation, and findings in a large sample of testicular cancer survivors. Qual Life Res. 2006;15(5):791–800.
67. Castillo EM, Goodman-Gruen D, Kritz-Silverstein D, Morton DJ, Wingard DL, Barrett-Connor E. Sarcopenia in elderly men and women: the Rancho Bernardo study. Am J Prev Med. 2003;25(3):226–31.
68. Hyatt RH, Whitelaw MN, Bhat A, Scott S, Maxwell JD. Association of muscle strength with functional status of elderly people. Age Ageing. 1990;19(5):330–6.
69. Giampaoli S, Ferrucci L, Cecchi F, Lo Noce C, Poce A, Dima F, et al. Hand-grip strength predicts incident disability in non-disabled older men. Age Ageing. 1999;28(3):283–8.
70. Onder G, Penninx BW, Lapuerta P, Fried LP, Ostir GV, Guralnik JM, et al. Change in physical performance over time in older women: the Women's Health and Aging Study. J Gerontol A Biol Sci Med Sci. 2002;57(5):M289–93.
71. Hladiuk M, Huchcroft S, Temple W, Schnurr BE. Arm function after axillary dissection for breast cancer: a pilot study to provide parameter estimates. J Surg Oncol. 1992;50(1):47–52.
72. Swedborg I, Wallgren A. The effect of pre- and postmastectomy radiotherapy on the degree of edema, shoulder-joint mobility, and gripping force. Cancer. 1981;47(5):877–81.
73. Tasmuth T, von Smitten K, Kalso E. Pain and other symptoms during the first year after radical and conservative surgery for breast cancer. Br J Cancer. 1996;74(12):2024–31.
74. Bendz I, Fagevik Olsen M. Evaluation of immediate versus delayed shoulder exercises after breast cancer surgery including lymph node dissection – a randomised controlled trial. Breast. 2002;11(3):241–8.
75. Gerber LH, Hoffman K, Chaudhry U, Augustine E, Parks R, Bernad M, et al. Functional outcomes and life satisfaction in long-term survivors of pediatric sarcomas. Arch Phys Med Rehabil. 2006;87 (12):1611–7.
76. Brown DJ, McMillan DC, Milroy R. The correlation between fatigue, physical function, the systemic inflammatory response, and psychological distress in patients with advanced lung cancer. Cancer. 2005;103(2):377–82.
77. Dodd MJ, Miaskowski C, Paul SM. Symptom clusters and their effect on the functional status of patients with cancer. Oncol Nurs Forum. 2001;28(3):465–70.
78. Given BA, Given CW, Sikorskii A, Hadar N. Symptom clusters and physical function for patients receiving chemotherapy. Semin Oncol Nurs. 2007;23(2):121–6.
79. Lorig KR, Sobel DS, Ritter PL, Laurent D, Hobbs M. Effect of a self-management program on patients with chronic disease. Eff Clin Pract. 2001;4(6):256–62.
80. Kessler RC, Greenberg PE, Mickelson KD, Meneades LM, Wang PS. The effects of chronic medical conditions on work loss and work cutback. J Occup Environ Med. 2001;43(3):218–25.
81. Bradley CJ, Oberst K, Schenk M. Absenteeism from work: the experience of employed breast and prostate cancer patients in the months following diagnosis. Psycho-Oncology. 2006;15(8):739–47.
82. Yabroff KR, Lawrence WF, Clauser S, Davis WW, Brown ML. Burden of illness in cancer survivors: findings from a population-based national sample. J Natl Cancer Inst. 2004;96(17):1322–30.

83. Bradley CJ, Neumark D, Luo Z, Schenk M. Employment and cancer: findings from a longitudinal study of breast and prostate cancer survivors. Cancer Invest. 2007;25(1):47–54.
84. Hansen JA, Feuerstein M, Calvio LC, Olsen CH. Breast cancer survivors at work. J Occup Environ Med. In press.
85. Taskila T, Lindbohm ML. Factors affecting cancer survivors' employment and work ability. Acta Oncol. 2007;46(4):446–51.
86. Hewitt M, Rowland JH, Yancik R. Cancer survivors in the United States: age, health, and disability. J Gerontol A Biol Sci Med Sci. 2003;58(1):82–91.
87. Satariano WA, DeLorenze GN. The likelihood of returning to work after breast cancer. Public Health Reports. 1996;111(3):236–41.
88. Bouknight RR, Bradley CJ, Luo Z. Correlates of return to work for breast cancer survivors. J Clin Oncol. 2006;24(3):345–53.
89. Greenwald HP, Dirks SJ, Borgatta EF, McCorkle R, Nevitt MC, Yelin EH. Work disability among cancer patients. Soc Sci Med. 1989;29(11):1253–9.
90. Bradley CJ, Bednarek HL. Employment patterns of long-term cancer survivors. Psychooncology. 2002;11(3):188–98.
91. Hoffman B. Cancer survivors at work: a generation of progress. CA Cancer J Clin. 2005;55(5):271–80.
92. National Institute for Occupational Safety and Health. Musculoskeletal disorders and workplace factors: a critical review of epidemiologic evidence for work-related musculoskeletal disorders of the neck, upper extremity, and low back. NIOSH Publication No. 97–141, DHHS: Cincinnati, 1997.
93. Peters J, Pickvance S, Wilford J, Macdonald E, Blank L. Predictors of delayed return to work or job loss with respiratory ill-health: a systematic review. J Occup Rehabil. 2007;17(2):317–26.
94. de Croon EM, Sluiter JK, Nijssen TF, Dijkmans BA, Lankhorst GJ, Frings-Dresen MH. Predictive factors of work disability in rheumatoid arthritis: a systematic literature review. Ann Rheum Dis. 2004;63(11):1362–7.
95. Feuerstein M. Cancer survivorship and work. J Occup Rehabil. 2005;15(1):1–2.
96. Arnetz BB, Sjogren B, Rydehn B, Meisel R. Early workplace intervention for employees with musculoskeletal-related absenteeism: a prospective controlled intervention study. J Occup Environ Med. 2003;45(5):499–506.
97. Booker HE, Cleeland CS. Sustained sensory input and epileptiform activity. Dis Nerv Syst. 1970;31(4):265–8.
98. Franche RL, Severin CN, Hogg-Johnson S, Cote P, Vidmar M, Lee H. The impact of early workplace-based return-to-work strategies on work absence duration: a 6-month longitudinal study following an occupational musculoskeletal injury. J Occup Environ Med. 2007;49(9):960–74.
99. Franche RL, Cullen K, Clarke J, Irvin E, Sinclair S, Frank J. Workplace-based return-to-work interventions: a systematic review of the quantitative literature. J Occup Rehabil. 2005;15(4):607–31.
100. Bos EH, Krol B, Van Der Star A, Groothoff JW. The effects of occupational interventions on reduction of musculoskeletal symptoms in the nursing profession. Ergonomics. 2006;49(7):706–23.
101. Lahiri S, Markkanen P, Levenstein C. The cost effectiveness of occupational health interventions: preventing occupational back pain. Am J Ind Med. 2005;48(6):515–29.
102. Rempel DM, Krause N, Goldberg R, Benner D, Hudes M, Goldner GU. A randomised controlled trial evaluating the effects of two workstation interventions on upper body pain and incident musculoskeletal disorders among computer operators. Occup Environ Med. 2006;63(5):300–6.
103. Rivilis I, Cole DC, Frazer MB, Kerr MS, Wells RP, Ibrahim S. Evaluation of a participatory ergonomic intervention aimed at improving musculoskeletal health. Am J Ind Med. 2006;49(10):801–10.

104. Robertson MM, O'Neill MJ. Reducing musculoskeletal discomfort: effects of an office ergonomics workplace and training intervention. Int J Occup Saf Ergon. 2003; 9(4):491–502.
105. Van der Molen HF, Sluiter JK, Hulshof CT, Vink P, Frings-Dresen MH. Effectiveness of measures and implementation strategies in reducing physical work demands due to manual handling at work. Scand J Work Environ Health. 2005;31(Suppl 2):75–87.
106. Chengalur SN, Rodgers SH, Bernard TE. Kodak's Ergonomic Design for People at Work. John Wiley & Sons: Hoboken, New Jersey, 2004.
107. National Research Council and Institute of Medicine. Musculoskeletal Disorders and the Workplace: Low Back and Upper Extremity Disorders. National Academies Press: Washington, DC, 2001.
108. Loisel P, Buchbinder R, Hazard R, Keller R, Scheel I, Van Tulder M, et al. Prevention of work disability due to musculoskeletal disorders: the challenge of implementing evidence. J Occup Rehabil. 2005;15(4):507–24.
109. Amell T, Kumar S. Work-related musculoskeletal disorders: design as a prevention strategy. A review. J Occup Rehabil. 2001;11(4):255–65.
110. Tompa E, de Oliveira C, Dolinschi R, Irvin E. A systematic review of disability management interventions with economic evaluations. J Occup Rehabil. 2008;18(1):16–26.
111. Smith MJ and Carayon PC. A balance theory of job design for stress reduction. Int J Ind Ergon. 1989;1(4):67–79.
112. Carayon P, Smith MJ. Work organization and ergonomics. Appl Ergon. 2000;31(6):649–62.
113. Kumar S. Perspectives in Rehabilitation Ergonomics. Bristol, PA: Taylor & Francis Ltd; 1997.
114. Brooker AS, Cole DC, Hogg-Johnson S, Smith J, Frank JW. Modified work: prevalence and characteristics in a sample of workers with soft-tissue injuries. J Occup Environ Med. 2001;43(3):276–84.
115. Vanderheiden G. Design for people with functional limitations. In: Salvendy G, ed. Handbook of Human Factors and Ergonomics. Hoboken, New Jersey: John Wiley & Sons; 2006.

Chapter 7
Cognitive Limitations

Tracy Veramonti and Christina Meyers

Introduction

Amongst some of the more common and distressing symptoms faced by individuals with cancer is that of neurocognitive dysfunction. While neurocognitive symptoms often herald the diagnosis when cancer directly affects the brain, survivors with systemic malignancies (e.g., breast cancer, lung cancer, leukemia) have also been found to have neurocognitive impairments, even prior to the initiation of treatment [1–4]. Additionally, oncologic successes are often dependent on a multimodal, aggressive treatment approach that frequently combines surgery, radiation, chemotherapy, and/or immunotherapy. The central nervous system may be vulnerable to these antineoplastic treatments, leading to a worsening of neurocognitive symptoms and/or emergence of new symptoms during and following treatment. Further, cancer survivors may be susceptible to neurocognitive symptoms as a side effect of medications commonly prescribed to manage concurrent medical complications (e.g., corticosteroids, antiepileptics, immuosuppressive agents, antiemetics, and opioid narcotics) or secondary to co-existing neurologic conditions unrelated to the diagnosis of cancer [3, 4].

Survivors have coined the term "chemobrain" or "chemofog" to capture the changes in neurocognitive functioning often noticed soon after initiating treatment for cancer. Cancer survivors may report difficulties with short term memory, exemplified by difficulties recalling something they were told, forgetting or confusing details of recent events, forgetting to pass on a message, misplacing or losing items in their home or office, or missing critical appointments. Other common complaints include word-finding difficulties and inefficiencies in attention, including trouble sustaining attention on one task for any length of time or a problem dividing attention between multiple tasks at the same time (i.e., "multi-tasking"). "Chemobrain" complaints likewise frequently

---

T. Veramonti (✉)
Department of Neuro-Oncology, Unit 431, University of Texas M.D. Anderson Cancer Center, Houston, TX 77230-1402, USA
e-mail: tlveramo@mdanderson.org

include problems with organization or keeping up with conversations and/or occupational responsibilities due to slowed mental processing speed.

Not infrequently, neurocognitive symptoms persist after treatment is completed. In a recent online survey, 96% of 471 cancer survivors responding reported changes in cognitive functioning during or following treatment. Moreover, 92% of respondents five or more years post-treatment reported persistence of cognitive deficits at some level, with 61% indicating that the severity of symptoms persisted at the same level they experienced immediately following treatment, and only 8% reporting that their symptoms wholly resolved [5]. While self-report data, in the absence of pre- and post-treatment objective assessment via neuropsychological testing, is problematic (See Section, "The Impact of Cognitive Symptoms on Work"), the number of patients who report persistent neurocognitive dysfunction in the years following treatment warrants further attention. In these cases, patients may be considered "cured" or "disease-free" but face the unexpected scenario of being distressed by a "memory problem" in the context of an otherwise "successful" treatment outcome. Despite limitations in our understanding of treatment-related neurotoxicities and their evolution over time, the unfortunate reality is that persistent neurocognitive symptoms can greatly compromise a survivor's ability to function in occupational pursuits. This realization, that many antineoplastic therapies have potential neurotoxicities and the importance of examining nature, course, and persistence of neurocognitive symptoms in cancer survivors, is underscored by numerous recent high-profile national reports in the arena of cancer survivorship [6].

Assessment of Cognitive Symptoms: The Role of the Neuropsychological Evaluation

For cancer survivors with treatment-related neurocognitive sequelae preventing or limiting success in return to work, neuropsychological assessment to examine strengths and weaknesses and to assist with rehabilitation planning is indicated [7]. Within the setting of oncology, neuropsychological evaluation provides a quantitative assessment of the cognitive and neurobehavioral symptoms that may arise as a consequence of cancer, treatment, and/or co-existing neurologic or psychiatric comorbidities. With the exception of documenting profound cognitive impairment, brief screens of global neurocognitive dysfunction, such as those afforded by the Mini-mental Status Examination (MMSE [8]) are insensitive to the types of neurocognitive disturbances most frequently seen in individuals with cancer [9] and inappropriate when the purpose of the evaluation is to assist with decisions about return to work and planning appropriate rehabilitation strategies. Additionally, as noted previously, sole reliance on patient self-report is likewise inappropriate as self-reported cognitive symptoms tend to correlate more significantly with indices of fatigue and mood than with objective evidence of cognitive impairment, as assessed by standardized neuropsychological tests [10–13].

Neuropsychological assessment in the setting of oncology is useful for: (1) appreciating any pre-treatment neurocognitive deficits, so as to intervene more proactively and to establish a baseline from which any neurotoxic effects of disease and treatment can be measured; (2) increasing understanding of the extent to which different treatment strategies improve neuropsychological functioning (secondary to improved tumor control) or have short- or long-term neurotoxicities; (3) improving patient care and management by providing information to assist with treatment decisions, including differential diagnostic assessment (e.g., depression versus impaired frontal lobe/executive functions); (4) guiding rehabilitative interventions, such as pharmacologic and behavioral strategies aimed at reducing functional disabilities and improving quality of life. The feasibility and tolerability of neuropsychological evaluation in cancer survivors has been well demonstrated and neurocognitive endpoints are being increasingly incorporated into new clinical trials [14].

The existing literature suggests that declines in learning and memory are among the most common neuropsychological impairments faced by cancer survivors. This is not unexpected as learning and memory are believed to depend heavily on frontal subcortical networks in the brain which have been found to be preferentially disrupted as a consequence of numerous treatments for both intracerebral and systemic malignancies, including cranial radiotherapy, chemotherapy, endogenous administration of cytokines, and hormonal therapies [3, 4, 15–17]. In addition to deficits in learning efficiency (i.e., acquisition of new information) and memory retrieval, there is often concurrent evidence of additional neuropsychological deficits associated with frontal subcortical network dysfunction, including inefficiencies in executive functions (e.g., planning and organization skills, mental flexibility, abstraction), word retrieval, cognitive processing speed, and bilateral fine motor speed. In this context, survivors with brain tumors or intracerebral metastases may additionally have focal or lateralizing findings (e.g., language deficits in patients with left hemispheric lesions) as a result of tumor impingement on critical neuroanatomic structures, though the nature of these focal deficits is typically less dramatic than what would be expected in survivors with lesions of more acute onset (e.g., secondary to cerebrovascular accident [18]). Depending on the nature and severity of neurocognitive deficits, there is potential for disruption in abilities to efficiently carry out many tasks involved in work.

The Impact of Cognitive Symptoms on Work

The following hypothetical case examples are provided to illustrate the nature of symptoms commonly reported by cancer survivors in the workplace:

Case 1: The patient was a 30-year-old gentleman, employed as a senior software engineer, who had undergone surgical resection followed by chemotherapy and radiation for a malignant brain tumor. Immediately post-surgery, he experienced some decline in right-sided motor functioning and during radiation suffered mild fatigue; both of these symptoms subsequently resolved. In the ensuing months, however, he started to become increasingly aware of changes in his cognitive functioning, including decreased ability to maintain attentional focus, forgetfulness, and trouble with multi-tasking and disorganization. The patient was quite vigilant to his cognitive symptoms and their interference on his work. Prior to his diagnosis, he supervised a team of five engineers, maintained multiple work projects, and earned numerous performance awards. Following treatment, he was having difficulty managing requirements to multi-task, got easily distracted, and could not complete time-sensitive projects. The patient self-initiated numerous attempts to compensate for his cognitive difficulties, one of which included extreme note-taking, such that he was filling one 90-page spiral bound notebook every two weeks. Unfortunately, the effectiveness of his copious note-taking practice was limited, as when forced to recall important information, he could not quickly locate requisite details within his notebook and became easily frustrated. He was forced to spend extra hours at work in the evening and on weekends to try to "make up" for work that he was unable to complete during the typical workday. Consequently, he had essentially ceased participation in any positively reinforcing leisure activities and his family was concerned. The patient reported decreased self-confidence and loss of self-esteem as well as discouragement over his perceived failure to meet pre-illness self-expectations for work performance.

Case 2: The patient was a 45-year-old woman with a history of breast cancer, diagnosed three years ago, who was currently without evidence of active disease. Her prior treatments included mastectomy followed by adjuvant chemotherapy and radiation. She was currently receiving hormonal therapy. The patient was referred for neuropsychological evaluation based on her complaints of changes in short-term memory and word-finding difficulties since receiving chemotherapy. She was concurrently being followed for complaints of significant fatigue which began upon completion of radiation. Regarding her cognitive abilities, the patient described going from an "intelligent, high functioning, independent woman" to being a "stupid, dimwitted person" since completing treatment for cancer. She reported significant changes in her ability to learn new information and recall conversations and tasks as well as slowed cognitive processing speed, lack of attention to detail, decreased ability to multi-task, and word-finding difficulties. She described her life as "no longer being on auto-pilot" as given by a need to exert increased mental effort to complete even mundane tasks (e.g., watch and follow a television show). She reported frequently misplacing objects around her home and avoided reading secondary to inability to sustain attention. She described indecisiveness and increased dependence on her husband and children secondary to decreased self-confidence emanating from her realization of her cognitive deficiencies. Overall, she believed that her cognitive symptoms had progressively worsened over time, and as a consequence of her cognitive symptoms she had been terminated from two jobs over the past 18 months. She specifically cited slow speed and difficulties learning new work procedures as her primary difficulties in work settings. Despite her age, she was extremely concerned that her cognitive decline may be indicative of the onset of a progressive dementia, such as Alzheimer's disease.

The impact of neurocognitive symptoms on the ability to work during and following treatment for cancer is an area of growing import, particularly as oncologic successes continue to mount, and with them, a growing number of survivors who wish or need to return to their previous occupational pursuits. The following section highlights the state of current knowledge regarding the impact of neurocognitive symptoms on the ability to work during and following treatment for cancer. The majority of studies presented are based on survey or interview methodologies in which neurocognitive deficits were measured via self-report. While self-report data are useful to highlight the concerns of cancer survivors about the potential cognitive sequelae associated with cancer treatments, objective assessment, in the form of neuropsychological evaluation, is considered the "gold standard" for determining the occurrence, pattern, and severity of cognitive symptoms. Moreover, virtually every study assessing self-report of cognitive functioning has found little to no relationship with objective neuropsychological test performance [12, 19–22]. Instead, self-reported cognitive symptoms tend to be correlated with indices of fatigue and emotional distress in these studies. Finally, for subsets of survivors with certain cerebral malignancies with known cognitive sequelae, reliance on self-report can be quite problematic secondary to diminished awareness into the nature, severity, or impact of specific cognitive symptoms on daily life. In the future prospective, longitudinal trials, which incorporate a pre-treatment neuropsychological evaluation, are necessary to objectively characterize the nature and severity of cancer and treatment-related cognitive changes and their association with work performance and productivity.

As an effort to gather information directly from cancer survivors about their experience of "chemobrain" during and following treatment, the online survey conducted by the Hurricane Voices Breast Cancer Foundation [5] specifically queried the impact of neurocognitive symptoms on a survivor's ability to work. Nearly two-thirds of the 471 survey respondents (the majority of whom were survivors of breast cancer) reported that cognitive changes had an adverse impact on their work functioning and/or relationships at work and there were 10 reported instances in which respondents left jobs or were terminated. A consistent theme from respondents emerged, namely that the work they engaged in prior to their diagnosis and treatment required greater effort and concentration than before. Respondents cited feelings of being overwhelmed by assigned tasks, inability to multi-task, or incapability to organize their daily work load as common experiences. Trouble learning new tasks, understanding novel concepts, and developing new skill sets was also highlighted. Respondents further noted that issues with memory forced heavy reliance on note-taking while word retrieval difficulties hampered effective written and verbal communication. The challenges described by patients in the workplace appeared to contribute to overall loss of self-confidence and feelings of inadequacy.

Nearly 300 of the 471 respondents felt their cognitive symptoms warranted discussion with a medical profession; however, their concerns were met with mixed reactions. Of the respondents 55% felt their oncologist was understanding, but 42% felt their doctors' response was dismissive and/or indifferent. Only 10% were offered assistance; 6% of respondents had neuropsychological testing and less than 8% were referred for an intervention against their cognitive symptoms. The authors concluded, "Despite the pervasive impact on patients' lives, cognitive changes are not adequately acknowledged and addressed by healthcare providers." Lack of familiarity on the part of oncologic professionals with research demonstrating that brain functioning is impacted by treatment was cited as a potential factor responsible for the current state of affairs. In addition, the criticism that neuropsychological testing isn't always sensitive to some subtle cognitive changes was also offered, and it was concurrently felt that because effective intervention strategies are not available, professionals are left with little options to help survivors cope.

Hansen and colleagues [23] also conducted a web-based survey that included a number of self-report measures of fatigue, cognitive limitations, mood, and work limitations. This study was focused on breast cancer survivors, who were an average of four years post-diagnosis. Survivors reported greater work limitations, more time off, higher levels of fatigue, affective symptoms, and self-reported cognitive limitations at work than a comparable group of patients without cancer. While cognitive limitations contributed univariately to work limitations, when considering symptom burden in a multivariable regression model, fatigue emerged as accounting for the majority of variance in work limitations and was more strongly related to limitations at work in the breast cancer group.

Recent interview studies have also documented work limitations in survivors who return to work following diagnosis and treatment for cancer. Bradley and Bednarek [24] examined the employment patterns of 253 long-term survivors of breast, colon, lung, or prostate cancer in the Detroit metropolitan area. Approximately 67% (n=95) of survivors employed at the time of their cancer diagnosis remained employed 5–7 years later. Of the survivors who were working, 22 reported at least one work limitation secondary to cancer and cancer treatment. In addition to limitations in performing physical tasks, survivors reported effects on their ability to perform cognitive tasks such as concentrating for long periods of time (12%), analyzing data (11%), and learning new things (14%). Amir et al. [25] conducted a qualitative study of interview responses collected from 41 individuals to examine their experiences in returning to work following a cancer diagnosis and treatment. At least one-third of interviewees acknowledged experiencing difficulties upon returning to work following treatment, including "fatigue and loss of confidence and cognitive function."

In a study of breast cancer survivors which included neuropsychological assessment prior to and at short- and long-term intervals following treatment with chemotherapy, Wefel and colleagues [26] reported that 33% of women had evidence of cognitive impairment prior to the initiation of systemic therapy. At the short-term post-chemotherapy time point (approximately six months after the pre-treatment assessment) 61% of the cohort exhibited cognitive decline relative to the pre-treatment assessment. Moreover, survivors who experienced cognitive decline reported greater difficulty working compared with those who did not. While 45% of the patients who showed an initial cognitive decline in cognitive functioning improved by one year post-treatment, 45% had stable functioning and 10% had a mixed pattern of results. Ability to work appeared to improve at long-term follow up suggesting some type of recovery of function over time specifically in relation to work reentry. However, the impact of cognitive limitations on work productivity remains unclear.

For brain tumor survivors specifically, prior research has underscored the particularly problematic nature of neurocognitive difficulties (as opposed to physical disabilities) in preventing these individuals from returning to work [27]. Generally speaking, for brain tumor survivors, maintaining employment after diagnosis and treatment has been found to be the exception, not the rule. Not unexpectedly, at least initially all brain tumor survivors employed at the time of diagnosis miss some work because of their treatment [28]. Following diagnosis and treatment, Fobair and colleagues [29] reported that only 18% of survivors return to full-time work and 10% to part-time work. Similar findings were echoed in recent online survey conducted by the National Brain Tumor Foundation [30]. While 91% of the 277 brain tumor respondents were employed prior to diagnosis, only 33% were employed following diagnosis. In this latter study, changes in employment paralleled changes in household income, with 48% of respondents reporting downward shifts in household income. Brain tumor survivors who do return to work report higher levels of work limitations and time off than their non-cancer peers as well as higher levels of symptom burden (including self-reported cognitive limitations), lower levels of health behaviors, and more negative problem solving orientation [31].

Higher rates of return to work have however been reported for highly selected samples of brain tumor survivors with stable disease following initial treatment [32, 33]. Giovagnoli [32] compared a sample of 57 brain tumor survivors who were stable following post-operative treatment with radiotherapy and chemotherapy to a group of 24 individuals with heterogeneous chronic disabling disorders of the central or peripheral nervous system (e.g., myasthenia, multiple sclerosis, peripheral neuropathy). Of the brain tumor survivors 73% resumed the work they ceased at the time of diagnosis compared to 58% of patients in the neurologic control group. The authors acknowledged that these results are not generalizable to the general brain tumor survivor population, as both untreated patients and patients with recurrent disease were excluded from analyses. Moreover, very few members of the study sample had glioblastoma (14%) or a grade IV tumor and none had seriously disabling motor or cognitive impairment.

The degree to which neurocognitive impairments adversely impact a patient's ability to function, including return to work, is dependent on numerous individual, environmental, and sociocultural factors. For example, the nature, extent, and severity of neurocognitive deficits, the aggressiveness of the patient's disease and treatment, whether or not the patient was working at the time of diagnosis, the type and pace of the patient's work, availability of employer accommodation (including supportive/flexible work environment), family and community supports, and access to services can influence a survivor's success in returning to work [34].

Management of Cognitive Symptoms: Limiting the Impact of Cognitive Impairments on Work

Despite the commonality of neurocognitive impairments in survivors with intracerebral and systemic malignancies, prior to, during, and following treatment, few interventions are offered that specifically target these symptoms. For some survivors, cognitive impairments are mild and subtle, as is often the case in high functioning individuals suffering with cancer associated cognitive symptoms secondary to neurotoxic effects of disease and treatment. In others, including those with aggressive brain tumors, neurocognitive deficits can be frankly debilitating. Either scenario can present challenges to a survivor's daily functioning, including their ability to work. The following sections will review behavioral and pharmacologic strategies aimed at minimizing the cognitive morbidities associated with cancer and its treatment, thereby maximizing a patient's functioning.

Non-Pharmacologic Strategies: Individualized, Focused Cognitive Compensatory Interventions

One criticism offered by the Hurricane Voices Breast Cancer Foundation survey [5] as to the reason for the lack of response of clinical providers to survivors' complaints of "chemobrain" was that since "effective intervention strategies are not available, professionals are left with little options to help patients cope." Primary cancer centers rarely offer cognitive rehabilitation services, even to brain tumor survivors, and traditional rehabilitation hospitals rarely focus on such individuals secondary to concerns over poor prognosis [27]. However, traditional rehabilitation related disciplines focusing on treating survivors of traumatic brain injury, stroke, and dementia have contributed a wealth of knowledge regarding effective behavioral practices against the types of cognitive impairments from which many of these survivors suffer [35, 36].

In fact, cognitive interventions may represent one very significant area in which there is a window of opportunity to improve the quality of a survivor's life, regardless of the extent or stage of their illness and for decreasing the costs and losses to survivors, their families, and society. In 2000, the Brain Tumor Progress Review co-sponsored by the National Cancer Institute and the National Institute of Neurological Disorders and Stroke called for a review of these existing rehabilitation interventions, to determine whether evidence-based strategies could be used successfully with brain tumor survivors and their caregivers [37]. To date, there has been a dearth of such clinical activity and clinically applied research. Although there is likewise a lack of evidence from prospective, randomized, controlled designs supporting the efficacy of targeted cognitive interventions for survivors with cognitive symptoms secondary to systemic malignancies and their treatment (i.e., patients with "chemobrain"), clinical experience suggests that these same approaches may be quite helpful, particularly in assisting these patients to compensate for cognitive deficits that impact their work. In cancer survivors, as in traditional rehabilitation populations, the specific goal of cognitive interventions involves increasing "skill or knowledge, a change in behavior, and/or the use of a compensatory strategy that will increase or improve some aspect of independent functioning" [38].

There are examples from rehabilitation-related disciplines of common, evidenced-based compensatory interventions that are applicable to survivors with cancer-related cognitive dysfunction. We focus on interventions designed to circumvent the impact of inefficiencies in learning and memory on daily life, since these are amongst the most common neuropsychological impairments cancer that survivors face [4]. While it is important to realize that memory impairments do not typically occur in isolation, but rather are often accompanied by neuropsychological evidence of other frontal subcortical symptoms in survivors with cancer-related cognitive dysfunction (i.e., slowed information processing speed, inefficiencies in attention and executive functions), in working with these patients, we have often observed that customized, practical interventions against a "memory" impairment involving implementation of an external aid, can be helpful for managing other commonly associated deficits. In fact, as highlighted below, the popularity of external memory aids in traditional rehabilitation settings is secondary to their effectiveness in minimizing not only the impact of a memory problem but also deficits in attention and executive functioning (e.g., planning, organization, time and goal management).

Neuropsychological interventions designed to minimize the interference of memory problems on everyday life are diverse and the reader is referred to recent reviews [36, 39] for a more complete discussion of the evidence of various approaches. Of the available techniques, external memory aids (e.g., checklists, planners or memory notebooks, wall calendars, pagers) have been among the most widely used interventions for individuals with significant memory impairments following acquired brain injury [40]. Their effectiveness has been well documented in the field of rehabilitation for increasing the independence and functionality of people with memory impairments [39]. The Brain Injury Interdisciplinary Special Interest Group (BI-ISIG) of the American Congress of Rehabilitation Medicine for the cognitive rehabilitation of people with traumatic brain injury and stroke has further recommended compensatory memory strategy training (e.g., through the use of a notebook or diary) as a practice standard for patients with memory impairment after traumatic brain injury or stroke [36].

External memory aids or cueing systems are customized specifically to meet the needs of the individual considering his/her common activities, everyday vulnerabilities to memory failures (and thus targets for intervention), and neuropsychological strengths and weaknesses. Depending on these factors, an external memory aid may range in its sophistication and reliance on technology (i.e., simple wall calendar versus preprogrammed paging systems and computerized organizational media) as well as in generalizability (i.e., to compensate for specific tasks or memory problems occurring across various tasks and settings). Depending on the individual survivor's neurocognitive strengths and weaknesses, an external aid may be regulated by the person himself (i.e., self-directed use of a memory notebook or day planner) or the environment (i.e., preprogrammed paging system [41]). Further, depending on targets for intervention, an external aid may be customized to address problems with both episodic (i.e., memory for events) and prospective (i.e., "remembering to remember," memory to act on future intentions) memory as well as deficits in executive functioning (e.g., planning, organization, initiation of a task, time estimation and management [38]). Systematic, explicit instruction involving supervised practice over multiple sessions has been recommended as a means of maximizing a patient's success with external aids [42–44].

For example, in patients for whom the target for intervention is to compensate for difficulties with everyday memory failures, disorganization, and disturbances in planning, a written or computerized day planner, which addresses the impact of neuropsychological difficulties across tasks and settings, may be implemented. In this case, intervention efforts would be directed toward systematic instruction and supervised practice in acquiring and refining the skills which facilitate use of the planner to compensate for deficits in planning and organization (e.g., planning daily activities after considering the importance of tasks to be completed, time requirements associated with each task, and other conflicting responsibilities) as well as memory (e.g., scheduling future appointments, recording notes of important events as they occur throughout the course of a day).

Although the precise nature of the interventions described above may differ in their target and scope, they all involve development of strategies to compensate for a cognitive deficit ("strategy training") rather than attempts to directly restore the underlying impaired cognitive function through repetitive practice or drills ("restitution training" [36]). In fact there has been no empirical support for the efficacy of drill-oriented approaches (e.g., repetitive massed practice or general mental stimulation exercises) for restoring memory [45]. There is no evidence that attempts to directly retrain impaired cognitive functions through repetitive practice on carefully selected exercises (commonly in the form of computer games) generalizes or transfers to tasks that differ considerably from those used in training. More specifically, while individuals may improve on a targeted outcome measure which is similar to that being trained (i.e., from one computer game to a similar computer game) there is no support for the assumption that improvement on a computer game will generalize or transfer to other tasks, and most importantly to the "real world" tasks cancer survivors are most vulnerable to err in, such as multi-tasking or forgetfulness in the workplace.

Pharmacologic Management of Cognitive Impairment

The predilection for frontal lobe dysfunction in survivors with brain tumors is secondary to adverse effects of both tumor and antineoplastic treatments. Frontal lobe dysfunction, including impairments in executive functioning manifested by apathy, diminished motivation and spontaneity together with neurobehavioral slowing and deficits in working memory, is likely secondary to disruption of the monoamine pathways of the frontal-brainstem reticular system. Additionally, catecholamines play an integral role in the modulation of attention and working memory. Stimulant therapy with methylphenidate hydrochloride, a mixed dopaminergic-noradrenergic agonist pharmacologically similar to amphetamines, has been associated with dramatic subjective and objective improvements in cognition and daily functioning (e.g., decreased fatigue, improved concentration, brighter mood, improved ambulation) in brain tumor survivors [46]. In a phase I trial of 30 survivors with malignant glioma using a single treatment group, dose-escalating design (10, 20, 30 mg Methylphenidate twice daily) brain tumor survivors demonstrated significant improvements in psychomotor speed, memory, visual-motor function, executive function, and bilateral motor speed without increased seizure activity and in conjunction with reductions in glucocorticoid dosage [46]. Adverse side effects (e.g., irritability, "shakiness") were minimal and resolved immediately upon discontinuation of the drug. Moreover, the findings could not simply be attributed to improved mood and were particularly powerful given evidence of ongoing neurologic injury secondary to tumor progression and/or progressive radiation injury in 50% of study patients.

Lower and colleagues [47] presented preliminary data from a phase III, randomized, placebo-controlled trial on the safety and efficacy of dexmethylphenidate (d-MPH, Focalin) for persistent fatigue and memory impairment in 132 adult survivors with extracerebral malignancies (predominantly patients with breast cancer). Treatment with d-MPH (mean highest dose 27.7 mg/day) was associated with improvements in fatigue and in memory (as assessed by the High Sensitivity Cognitive Screen). Future studies, incorporating comprehensive neuropsychological assessment to capture the breadth and extent of cognitive impairment typically documented in survivors with "chemobrain" are clearly warranted.

Modafinil, an oral wakefulness-promoting agent initially approved for use in narcolepsy, has also been investigated as an agent to alleviate fatigue and improve quality of life in brain tumor survivors. In a small pilot study of 15 survivors with primary brain tumor, Nasir [48] documented moderate to significant improvements in cancer-related fatigue in approximately two-thirds of survivors after treatment with Modafinil (200 mg daily, increased to 300 mg after four weeks in non-responders). One survivor had to discontinue treatment due to side effects of encephalopathy; otherwise side effects were mild (anxiety, dizziness) and did not necessitate discontinuation or drug dose reduction. Two recent reviews can provide the reader with more information on the use of pharmacological approaches used to manage fatigue, mood, and cognitive limitations in cancer survivors [49, 50].

Survivors with nasopharyngeal carcinoma are particularly susceptible to temporal lobe radionecrosis after undergoing standard treatment with unilateral or bilateral temporal lobe radiation [51]. The cognitive consequence of this unfortunate but common side effect primarily involves an impairment in memory. Recently, Chan and colleagues [52] examined the effect of mega dose Vitamin E (1000 IU, twice daily) using an open-label, non-randomized, treatment versus control design, on cognitive functioning in patients with temporal lobe radionecrosis. After one year of dietary supplementation with megadose Vitamin E, patients in the treatment group demonstrated significant improvements in memory and executive functioning.

Future Directions

There is a burgeoning body of research utilizing pre-clinical and animal models of neurocognitive functioning to better elucidate the mechanisms of chemotherapy related neurocognitive impairment. Several researchers have found memory impairments following exposure to widely used chemotherapy agents [53, 54]. These impairments may be related to treatment-induced oxidative stress in the brain, leading to cell dysfunction or cell death [55], and/or decreased neurogenesis in areas where proliferation is essential to normal brain function (subventricular zone, hippocampus, and corpus callosum [56–58]). There is also new evidence that exposure to chemotherapy may cause delayed brain injury. Han et al. [58] found that therapeutic levels of 5-fluorouracil, an agent widely used in breast and colon cancers among others, is associated with delayed damage to myelin, and that the myelin damage was associated with functional changes in the auditory brainstem response in animals. The time at which the delayed myelin damage was measured was 56 days post-exposure. These findings support the notion of delayed white matter injury due to chemotherapy exposure that is consistent with the clinical syndrome observed in survivors. With improved understanding of the pathogenesis underlying treatment-induced neurotoxicities, the possibility for targeted interventions against common neurocognitive sequelae emerges.

Ideally as the evidence base regarding effective rehabilitation for cancer survivor specific cognitive deficits emerges, the impact of these approaches on return to work, work retention, and maximizing abilities at work will be determined.

Rehabilitation studies must include this important aspect of recovery of function. There is also a need for the increased use of valid neuropsychological assessment to examine specific patterns of deficits and their proposed impact on work tasks. Tailored interventions either of the compensatory type discussed earlier and/or specific work place accommodations can be implemented and evaluated. The development of workplace accommodations that can address very specific neuropsychological deficits that can impact work performance represents a reasonable next step. The focus up to now has been assessment of deficits and use of compensatory strategies. While this approach has generated useful strategies, the combination of this (which is primarily focused on the worker and accommodations which also considers changes at the workplace) may represent an ideal approach to optimizing work outcomes (Table 7.1).

Table 7.1 Mean values, standard deviations, and paired t test results for measures of cognitive (table adapted with permission from Wefel, J.S., Lenzi, R., Theriault, R.L., Davis, R.N., & Meyers, C.A. 2004, "The Cognitive Sequelae of Standard-Dose Adjuvant Chemotherapy in Women with Breast Carcinoma: Results of a Prospective, Randomized, Longitudinal Trial" Cancer, 100(11), p. 2297)

Measure	Baseline Mean (SD)	No. of patients	Short-term postchemotherapy Mean (SD)	No. of patients	Long-term postchemotherapy Mean (SD)	No. of patients
Digit Span[a]	11.06 (2.69)	18	10.72 (3.29)	18	11.29 (3.02)	14
Arithmetic[a]	10.22 (2.56)	18	11.12 (3.02)	17	11.00 (2.80)	14
Digit Symbol[a]	11.61 (2.55)	18	12.67 (2.77)[b]	18	13.27 (3.17)	15
TMTA[c]	0.41 (0.89)	18	0.51 (1.05)	18	0.55 (0.89)	15
VSRT LTS[c]	−0.76 (1.20)	18	−0.26 (1.30)[d]	18	−0.24 (1.01)	15
NVSRT LTS[c]	0.11 (0.83)	18	0.66 (0.84)[d]	18	0.54 (1.06)	15
VSRT DR[c]	−1.03 (2.14)	18	−0.90 (1.50)	18	−0.25 (0.81)	15
NVSRT DR[c]	0.00 (1.04)	18	0.45 (1.40)	18	0.28 (1.43)	14
COWA[c]	0.29 (1.06)	18	0.41 (0.84)	18	0.86 (0.76)	15
TMTB[c]	0.56 (0.88)	18	0.78 (1.02)	18	0.79 (1.12)	15
CT[c]	0.04 (0.94)	17	0.85 (0.75)[b]	17	1.06 (0.87)	14
Similarities[a]	11.11 (2.59)	18	11.72 (2.74)	18	11.07 (2.70)	14
Block Design[a]	11.44 (2.85)	18	12.39 (3.36)[d]	18	12.71 (3.77)	14
GP–dominant hand[c]	0.20 (1.32)	18	0.04 (1.59)	18	0.23 (1.41)	15
GP–nondominant hand[c]	−0.23 (0.97)	18	0.09 (0.98)	18	0.21 (1.07)	15

SD: standard deviation; TMTA: Trail Making Test Part A; TMTB: Trail Making Test Part B; VSRT: Verbal Selective Reminding Test; NVSRT: Nonverbal Selective Reminding Test; LTS: Long-Term Storage; DR: Delayed Recall; COWA: Controlled Oral Word Association Test; CT: Booklet Category Test; GP: Grooved Pegboard Test.
[a] Scaled scores (mean, 10; standard deviation, 3).
[b] $P \leq 0.01$, indicating a significant change relative to baseline.
[c] z scores (mean, 0; standard deviation, 1).
[d] $P \leq 0.05$, indicating a significant change relative to baseline.

Refences

1. Meyers C, Albitar M, Estey E. Cognitive impairment, fatigue, and cytokine levels in patients with acute myelogenous leukemia or myelodysplastic syndrome. Cancer. 2005;104:788–93.
2. Meyers CA, Byrne KS, Komaki R. Cognitive deficits in patients with small cell lung cancer before and after chemotherapy. Lung Cancer. 1995;12:231–5.
3. Wefel J, Lenzi R, Theriault R, Buzdar A, Cruickshank S, Meyers C. 'Chemobrain' in breast carcinoma: A prologue. Cancer. 2004; 101:466–75.
4. Wefel JS, Kayl AE, Meyers CA. Neuropsychological dysfunction associated with cancer and cancer therapies: A conceptual review of an emerging target. British Journal of Cancer. 2004;90:1691–6.
5. Hurricane Voices Breast Cancer Foundation. Cognitive Changes Related to Cancer Treatment 2007 cited 2008; Available from: www.hurricanevoices.org.
6. Rowland J, Hewitt M, Ganz P. Cancer survivorship: A new challenge in delivering quality cancer care. Journal of Clinical Oncology. 2006;24:5101–4.
7. Vargo MM, Smith RG, Stubblefield MD. Rehabilitation of the cancer patient. In: DeVita VT, Lawrence TS, Rosenberg SA, eds. *Cancer: Principles and Practice of Oncology.* Philadelphia, PA: Lippincott Williams & Wilkins 2008:2857–84.
8. Folstein MF, Folstein SE, McHugh PR. "Mini-mental state." A practical method for grading the cognitive state of patients for the clinician. Journal of Psychiatric Research. 1975;12:189–98.
9. Meyers CA, Wefel JS. The use of the Mini-Mental State Examination to assess cognitive functioning in cancer trials: No ifs, ands, buts, or sensitivity. Journal of Clinical Oncology. 2003;21:3557–8.
10. Castellon S, Ganz PA, Bower J, Petersen L, Abraham L, Greendale G. Neurocognitive performance in breast cancer survivors exposed to adjuvant chemotherapy and tamoxifen. Journal of Clinical and Experimental Neuropsychology. 2004;26:955–69.
11. Cull A, Hay C, Love S, Mackie M, Stewart M. What do cancer patients mean when they complain of memory problems? British Journal of Cancer. 1996;74:1674–979.
12. Jenkins V, Shilling V, Deutsch G, Bloomfield D, Morris R, Allan S, et al. A 3-year prospective study of the effects of adjuvant treatments on cognition in women with early stage breast cancer. British Journal of Cancer. 2006;94(6):828–34.
13. Schagen S, Muller M, Boogerd W, van Dam F. Cognitive dysfunction and chemotherapy: Neuropsychological findings in perspective. Clinical Breat Cancer Supplement. 2002;3(3):S100–S8.
14. Meyers C, Brown P. Role and relevance of neurocognitive assessment in clinical trials of patients with CNS tumors. Journal of Clinical Oncology. 2006;24:1305–9.
15. Meyers CA, Kudelka AP, Conrad CA, Gelke CK, Grove W, Pazdur R. Neurotoxicity of CI-980, a novel mitotic inhibitor. Clinical Cancer Research. 1997;3:419–22.
16. Meyers CA, Abbruzzese JL. Cognitive functioning in cancer patients: Effect of previous treatment. Neurology. 1992;42:434–6.
17. Crossen JR, Garwood D, Glatstein E, Neuwalt EA. Neurobehavioral sequelae of cranial irradiation in adults: A reivew of radiation-induced encephalopathy. Journal of Clinical Oncology. 1994;12:627–42.
18. Anderson SW, Damasio H, Tranel D. Neuropsychological impairments associated with lesions caused by tumor or stroke. Archives of Neurology. 1990;47.
19. Hermelink K, Untch M, Lux MP, Kreienberg R, Beck T, Bauerfeind I, et al. Cognitive function during neoadjuvant chemotherapy for breast cancer: Results of a prospective, multicenter, longitudinal study. Cancer. 2007;109(9):1905–13.
20. Jacobs SR, Jacobsen PB, Booth-Jones M, Wagner LI, Anasetti C. Evaluation of the Funtional Assessment of Cancer Therapy Cogntive Scale with Hematopoetic Stem Cell Transplant Patients. Journal of Pain and Symptom Management. 2007;33(1):13–23.

21. Mehnert A, Scherwath A, Schirmer L, Schleimer B, Petersen C, Schulz-Kindermann F, et al. The association between neuropsychological impairment, self-perceived cognitive deficits, fatigue, and health related quality of life in breast cancer survivors following standard adjuvant versus high-dose chemotherapy. Patient Education and Counseling. 2007;66(1):108–18.
22. Vardy J, Wong K, Yi QL, Park A, Maruff P, Wagner L, et al. Assessing cognitive function in cancer patients. Supportive Care in Cancer. 2006;14(11):1111–8.
23. Hansen JA, Feuerstein M, Olsen CH, Calvio LC. Breast cancer survivors at work. Journal of Occupational and Environmental Medicine. in press.
24. Bradley CJ, Bednarek HL. Employment patterns of long-term cancer survivors. Psycho-Oncology. 2002;85:188–98.
25. Amir Z, Neary D, Luker K. Cancer survivors' veiws of work 3 years post diagnosis: A UK perspective. European Journal of Oncology Nursing. 2008;12(3):190–7.
26. Wefel JS, Lenzi R, Theriault RL, Davis RN, Meyers CA. The cognitive sequelae of standard-dose adjuvant chemotherapy in women with breast carcinoma: Results of a prospective, longitudinal trial. Cancer. 2004;100(11):2292–9.
27. Meyers C, Boake C. Neurobehavioral disorders in bran tumor patients: Rehabilitation strategies. The Cancer Bulletin. 1993;45:362–4.
28. Bradley S, Sherwood PR, Donovan HS, Hamilton R, Rosenzweig M, Kricik A, et al. I could lose everything: Understanding the cost of a brain tumor. Journal of Neuro-Oncology. 2007;85:329–38.
29. Fobair P, Mackworth N, Varghese A, Prados M. Quality of life issues among 200 brain tumor patients treated at the University of California in San Francisco, interviewed 1988. *Brain Tumor Conference*: A Living Resource Guide 1990.
30. Patterson H. Nobody can afford a brain tumor... The financial impact of brain tumors on patients and familiers: A summary of findings. Report from the National Brain Tumor Foundation 2007.
31. Feuerstein M, Hansen JA, Calvio LC, Johnson L, Ronquillo JG. Work productivity in brain tumor survivors. Journal of Occupational and Environmental Medicine. 2007;49(7):803–11.
32. Giovagnoli AR. Quality of life in patients with stable disease after surgery, radiotherapy, and chemotherapy for malignant brain tumor. Journal of Neurology, Neurosurgery, and Psychiatry. 1999;67:358–63.
33. Kleinberg L, Wallner K, Malkin MG. Good performance of long-term disease-free survivors of intracranial gliomas. International Journal of Radiation Oncology Biology and Physics. 1993;26:129–33.
34. Taskila T, Lindbohm M. Factors affecting cancer survivors' employment and work ability. Acta Oncology. 2007;46(6):446–51.
35. Cicerone KD, Dahlberg C, Kalmar K, Langenbahn DM, Malec JF, Bergquist TF, et al. Evidence-based cognitive rehabilitation: Recommendations for clinical practice. Archives of Physical Medicine and Rehabilitation. 2000;81(12):1596–615.
36. Cicerone KD, Dahlberg C, Malec JF, Langenbahn DM, Felicetti T, Kneipp S, et al. Evidence-based cognitive rehabilitation: Updated review of the literature from 1998 through 2002. Archives of Physical Medicine and Rehabilitation. 2005;86(8):1681–92.
37. Brain Tumor Progress Review Group. Report of the Brain Tumor Progress Review Group. NIH Publication No. 01-4902: National Cancer Institute and National Institute of Neurological Disorders and Stroke; 2000.
38. Sohlberg MM, Mateer CA. *Cognitive Rehabilitation: An Integrative Neuropsychological Approach*. New York: Oxford University Press 2001.
39. Sohlberg MM. External Aids for Management of Memory Impairment. In: High WM, Sander AM, Struchen MA, Hart KA, eds. *Rehabilitation for Traumatic Brain Injury*. New York: Oxford University Press 2005.

40. Evans JJ, Wilson BA, Needham P, Brentnall S. Who makes good use of memory aids? Results of a survey of people with acquired brain injury. Journal of the International Neuropsychological Society. 2003;9:925–35.
41. Malec J, Cicerone K. Cognitive rehabilitation. In: Evans R, ed. *Neurology & Trauma*. Second ed. New York: Oxford 2005:238–61.
42. Sohlberg MM, Mateer CA. Training the use of compensatory memory books: a three stage behavioral approach. Journal of Clinical and Experimental Neuropsychology. 1989;11:871–91.
43. Donaghy S, Williams W. A new protocol for training severely impaired patients in the usage of memory journals. Brain Injury. 1998;12(12):1061–70.
44. Schmitter-Edgecombe M, Fahy J, Whelan J, Long C. Memory remediation after severe closed head injury. Notebook training versus supportive therapy. Journal of Consulting and Clinical Psychology. 1995;63:484–9.
45. Sohlberg MM. External Aids for Management of Memory Impairment. In: High WM, Sander AM, Struchen MA, Hart KA, eds. *Rehabilitation for Traumatic Brain Injury*. New York: Oxford University Press 2005.
46. Meyers CA, Weitzner MA, Valentine AD, Levin VA. Methylphenidate therapy improves cognition, mood, and function of brain tumor patients. Journal of Clinical Oncology. 1998;16(7):2522–7.
47. Lower E, Fleischman S, Cooper A, Zeldis J, Faleck H, Manning D. A phase III, randomized placebo-controlled trial of the safety and efficacy of d-MPH as new treatment of fatigue and "chemobrain" in adult cancer patients. (Abstract). Journal of Clinical Oncology. 2005;23:8000.
48. Nasir S. Modafinil improves fatigue in primary brain tumor patients (Abstract). Society of Neuro Oncology. 2003;5:335.
49. Breitbart W, Alici Evcimen Y. Update on psychotropic medications for cancer related fatigue. Journal of the National Comprehensive Cancer Network. 2007;5(10):1081–91.
50. Caroll JK, Kohli S, Mustian KM, Roscoe J, Morrow GR. Pharmacologic treatment of cancer related fatigue. Oncologist. 2007;12(Suul 1):43–51.
51. Cheung M, Chan AS, Law SC, Chan JH, Tse VK. Cognitive function of patients with nasopharyngeal carcinoma with and without temporal lobe radionecrosis. Archives of Neurology. 2000;57:1347–52.
52. Chan AS, Cheung M-C, Law SC, Chan JH. Phase II study of Alpha-Tocopherol in improving the cognitive function of patients with temporal lobe radionecrosis. Cancer. 2003;100(2):398–404.
53. Winocur G, vardy J, Binns MA, Kerr L, Tannock I. The effects of the anti-cancer drugs, methotrexate and 5-fluorouracil, on cognitive function in mice. Pharmacology, Biochemistry, and Behavior. 2006;85(1):66–75.
54. Reiriz AB, Reolon GK, Preissler T, Rosado JO, Henriques JA, Roesler R, et al. Cancer chemotherapy and cognitive function in rodent models: Memory impairment induced by cyclophosphamide in mice. Clinical Cancer Research. 2006;12(1):198–205.
55. Joshi G, Sultana R, Tangpong J, Cole MP, St Clair DK, vore M, et al. Free radical mediated oxidative stress and toxic side effects in brain induced by the anti cancer drug adriamycin: Insight into chemobrain. Free Radical Research. 2005;39:1147.
56. Crandall J, Sakai Y, Zhang J, Koul O, Mineur Y, Crusio WE, et al. 13-cis-retinoic acid suppresses hippocampal cell division and hippocampal-dependent learning in mice. Proceedings of the National Academy of Sciences of the United States of America. 2004;101:5111.
57. Dietrich J, Han R, Yang Y, Mayer-Proschel M, Noble M. CNS progenitor cells and oligodendrocytes are targets of chemotherapeutic agents in vitro and in vivo. Journal of Biology. 2006;5:22.
58. Han R, Yang YM, Dietrich J, Luebke A, Mayer-Proschel M, Noble M. Systemic 5-fluorouracil treatment causes a syndrome of delayed myelin destruction in the CNS. Journal of Biology. in press.

Chapter 8
Young Survivors of Childhood Cancer

Angela de Boer, Jos Verbeek, and Frank van Dijk

Introduction

Due to recent advances in new and successful treatments the consequences of receiving a diagnosis of cancer in childhood have dramatically changed. Children and adolescents with cancer, who may have had a limited life expectancy a few decades ago, are now often surviving into adulthood. The overall five-year survival was over 72% for all pediatric malignancies in 19 European countries in the period 1978–1997 [1]. In the UK, the overall survival was 75% between 1992 and 1996 [2] with the highest survival for survivors of Hodgkin's disease (95%) and retinoblastoma (95%) and the lowest for primitive neuroectodermal tumors (50%) and neuroblastoma (55%). The overall survival in the US was 80% in the period 1996–2003 compared to 62% in 1975–1977 [3]. The highest survival rates in the US were found for survivors of Hodgkin's disease (95%) and Wilm's tumor (92%), while the lowest survival rate of 50% was found for survivors of acute myeloid leukemia [3].

There is an increasing large cohort of at-risk patients who have a potential life expectancy that should extend well into old age and within a setting where complications of therapy may not become apparent until many years after cancer treatment [4]. With the sustained improvement in survival and the increasing number of survivors of childhood cancer, there is a need to develop and improve management of adverse long-term effects and their influence on employment.

Late Effects

Many survivors are doing well in general terms, although two recent publications reported that the majority of survivors had at least one chronic disease or adverse health condition. The U.S. Childhood Cancer Survivor Study (CCSS) is

---

A. de Boer (✉)
Coronel Institute of Occupational Health, AMC/Academic Medical Centre,
Meibergdreef 9/K0-105, 1105 AZ Amsterdam, The Netherlands
e-mail: a.g.deboer@amc.uva.nl

a retrospective cohort study of 10, 397 childhood cancer survivors with leukemia (30%), Hodgkin's disease (18%), central nervous system tumors (13%), bone tumors (11%) or sarcoma (10%). The CCSS found that 62% of these adult survivors of childhood cancer with a mean age of 27 years suffered from at least one chronic condition [5]. These included second primary tumors, cerebrovascular disease, cardiovascular disease, renal disease, hearing loss, visual handicaps, cognitive dysfunction, and major joint replacement. A similar result was found in the Emma Children's Hospital/Academic Medical Centre in the Netherlands [6]. Seventy five percent of the adult survivors of childhood cancer with a median age of 24 years had one or more adverse health or functional outcome. These included orthopedic (in 30% of the patients), neurologic (19%), cardiovascular (13%), endocrine (18%), nephrologic (11%), cognitive (36%), and fertility problems (14%). A high or severe burden of adverse events was observed in 55% of survivors who received radiotherapy only, compared to 25% of survivors who had surgery only and in 15% of survivors who received chemotherapy only [6].

In addition to the medical assessment of the chronic health condition of young survivors of childhood cancer, a growing number of studies have documented the substantial impact of childhood cancer and treatment on quality of life and emotional well-being. Although most long-term survivors of childhood cancer have been found to function psychologically well, a subgroup of survivors reported depression, anxiety, post-traumatic stress, anger, and confusion [7, 8]. The autonomy and social development of survivors was also found to be hampered compared to the development of their healthy peers [9].

These long-term medical and psychological effects of childhood cancer or its treatment may cause impairments that diminish social functioning such as school attendance, social activities and obtaining employment [10]. It can be especially difficult for young survivors of childhood cancer to obtain a job, given the possible late physical effects of childhood cancer such as cardiovascular and pulmonary damage, scoliosis, fatigue or visual handicap. Potential cognitive effects such as impaired attention capabilities and the increased risk of depression or post-traumatic stress are particularly related to problems with work in adults with childhood cancer [11]. Furthermore, job rejection because of cancer and job discrimination might prevail [12]. Finally, the impact of health care insurance companies through acceptance rules and social security schemes on obtaining work or on access to a work disability pension scheme is not clear.

Importance of Work for Young Survivors of Childhood Cancer

Obtaining employment appropriate to one's education and interests is an important and challenging life goal for anyone. It is even more significant for cancer survivors, because as reported in the previous chapter a patient's self-image and sense of competence is often closely tied to career and daily work experiences [13]. Badell et al. [14] found that for 19% of the childhood survivors of bone marrow transplantation the main concern in life was work, whereas for their age-matched controls this figure was only 2%. A study of Seitzman et al. [15] on self-concept in adult survivors of childhood acute lymphoblastic leukemia also showed the difference between survivors and healthy controls in the effect of being employed. Unemployed survivors reported lower global self-worth scores than employed survivors, whereas employment status had no impact on self-worth in the sibling controls. But being employed is not only important for the survivor's self-image and self-concept. Work performance after cancer treatment is frequently seen as a measure of recovery and being cured in its own right. Furthermore, employment provides financial support and can include access to health insurance which might cover or help to compensate for the increased costs many young cancer survivors are still dealing with. Being able to work and stay at work is not only important for the individual but from a societal point of view it is also important to reduce avoidable work incapacity [16].

Finally, the issue of obtaining work is especially important for the young survivors. Because of their long-life expectancy they still have a complete working life ahead of them. A failed transition from school to the adult working life might result in an entire working life lost.

Unemployment in Young Survivors of Childhood Cancer: Meta-analysis

Over the course of almost a forty year period, studies have been conducted into the occupational rehabilitation of adult cancer patients [16]. For the group of young survivors of childhood cancer, however, it took almost a decade longer before research on their vocational status was initiated. Although a body of information on the adjustment of pediatric and adult cancer patients was available by the mid-1980s, research in this area had rarely focused on the long-term vocational adjustment of young cancer survivors [17].

The first years of research on employment of adult survivors of childhood cancer were dominated by the United States, placing the emphasis on legal issues such as discrimination and obtaining health insurance. Two major reports from the early 1980s describe high rates of discrimination against the survivors of childhood cancer. Survivors of childhood cancer were perceived as ordinarily lacking a record of employment or established skills. [18, 19] Toward the 1990s, more research on the employment of adult survivors of childhood cancer was initiated and the use of control groups became more common. There has been a steady flow of studies on the occupational achievements of this group ever since. Increasingly these studies were also conducted outside the United States in the United Kingdom, Austria, Sweden, Israel, Brazil, the Netherlands, Slovenia, Italy, Canada, Norway, and Germany [20].

In 2006, we published a meta-analysis in which we provided an overview of the articles which assessed the employment rates of adult survivors of childhood cancer [20]. The main aim of our meta-analysis was to assess the risk of unemployment of adult survivors of childhood cancer compared to healthy controls. We also described the unemployment rates found in uncontrolled studies and we explored prognostic factors for unemployment.

Method of Literature Search of the Meta-analysis

A series of literature searches was conducted using the electronic databases of Medline, CINAHL, EMBASE, ClinPSYCH, PsycINFO and OSHROM. Studies published from 1966 to January 2006 were retrieved, with no restrictions on the language.

For the search, we combined words related to employment (such as employment, unemployment, absenteeism, work, occupational) with words on survivors (survivor(s)), cancer (such as neoplasm(s), cancer(s), carcinoma(s)) and childhood (child(ren)(hood), adolescent). When available, subject headings such as MeSH terms were also added in all searches. Subsequently, the results of the employment search were combined with the results of the search on survivors of childhood cancer. Finally, all included publications and review articles were hand searched for additional references. The quality of the included studies varied considerably depending on study design and objectives. In some studies the unemployment rates were only secondary outcomes to clinical outcomes while other studies have been designed to find the best estimate of the unemployment risk in cancer survivors, by means of an age- and sex-matched control group and the provision of follow-up data. However, we felt that we had selected the outstanding part of unemployment studies by our inclusion criteria.

For the meta-analysis we used only studies which included a control group. We used the proportion of unemployed cancer survivors in uncontrolled studies to explore the external validity of the reported controlled studies. First, the overall meta-analysis of all controlled studies was performed. Next, the difference in risk of unemployment between the survivors living in the USA and Europe was analyzed because of expected differences between the labor markets in the USA and Europe. Finally, separate meta-analyses for four cancer diagnoses were performed.

Results of the Meta-analysis

A total of 34 papers was found in which 40 original empirical studies were reported of which 24 were controlled studies. The overall meta-analysis of these 24 controlled studies showed that survivors of childhood cancers were almost twice as likely to be unemployed in later life than healthy controls (odds ratio (OR) = 1.85 [95% confidence interval (CI) 1.27–2.69) [20]. In the meta-analysis, we excluded students from the data. Twelve of the controlled studies were performed in the USA and the other twelve controlled studies were from countries in Europe and one from Israel. We found that in the USA, the overall risk to become unemployed after childhood cancer was over three times higher than in the control group (OR 3.24 [95% CI, 2.16–4.86]), see Fig. 8.1. However, no difference in unemployment was found between the patient and control groups in Europe (OR 1.00 [95% CI, 0.58 to 1.70]), see Figure 8.2.

This difference was not related to differences in diagnosis groups of the studies performed in the United States or in Europe. A possible explanation might be that in the USA, the viewpoint of the society and employers regarding long-term survivors of cancer is different compared to that in Europe. Earlier studies provide support for this idea as the job rejection rates for adult survivors of childhood cancer have been reported to be 6% in the UK [21] and 7–45% in the USA [22–26]. Another possibility might be that many teenagers in the USA are involved in part-time temporary jobs and that the experience of cancer treatment might easily displace young cancer survivors from this marginal workforce. However, the same situation occurs in Europe where many young people achieve essential work experience in part-time temporary jobs as well. Alternatively, it might be possible that despite the Americans with Disabilities Act (ADA), there is more discrimination regarding cancer in the USA. Earlier studies in the USA have shown that discrimination at the workplace prevails [22–23]. Employers in the USA might be more cautious about employing cancer survivors because they expect them to have greater time off or they anticipate problems at work including lower productivity (see Chapter 3). In a recent study of Feuerstein et al. [27] the pattern of 59,981 ADA disputes among survivors of adult-onset cancers and non-cancer related impairments was investigated. The results indicated that claims related to termination and

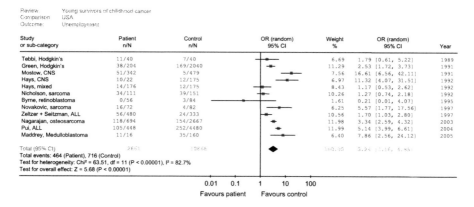

Fig. 8.1 USA: Unemployment in young survivors of childhood cancer

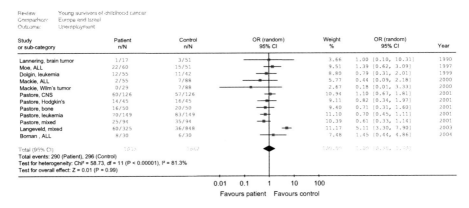

Fig. 8.2 Europe: Unemployment in young survivors of childhood cancer

employment policies and benefits were more common from employees who were cancer survivors than from employees with other types of impairments. The authors conclude that alleged discrimination-related dismissal, inequities in the application of workplace policies and relationships are potential sources of workplace stress that need to be addressed through policy, operational, employer and employee change [27]. Finally, many employers in the USA pay for health insurance whereas employers in Europe usually do not. This might be an explanation for the differences where some employers may avoid risks for health care costs.

Young Survivors of Blood Cancers

Ten controlled studies reported in nine articles provided data on unemployment of adult survivors of childhood blood cancers [17, 22, 28–34]. Figure 8.3 shows

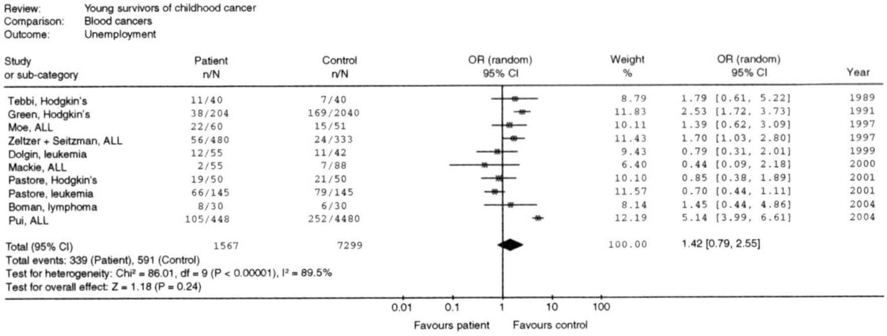

Fig. 8.3 Unemployment in young survivors of blood cancers

the results of the meta-analysis of these ten controlled studies concerning 1567 survivors of blood cancers and their controls. Adult survivors of blood cancers were almost one and a half times more likely to become unemployed than the controls, but the result was not statistically significant (OR, 1.42 [95% CI, 0.79–2.55]). The unemployment rate was on average 22% for the survivors of blood cancer. A similar pattern of unemployment was found in the four uncontrolled studies [24, 35, 36]: unemployment rates of around 30% for the survivors of leukemia.

Although the difference in unemployment between survivors and controls was relatively small in most studies, we found other employment issues. Having survived childhood blood cancer might result in working part-time. Three studies have found that controls were more likely than childhood cancer survivors to be employed full-time rather than part-time. Zeltzer/Seitzman [15, 34] found that 49% of the survivors and 61% of the controls worked full-time, while Zevon et al. [24] found percentages of 66% versus 83%, respectively, and Boman and Bodegard [28] reported 83% of survivors working full-time versus 87% of the controls. However, no differences between survivors and controls were found in hours worked per week in another study [31].

In the Swedish study of Boman and Bodegard [28] it was reported that only a small proportion of the survivors (30%) reported concrete plans for occupational advancement in the future versus 47% of the controls. Finally, no differences in job satisfaction and job appropriateness were found between survivors and controls [29] in an Israeli study.

Young Survivors of CNS and Brain Tumors

We found ten studies on the employment of adult survivors of childhood tumors of the central nervous system or brain tumors [11, 23, 32, 37–43]. The results for the five controlled studies [23, 32, 40–42] in the meta-analysis for unemployment of survivors of CNS and brain tumors are depicted in Fig. 8.4.

Review:	Young survivors of childhood cancer						
Comparison:	CNS and brain tumors						
Outcome:	Unemployment						
Study or sub-category	Patient n/N	Control n/N	OR (random) 95% CI	Weight %	OR (random) 95% CI	Year
Lannering, brain tumors	1/17	3/51		14.07	1.00 [0.10, 10.31]	1990
Mostow, CNS	51/342	5/479		21.42	16.61 [6.56, 42.11]	1991
Hays, CNS	10/22	12/175		20.98	11.32 [4.07, 31.51]	1992
Pastore, CNS	57/123	54/123		23.03	1.10 [0.67, 1.82]	2001
Maddrey, medulloblastoma	11/16	35/160		20.50	7.86 [2.56, 24.12]	2005
Total (95% CI)	520	983		100.00	4.74 [1.23, 18.65]	
Total events: 130 (Patient), 109 (Control)						
Test for heterogeneity: Chi² = 38.80, df = 4 (P < 0.00001), I² = 89.7%						
Test for overall effect: Z = 2.23 (P = 0.03)						

0.01 0.1 1 10 100
Favours patient   Favours control

Fig. 8.4 Unemployment in young survivors of CNS and brain cancers

Survivors of CNS and brain tumors in childhood are almost five times more likely to be unemployed as adults (OR, 4.74 [95% CI, 1.21–18.65]). The unemployment rate was 25% in the controlled studies, but the five uncontrolled studies reported a higher unemployment rate of around 50% [11, 37–39, 43]. Jenkin [38] concludes that a broad generalization of their results is that only one of every three adult survivors of an irradiated early childhood brain tumor will be capable of competitive full-time employment and have a life-style within the normal range. One of the three will be employable with support, and one will not be employable (see Chapter 2).

Thus there is a highly elevated risk of unemployment for adult survivors of CNS and brain tumors. Symptom burden can impact work. A wide range of these sequelae prevail: 38% have cognitive, 25–77% motor, 20–24% visual, 21% epilepsy, 50% memory and 14% psychological emotional dysfunction [11, 40, 41].

The health condition of the survivors of childhood CNS tumors can also have an effect of job change or the decision to stop working. In the study of Mostow [42], 37% of the CNS tumor survivors who were 20 years post-diagnosis on average, changed jobs or stopped working because of cancer, versus only 4% of their healthy siblings.

Young Survivors of Bone Cancers

The employment of adult survivors of childhood bone cancers was reported in seven studies. Figure 8.5 reflects the results for the meta-analysis for the survivors of bone tumors such as osteosarcoma and Ewings sarcoma. The four controlled studies [32, 44–46] showed a doubled risk on unemployment for the group of survivors of childhood bone cancers, but the estimate was not statistically significant (OR, 1.97 [95% CI, 0.88–4.40]). The unemployment rate in the controlled studies was 20% while the average unemployment rate of the uncontrolled studies was approximately 40%.

Having experienced bone cancer in childhood can not only influence the chance on employment but also the choice of work. Of the young survivors of

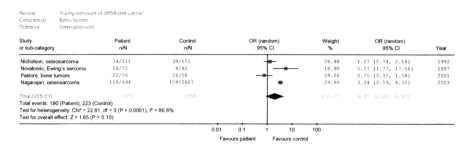

Fig. 8.5 Unemployment in young survivors of bone cancers

bone cancer in the study of Eiser et al., the majority (44%) felt that their opportunities were limited as a result of the illness. All of them reported that restricted mobility was a limitation on job opportunities. Another 25% of the survivors reported that their experiences had directed their choice of work. All of them were employed in social or health environments. Finally, 31% reported that the illness made no difference to their choice of work [47]. Similar results were found by Felder et al. Due to consequences of treatment, 18% of the survivors had to give up their jobs and another 27% reported changes in job orientation implying they had to choose another profession than what they would have liked to have. However, although they were originally not inspired they were satisfied with their current occupations [48].

Young Survivors of Other Cancers

We found no overall increased risk of unemployment in the five controlled studies of Langeveld, Pastore, Mackie, Byrne, and Hays [23, 30, 32, 49, 50] on survivors of other or mixed diagnoses (OR 0.97 [0.27–3.53]), see Fig. 8.6. Results of the five controlled studies showed that 15% of the patients were unemployed whereas the uncontrolled studies reported an unemployment rate of around 30%.

The survivors who do work are not always willing to disclose their cancer history at their work. About half of the survivors (23% with Wilm's tumor, 19% leukemia) in the study of Meadows et al. [51] had not told any coworkers or employers of their cancer history whereas only 12% said that they told all of their coworkers and employers. In this group of survivors, promotions were not seen as being affected by their health histories, although 10% noted that they had difficulty in job performance related to cancer. The majority of these people experienced problems with coworkers, which they attributed to their history of cancer.

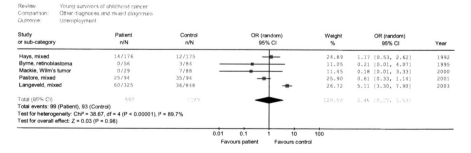

Fig. 8.6 Unemployment in young survivors of other cancers

Developments Since the Meta-analysis

A new literature search regarding employment of survivors of childhood cancer in March 2008 resulted in 107 new abstracts over the past two years. After reading the abstracts and articles, we found seven new studies on employment status of adult survivors of childhood cancer.

In 2008, data on the employment status of a very large cohort of young cancer survivors as part of the Childhood Cancer Survivor Study were published. In this article of Pang et al. [52], the employment status and risk factors for unemployment were described for 10,399 childhood cancer survivors compared with 3,083 siblings. Most prevalent diagnoses were leukemia (29%), Hodgkin's disease (19%), CNS tumors (12%) and bone cancer (11%). The median age in this study from the United States was 26 years and the median follow-up from diagnosis was 16 years. Survivors reported a 5.6% unemployment rate, compared with 1.2% of siblings. Compared to siblings, survivors had an increased risk of having never been employed of 3.7 (OR 3.7 [2.6–5.1]). In comparison with our meta-analysis (OR 1.8 [1.3–2.7]) this is a higher overall unemployment risk, but it is similar to our risk of 3.2 of the 12 controlled studies from the United States (OR 3.2 [2.2–4.9]). Pang et al. think that the difference may reflect that the Childhood Cancer Survivor Study uses a relatively unselected cohort with large individual disease groups and large sibling control groups. In their study it was also found that the risk of unemployment was increased for all childhood cancer diagnoses, but the greatest risk was reported for the 1,148 CNS tumor survivors who were ten times more likely to be unemployed (OR 9.9 [6.9–14.2]). The 2,875 survivors of leukemia were three times more likely to be unemployed (OR 3.2 [2.2–4.5]), the 1,831 survivors of Hodgkin's disease were twice as likely (OR 2.4 [1.4–3.7]), and the risk for the 1,080 survivors of bone cancer was almost four times higher (OR 3.6 [2.2–5.4]). Of the employed survivors in this study, 13% had ever been rejected for a job due to medical history, versus 3% of their healthy siblings [52]. In another report of the Childhood Cancer Survivor Study on survivors of rhabdomyosarcoma, Punyko et al. found that survivors were less likely ever to have had a job than healthy controls (3% versus 1%). They also reported that survivors of rhabdomyosarcoma were more likely to have sickness absence than their siblings, to be turned down for a civilian job, and to be turned down for a military job, but not for the police force or fire fighting [53]. In a recent study from the St. Jude's Children's Hospital in the United States, 1,437 survivors of childhood cancer were compared to U.S. normative data. Most were survivors of hematologic malignancies (71%), embryonal tumors (15%) and sarcomas (11%), with an average age of 30 years. Half of the survivors were male and most (61%) were working full-time. Full-time employment among survivors was lower than national norms, except among survivors of hematologic malignancies who had not received radiation therapy [54].

In 2008, a Greek study on 103 survivors of mainly leukemia and non-Hodgkin's disease with a mean age of 20 years, reported that 27% were employed. More than a third (36%) of them said that they had altered their vocational aspirations due to reduced abilities. Compared to healthy controls, significantly lower percentage of survivors reported having high professional expectations and ambitions (50% versus 63% controls) [55].

In contrast with earlier studies on CNS survivors, the United States study of Gerhardt et al. [56] found no differences in (temporary) employment between 18-year old survivors (79%) and their classmates (67%). However, these survivors were much younger than in other studies and were still in school. This study found no differences in hours worked per week (12 hours), ever being fired (14% versus 15% survivors) or in job performance. Nonetheless, there was a trend for fewer survivors to report plans for work after high school (76%) compared to comparison peers (88%). In a study of the Norwegian Cancer registry of Johannesen et al. the authors did find a considerable effect of surviving childhood CNS tumors on employability. More than a third of the 548 CNS survivors (36%) were not working, versus 4% of the population. Twenty percent of the CNS survivors received a disability pension. In comparison, only 4% of the 596 survivors treated for hematological malignancies received a disability pension and just 6% of them were not working [57]. Finally, 32 long-term survivors of pediatric sarcomas in the study of Gerber et al. [58] in the United States reported that health affected their career. Sixty-five percent of them said that their tumor had a negative impact on their vocational plans.

We conclude that in the studies on employment of young survivors of childhood cancer published since our meta-analysis of 2006, the pattern we described of employment and work ability is confirmed. Similar rates of unemployment were found and the survivors of CNS tumors were, on average, again found to be the patients with a very high risk of unemployment.

The Effect of Prognostic Factors on Employment

The results we described above indicate that there is a group of patients who experience difficulties with work in spite of the general positive findings. Successful transition to employment was seen to be influenced by diagnosis and country. The effects of some other demographic, illness- and treatment related factors predictive of employment have also been explored and thus groups at risk for problems with employment can be identified. Six studies analyzed the effect of demographic, illness- and treatment related factors on later employment and unemployment. The prognostic factors are summarized in Table 8.1.

Over the years (in 1991, 2003 and 2008), young men were consistently found to be more often employed than young female survivors [22, 44, 52]. Younger survivors were more likely to be unemployed [22, 52] which is explicable because

Table 8.1 Prognostic factors for employment of adult survivors of childhood cancer

Factor	Effect (n studies)
Demographic	
Male	Positive (3)
Younger age	Negative (2)
Younger age at diagnosis	Negative (2)
Disease-related	
Radiotherapy	Negative (2)
Limited physical performance	Negative (1)
Motor impairment	Negative (1)
Epilepsy	Negative (1)
Less cognitive control	Negative (1)
Diminished emotional health	Negative (1)
Person-related	
High school or college	Positive (1)
Lower IQ	Negative (1)

younger survivors are still studying. Younger age at diagnosis was related to never being employed [12, 52].

The cancer treatment can also have a considerable effect on later employment. Survivors who ever received radiotherapy [44] or were ever treated with cranial radiotherapy > 30 Gy [52] were four times more likely to be never employed. In addition, adult survivors with problems with executive function such as cognitive control and behavioral regulation, and with diminished emotional health such as depressive symptoms, somatization and anxiety, were also less likely to be employed [10]. Employment was associated inversely with motor impairment and epilepsy [11] and patients with limited physical performance and activity levels [10] were found to be unemployed more often.

Finally, young survivors who had graduated from high school or college [44] were more likely to have been employed in the past year and more likely to ever have a job. Lower IQ [11] on the other hand, was associated with higher unemployment rates.

Educational Outcomes Among Survivors of Childhood Cancer and the Impact on Work

Educational achievements do effect the transition into adult employment in young adult survivors of childhood cancer. However, achieving a successful school career is not always straightforward for adolescent cancer patients. It is not surprising that research has found that some groups of survivors of childhood cancer may not complete their education or are placed in special education programs, given the significant risk for cognitive and functional deficits after treatment. For instance, Mitby et al. [59] analyzed the educational achievements of 12,430 survivors of childhood cancer and 3,410 full siblings. They concluded that survivors of leukemia, CNS tumors, non-Hodgkin lymphoma, and neuroblastoma were significantly less likely to finish high school compared with siblings; however, when survivors received special education services, the chances to finish high school were close to those of the sibling population. The use of special education services was reported in 23% of survivors and 8% of siblings, which is comparable to the 20% vs. 8% found in the Canadian study of Barrera et al. [60]. Intrathecal methotrexate and cranial radiation, administered alone or in combination, significantly increased the likelihood that a survivor would use special education [59] or to experience educational difficulties [60]. Hence, young survivors of CNS tumors such as medulloblastoma continue to experience academic failure and significant learning delays despite steps to reduce radiation dose exposure [61, 62].

Furthermore, young survivors of childhood cancer often miss school for a considerable amount of time due to long treatment and follow-up appointments in the clinic. These circumstances could result in poorer educational results such as grade retention [60] in spite of the use of special education services. However, findings do indicate that survivors may experience delays during their school years but these difficulties do not always necessarily affect their ultimate level of educational or occupational achievement. The purpose of the study of Gerhardt [56] was to examine educational and occupational outcomes among survivors of childhood cancer and peers during the transition from adolescence to emerging adulthood. Families were recruited when children with cancer were 8–15 years old and receiving initial treatment for a malignancy that did not primarily affect the central nervous system. At that time, each child with cancer was matched to a classmate of similar age, gender, and race for inclusion in a comparison group. For the follow-up at 7 years post-diagnosis, 56 survivors, 60 peers, and their parents completed questionnaires soon after the youths' 18th birthday. Survivors were more likely to report repeating a grade and having more school absences. However, the proportion of participants who graduated from high school, were (temporary) working, and expressed plans to attend postsecondary education or seek employment were similar between groups. Initial treatment intensity, time since diagnosis, and severity of late effects were associated with several indices of educational and occupational attainment [56]. Young leukemia patients in a Dutch study showed lower educational level of secondary education than their siblings [63]. In another Dutch study on survivors of leukemia, solid tumors and brain/CNS tumors, no overall differences in educational level (low, high) were found, compared to their age and sex-matched controls. Yet again, survivors of brain/CNS tumors did have a significantly lower educational level [49]. In a Finnish study on the scholastic achievements of 16-year old childhood leukemia patients, the information on their ninth-grade school report was obtained from Statistics Finland and compared to five matched controls. The patients whose treatment included cranial irradiation had a lower overall mark average and lower marks for all assessed school subjects compared with their controls. Of the patients treated with chemotherapy alone, only the females with leukemia diagnosed before 7 years of age had lower school marks than their controls [64].

However, educational difficulties do not necessarily occur. In a Swedish Study on young adult survivors of mainly lymphoma and leukemia, no differences were found between the survivors and their age- and sex-matched controls [28]. With respect to number of school years, total length of education, higher education, and vocational education the two groups did not differ.

As the data show, many survivors are capable to compensate for the difficulties, which is also an encouraging finding. For health policy reasons and future research it is important to analyze which subgroups of survivors may be at greater risk for difficulties than others and therefore require a greater level of support or services. On the basis of the literature, it can be concluded that survivors of brain or CNS tumors and/or patients who received cranial irradiation are at risk of educational difficulties and could need extra support.

Interventions to Improve Employment

Unfortunately, no interventions specifically aimed at improving employment or work participation in young survivors of childhood cancer have been developed and evaluated so far. Some attention was given to the problems the survivors might have with their careers in an "adventure therapeutic activity" in which young adult cancer survivors participate in a jeep trip safari in Israel [65]. Because the survivors' main areas of concern included occupation, after the trip, a group activity was organized involving private businesses and job placement organizations. Furthermore, to raise the level of awareness of potential employers to the needs of young adult cancer survivors, a list of recommendations was sent to more than 1,500 managers of various organizations.

In a similar program in the United States, young survivors went to a 4-day retreat designed to provide an educational and support experience. The camp took place at a buffalo ranch in the United States and results showed that participants discussed several areas of concern among each other including social exclusion and career options [66]. Another possible support for survivors could be information. In Britain, an information booklet was developed for adult survivors of cancer in childhood which included information about employment [67]. The leaflet was given to 50 attendees of a long-term follow-up clinic and they were interviewed about the leaflet afterwards. Many patients (41%) were interested in the information about jobs given in the leaflet. Half of the patients thought the illness could have a negative effect on their future and they were especially concerned about limited job opportunities. The results suggested that written information is likely to be an acceptable and effective supplement to discussions with medical professionals. The effects of these interventions on employment were not evaluated.

New research preferably could include new intervention studies. Right now there are already new initiatives for programs to help adult survivors of childhood cancer obtain a job. Young survivors often do not have the experience of small temporary jobs during their adolescence. Their healthy peers usually work temporarily in minor jobs and thus gain experience in the everyday demands of employment. In order to help young patients, the Emma's Children's Hospital of the Academic Medical Center (AMC) in Amsterdam founded a special agency for temporary jobs for chronically ill children. This initiative has not been (scientifically) evaluated yet, but for 27 of the 57 adolescents and young adults who applied in 2007, a temporary job was found.

Other hospitals have special survivorship programs for young survivors, and some of these include employment issues. The Hayashi's Late Effects Program at St. Louis Children's Hospital and The Washington University School of Medicine teaches young survivors to admit to their disabilities and develop techniques to get around them as best they can. They are taught not to hide their disabilities from potential employers or admitting to problems but not explaining why they have them. This Late Effects Program was established to provide comprehensive care for patients experiencing medical, emotional and quality of life difficulties as a consequence of their cancer therapy [68]. The Texas Children's Cancer Center in Houston, USA offers a website on long-term effects of childhood cancer treatment. It also gives information and tips about employment [69].

Future Research

Given the potential occurrence of late educational and vocational effects in adult survivors of childhood cancer there is an urgent need for intervention programs which focus on these problems. Recent research suggests that vocational services have been associated with positive vocational outcomes in adults [70] and similar approaches should be investigated in young adults. Especially young survivors of CNS or brain tumors, those who received cranial irradiation, female survivors, those with motor impairment, epilepsy or cognitive problems, could benefit from additional assistance. Furthermore, attention should be given to the development and validation of outcome measures. Finally, the identification of prognostic factors and studies describing the viewpoint of young survivors require future research.

What Interventions Could We Develop?

The WHO model of functioning, disability and health can serve as a theoretical framework from which interventions to improve the employment and

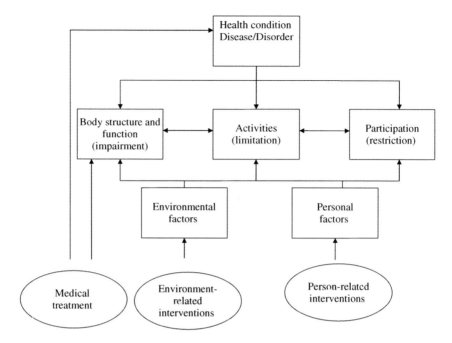

Fig. 8.7 The International classification of functioning, disability and health of the WHO and points of intervention

functioning at work can be developed. Figure 8.7 depicts the International Classification of Functioning, Disability and Health of the WHO, a model illustrating elements that impact function and interventions [71].

In the model, employment is one of the roles in which one can participate in society. Patients can be restricted in their participation, such as working, due to their limitations in performing certain activities. The ability to perform activities is strongly influenced by impairments of body structure and functioning of the body. As is seen in the figure, diseases or disorders affect the body function as well as activities and participation, possibly leading to disability, work disability and unemployment. Environmental and personal factors essentially condition this process of disease, impairment, limitation in activities and participation in society.

Three types of possible interventions can be devised from the WHO model: medical treatment, environment-related interventions and person-related interventions. For each category, several interventions could be developed, as is shown in Table 8.2.

The first category relates to development of better medical treatments. With successful treatment, the disease and its consequences will disappear. For example, a change in the treatment of childhood leukemia into a therapy without cranial radiation in the 1970s and 1980s greatly influenced its related disability [72].

8 Young Survivors of Childhood Cancer 179

Table 8.2 Future research: possible interventions to improve the workability and employability in young survivors of childhood cancer

Medical treatment	Environment-related interventions	Person-related interventions
Interventions to: – prevent late or long term effects of cancer treatment on function – treat late and long term effects – maintain optimal overall health condition necessary to work – improve functional capacities	Interventions to: – adapt working environment – include work issues in cancer surveillance – improve communication between physicians – optimize implementation of anti-discrimination laws	Interventions to: – selectively offer special education – improve work experience by providing temporary jobs – alter misconceptions regarding work – enhance adolescent employment readiness

The second type is environment-related interventions, which are aimed at factors within the workplace. First of all, it is important to develop interventions which adapt the working environment. If the working environment of young adults who survived childhood cancer can be adapted to their impairments and limitations, it could make the difference between a young disability retirement for forty years or living an everyday working life. In ergonomics, the concept of adapting the environment to workers has always been important and this has been a strong incentive for occupational physicians to promote workplace adaptations to prevent restrictions in participation. Workplace adaptations also include an adjusted workplace, adjusted working hours, and flexible working times. A recent study of Bouknight et al. showed that a high percentage of employed breast cancer patients returned to work after treatment, and workplace accommodations played an important role in their return [73]. Therefore, interventions should be developed to enable young cancer survivors to succeed in appropriate employment. However, many young adults who start their first job do not have an occupational physician who can help them with necessary adaptations. Neither do they have an employer who will provide these adjustments to them. Therefore, alternative routes to provide these young people with a workplace which is adapted to their needs should be sought. One of the possibilities would be to get these adaptations organized through the hospital where the young survivors were treated.

In recent years, special surveillance programs for children who have survived cancer, have been organized and executed in children's hospitals [74]. The principal goal of these long-term follow-up of survivors is to decrease the severity of late treatment complications by performing appropriate surveillance to detect incipient toxicity, and by facilitating timely diagnosis and management of emerging or established late effects. Moreover, long-term follow-up allows provision of survivor education, psychosocial support and health promotion advice. There is an increasing utilization of multidisciplinary teams, and recognition of the importance of effective transition strategies. Interventions to include work issues in these surveillance programs could help young survivors of childhood cancer to increase their employability. Up till now, workplace interventions were beyond the scope of clinicians and nurses. Making the young adult aware of work issues and helping him or her to find a job in which workplace adjustments, including flexible working times and physical adjustments could be part of a long-term follow program.

When young survivors do have a job but have difficulties maintaining it because of established or emerging late effects, general practitioners, occupational physicians or employee assistance programs could help with workplace adjustments and social support. Yet, many general practitioners, occupational physicians or employee assistants do not have the specialist knowledge of late effects of childhood cancer and they should therefore be more encouraged to contact the pediatrician or oncologist for information. Clinicians on the other hand, should provide occupational physicians with medical information more often in order to provide better care [75].

Finally, we have seen that it matters in which country the young survivors live and therefore national laws might have an impact on the employability of young survivors of childhood cancer. In the study of Bouknight et al. on breast cancer patients it was shown that perceived employer discrimination because of cancer was negatively associated with return to work [73]. Better anti-discrimination laws in combination with a national campaign and a serious and thorough reconsideration of the arrangements in the health insurance system linked to employment status may improve the employment conditions of many young cancer survivors.

Third, person-related factors can be the focus of an intervention. Although most long-term survivors of childhood cancer will complete high school successfully and many will go on to college and university, some survivors will have significant difficulty doing so [59]. By identifying the individuals most at risk for problems with school performance, clinicians and educators will be able to foresee potential problems better and can choose to initiate special education services early on in these children's education. Several long-term follow-up clinics have created models for the interaction between physicians, nurses, and school staff members to better serve the increasing population of cancer patients and survivors at risk for cognitive impairment. An intervention in which survivors at risk are selected and offered a special education program has not yet been evaluated with regard to work-related outcomes.

Many young cancer survivors do not have the experience of small temporary jobs during their adolescence. Their healthy peers frequently work in part time jobs and thus gain experience and skills in the everyday demands of employment. An intervention offering temporary jobs to young survivors of childhood cancer could help them in acquiring work experience which is vital for a successful career. Such an intervention could be part of the long-term follow-up programs already offered to survivors in many clinics.

From our research we know that among adult cancer survivors the severity of the disease in terms of diagnosis and treatment has a large influence on the time needed to return to work. Moreover, we have found that self-assessed work ability is an important factor in the return to work process of adult cancer patients as well and that it predicts future return to work independent of age and clinical factors [76]. Our results are congruent with Leventhal's "model of illness representations" [77]. It states that people's cognitive representations of illness play an important role in influencing their strategies for coping which in turn influence illness outcome. Based on this model the functional outcome might be worse or better, relatively independent of the objective medical seriousness of the illness. The most important features of the illness representation are the cause (biological versus functional), the timeline (long versus short), and the consequences for functioning. If the illness representations are deviant from current realistic medical knowledge, they can also be called misconceptions. Earlier research showed that if these misconceptions of the illness could be changed by a cognitive behavioral intervention, the return to work rate was twice as fast [78]. This could be a promising approach for young survivors of childhood cancer. It is very understandable that many young survivors have been protected by their environment because of their life-threatening disease. However comprehensible, this might have given misconceptions about the possibilities of employment and career, work ability and job prospects of these youngsters. Misconceptions might be interrelated with avoiding or passive behavior toward education and jobs. An intervention on changing these "illness representations" and behavior, with regard to education and employment, might help young survivors in obtaining an ordinary career.

Finally, vocational counseling programs have been successfully developed for adults with congenital heart disease [79] and with juvenile arthritis [80]. The program for heart disease patients included initial work skills training, development of personal and social skills, preparation for individual career decisions, and job finding skills and job placement [79]. The program for adolescents with juvenile arthritis was organized from a special adolescent employment readiness center in the Children's National Medical Center in Washington. In a prevocational team including the referring physician, vocational rehabilitation counselor, job placement coordinator, physical and occupational therapist and education coordinator, services were offered such as career counseling, work life orientation programs and assistance in summer job placement. They also used a job category oriented screening tool to assist the adolescent in identifying their physical strengths and weaknesses as they relate to work activities [80]. Such an adolescent employment readiness program could also greatly benefit the young survivors of childhood cancer in their careers.

What Outcomes Are Important?

In future research on employment of adult survivors of childhood cancer, two types of outcomes are important: employment and functioning at work. Table 8.3 gives an overview of both types of outcomes.

Table 8.3 Future research: possible outcomes of employment and functioning at work

Employment	Functioning at work
– employment rate	– functioning at work
– job retention	– work ability
– disability pension	– job appropriate for education level
– sickness absence	– job experience
– full-time / part-time	– attitude towards work

The rate of employment should be the main outcome measure. Since we found in our meta-analysis that young survivors of childhood cancer are more likely to be unemployed than healthy controls and this result was confirmed in later and larger studies, we argue that trying to narrow this gap should be the first target of interventions. A second outcome could be to decrease the number of cancer survivors that stop working and/or enter disability pension programs because of disease-related problems. Differences in sickness absence between survivors of childhood cancer and healthy controls do also prevail and thus they should also be an outcome measure in intervention research. Finally, cancer survivors sometimes adjust their working hours because of their illness history and therefore an important outcome should be working full-time or part-time or number of hours worked per week.

Furthermore, it is essential to assess if young survivors are functioning well at work, because it is important to assess how well young survivors of childhood cancer are actually doing at work. The first outcome could be functioning at work which includes good functioning and performance, accuracy, good social contacts, cooperation, good-quality future perspectives, ongoing education and working with competence and pleasure. No reliable and validated instrument of work functioning in cancer patients exists and it should be developed in future research. Another outcome could be work ability: how does the worker judge his or her working capacities? Again, no cancer-specific work ability measurement has been developed so far and this could be the focus of future research as well. In addition, the job that young survivors are holding should be corresponding to the educational level they have achieved so this should be an outcome in forthcoming projects.

Do the interventions we offer improve work functioning, work ability, job experience, and attitude toward work ? These are issues that should be addressed in future research and practice of young cancer survivors.

Other Issues in Future Research

Apart from the development and evaluation of new interventions and the development of new outcome measurements, knowledge on prognostic factors and knowledge on the viewpoint of adult survivors of child cancer themselves should be improved. For survivors of adult-onset cancer, two reviews of factors affecting cancer survivors' employment and work ability have been written, resulting in dozens of predictors [81, 82]. However, we only found a few predictors of employment for young survivors for childhood cancer. More research should be performed on prognostic factors because these factors can be used for selection of young survivors at risk for unemployment and for the development of new interventions. Finally, no research so far has focused on the viewpoint of young cancer survivors themselves with regard to work. For adult survivors several qualitative studies have been published which included focus groups [83–86]. Many aspects of employment and the return-to-work process were discussed in these groups and the problems the patients encountered were evaluated extensively. Future qualitative research on work-related issues from the viewpoint of the young survivors themselves could help develop interventions for their benefit with elements they find important.

Conclusion

Recent advances in new and successful treatments the consequences of receiving a diagnosis of cancer in childhood have dramatically changed. The overall five-year survival is now 72–80% for all pediatric malignancies.

Many survivors are doing well in general terms, although the majority of survivors have at least one chronic disease or adverse health condition. These long-term medical and psychological effects of childhood cancer or its treatment may cause impairments, misconceptions or inadequate behavior that diminish social functioning such as school attendance, social activities and obtaining employment. It can be especially difficult for young survivors of childhood cancer to obtain a job, given the possible late physical effects of childhood cancer such as orthopedic, neurologic, cardiovascular, and cognitive problems.

We found in our meta-analysis of 24 controlled studies that survivors of childhood cancers are almost twice as likely to be unemployed in later life as healthy controls. Survivors in the USA had an overall threefold risk of being unemployed, whereas no such risk was found for survivors in European countries. We found that survivors of CNS and brain tumors were almost five times more likely to be unemployed, while the risks for survivors of blood or bone cancers were somewhat elevated. These findings are consistent over time and have been confirmed in recent research. Apart from type of diagnosis and country (USA versus Europe), we found that predictors of unemployment were younger age, lower education or IQ, female gender, motor impairment or epilepsy and (cranial) radiotherapy.

Educational achievements can effect the transition into adult employment in young adult survivors of childhood cancer. The literature showed that many survivors are capable of compensating for the difficulties, which is also a very encouraging finding. For health policy reasons and future research it is important to analyze which subgroups of survivors may be at greater risk for difficulties than others. We concluded that survivors of brain/CNS tumors and patients who received cranial irradiation are at risk of educational difficulties and could need extra support. Unfortunately, no interventions specifically aimed at gaining employment for survivors of childhood cancer have been developed or evaluated as yet.

Future research on employment in adult survivors of childhood cancer should focus on the development and evaluation of new interventions. We think that new interventions should be multifaceted. They may focus on work-place adjustments and actions against discrimination where and when this exists, but also on education, stimulating work experience and attention to inadequate illness perceptions and behavior. Environment-related interventions should focus on interventions to adapt the working environment, include work issues in surveillance, improved communication between physicians and effective implementation of anti-discrimination laws. Person-related interventions should encompass interventions to selectively offer special education, improve work experience by providing temporary jobs, alter misconceptions regarding work and enhance adolescent work readiness. These interventions should support the employability and functioning at work of young cancer survivors.

Furthermore, attention should be given to the development and validation of outcome measures such as functioning at work and workability. More research should be performed on prognostic factors because these factors can be used for selection of young survivors at risk for unemployment and for the development of new interventions.

Finally, future qualitative research on work-related issues from the viewpoint of the young survivors themselves could help develop interventions for their benefit with elements they find important. We feel that in this way the needs of the survivors are best met, keeping in mind that with a successful transition from school to the adult working life an entire working life is saved. Given the success in keeping these children alive to be young adults, we can surely figure out how to help them create meaningful, age appropriate adaptations such as a meaningful career or work experience.

References

1. Pritchard-Jones K, Kaatsch P, Steliarova-Foucher E, Stiller CA, Coebergh JW. Cancer in children and adolescents in Europe: developments over 20 years and future challenges. Eur J Cancer. 2006; 42(13):2183–90.
2. UK stat: http://info.cancerresearchuk.org/cancerstats/childhoodcancer/survival/?a=5441 Accessed at 4th March 2008.
3. Ries LAG, Melbert D, Krapcho M, Mariotto A, Miller BA, Feuer EJ, et al. (eds.) SEER Cancer Statistics Review, 1975–2004, National Cancer Institute. Bethesda, MD: http://seer.cancer.gov/csr/1975_2004/, based on November 2006 SEER data submission, posted to the SEER web site, 2007. Accessed at 4th March 2008.

4. Robison LL, Hudson MM. Medical surveillance of long-term survivors of childhood cancer. Eur J Cancer. 2007; 43:2629–30.
5. Oeffinger KC, Mertens AC, Sklar CA, Kawashima T, Hudson MM, Meadows AT, et al. Childhood Cancer Survivor Study. Chronic health conditions in adult survivors of childhood cancer. N Engl J Med. 2006; 355:1572–82.
6. Geenen MM, Cardous-Ubbink MC, Kremer LC, van den Bos C, van der Pal HJ, Heinen RC, et al. Medical assessment of adverse health outcomes in long-term survivors of childhood cancer. JAMA. 2007; 297:2705–15.
7. Eiser C, Hill JJ, Vance YH. Examining the psychological consequences of surviving childhood cancer: systematic review as a research method in pediatric psychology. J Pediatr Psychol. 2000; 25:449–60.
8. Langeveld NE, Stam H, Grootenhuis MA, Last BF. Quality of life in young adult survivors of childhood cancer. Support Care Cancer. 2002; 10:579–600.
9. Stam H, Grootenhuis MA, Last BF. The course of life of survivors of childhood cancer. Psycho-oncology. 2005; 14:227–238.
10. Ness KK, Mertens AC, Hudson MM, et al. Limitations on physical performance and daily activities among long-term survivors of childhood cancer. Ann Inter Med. 2005; 143:639–47.
11. Macedoni-Luksic M, Jereb B, Todorovski L. Long-term sequelae in children treated for brain tumors: impairment, disability and handicap. Ped Hematol Oncol. 2003; 20:89–101.
12. Hays DM. Adult survivors of childhood cancer. Employment and insurance issues in different age groups. Cancer. 1993; 71(10 Suppl):3306–9.
13. Henrichs MH. Principles of psychosocial oncology. In: Rubin P (ed). Clinical Oncology. Philadelphia: WB Saunders, 1993.
14. Badell I, Igual L, Gomez P, Bureo E, Ortega JJ, Cubells J, et al. Quality of life in young adults having received a BMT during childhood: a GETMON study. Bone Marrow Transplant. 1998; 21 (Suppl 2):S68–71.
15. Seitzman RL, Glover DA, Meadows AT, Mills JL, Nicholson HS, Robison LL, et al. Self-concept in adult survivors of childhood acute lymphoblastic leukemia: a cooperative Children's Cancer Group and National Institutes of Health study. Pediatr Blood Cancer. 2004; 42:230–240.
16. Verbeek J, Spelten E. Work. In: Feuerstein, M. (ed). Handbook of cancer survivorship. Berkely: Springer, 2007.
17. Tebbi CK, Bromberg C, Piedmonte M. Long-term vocational adjustment of cancer patients diagnosed during adolescence. Cancer. 1989; 63:213–8.
18. Feldman, FR. Work and cancer health histories: work expectations and experiences of youth with cancer histories (ages 13–23). Oakland, CA: California Division, American Cancer Society, 1980.
19. Koocher GP. Surviving childhood cancer: issues in living. In: Spinetta JJ, Deasy-Spinetta P, (eds). Living with childhood cancer. St. Louis: CBV Mosby, 1981; 171–83.
20. de Boer AG, Verbeek JH, van Dijk FJ. Adult survivors of childhood cancer and unemployment: A meta-analysis. Cancer. 2006; 107:1–11.
21. Evans SE, Radford M. Current lifestyle of young adults treated for cancer in childhood. Arch Dis Child. 1995; 72:423–6.
22. Green DM, Zevon MA, Hall B. Achievement of life goals by adult survivors of modern treatment for childhood cancer. Cancer. 1991; 67:206–13.
23. Hays DM, Landsverk J, Sallan SE, Hewett KD, Patenaude AF, Schoonover D, et al. Educational, occupational, and insurance status of childhood cancer survivors in their fourth and fifth decades of life. J Clin Oncol. 1992; 10:1397–1406.
24. Zevon MA, Neubauer NA, Green DM. Adjustment and vocational satisfaction of patients treated during childhood or adolescence for acute lymphoblastic leukemia. Am J Pediatr Hematol Oncol. 1990; 12:454–61.
25. Wasserman AL, Thompson EI, Wilimas JA, Fairclough DL. The psychological status of survivors of childhood/adolescent Hodgkin's disease. Am J Dis Child. 1987; 141:626–31.

26. Teta MJ, Del Po MC, Kasl SV, Meigs JW, Myers MH, Mulvihill JJ. Psychosocial consequences of childhood and adolescent cancer survival. J Chronic Dis. 1986; 39:751–9.
27. Feuerstein M, Luff GM, Harrington CB, Olsen CH. Pattern of workplace disputes in cancer survivors: a population study of ADA claims. J Cancer Surv. 2007; 1:185–192.
28. Boman KK, Bodegard G. Life after cancer in childhood: social adjustment and educational and vocational status of young-adult survivors. J Pediatr Hematol Oncol. 2004; 26:354–362.
29. Dolgin MJ, Somer E, Buchvald E, Zaizov R. Quality of life in adult survivors of childhood cancer. Soc Work Health Care. 1999; 28:31–43.
30. Mackie E, Hill J, Kondryn H, McNally R. Adult psychosocial outcomes in long-term survivors of acute lymphoblastic leukaemia and Wilms'tumor: a controlled study. Lancet. 2000; 355:1310–4.
31. Moe PJ, Holen A, Glomstein A, Madsen B, Hellebostad M, Stokland T, et al. Long-term survival and quality of life in patients treated with a national all protocol 15–20 years earlier: IDM/HDM and late effects? Pediatr Hematol Oncol. 1997; 14:513–24.
32. Pastore G, Mosso ML, Magnani C, Luzzatto L, Bianchi M, Terracini B. Physical impairment and social life goals among adult long-term survivors of childhood cancer: a population-based study from the childhood cancer registry of Piedmont, Italy. Tumori. 2001; 87:372–8.
33. Pui CH, Cheng C, Leung W, Rai SN, Rivera GK, Sandlund JT, et al. Extended follow-up of long-term survivors of childhood acute lymphoblastic leukemia. N Engl J Med. 2003; 349:640–9.
34. Zeltzer LK, Chen E, Weiss R, Guo MD, Robison LL, Meadows AT, et al. Comparison of psychologic outcome in adult survivors of childhood acute lymphoblastic leukemia versus sibling controls: a cooperative Children's Cancer Group and National Institutes of Health study. J Clin Oncol. 1997; 15:547–56.
35. Felder-Puig R, Peters C, Matthes-Martin S, Lamche M, Felsberger C, Gadner H, et al. Psychosocial adjustment of pediatric patients after allogeneic stem cell transplantation. Bone Marrow Transplant. 1999; 24:75–80.
36. Haddy TB, Adde MA, Magrath IT. Health lifestyles, risk-taking behavior and attitudes of long-term survivors of non-Hodgkin's lymphoma. Int J Ped Hematol/Oncol. 2001; 7:57–70.
37. Fischer EG, Welch K, Shillito J, Winston KR, Tarbell NJ. Craniopharyngiomas in children. J Neurosurg. 1990; 73:534–40.
38. Jenkin D, Danjoux C, Greenberg M. Subsequent quality of life for children irradiated for a brain tumor before age four years. Med Pediatr Oncol. 1998; 31:506–11.
39. Kiltie AE, Lashford LS, Gattamaneni HR. Survival and late effects in medulloblastoma patients treated with craniospinal irradiation under three years old. Med Pediatr Oncol. 1997; 28:348–54.
40. Lannering B, Marky I, Lundberg A, Olsson E. Long-term sequelae after pediatric brain tumors: their effect on disability and quality of life. Med Pediatr Oncol. 1990; 18: 304–10.
41. Maddrey AM, Bergeron JA, Lombardo ER, McDonald NK, Mulne AF, Barenberg PD, et al.. Neuropsychological performance and quality of life of 10 year survivors of childhood medulloblastoma. J Neuro-Oncol. 2005; 72:245–53.
42. Mostow EN, Byrne J, Connelly RR, Mulvihill JJ. Quality of life in long-term survivors of CNS tumors of childhood and adolescence. J Clin Oncol. 1991; 9:592–9.
43. Sutton LN, Radcliffe J, Goldwein JW, Phillips P, Janss AJ, Packer RJ, et al. Quality of life of adult survivors of germinomas treated with craniospinal irradiation. Neurosurgery. 1999; 45:1292–7.
44. Nagarajan R, Neglia JP, Clohisy DR, Yasui Y, Greenberg M, Hudson M, et al. Education, employment, insurance, and marital status among 694 survivors of pediatric lower extremity bone tumors: a report from the childhood cancer survivor study. Cancer. 2003; 97:2554–64.

45. Novakovic B, Fears TR, Horowitz ME, Tucker MA, Wexler LH. Late effects of therapy in survivors of Ewing's sarcoma family tumors. J Ped Hematol Oncol. 1997; 19:220–5.
46. Nicholson HS, Mulvihill JJ, Byrne J. Late effects of therapy in adult survivors of osteosarcoma and Ewing's sarcoma. Med Pediatr Oncol. 1992; 20:6–12.
47. Eiser C, Cool P, Grimer RJ, Carter SR, Cotter IM, Ellis AJ, et al. Quality of life in children following treatment for a malignant primary bone tumor around the knee. Sarcoma. 1997; 1:39–45.
48. Felder-Puig R, Formann AK, Mildner A, Bretschneider W, Bucher B, Windhager R, et al. Quality of life and psychosocial adjustment of young patients after treatment of bone cancer. Cancer. 1998; 83:69–75.
49. Langeveld NE, Ubbink MC, Last BF, Grootenhuis MA, Voute PA, de Haan RJ. Educational achievement, employment and living situation in long-term young adult survivors of childhood cancer in the Netherlands. Psycho-oncology. 2003; 12:213–25.
50. Byrne J, Fears TR, Whitney C, Parry DM. Survival after retinoblastoma: long-term consequences and family history of cancer. Med Pediatr Oncol. 1995; 24:160–5.
51. Meadows AT, McKee L, Kazak AE. Psychosocial status of young adult survivors of childhood cancer: a survey. Med Pediatr Oncol. 1989; 17:466–70.
52. Pang JW, Friedman DL, Whitton JA, Stovall M, Mertens AC, Robison LL, et al. Employment status among adult survivors in the Childhood Cancer Survivor Study. Pediatr Blood Cancer. 2008; 50:104–10.
53. Punyko JA, Gurney JG, Scott Baker K, Hayashi RJ, Hudson MM, Liu Y, et al. Physical impairment and social adaptation in adult survivors of childhood and adolescent rhabdomyosarcoma: a report from the Childhood Cancer Survivors Study. Psychooncology. 2007; 16:26–37.
54. Crom DB, Lensing SY, Rai SN, Snider MA, Cash DK, Hudson MM. Marriage, employment, and health insurance in adult survivors of childhood cancer. J Cancer Surviv. 2007; 1:237–45.
55. Servitzoglou M, Papadatou D, Tsiantis I, Vasilatou-Kosmidis H. Psychosocial functioning of young adolescent and adult survivors of childhood cancer. Support Care Cancer. 2008; 16:29–36.
56. Gerhardt CA, Dixon M, Miller K, Vannatta K, Valerius KS, Correll J, et al. Educational and occupational outcomes among survivors of childhood cancer during the transition to emerging adulthood. J Dev Behav Pediatr. 2007; 28:448–55.
57. Johannesen TB, Langmark F, Wesenberg F, Lote K. Prevalence of Norwegian patients diagnosed with childhood cancer, their working ability and need of health insurance benefits. Acta Oncol. 2007; 46:60–6.
58. Gerber LH, Hoffman K, Chaudhry U, Augustine E, Parks R, Bernad M, et al. Functional outcomes and life satisfaction in long-term survivors of pediatric sarcomas. Arch Phys Med Rehabil. 2006; 87:1611–7.
59. Mitby PA, Robison LL, Whitton JA, Zevon MA, Gibbs IC, Tersak JM, et al. Childhood Cancer Survivor Study Steering Committee. Utilization of special education services and educational attainment among long-term survivors of childhood cancer: a report from the Childhood Cancer Survivor Study. Cancer. 2003; 97:1115–26.
60. Barrera M, Shaw AK, Speechley KN, Maunsell E, Pogany L. Educational and social late effects of childhood cancer and related clinical, personal, and familial characteristics. Cancer. 2005; 104:1751–60.
61. Palmer SL, Reddick WE, Gajjar A. Understanding the cognitive impact on children who are treated for medulloblastoma. J Pediatr Psychol. 2007; 32:1040–9.
62. Upton P, Eiser C. School experiences after treatment for a brain tumor. Child Care Health Dev. 2006; 32:9–17.
63. Kingma A, Rammeloo LA, van Der Does-van den Berg A, Rekers-Mombarg L, Postma A. Academic career after treatment for acute lymphoblastic leukaemia. Arch Dis Child. 2000; 82:353–7.

64. Harila-Saari AH, Lähteenmäki PM, Pukkala E, Kyyrönen P, Lanning M, Sankila R. Scholastic achievements of childhood leukemia patients: a nationwide, register-based study. J Clin Oncol. 2007; 25:3518–24.
65. Elad P, Yagil Y, Cohen L, Meller I. A jeep trip with young adult cancer survivors: lessons to be learned. Support Care Cancer. 2003; 11:201–6.
66. Zebrack BJ, Oeffinger KC, Hou P, Kaplan S. Advocacy skills training for young adult cancer survivors: the Young Adult Survivors Conference at Camp Māk-a-Dream. Support Care Cancer. 2006; 14:779–82.
67. Blacklay A, Eiser C, Ellis A. Development and evaluation of an information booklet for adult survivors of cancer in childhood. The United Kingdom Children's Cancer Study Group Late Effects Group. Arch Dis Child. 1998; 78:340–4.
68. St. Louis Late Effects Program. http://www.stlouischildrens.org/tabid/211/itemid/4221/Late-Effects-Program.aspx. Accessed at April 1st 2008.
69. Texas Children's Center. http://www.cancersurvivorchild.org/frame_dyn.html?future/index.html. Accessed at April 1, 2008.
70. Chan, F, Strauser, D, Cardoso, EdS, Zheng, LX, Chan, JYC, Feuerstein, M. State vocational services and employment in cancer survivors. J Cancer Surviv. 2008; 2:169–78.
71. WHO. International Classification of Functioning, Disability and Health. Geneva: WHO; 2001.
72. Cole PD, Kamen BA. Delayed neurotoxicity associated with therapy for children with acute lymphoblastic leukemia. Ment Retard Dev Disabil Res Rev. 2006; 12:174–83.
73. Bouknight RR, Bradley CJ, Luo Z. Correlates of return to work for breast cancer survivors. J Clin Oncol. 2006; 24:345–53.
74. Skinner R, Wallace WH, Levitt G. Long-term follow-up of children treated for cancer: why is it necessary, by whom, where and how? Arch Dis Child. 2007; 92:257–60.
75. Verbeek J, Spelten E, Kammeijer M, Sprangers M. Return to work of cancer survivors: a prospective cohort study into the quality of rehabilitation by occupational physicians. Occup Environ Med. 2003; 60:352–7.
76. de Boer AG, Verbeek JH, Spelten ER, Uitterhoeve AL, Ansink AC, de Reijke TM, et al. Work ability and return-to-work in cancer patients. Br J Cancer. 2008; 98:1342–7.
77. Leventhal H, Nerenz DR, Steele, DJ. Illness representations and coping with health threats. In: Baum A, Taylor SE, Singer JE (eds). Handbook of psychology and health, Erlbaum: London, 1984.
78. Petrie KJ, Cameron LD, Ellis CJ, Buick D, Weinman J. Changing illness perceptions after myocardial infarction: an early intervention randomized controlled trial. Psychosom Med. 2002; 64:580–6.
79. McGrath KA, Truesdell SC. Employability and career counseling for adolescents and adults with congenital heart disease. Nurs Clin North Am. 1994; 29:319–30.
80. White PH, Shear ES. Transition/job readiness for adolescents with juvenile arthritis and other chronic illness. J Rheumatol Suppl. 1992; 33:23–7.
81. Spelten ER, Sprangers MA, Verbeek JH. Factors reported to influence the return to work of cancer survivors: a literature review. Psychooncology. 2002; 11:124–31.
82. Taskila T, Lindbohm ML. Factors affecting cancer survivors' employment and work ability. Acta Oncol. 2007; 46:446–51.
83. Main D, Nowels C, Cavender T, Etschmaier M, Steiner J. A qualitative study of work and work return in cancer survivors. Psycho-Oncology 2005; 14:992–1004.
84. Nachreiner N, Dagher CR, McGovern P, Baker B, Alexander B, Gerberich S. Succesfull return to work for cancer survivors. Business and Leadership 2007; 55:290–5.
85. Maunsell E, Brisson C, Dubois L, Lauzier S, Frazer A. Work problems after breast cancer: an exploratory qualitative study. Psycho-Oncology 1999; 8:467–3.
86. Kennedy F, Haslam C, Munir F, Pryce J. Returning to work following cancer: a qualitative exploratory study into the experience of returning to work following cancer. Eur J Cancer Care 2007; 16:17–25.

Section IV
Primary and Secondary Prevention

Chapter 9
Primary and Occupational Health Care Providers

Jos Verbeek, Angela de Boer, and Taina Taskila

Introduction

Cancer survivors visit many different physicians and health care professionals. Contacts between cancer survivors and their primary care physicians or their occupational physicians are, however, not self-evident. Usually a patient goes to his or her primary care physician with complaints of first symptoms. Then, either a diagnosis is made in primary care or the patient is referred to a specialist in a hospital where the disease is diagnosed. From that time on, the focus of care is in the hospital with the surgeon, oncologist, and radiotherapist. Outpatient management of elements of this care have evolved as well over the years. Coordinating the care among these specialties is difficult enough, so one may wonder if there is still a role for the primary care physician. For the occupational physician, the case is even more complicated. An occupational physician is not involved in the diagnosis or treatment of the cancer patient. He or she might see the patient before or during treatment, but this is not always commonplace. Therefore, visits to the occupational physician often turn into a routine at the end of the treatment only when return to work becomes important or is questioned. In this chapter we will discuss when and how the primary care and occupational health physician can contribute to the area of work among cancer survivors.

The involvement of primary care physicians is important because they can facilitate return to work and help their patients to overcome barriers for work resumption [1]. Sisler et al. asked 202 cancer survivors about the role of primary care physicians in cancer treatment but problems with work were not mentioned in their questionnaire [2]. In a recent follow-up study on adult survivors of childhood cancer in the Northern Netherlands, the majority (64%) of 358 general practitioners felt it was their responsibility to be in charge of childhood

---

J. Verbeek (✉)
Team leader, Finish Institute of Occupational Health, Center of Good Practices, Knowledge Transfer Team, Cochrane Occupational Health Field, Kuopio, Finland
e-mail: jos.verbeek@ttl.fi

cancer survivors. However, the main requirements for participation in survivor care were the availability of guidelines and sufficient information [3, 4].

In most countries, it is one of the tasks of the occupational health physician to facilitate return to work or to assist in rehabilitation in the sense of helping patients to regain the roles in society that they had before their disease. We will deal with this role of both the primary care physician and the occupational physician in this chapter assuming that they are more or less similar with regard to return to work. However, one substantial difference between the primary care and the occupational physician is that the occupational physician has access to the workplace far more easily. Especially in large employers, the occupational physician should have established contacts with the company in which the cancer survivor is working. Contacting the workplace and arranging workplace accommodations for example should be fairly easy and routine in other illnesses for the occupational physician. Further on we will, for the sake of readability, only refer to the occupational health physician but this includes similar tasks of the primary care physician.

In general, work resumption is self-evident and unproblematic for most patients after they have been cured and they feel well again. Although a classic 'cure' often does not occur, this applies to cancer survivors as well and once they have been treated successfully the majority of them return to work and remain employed. For example, in Finland, the rate of unemployment was only 9% higher among cancer survivors than among comparable healthy controls two to three year after diagnosis [5]. Also, in Canada, a similar difference of 7% higher unemployment of breast cancer survivors was found several years after diagnosis and many of those who were out of work stated that this was their own wish [6].

This means that no assistance from physicians regarding return to work is needed in many cases. There is even some evidence that interference of physicians would increase sick leave because of the necessary administrative procedures involved and the lack of interventions to alter the natural course of minor disorders [7]. But it is also clear that there is a minority of cancer survivors with problems and sometimes severe work limitations that cause partial or total disablement. Moreover, there is a substantial variation in return to work depending on the type of cancer. Patients with testicular cancer, for example, do not differ in employment status from healthy controls, but survivors of blood cancer and cancer of the central nervous system do [5]. In those cases, the occupational health physician and also the primary care physician can help patients to get back to work by trying to remediate the cause of disability [8]. In this chapter, we will deal with screening for problematic return to work, the timing of offering help, and what can be done to help patients to return to work and to remain employed.

The individual variation in time to return to work is considerable even when patients with the same diagnosis and treatment are compared. From our study on return to work in cancer patients, we extracted data on a consecutive series of women with breast cancer and men with testicular cancer and their time to return to work. The groups were homogenous with regard to treatment: the women with breast cancer had received an operation, radiation therapy, and chemotherapy and the men with testicular cancer had all been operated on [9]. As can be seen from the figures, only very few of the women with breast cancer had a few weeks of sick leave during their treatment but many others did not return to work after the one-and-a-half-year follow-up. The median time being off work for the breast cancer survivors was one year. For the men with testicular cancer, this was the opposite with most of them hardly being off work and a few being away for more than a year (Fig. 9.1). In comparison with data from Canada, sick leave in the Netherlands seems to be much longer. Drolet reports that 20% of their sample of breast cancer survivors interviewed three years after diagnosis reported that they kept on working during treatment and that only 12% were on sick leave longer than 12 months. The difference between the two countries must be due to differences in social security. In the Netherlands, there is a paid sick leave up to two years and in Canada there is only a 15-week federal employment insurance. Drolet reports that three-quarters of the cancer survivors in their sample exceeded this 15-week limit [6]. This is in line with qualitative research from which we know that some of the cancer survivors stated that work helped them to maintain a sense of normality during their treatment and other persons stated that work was a big additional burden. Others stated that they had to stay at work for financial reasons [10]. While treating patients, there is no systematic attention to this variation in sick leave. This may mean that some of these survivors are off work unnecessarily. It should be part of the task of the occupational physician to assess which patients benefit from work and help them to stay at work.

Depending on the way health care and social security is organized, primary care and occupational health physicians have an important role in sickness certification in many countries. This means that a cancer survivor would be required to see either one of these physicians for getting their sickness absence legitimized or before return to work or for both of these reasons.[1] In both these roles, legitimizing sick leave and assessing fitness for work, there can be a tension between patients', society's and employers' interests [11]. This tension is often felt by cancer survivors as a pressure by the physician to get them back to work where they themselves do not feel well enough to return [10]. Of course, this depends highly on how cancer survivors perceive their work. Some survivors see work as a source of energy and distraction while for others it is only a burden that consumes the precious little energy that they have left after a devastating disease and treatment. In some countries it is the specialist in hospital who legitimizes sick leave but it will put them in a similar position as

---

[1] In the Netherlands most patients that are on sick leave for some time are seen by occupational physicians to support their return to work. At the same time they provide 'sick notes' to legitimize absence from work for medical reasons. In the UK the primary care physician provides 'sick notes,' a policy currently very much under debate.

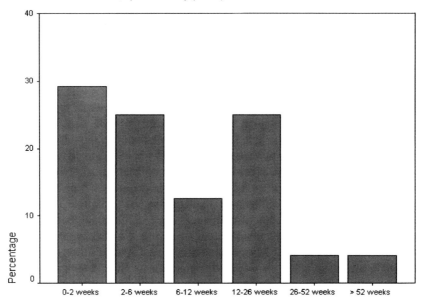
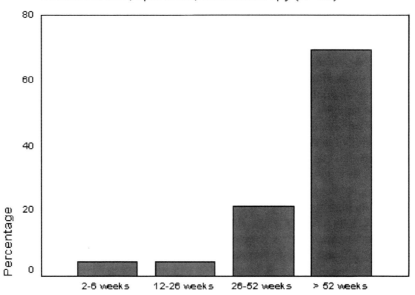

Fig. 9.1 Consecutive series of cancer survivors with breast cancer (n=23) and testicular cancer (n=24) and the time to return to work in weeks. Unpublished data from Spelten et al. 2003

the occupational health physician with regard to return to work.² We will deal with this role tension of the occupational health physician later in this chapter.

The advice of physicians about return to work is influential. In Drolet's study among breast cancer survivors 3 years after diagnosis, work absence lasted longer if a physician had advised to take sick leave, independent from other predictors [6]. In another study, the opposite was found: if patients had received advice about return to work from their doctor they returned to work sooner [12]. This was a cross-sectional study and it might be that those who returned to work remembered better getting advice then those who did not return. Nevertheless, these studies show that a physician's advice about sick leave is not trivial and can have substantial influence.

Our understanding and possibilities for offering support are seriously hampered by a lack of research. Searching Medline through PubMed yields hardly any articles on the topic of return to work and the primary care or occupational health physician. Only occupational health nurses have since long been involved with return to work issues of cancer survivors [13, 14]. This has not resulted in many studies on which issues to address and the effectiveness of these interventions. We will use what is available but also draw heavily upon the literature on return to work in general and the empowerment of patients with chronic diseases.

In a minority of cases, where the cancer is occupational in origin, there is an automatic involvement of the occupational physician or other occupational health specialists. Here, we will not deal with the problems of diagnosing cancer as an occupational disease but later in this chapter we will briefly go into issues of return to work when the cause is occupational. Recently, for example, shift work has been indicated as a potential carcinogenic for breast cancer by the International Agency on Research on Cancer being the authority in this area [15]. This might complicate the return to work process.

When to Provide Help for Problematic Return to Work

The best moment to discuss work issues with a patient is probably when a firm diagnosis has been made and a treatment plan has been established. At this stage it will be clear how much room there will be for work in addition to the burden of disease and treatment and how long the treatment process will take. Then, there can also be an assessment of the potential problems that might occur depending on the type of work, the kind of contract a patient has with the employer, and the kind of health and social security insurance the patient has. A teacher with a permanent position, good health, and social insurance diagnosed with cancer is at less risk of running into work or financial problems than a

---

² In Finland, for example, the treating specialist in hospital prescribes the number of weeks a patient is allowed to stay off work on sick leave

brick layer without good health and social insurance, who is on a temporary contract. It has been shown that cancer survivors with lower social economic status run a greater risk of not working as a result of their disease [5].

It is also important to assess at this early stage what the meaning of work is for a patient. We think that the following four questions have to be answered.

- Is work, an important part of their identity and will it help a patient to stay "normal"?
- How likely is it that there will be financial problems if a patient is not at work?
- How mentally, emotionally, and physically demanding is the job and is there a need for work accommodations?
- What is the relationship with supervisor and is the patient able to talk about his/her disease at the workplace?

From qualitative research it is also known that the answers to these questions may change during the course of the disease and treatment [10, 16]. See also the chapter in this book on the meaning of work (Chapter 6). Work that previously was very important may loose its importance in the light of the experience of a life-threatening disease. Furthermore, the financial situation is different at various times in one's career. A teacher just before retirement probably views his work differently than a busy lawyer in her forties.

It seems that the treating physician, usually the oncologist, is in the best position at this stage of the disease and treatment process to uncover these problems and refer the patient for appropriate help. In many hospitals, an oncology nurse has the role of coordinating the care among treating physicians and he or she would be in the best position to refer the patient to the occupational or primary care physician if needed. This has the great advantage that the number of health care workers involved is limited for most patients [17]. As research from the past decade shows, it seems that oncology nurses are not involved in all matters and that treating physicians do not take up work issues routinely [18, 19]. For this reason occupational and primary care physicians should communicate better with the physicians and nurses involved in cancer treatment. They should make clearer what kind of help they can offer to the cancer survivor. Finally, clinical practice guidelines will be needed in which the tasks and roles of the various specialists, primary care physicians, and occupational physicians involved are described [4].

Additionally, the supervisor at the patient's workplace could possibly refer patients to the occupational physician for help in dealing with work problems if the workplace has such a service or outside consultant. However, it is difficult to rely on the supervisor unless clear agreements have been made. Referral by the supervisor is dependent on the perception of the occupational physician's role by the supervisor and the supervisor's evaluation of the impact of the disease. Sometimes they are compassionate and they want as few problems for the cancer survivor as possible and so they may keep the patient away from the occupational physician. In other cases, a conflict at work already exists and the supervisor won't put any effort into the return to work process. The supervisor is therefore an unreliable source of referral if there are no clear instructions. Self-employed entrepreneurs will usually neither have supervisors nor an occupational physician. Especially here, the primary care physicians could have an important role in the return to work process.

How to Assess Which Survivors Need Most Help?

Ideally, the assessment of the need for help should be based on effective interventions that we can offer. Unfortunately, we are not aware of studies in which interventions to enhance return to work have been evaluated. There are a number of studies on prognostic factors for return to work, both quantitative and qualitative. The best strategy seems to concentrate and put most efforts on patients with a high risk of loosing their job, based on known risk factors of prognostic factors. It is not easy to draw valid inferences from studies on prognostic factors. The outcome is highly dependent on which factors are studied, the prevalence of these factors and if a multivariate analysis has been applied.

From studies among various types of cancer patients, we know that prognosis of return to work depends in part on diagnosis and treatment (Tables 9.1 and 9.2). In our literature survey, we found six studies among a variety of cancer survivors from which it can be inferred that cancer site, disease stage, and treatment are important predictors [20]. Since then, more studies with valid research design and analysis have been reported. Taskila studied prognostic factors for employment two to three years after diagnosis in a retrospective cohort study and Short did the same for a cohort of survivors one to five years after diagnosis [5, 21]. Also in these studies, testicular cancer is consequently reported to have a more favourable prognosis of return to work than cancers at other sites. Leukaemia, lung cancer, and cancer of the central nervous system are reported as having a worse than average prognosis for return to work. Breast cancer patients take an intermediate position. Treatment including surgery only will be less of a hindrance for work resumption than those treatments that also include chemotherapy and radiation. For other clinical and personal factors the picture is less clear. Fatigue and depression often coincide and also from other diseases these are known as barriers for return to work. Apart from having more physical complaints or chronic conditions, other clinical factors are not yet reported as having an influence. Sometimes older age is reported as hindering return to work and sometimes not. In none of the studies is there an influence of marital status or having children in the household. Physically heavy work is sometimes reported as an independent prognostic factor but not always. Other working conditions have not been found to be associated with return to work in one of the recent studies. In one study, having sick leave benefits was associated with a shorter time to return to work compared to those patients who did not have benefits [22].

Table 9.1 Factors predicting or associated with time to return to work reported in the literature in studies involving multiple cancer types after one to five year follow-up

Study	Type of research design	Personal, clinical, and work-related factors increasing the risk of staying off work	Factors examined but not related to a longer return to work
Spelten 2003	Prospective cohort of 235 survivors followed until 1.5 years after diagnosis: 36% not returned to work	Older age, diagnosis, more extensive treatment, heavy physical work load, more physical complaints, higher depression score, higher fatigue score	Work hours per week, gender, children in household, marital status, breadwinner status, sleep problems, cognitive problems, stress at work
Taskila 2004	Retrospective cohort of 12542 survivors three to six years after diagnosis and healthy referents: survivors 9% lower employment rate than referents	Diagnosis, occupation with heavy physical load, lower education	
Short 2004	Retrospective survey among 1433 survivors one to four years after diagnosis: 13% survivors quit work after four years	Diagnosis of cancer of the central nervous system, head and neck, blood and lymph, stage, recurrence, female, less than college education, chronic conditions	Age, race, marital status, children at home, physically demanding job
Poirier 2005	Prospective cohort of 77 cancer survivors attending > 4 weeks radiotherapy with follow-up one month after treatment: 18% not working at follow-up	Older age, more pain, more fatigue, more side effects, female, no sick leave benefits	

Several authors reported on prognostic factors for return to work in patients with one cancer type only. Breast cancer has been examined most often and provides similar information as the studies that have included different cancer types. Workplace accommodations consistently facilitate return to work in cancer survivors [6, 23, 24].

A study among survivors of rectal cancer reported similar results with older age, lower educational level, shorter time since surgery, radiotherapy, lower overall health, more physical symptoms, and more limitations being reported as predictors of longer time to return to work [25]. Among survivors of prostate cancer, being a white collar worker and married were favourable for return to work, but lower hematocrit levels and longer catheter indwelling hindered return to work in a multivariate analysis [26].

Table 9.2 Factors predicting or associated with return to work or work absence due to cancer in breast cancer patients in multivariate analyses after one to three years follow-up

Study	Type of research design	Personal, clinical, and work-related factors increasing the risk of staying off work	Factors examined but not related to a longer return to work
Drolet 2005	Retrospective assessment of absence in 611 newly treated breast cancer survivors three years after diagnosis: 20% unemployed	Age, union-member, chemotherapy, physician advised work absence	Income level, education, blue collar, employment duration, hours per week, radiotherapy, hormone therapy, node involvement
Bouknight 2006	Retrospective assessment of work in 416 newly treated breast cancer survivors 12 months after diagnosis: 18% not working	Older age, self-assessed poorer health, regional node involvement, heavy lifting, less accommodation, cancer discrimination	Age, income, race, education, marital status, radiation, chemotherapy, blue collar, sick leave
Johnsson 2008	Prospective assessment of return to work two years after start treatment in 222 breast cancer patients: 16% had not returned to work	Chemotherapy or nodal involvement	Age, marital status, education, having children at home

We studied an additional predictive factor in a reanalysis of our cohort study [27]. At first in our follow-up study we were mainly interested in clinical and psychosocial factors. In the literature, it is reported that workers' expectations for recovery are important predictors for return to work [8]. This caused us to reanalyse the data of our follow-up study. In that study, we had also measured the perceived work ability using a simple visual analogue scale. The anchors of this very simple 10-point scale were "not being able to work at all" on the left side, and "the best work ability ever" on the right side [28].

In the reanalysis, we found that a higher score of self-reported work ability at six months was a strong predictor of a shorter time to return to work, independent from diagnosis, treatment, performing heavy physical work, fatigue, and age. It is especially interesting that the prediction is independent from the other factors reported earlier. This means that self-assessed work ability is not just an overall assessment in which the patient takes the other factors into account but that there is apparently a separate dimension that has to be taken into account. That is, the beliefs of the cancer survivor regarding the possibility or expectation they will return to work are captured in an overall rating of their work ability. The rating is probably based on the expectation of the positive impact of work and work as an opportunity to keep a sense of normal life to a very

Table 9.3 Items to assess for risk of unemployment in cancer survivors criteria to discern high from low risk

Item	Risk Factor	Criteria
Clinical items	Cancer site	Blood, Lymph, Lung, CNS, Head-neck
	Treatment	Chemotherapy and/or Radiotherapy
	Cancer/treatment related symptoms	Severe fatigue, depression score
Persons at risk	Age	Over 50
Job/Work items	Physical work load	Demanding
	Self-assessed work ability	VAS Score less than 5
	Social security	No formal leave/benefits less than 12 weeks
	Attachment to job	Low
	Value of work	Does not give sense of normality
	Relation with supervisor	No normal communication

unpredictable situation [10, 14, 16, 18, 29]. Finally, those survivors with a lower social-economic status are less likely to return to work [5]. These cancer survivors are probably more often exposed to heavy physical work and have less attachment to work. This increases the risk of loosing their jobs during the cancer treatment period.

What does this mean for the occupational physician for the assessment of a prognosis of return to work? (Table 9.3) In the first place, the occupational physician should obtain details regarding the cancer diagnosis and treatment plan. Since a variety of cancer diseases exists with varying treatment schedules and side effects, it is impossible for the occupational physician to make a proper assessment of the work issues without information from the treating physician. The next step should be to inquire with the patient about the meaning of work, potential job insecurity, health insurance, and social insurance coverage. Subsequently, the patient can be asked to complete a simple work ability index visual analogue scale. Taken together the prognostic factors function as a prediction rule. While these factors need further evaluation for their prospective predictive ability from a practical perspective, the more prognostic factors that are present, the higher the risk for not returning to work and/or eventually losing employment.

What Interventions Should the Occupational Physician Carry Out?

When a patient is assessed as running a high risk of loosing her or his job as a consequence of cancer, treatment, or residual symptom burden, the physician should try to ameliorate or remediate the problems. Even though many interventions seem trivial and there is hardly any evidence on their effectiveness at this point, it is good to keep in mind that even modest interventions can have beneficial effects. McQuellon showed that a one-hour orientation programme in their clinic reduced anxiety and depression levels one week later [30]. Stanton, in her review of psychosocial interventions, provides more examples of relatively minimal interventions which can be adopted readily in practice and still are effective [31]. She also states that interventions explicitly designed to enhance capacities to monitor and alter cancer-relevant thoughts, emotions, and behaviours (coping skills, goal setting, problem solving) produce larger effect size than those without those components. This implies that structured help for work-related problems can be relatively simple and could be effective if directed towards better assessment of work ability and problem solving.

The following interventions are based on problems that are mentioned by patients as being facilitators or barriers of their return to work in qualitative studies and that are within the competence of the occupational and primary care physician.

Recommendation for Return to Work

From the previously mentioned studies on prognosis it is clear that the simple fact of giving advice about return to work is associated with a longer or shorter duration of sick leave. Since it is not known from these studies what the content of the advice was, we cannot make inferences about the content of the advice.

Based on the literature on return to work in general, we made a ten-step return to work plan for cancer survivors including a return to work advice [32] (Table 9.4). The treating radiotherapist handed it over to the patients at the end of radiotherapy treatment and advised them to discuss it with their occupational physician. In general, patients were satisfied with the advice but the impact on return to work remains to be determined. This finding, however, is in line with literature on patient preferences in back pain patients for example [33]. Patients appreciate concrete information about functioning. We advised patients to resume work when they could go out for a long walk or receive visitors for a couple of hours. Work resumption is made easier if it is part-time, with lighter tasks, and according to a fixed schedule. There is no reason to advise all patients to stop working during treatment as studies indicate that patients who continue to work during treatment obtain benefit such as being distracted from cancer [29]. However, if patients want to continue working it is good to advise them to make arrangements that will allow flexibility for medical treatment. If the treating physician would discuss these items with every employed patient this would probably reduce uncertainty on work issues and increase quality of life.

There is a dilemma if the prognosis for survival is not good and the patient wants to continue ordinary life, including work, as much as possible. Our feeling is that also these patients should be able to use work as an "energy source" if they want to and not automatically be told to stop working. In this case, extra communication with the supervisor is needed because some

Table 9.4 Ten steps for cancer survivors to return to work

1. Schedule an appointment with your occupational health physician or primary care physician as the professional who is there to help you with return to work
2. Keep in contact with your employer. You will need him or her to get back to work and to realize work accommodations if needed.
3. Keep in contact with your co-workers. Go to work to see them and tell them how you are doing.
4. Draw up a return-to-work plan in consultation with your supervisor and occupational physician. For all involved, supervisor and colleagues, the plan will make your situation more transparent and at ease.
5. Start to return to work before full recovery, but start with a limited number of hours. Starting with a small number of hours brings the reassurance that this will succeed. This has been shown to facilitate return to work. Discuss which further work accommodations are needed to make working feasible such as lighter tasks.
6. Make sure the return-to work plan encompasses the date and number of hours of the start, which days of the week will be worked, the timing of the expansion of hours, the tasks and number of hours of this expansion, and the proposed date of full return to work.
7. How to set a goal for the time needed for complete return to work? Depending on the number and severity of physical complaints and the physical or emotional demands of work, this can range from a couple of weeks to a number of months.
8. Evaluate the return-to-work plan with your supervisor every two weeks. Adjust the plan according to your evaluation.
9. If unsure, draw up a second, less ambitious return-to-work plan that may be used if the first plan fails.
10. An example of a return to work plan is gradual return to work in 12 weeks for a nurse who has survived breast cancer starting with two times four hours per week.

supervisors might be of the opinion that the physician should have stopped the worker with advanced cancer from returning to work.

Work Accommodations

Patients mention most often that having a flexible work schedule or being given tasks that make it easier to cope with the treatment schedule have helped them to stay at work. The occupational physician is in a position and often has the relationship with work sites to help patients implement work accommodations. It is good to realise that sometimes cancer survivors have mixed feelings about getting other tasks as part of their disease management, especially if these tasks are less valued. Some cancer survivors report that being assigned minor tasks is an additional "punishment" [10]. There are, in general, few studies that have evaluated the impact of work accommodations on return to work or management of chronic diseases but there is some evidence that training patients in realising work accommodations is effective [34]. Work accommodations is covered in more depth in Chapter 12 of this volume.

Managing Fatigue and Other Disease- or Treatment-Related Symptoms

Several studies have shown that symptoms that can be easily regarded as minor compared to those related to cancer can have a substantial impact on work ability. In breast cancer patients, hot flashes have considerable impact on quality of life. In brain tumor survivors, depressive symptoms, fatigue, cognitive limitations, and sleep problems accounted for 65% of the variance in work limitations [35]. The occupational physician should see to it that these symptoms are properly attended to. More guidance can be found in the Handbook of Cancer Survivorship and in other chapters of this book [36].

Involvement of Supervisors and Colleagues and Disclosure of Diagnosis

Involvement of supervisors and relations with colleagues have since long been mentioned as a possible hindrance for return to work [9]. In our own study on the quality of rehabilitation by occupational physicians, the physicians assessed that in more than 80% of the cases the attitude of colleagues and supervisor did not hamper return to work [19]. The patients' own assessment of relations with colleagues and superiors was quite favourable with a score of more than 80 out of a maximum of 100. The prevalence of problems with supervisors or colleagues is much less than of the clinical symptoms. Most workers can communicate normally with their supervisors. Disclosure of the diagnosis and return to work should be part of that normal communication. Therefore, it is not surprising that Pryce found a positive association between disclosure of diagnosis to colleagues and working during treatment [12].

However, being affected by cancer can coincide with a conflict at work or relations that are strained already. In a qualitative study among long-term beast cancer survivors, 5% of the respondents reported that disclosure of the diagnosis had caused work- or job-related problems [37]. This might indicate that few situations occur in which problems at work coincide with a diagnosis of cancer. In such a situation, it can be difficult to manage return to work. Since the occupational physician has an optimal position between work and health care, he or she should mediate between patient and supervisor even though in this case it might be difficult to achieve satisfactory results.

Occupational Cancer

Cancers such as mesothelioma and lung cancer that are most associated with work still have quite a grave prognosis. In these cases, return to work is seldom an issue. Recently, breast cancer has been associated with shift work [15]. This can raise the question whether it is wise to return to the same work that has been associated, at least partially, to the breast cancer. The consequences of working or not working should be discussed with the patient so that she can make an informed decision. It is important to note the difference in decision making at a societal level and at the individual level because the costs and benefits will be different. For most people resuming work, the decision would depend on the benefits and harms of the alternatives. If the alternative is no exposure to the risk of breast cancer but also no income from work, it is quite clear that no work would be much more damaging to health. To get a clearer picture of the risks of continuing with shift work for a survivor of breast cancer, one can point out that the association is only reported for those with a long duration of exposure of more than 20 years. Moreover, the absolute risk of breast cancer for an individual woman is still relatively small. Schernhammer observed women between the ages of 40 and 50 for a period of little over ten years and found a risk of breast cancer in only 1 of every 1000 women per year [38]. The reported relative risk for breast cancer after 20 years of shift work is 1.8 and means an almost doubling of the risk, but for the absolute risk it means an increase from 1 to 2 per 1000 per year. Even though these risks are important from a public health point of view, they are relatively small from an individual point of view.

Physician and Fitness for Work Dilemmas

Assessment of work disability or fitness for work can cause ethical dilemmas. An oncologist once told us that she always followed the patients' wishes in return to work recommendations. She was of the opinion that she should support any wish the patient had about work. When we discussed the social security issues involved, it turned out that she was not aware that keeping a patient off work in the Netherlands for longer than two years will almost automatically mean that the employment contract is ended and the patient cannot return to his or her old job anymore. This means that blindly following the patients' wishes can turn against their own interests in the long run.

Important ethical principles to be taken into account in decisions like these are patient autonomy, beneficence or doing no harm, and equity and solidarity [39]. The oncologist followed two important ethical principles. First, she gave high priority to patient autonomy. Then she tried to follow the principle of beneficence which is an important ethical lead for physicians, but she was not well informed and her advice could also have harmed the patient. It is clear that in a case where the patient gets a disability benefit, the principle of equity and solidarity is important. Since resources are not endless, allowing benefits to one person will mean withholding benefits for another patient. If this is not done in a professional way, this would mean that the principle of equity and solidarity would be violated. In many European countries, the growing numbers of disabled workers and expenditure for disability benefits is a major political problem [40]. In our view, there has to be a fair assessment of work disability including recommendations for return to work based on the principles outlined above.

For many occupational physicians and also treating specialists, these are difficult dilemmas. The wish to be nice to a patient who has gone through the experience of cancer and its treatment can be very strong. Often, it results in the recommendation to be on sick leave because it is assumed that work will be a burden to the patient and the physician is in the position to legitimize sick leave. As outlined above, these decisions can do more harm than good. We need better tools to make decisions as to who is able to work and who is not.

How Well Are Occupational Physicians Doing?

We were able to measure the quality of care provided by occupational physicians in the Netherlands in a cohort of 100 cancer survivors about one to two years after diagnosis [19]. The patients completed a questionnaire regarding their disease, complaints, working conditions, and sick leave. The physicians of the patients were interviewed about the problems hindering return to work in their patients and how they had solved them. Based on the literature and in line with the ideas mentioned above, we had conceived four indicators for the quality of rehabilitation by the occupational physician (Table 9.5). These indicators were based on general principles of quality of care such as continuity of care and knowledge of return to work processes in cancer survivors. In addition, the patients filled in a satisfaction questionnaire resulting in a score between zero and 100. We were finally able to relate the quality of care to the time it took for the patients to return to work.

To our surprise, there was hardly any communication between the occupational physician and the specialists that treated the cancer survivors. In only six cases there had been a formal exchange of information. As to the continuity of care, most patients had seen the same physician but there was a lack in follow-up, leaving almost 40% without a new appointment. In 80% of the cases, the

Table 9.5 Quality indicators and their criteria for good quality of occupational rehabilitation of cancer survivors by occupational health physicians

Quality Indicator	Criteria for Good Quality
1 Medical information of the diagnosis and treatment	Information from treating physician
2 Continuity of care	Regular contact with same physician
3 Information on disease and treatment related complaints and appropriate interventions	At least two of these problems like fatigue mentioned and taken appropriate action such as referral to a treating physician
4 Information on relations with the supervisor and colleagues at work and appropriate interventions	Problems mentioned and in case of problems contact with the supervisor or other employees of the firm of the cancer survivor

physicians had knowledge of disease and treatment related complaints and taken one or more measures for improvement. The same held for relations with supervisor and colleagues. We concluded that quality was reasonable but that especially communication with the specialists was open for improvement. In line with the quality of care, the patients rated their satisfaction with an average score of 77 (SD = 16). Higher quality of care was associated with a shorter time to return to work in a multivariate analysis in which the effect of a great number of confounders was taken into account [19].

In Finland, Taskila studied the amount of social support that 640 cancer survivors two to three years after diagnosis and back at work had actually received from occupational health services and others [41]. The patients filled in a questionnaire about the amount of social support from co-workers, supervisors, and occupational health services and if they had hoped for more from any of these resources. Most support was received from colleagues and least from occupational health services. The patients, especially those who had received chemotherapy, indicated that they had hoped for more support from the occupational health services. The authors conclude that their study indicates a clear need to better organize occupational health services for cancer survivors.

Conclusions and Directions for the Future

Physicians' recommendations on return to work do influence the time to return to work in cancer survivors. However, it is not always clear if this is increasing or decreasing the barrier for work resumption. Therefore, we argued that physicians should assess which patients are most in need of support for return to work based on patient preferences and established predictors for return to work. Those most in need can be supported through recommendations about work resumption, work accommodations, communication with work, and attending to cancer and treatment related symptoms.

Occupational health professionals and primary care physicians have a place in survivorship care. What place they have depends partly on the organization of health care and also to a great extent on the organization of survivorship care. Oeffinger describes a shared-care model in which care is shared between the oncologist and the primary care physician [17]. To improve return to work such a shared-care model is very much needed. With an increased likelihood of survival among many cancer patients, perhaps it is time for the oncologist or more likely the oncology nurse practitioner as part of cancer care to assess the need for return to work support at an early stage of treatment and communicate with the primary care or occupational health physician. Even though we have positive experiences with such a model in a pilot study, at present this is not commonly accepted practice. Multidisciplinary guidelines are needed to implement the shared-care model in practice. The fact that in the Netherlands a multidisciplinary guideline development process has just started shows that the prospects for such a model are good. Another model described by Oeffinger is the Comprehensive Survivor Programme in Academic Institutions in which the oncology nurse practitioner has a pivotal role. In our view, the oncology nurse could play a pivotal role in both establishing the risk of loosing employment, communicating with the occupational physician and primary care physician and remediating return to work problems and work optimization and retention to a certain extent.

There is a clear need for research into effective interventions to enhance return to work and work retention for those survivors who need it. Simple recommendations for return to work by physicians can be influential. We need recommendations in which patient preferences and patients' perceived work ability are taken into account. Also, cancer specific work accommodations for symptom burden need to be developed and evaluated. The evaluation of such recommendations in randomised trials will greatly enhance our understanding of the work outcomes in cancer survivors.

References

1. Guzman J, Yassi A, Cooper JE, Khokhar J. Return to work after occupational injury. Family physicians' perspectives on soft-tissue injuries. Canadian Family Physician. 2002; 48:1912–9.
2. Sisler JJ, Brown JB, Stewart M. Family physician's roles in cancer care. Survey of patients on a provincial cancer registry. Canadian Family Physician. 2004; 50:889–96.
3. Blaauwbroek R, Tuinier W, Meyboom-de Jong B, Kamps W, Postma A. Shared care by paediatric oncologists and family doctors for long-term follow-up of adult childhood cancer survivors: A pilot study. Lancet Oncology. 2008; 9 (3):232–8.
4. Blaauwbroek R, Zwart N, Bouma M, Meyboom-de Jong B, Kamps W, Postma A. The willingness of general practitioners to be involved in the follow-up of adult survivors of childhood cancer. Journal of Cancer Survivorship. 2007; 1:292–7.
5. Taskila-Abrandt T, Martikainen R, virtanen SV, Pukkala E, Hietanen P, Lindbohm ML. The impact of education and occupation on the employment status of cancer survivors. European Journal of Cancer. 2004; 40(16):2488–93.
6. Drolet M, Maunsell E, Brisson J, Brisson C, Masse B, Deschenes L. Not working 3 years after breast cancer: Predictors in a population-based study. Journal of Clinical Oncology. 2005; 23(33):8305–12.
7. Vrijhof BJ. Effectiveness of faster control of sickness absence, an experiement (in Dutch). Tijdschrift voor Bedrijfs – en Verzekeringsgeneeskunde. 1996; 4(1):13–21.
8. Verbeek JH. How can doctors help their patients to return to work? PLoS Medicine. 2006; 3(3):e88.
9. Spelten ER, Verbeek JH, Uitterhoeve AL, Ansink AC, van der Lelie J, de Reijke TM, et al. Cancer, fatigue and the return of patients to work – A prospective cohort study. European Journal of Cancer. 2003; 39(11):1562–7.
10. Kennedy F, Haslam C, Munir F, Pryce J. Returning to work following cancer: A qualitative exploratory study into the experience of returning to work following cancer. European Journal of Cancer Care. 2007; 16(1):17–25.
11. Verbeek J, Hulshof C. Work disability assessment in the Netherlands. In: Westerholm P, Nilstun T, Ovretveit J, eds. *Practical Ethics in Occupational Health*. 1 ed. San Francisco, CA: Radcliffe Medical Press 2004; 105–14.

12. Pryce J, Munir F, Haslam C. Cancer survivorship and work: Symptoms, supervisor repsonse, co-worker disclosure and work adjustment. Journal of Occupational Rehabilitation. 2007; 17(1):83–92.
13. Clark JC, Landis L. Reintegration and maintenance of employees with breast cancer in the workplace. AAOHN Journal. 1989; 37(5):186–93.
14. Nachreiner NM, Dagher RK, McGovern PM, Baker BA, Alexander BH, Gerberich SG. Successful return to work for cancer survivors. AAOHN Journal. 2007; 55(7):290–5.
15. Kolstad HA. Nightshift work and risk of breast cancer and other cancers – A critical review of the epidemiologic evidence. Scandinavian Journal of Work, Environment and Health. 2008; 34(1):5–22.
16. Amir Z, Neary D, Luker K. Cancer survivors' views of work 3 years post diagnosis: A UK perspective. European Journal of Oncology Nursing. 2008: 12(3):190–7.
17. Oeffinger KC, McCabe MS. Models for delivering survivorship care. Journal of Clinical Oncology. 2006; 24(32):5117–24.
18. Maunsell E, Brisson C, Dubois L, Lauzier S, Fraser A. Work problems after breast cancer: An exploratory qualitative study. PsychoOncology. 1999; 8(6):467–73.
19. Verbeek J, Spelten E, Kammeijer M, Sprangers M. Return to work of cancer survivors: A prospective cohort study into the quality of rehabilitation by occupational physicians. Occupational and Environmental Medicine. 2003; 60(5):352–7.
20. Spelten ER, Sprangers MA, Verbeek JH. Factors reported to influence the return to work of cancer survivors: A literature review. PsychoOncology. 2002; 11(2):124–31.
21. Short PF, Vasey JJ, Tunceli K. Employment pathways in a large cohort of adult cancer survivors. Cancer. 2005; 103(6):1292–301.
22. Poirier P. Policy implications of the relationship of sick leave benefits, individual characteristics, and fatigue to employment during radiation therapy for cancer. Policy, Politics, and Nursing Practice. 2005; 6(4):305–18.
23. Bouknight RR, Bradley CJ, Luo Z. Correlates of return to work for breast cancer survivors. Journal of Clinical Oncology. 2006; 24(3):345–53.
24. Johnsson A, Fornander T, Olsson M, Nystedt M, Johansson H, Rutqvist LE. Factors associated with return to work after breast cancer treatment. Acta Oncologica. 2007; 46(1):90–6.
25. van den Brink M, van den Hout WB, Kievit J, Marijnen CA, Putter H, van de Velde CJ, et al. The impact of diagnosis and treatment of rectal cancer on paid and unpaid labor. Diseases of the Colon and Rectum. 2005; 48(10):1875–82.
26. Sultan R, Slova D, Thiel B, Lepor H. Time to return to work and physical activity following open radical retropubic prostatectomy. Journal of Urology. 2006; 176(4 Pt 1):1420–3.
27. de Boer AG, Verbeek JH, Spelten ER, Uitterhoeve AL, Ansink AC, De Reijke TM, et al. Work ability and return-to-work in cancer patients. British Journal of Cancer. 2008; 98(8):1342–7.
28. Tuomi L, Ilmarienen J, Jahkola A, Katajarinne L, Tulkki A. Work Ability Index. Helsinki: Finnish Institute of Occupational Health 1998.
29. Main DS, Nowels CT, Cavender TA, Etschmaier M, Steiner JF. A qualitative study of work and work return in cancer survivors. PsychoOncology. 2005; 14(11):992–1004.
30. McQuellon RP, Wells M, Hoffman S, Craven B, Russell G, Cruz J, et al. Reducing distress in cancer patients with an orientation program. PsychoOncology. 1998; 7(3):207–17.
31. Stanton AL. Psychosocial concerns and interventions for cancer survivors. Journal of Clinical Oncology. 2006; 24(32):5132–7.
32. Nieuwenhuijsen K, Bos-Ransdorp B, Uitterhoeve AL, Sprangers MA, Verbeek JH. Enhanced provider communication and patient education regarding return to work in cancer survivors following curative treatment: A pilot study. Journal of Occupational Rehabilitation. 2006; 16(4):647–57.

33. Verbeek J, Sengers MJ, Riemens L, Haafkens J. Patient's expectations of treatment for back pain: A systematic review of qualitative and quantitative studies. Spine. 2004; 29(20):2309–18.
34. Varekamp I, Verbeek JH, van Dijk FJ. How can we help employees with chronic diseases to stay at work? A review of interventions aimed at job retention and based on an empowerment perspective. International Archives of Occupational and Environmental Health. 2006; 80(2):87–97.
35. Feuerstein M, Hansen JA, Calvio LC, Johnson L, Ronquillo JG. Work productivity in brain tumor survivors. Journal of Occupational and Environmental Medicine. 2007; 49(7):803–11.
36. Feuerstein M. Handbook of Cancer Survivorship. New York, NY: Elsevier 2007.
37. Stewart DE, Cheung AM, Duff S, Wong F, McQuestion M, Cheng T, et al. Long-term breast cancer survivors: Confidentiality, disclosure, effects on work and insurance. PsychoOncology. 2001; 10(3):259–63.
38. Schernhammer ES, Kroenke CH, Laden F, Hankinson SE. Night work and risk of breast cancer. Epidemiology. 2006; 17(1):108–11.
39. Westerholm P, Nilstun T, Ovretveit J. Practical Ethics in Occupational Health. San Francisco, CA: Radcliffe Medical Press 2004.
40. Verbeek J, van Dijk F. Assessing the ability to work. BMJ. 2008; 336(7643):519–20.
41. Taskila T, Lindbohm ML, Martikainen R, Lehto US, Hakanen J, Hietanen P. Cancer survivors' received and needed social support from their work place and the occupational health services. Supportive Care in Cancer. 2006; 14(5):427–35.

Chapter 10
Rehabilitation

Michael J.L. Sullivan, Maureen Simmonds, David Butler, Shirin Shalliwani, and Mahnaz Hamidzadeh

Introduction

The treatment of cancer will frequently require that individuals temporarily modify or discontinue their occupational activities. Following the successful management of disease activity in individuals diagnosed with cancer, issues concerning the resumption of occupational responsibilities are often raised. Rehabilitation interventions might be considered as a viable option to assist cancer survivors in resuming occupational involvement [1].

As will be highlighted in this chapter, rehabilitation for the cancer survivor is particularly challenging. Rehabilitation efforts will likely be initiated within the context of ongoing medical care. Yet the goals of medical treatment and the goals of rehabilitation are quite distinct and respective interventions might be offered within treatment orientations that proceed from very different assumptions and philosophies. Clashes of paradigms might have important implications for outcomes of rehabilitation efforts for cancer survivors.

The field of rehabilitation for the cancer survivor is still in its infancy and might benefit from advances or lessons learned from other domains of rehabilitation. Yet the experience of the cancer survivor might also be sufficiently unique that novel approaches will need to be developed in order to ensure that the cancer survivor can continue to participate, as fully as possible, in all important domains of his or her life.

This chapter briefly describes what is currently known about disability in cancer survivors and examines the different rehabilitation models that have guided interventions provided for cancer survivors. The chapter also describes emerging trends in interventions being used to address the rehabilitation needs of the cancer survivor. Finally directions for future research and clinical development are discussed.

M.J.L. Sullivan (✉)
Professor, Departments of Psychology, Medicine and Neuroscience, Canada Research Chair in Behavioral Health, McGill University, 1205 Dr. Penfield Avenue, Montreal Quebec, Canada, H3A 1B1
e-mail: michael.sullivan@mcgill.ca

Cancer, Residual Symptoms and Disability

Currently, more than 70% of all cancer patients will survive more than 5 years following initial diagnosis. Recent surveys of cancer survivors indicate that the majority of cancer survivors are of working age (< 55 years) [2]. For men, individuals with prostate cancer comprise the largest group of cancer survivors; for women, individuals with a diagnosis of breast cancer comprise the largest group of cancer survivors.

As a function of improved detection and treatment procedures, the death rates, per year, due to prostate and breast cancer continue to decline [3]. Death rates due to colon, rectal, uterine and pancreatic cancer have also declined significantly over the past two decades [2]. Improved treatment outcomes inevitably translate into a growing population of cancer survivors. It is estimated that there are more than 25 million people worldwide alive with a diagnosis of cancer [1].

One of the major changes in cancer has been its transformation from a death sentence to a chronic illness. As life expectancies for cancer survivors continue to increase, questions of disability, rehabilitation and participation are beginning to be addressed. Research is accumulating addressing the residual symptoms associated with cancer survivorship, the unmet clinical needs of cancer survivors and the impact of post-cancer symptoms on functional abilities [4].

Cancer survivorship does not imply that individuals are symptom-free. Even when the symptoms of cancer have been successfully treated, the cancer survivor is likely to continue to experience a variety of troubling and debilitating symptoms. The residual symptoms that have been reported most frequently by cancer survivors include pain, fatigue and depression [5]. The persistence of these symptoms in cancer survivors is central to issues of rehabilitation since, across various debilitating health conditions, symptoms of pain, fatigue and distress have been shown to be significant determinants of work disability [6, 7].

Pain symptoms in cancer survivors can arise from multiple causes including adverse effects of cancer treatment, infection and musculoskeletal problems [8–11]. Research suggests that 30–60% of individuals with cancer will continue to experience pain symptoms that will persist in the post-treatment period [12–19]. Neuropathic pain and somatic pain conditions are the most common pain diagnoses in cancer survivors [20–22].

Considerable research shows that fatigue is a significant component of residual symptomatology following the treatment of cancer [23]. Fatigue has been discussed as one of the most debilitating symptoms of cancer treatment [5]. Symptoms of fatigue often persist beyond the treatment period and can continue to interfere with functioning for months or years. Surveys suggest that 60–90% of cancer survivors might experience debilitating symptoms of fatigue [24, 25]. Fatigue may interfere with the ability to participate in social and recreational activities that might otherwise act as a buffer to the stress and strain of life as a cancer survivor [24, 26]. Fatigue overlaps to some degree with depression, and might be misattributed to a depressive state [5, 27, 28]. Given that the task of coping with cancer is resource demanding, the cancer survivor with significant symptoms of fatigue might be particularly vulnerable to the adverse effects of other residual symptoms or life stresses associated with cancer [29].

There is considerable research indicating that prevalence rates of depressive disorders are higher in cancer survivors than in the general population [30–32]. It is clear that cancer pain can exert a significant negative impact on emotional functioning [33, 34]. The chronic stresses associated with cancer might eventually deplete the coping resources of many cancer patients, leaving them more vulnerable to the development of mental health problems. High levels of pain and fatigue have been associated with reductions in quality of life in cancer survivors [35–37]. Higher levels of pain and fatigue have also been associated with more severe depressive symptoms in cancer survivors [38–40]; [41].

Across a wide range of health and mental health conditions, symptoms of pain, fatigue and emotional distress have been linked with heightened risk of disability. It is not surprising therefore that research reveals that cancer survivors report a wide range of functional limitations. More than 50% of breast cancer survivors report limitations for physical activities such as lifting, reaching and carrying [42]. Reductions in grip strength have been reported in breast cancer survivors as much as two years post-treatment [43]. Functional limitations can impact to a significant degree on an individual's participation in different life role domains, including work [44].

There is a growing literature on work disability associated with cancer survivorship [45, 46]. There are indications that the majority of cancer survivors return to work once cancer symptoms have been effectively managed [44]. One study reported that breast cancer survivors were only 7% more likely to be unemployed three years after diagnosis than health controls [47]. Other studies suggest that 10–30% of cancer survivors might remain occupationally disabled more than one year following termination of treatment [26, 48–50]. Even when cancer survivors return to work, many do not maintain employment [26, 51].

It is clear that the cancer survivor might benefit from interventions that reduce the severity of residual symptoms of pain, fatigue or emotional distress. To the extent that these symptoms will persist, the cancer survivor might benefit from interventions aimed at minimizing the impact of these symptoms on daily functioning. The cancer survivor might present with a profile of risk factors that augment the probability of prolonged disability. In such cases, the cancer survivor might benefit from risk-factor targeted interventions programs. Finally, the cancer survivor might benefit from interventions designed to modify the work environment in order to better accommodate the cancer survivor with limitations.

As will be discussed in the next section, rehabilitation goals can vary considerably across cancer survivors, and also within cancer survivors over time. In order to appreciate what has been learned about key elements of successful rehabilitation of cancer survivors and the unmet rehabilitation needs of the cancer survivor, it is useful to briefly review different conceptualizations of the nature of disability and different intervention orientations in rehabilitation.

The Nature of Disability

Examination of the rates of disability associated with various chronic health conditions reveals the same pattern; in spite of all policy and interventions efforts, the magnitude of the disability problem in industrialized societies continues to grow at an alarming rate. Disability insurers report rates of chronic or permanent disability that are rising at approximately 5% per year [52, 53]. State social security or social assistance agencies report increases in permanent disability of approximately 10% each year [6, 53]. In North America, cancer survivors represent one of the fastest growing disability populations opting for assistance from state social security plans [54].

Similar increases in disability rates are observed whether countries operate under private or public health insurance schemes [55, 56]. Economic projections suggest that the rising prevalence and associated costs of disability will reach crisis proportions in many countries within a decade [54]. There is a basis for arguing that part of the problem emerges from misguided assumptions about the basic nature of disability.

In 1980, the World Health Organization published the International Classification of Impairments, Disabilities and Handicaps (ICIDH) as the first major classification system to focus specifically on disability [57] (Fig. 10.1). The ICIDH framework presented disability as a linear process that begins with an underlying cause, which brings about an impairment, which in turn causes a disability that may result in a handicap. The WHO model of disability was criticized for being overly linear, and for its relative neglect of social or economic factors that might contribute to disability.

In response to criticism leveled at the ICIDH classification system, the WHO [58] proposed a revision of its model, entitled the *International Classification of Functioning, Disability and Health (ICF)*. In the revised model, the term *functioning* replaced *impairment* but the model remained essentially linear, and still considered disability to arise from some disruption in physical or mental health processes.

Models such as the ICIDH, or the ICF have been useful in drawing attention to the forces that might impact on disability, and how disability can impact negatively on quality of life. These models however suffer from their emphasis

Fig. 10.1 WHO (1980) international classification of impairments, disabilities and handicaps. Geneva, Switzerland., World Health Organization

on the role of an impairment, or dysfunction, whether injury-related or illness-related as the underlying cause of disability.

Despite the broad acceptance of models of disability proposed by the WHO, the view that disability emerges from impairment has garnered only weak support from the empirical literature. Research in this area shows that, underlying medical symptoms do not have a direct impact on disability, and when they do, the observed magnitude of the relation is more modest than these models would suggest. Across individuals, wide variations in levels of disability are observed in spite of comparable medical symptoms. Numerous research investigations suggest that symptom severity typically accounts for only 10–30% of the variance in the severity of disability [49, 50, 56, 59–62].

The weak relationship between underlying symptoms and disability is seen across various debilitating health and mental conditions. For example, the severity of pain symptoms is a weak predictor of who will and who will not return to work in individuals with musculoskeletal conditions [63]. There are indications that treatments aimed at reducing pain symptoms are actually more likely to prolong disability than to facilitate return to work [64, 65]. Similarly, symptomatic treatment of depression has been shown to have little or no effect on return to work for individuals with a depressive condition [66]. Symptomatic treatment of other debilitating health or mental conditions does not contribute meaningfully to improved return to work outcomes [67]. Research is accumulating showing that, regardless of the individual's debilitating health or mental health condition, if return to work (or disability reduction) is the objective of treatment, symptomatic treatment alone is unlikely to achieve that outcome [68, 69]. Increasingly, it is becoming clear that if return to work is the objective, treatment must specifically target the factors that are contributing to work disability [70].

In spite of evidence suggesting that symptoms only partially explain disability, it has been difficult to reorient our targets of intervention to be more in line with clinical science. Rehabilitation professionals continue to focus most of their intervention efforts on symptom reduction. Our traditional medical heritage biases even our conceptual models of disability, and we pursue avenues of intervention that are unlikely to yield the outcomes we seek. The medical heritage of rehabilitation causes us to persist, sometimes indefinitely, in the application of ineffective treatment, as we aim to eradicate the source of the client's disability.

From a pragmatic perspective, disability is fundamentally a 'behavior' [71]. In other words, someone who is disabled behaves differently than someone without a disability. The behavior of disability typically involves reduced participation in activities of daily living and life role activities. In other words, compared to a time before the onset of illness or injury, individuals who are disabled engage in fewer social, recreational or occupational activities. From this pragmatic perspective, it follows that effective reduction in disability would entail the identification of barriers to participation and use of intervention techniques designed to increase participation.

The Nature of Rehabilitation

A chapter on cancer survivorship and rehabilitation presents a number of significant challenges. Rehabilitation encompasses a wide range of client populations and diverse intervention orientations. So marked are some of the differences across client populations and intervention orientations that it seems difficult at times to subsume these under a unitary perspective on rehabilitation.

Rehabilitation as a health discipline evolved in the early 1900s, originally to deal with injured soldiers returning from combat [24]. In the 1920s and 1930s, several institutions arose across North America that would take on the responsibility of caring for these injured soldiers, as well as other individuals with disabling health conditions. Partly due to lack of knowledge, and partly out of feelings of indebtedness, individuals with disabilities were offered palliative interventions, they were sheltered, and they were absolved of further responsibilities. It seemed that 'care and protection' was the best that could be offered for individuals who were not expected to recover from their condition. Care and protection often entailed removing the individual from active participation in various domains of life.

At least five intervention orientations can currently be identified in rehabilitation. These can be descriptively termed curative, palliative, restorative, compensatory and accommodative. Curative and palliative interventional approaches are most closely linked to the medical roots of rehabilitation. Traditional medical approaches proceed from the view that some form of pathology underlies dysfunctional states, and the objective of intervention is to identify and eradicate the underlying pathology. Although traditional medical approaches have been shown to be ill-suited for the management of disability, symptom-focused or symptom-soothing interventions still hold a prominent place in the rehabilitation of many debilitating health conditions, including cancer. Vestiges of the conceptual origins of rehabilitation also persist in the 'sick care' and 'protection' characteristics of many rehabilitation interventions.

Restorative rehabilitation approaches have been emerging as dominant models of rehabilitation for a variety of debilitating health conditions. These orientations proceed from the view that, for many debilitating health conditions, underlying pathology cannot be effectively eliminated by traditional medical means. As such, rehabilitation efforts are aimed at restoring or maximizing function through endurance or strengthening interventions.

More recently, compensatory and accommodative interventions have been gaining prominence in the repertoire of rehabilitation services available to individuals with various debilitating health conditions. Compensatory approaches are aimed at assisting the individual in compensating for impairments that cannot be changed. Accommodative interventions are characterized as rehabilitation approaches that target barriers to rehabilitation progress. Barriers to rehabilitation progress or barriers to resumption of occupational activities can exist at a multitude of levels and might include psychosocial risk factors, organizational and policy-related factors.

Table 10.1 Major rehabilitation orientations

Orientation	Description	Indications	Limitations
Curative	Intervention approaches designed to eliminate the source of the symptom or health condition. Curative approaches still dominate the rehabilitation of persistent pain conditions in spite of limited support for their efficacy.	There are not many indications for the use of curative approaches in the management of most chronic health conditions. The lack of knowledge about cause-effect relations in the etiology of most debilitating health conditions precludes the application of effective curative interventions.	Probably the least evidence-based approaches in the field of rehabilitation. Most efforts to discern and eradicate the source of ongoing symptoms have led to the application of unnecessarily prolonged and ineffective interventions.
Palliative	Intervention approaches designed to reduce the severity of residual symptoms. These might include pharmacological, physical therapy and psychological interventions where the primary objective is symptom severity reduction.	Palliative interventions can be an important component of rehabilitation under conditions where individuals suffer from significant physical or emotional distress.	Palliative interventions can be useful in reducing symptom severity but rarely have a significant impact on return to work. Research suggests that excessive focus on palliative interventions might actually prolong disability.
Restorative	Intervention approaches designed to restore function to limbs or other bodily systems that might have deteriorated as a result of debilitating symptoms or treatment (e.g. deconditioning).	When long periods of convalescence or inactivity lead to physical deconditioning, restorative interventions can be a useful component of a rehabilitation plan.	Restoration of function through increased physical activity or exercise occurs within a relatively short period of time. Lack of recognition to the upper limits of restoration of function has often led to excessively prolonged treatment.
Compensatory	Intervention approaches designed to maximize participation in spite of ongoing symptoms or limitations. The focus of many compensatory interventions is the	When complete restoration of function cannot be achieved, compensatory approaches can promote	While a number of psychological barriers to participation have been identified, not all are modifiable. Effective

Table 10.1 (continued)

Orientation	Description	Indications	Limitations
	development of alternate approaches to task completion or activity participation.	participation by assisting individuals in learning new ways of participation. These may include strategies for overcoming psychological or physical barriers.	intervention requires the ability to distinguish between modifiable and non-modifiable psychological and physical barriers to participation.
Accomodative	Intervention approaches designed to reduce barriers to participation. Have emerged from research highlighting the role of extra-individual (e.g., policy, organization, workplace) factors as barriers to participation.	When complete restoration of function cannot be achieved, accommodative approaches can promote reintegration into the workplace by removing structural barriers to participation.	Despite growing evidence of the efficacy of accommodative interventions, workplace inflexibility and various myths about the risks of hiring individuals with disabilities continue to impede the application of accommodative interventions.

In the following sections, research on the effects of different rehabilitation orientations for cancer survivors will be briefly reviewed. Where possible, parallels will be drawn between rehabilitation interventions for cancer survivors and those that have been studied in individuals with other debilitating health conditions. Cautions will be raised about rehabilitation approaches currently being used for cancer survivors that have been shown to be ineffective in other domains of disability. Finally, promising directions for future development will be highlighted.

Exercise and Rehabilitation

Exercise has been the most researched rehabilitation intervention for cancer survivors [72]. The health benefits of exercise have been documented across a wide range of cancer diagnoses. A number of studies have examined the effects of exercise on symptom severity and function of individuals who were diagnosed with cancer [73]. Exercise interventions have been used at various stages of the cancer experience.

Anecdotal accounts of the positive affects of exercise have been described by athletes who were diagnosed with cancer. Sarah Gordon describes how exercise was a key part of her cancer survivorship [74]. At the age of 21, cancer treatment would require removal of significant muscle mass from her right leg. She was told by her physicians she would never run or bike again. In 2007, she completed her first marathon as a cancer survivor.

At the age of 19, Douglas Ulman underwent back surgery for the removal of a large tumor. He was told that his ability to return to athletic activity was doubtful. On the 10-year anniversary of his cancer survivorship, Douglas Ulman completed the New York marathon, finishing just slightly behind his friend, Lance Armstrong, also a cancer survivor [75].

These anecdotal accounts illustrate both the discouraging messages frequently communicated by heath care professionals, and the strength and determination that will allow individuals to make dramatic progress in their rehabilitation. The stories of Sarah and Douglas illustrate what can be achieved through determination, commitment and exercise. However, it is important to consider that such dramatic athletic exploits will not characterize the recovery trajectories of most cancer survivors.

Exercise and Disease Activity: Curative Rehabilitation

There are some indications that physical activity following diagnosis of cancer might lead to reductions in disease activity and might also reduce the risk of recurrence [76, 77]. The potential protective effects of exercise have been reported in epidemiological studies as well as intervention trials [78].

The bulk of research pointing to a potential link between exercise and disease activity (e.g., mortality, recurrence) stems from prospective cohort studies. For example, it has been shown that individuals who reported exercising at least once per week prior to a diagnosis of colorectal cancer had a 10% better 5-year survival rate than individuals who did not exercise [79]. In a study of patients with colon cancer, frequent physical activity (e.g., approximately one hour per day) was associated with a 49% reduction in risk of recurrence or mortality [77].

Albeit suggestive of a protective effect of exercise, the correlational nature of these studies limits the nature of 'causal' conclusions that can be drawn. Higher levels of physical activity might represent a marker or proxy for pre-cancer health status. For example, only individuals who are healthy are able to walk for one hour per day. As a function of better overall health, these individuals might have been more resilient to cancer, regardless of their level of activity.

Several investigations have been conducted to examine the degree to which exercise interventions might be useful to reduce the severity or impact of residual cancer symptoms such as nausea, fatigue or pain [80]. Reductions in the severity of symptoms of nausea have been reported, following participation in an exercise program, in women with breast cancer undergoing chemotherapy [81]. Several investigations have shown that cancer survivors can improve the cardiovascular fitness through participation in a regular exercise program [82]. Resistance exercise has been shown to yield significant reductions in shoulder pain in individuals treated for head and neck cancer [83]. Aerobic exercise has been shown to reduce fatigue in men receiving treatment for prostate cancer [84]. Exercise training programs have also been shown to reduce the severity of symptoms of fatigue in breast cancer survivors [85, 86].

Exercise, Strength and Function: Restorative Rehabilitation

Both the symptoms of cancer and the effects of cancer can limit an individual's participation in physical activity. Long periods of inactivity during the treatment period can contribute to disuse and deconditioning. Muscle wasting and decreased muscle strength have been reported in more than 50% of cancer survivors [24, 87]. Prior to considering resumption of occupational activities, the cancer survivor might require interventions aimed at improving physical strength, flexibility and endurance [72].

Research on functional outcomes of exercise training can be assessed in terms of self-reported improvements in functioning, or objective measures of functional improvement. Quality of life measures have been the most frequently used indices of self-reported level of functioning. The results of several investigations have shown that participation in physical exercise can increase quality of life in cancer survivors [85, 86].

There is evidence that resistance training can yield significant increases in muscle mass in men with prostate cancer [88]. One study showed a home-based physical therapy intervention to be more effective in reducing upper-body disability in breast cancer survivors than group-based exercise or a pain management intervention [89].

The effects of exercise on muscle strength and role resumption have been more modest than those observed for symptom severity reduction or aerobic capacity. A meta-analysis of exercise interventions for cancer survivors concluded that effect sizes for muscle strength and role function were small or near-zero [90].

The Place of Exercise Training in Occupational Rehabilitation of the Cancer Survivor

Research on the effects of exercise on residual symptoms, strength, endurance and functional abilities has yielded generally positive outcomes. Research in this area suggests that exercise interventions could be usefully incorporated in rehabilitation programs for cancer survivors. Exercise training might be effective in reducing the severity of symptoms of nausea, fatigue and pain. Exercise training might be effective in restoring strength and function in regions of the body that have been adversely affected by deconditioning or surgery. Exercise training might facilitate resumption of important life activities and in turn, contribute to enhanced quality of life.

However, it is important to consider that reductions in symptoms, or increases in functional abilities observed following exercise training, may not necessarily contribute to enhanced return to work outcomes. In the research reviewed on the potential beneficial effects of exercise, return-to-work outcomes were not assessed. It is unclear therefore whether the use of exercise interventions, whether curative or restorative in their orientation will have a significant impact of return to work outcomes.

Exercise interventions often proceed from traditional medical models of disability. Whether aimed at reducing disease activity, or whether aimed at increasing functional abilities, the underlying assumption is that symptom reduction will translate into reduced disability. As noted earlier, research with individuals with other debilitating health conditions suggests that symptom reduction does not automatically translate into reduced disability. Failure to recognize the partial independence of symptoms and disability will necessarily compromise the effectiveness of rehabilitation efforts.

In recent years, numerous investigations have pointed to the role of psychosocial risk factors as determinants of occupational disability in individuals with persistent pain conditions, and other chronic health conditions. For example, several studies have been conducted addressing the role of psychosocial factors in the prediction of prolonged pain and disability associated with work-related musculoskeletal conditions [6]. Systematic reviews of prospective cohort studies indicate that initial levels of perceived pain and perceived functional disability are predictive of prolonged work disability [91]. Gheldolf et al. [92] found that pain-related fears were significant determinants of the inability to work in individuals with back pain. Cross-sectional and prospective studies have shown that high levels of pain catastrophizing are associated with longer periods of bed rest following injury, greater analgesic intake, longer periods of hospitalization and more prolonged work absence [60, 93, 94]. Lack of confidence in the ability to perform work-related activities has been associated with prolonged work disability [95, 96]. In research on work-related back injury, variables such as pain catastrophizing, pain-related fears (i.e., fear of movement/re-injury), self-efficacy, and outcome expectancies have been discussed as psychosocial risk factors for the prolonged pain and disability [6, 97, 98].

Little is currently known about the role of psychological factors in determining the trajectory of recovery following cancer treatment. Although numerous investigations have addressed the role of psychological risk factors for chronicity in low back disorders, only recently have rigorous investigations begun to examine psychological risk factors for chronicity in individuals treated for cancer [48, 99]. Given that a significant proportion of cancer survivors will experience debilitating symptoms of pain, psychosocial risk factors that have been identified in individuals with primary pain conditions might be similar in cancer survivors. It is therefore possible that rehabilitation interventions that have been used to target psychosocial risk factors for pain-related disability might also be of benefit to work-disabled cancer survivors.

Targeting Risk Factors for Disability in Cancer Survivors: Compensatory and Accommodative Interventions

One promising compensatory and accommodative intervention designed to reduce disability is the Progressive Goal Attainment Program (PGAP) [100]. PGAP was designed to specifically target the psychosocial factors that contribute to disability. The development of PGAP was originally based on research on the determinants of disability associated with pain conditions [60, 101]. The underlying rational was that, an intervention specifically targeting the psychosocial factors that contributed to disability might yield positive outcomes for individuals who were work-disabled due to a musculoskeletal condition [102].

Ongoing research has suggested that the psychosocial determinants of disability show striking similarity across a wide range of debilitating health and mental health conditions [70, 103, 104]. Individuals who have an alarmist orientation to their symptoms, individuals who are fearful of symptom exacerbations, and individuals who believe they are helpless to overcome the challenges of their health condition are more likely to exhibit high levels of disability [70]. These risk factors contribute to heightened disability in individuals regardless of their nature of their debilitating health or mental health condition. These are the psychosocial risk factors targeted by PGAP.

PGAP was originally designed to be provided in person but a telephonic version was developed for use in more remote locations. The telephonic version of PGAP is now also being used in a large national random assignment demonstration project being conducted in the United States (see below). The program consists of 10-weekly telephone contacts between a trained PGAP provider and a client. An educational video and Client Workbook are mailed to the client and serve as the platforms for the intervention techniques that will be used. The primary goals of PGAP are to reduce psychosocial barriers to rehabilitation progress, promote reintegration into life-role activities, increase quality of life, and facilitate return-to-work. These goals are achieved through targeted treatment of psychosocial risk factors, structured activity scheduling, graded-activity involvement, goal-setting, problem-solving, and motivational enhancement. In the initial weeks of the program, the focus is on developing a structured activity schedule for the client in order to facilitate resumption of pre-injury activities. Activity goals are established in order to promote resumption of family, social and occupational roles. Intervention techniques are invoked to target specific obstacles to rehabilitation progress (e.g. fear of symptom exacerbation, catastrophic thinking, and disability beliefs). In the final stages of the program, the intervention focuses on activities that will facilitate reintegration into the workplace [100]. PGAP is somewhat unique among disability reduction interventions in that all the techniques included in the intervention have activity resumption as their primary objective. There are no symptom-focused or symptom-reduction techniques included in the intervention. PGAP is also unique in its ability to successfully meet the accessibility challenge. As highlighted earlier in this chapter, disability is a population health problem. This population health problem will not be solved by interventions that can only be accessed in certain clinics or in centres based in large urban centres. Effective disability management occurs when disability is treated in the client's community of residence. With the development of the telephonic version of PGAP, PGAP can be offered to anyone in the world who owns a telephone.

Table 10.2 The main components of the Progressive Goal Attainment Program

(1) Education and Reassurance

The PGAP Video is used to provide the client with education about the nature of residual symptoms associated with cancer (e.g., pain, fatigue, emotional distress). Interviews with medical experts depicted in the PGAP Video are intended to convey reassurance about the benign nature of residual symptoms, and the importance of maintaining involvement in physical activities in order to promote progress in rehabilitation.

(2) Maintaining an Activity Log

Since one of the goals of PGAP is to maximize activity involvement, the client is asked to complete the Activity Log in the PGAP Client Workbook throughout the course of treatment.

(3) Activity Scheduling

Working with the PGAP clinician, the client develops an activity schedule that is designed to keep him or her as active as possible. Activities may include household activities, running errands, social and recreational activities. Activities are scheduled in relation to the client's chosen participation goals and are intended to create an activity structure that will ultimately facilitate resumption of occupational activities.

(4) The Walking Program.

A main component of the PGAP Program is the development of a walking program. The walking program starts with one 15-minute walk each day. As the PGAP Program moves forward, the PGAP clinician works with the client to steadily increase the distance walked each day.

(5) Increasing Activity Involvement

Through the course of the treatment program, the PGAP clinician assists the client in ways to increase activity involvement. The client is taught principles of graded activity participation to maintain momentum of recovery while minimizing the risk of symptom flare-ups. It is through graded activity participation that the client is first introduced to psychosocial strategies that can assist in overcoming the challenges of disability. Activity planning offers opportunities for the experience of success and achievement experiences; elements that are critical for the maintaining a positive and engaged orientation toward rehabilitation.

(6) Overcoming Psychological Obstacles to Activity Involvement

In the second phase of the program, the client develops skills to overcome fears of re-injury, learns to monitor and modify catastrophic thinking that may accompany symptoms, and learns to challenge his or her perceived limitations. Activity involvement is the primary tool for targeting psychosocial obstacles; activity involvement decreases attention to self-defeating thoughts, repeated exposure to discontinued activities reduces fears of symptom exacerbation and progressively increasing activity ultimately creates a reality that is incompatible with disability beliefs. Finally, the client learns communication skills and problem-solving strategies that will assist him or her in meeting the challenges associated with resumption of occupational activities.

As noted above, PGAP is being included as a component of an intervention that is now being tested in a large random assignment evaluation sponsored by the Social Security Administration of the United States and conducted by MDRC (a social policy research organization). The goal of the demonstration is to examine the effects of immediate access to health benefits, and other supports for new Social Security Disability insurance beneficiaries who have no health insurance. Cancer survivors make up one of the disability populations included in the evaluation, estimated to be about 10% of the total sample. Additional disability populations enrolled in the evaluation include individuals with persistent pain conditions related to back and other musculoskeletal disorders, individuals with a primary mental health diagnosis, and other chronic health problems such as cardiovascular, metabolic and neurologic conditions. There are three arms to the trial, 800 individuals are being assigned to a no intervention control group, 400 individuals will be provided with access to health care benefits and 800 individuals will be provided with a comprehensive rehabilitation program that will include health care benefits enhanced with medical care management, PGAP, and employment and benefits counseling. The medical care management, disability reduction intervention and the employment and benefits counseling are provided telephonically.

Medical care management guides clients toward appropriate health care services and ensures follow through on recommended treatment plans. Employment and benefits counselling services help clients to develop an employment plan and to understand how employment will affect their disability benefits. The program also provides referrals to local employment and other services to help individuals with disabilities reenter the labor market and access other financial and health supports they may be eligible to receive.

The evaluation will compare the outcomes of the three arms on a number of employment, health and disability measures. While the sample sizes may be too small to reliably determine impacts in these domains on cancer survivors and other sub-populations, the process component of the research will provide a rich source of data about the program experience and levels of participation among cancer survivors and other impairment groups in PGAP and the other components of the intervention. Interim results are likely to be available in 2009 and final results in early 2011.

Compensatory and Accommodative Interventions in the Workplace

As research revealed that work disability was not strictly a clinical problem, investigators turned their attention to workplace barriers impacting negatively on return to work outcomes. It became clear that functional limitations, residual symptoms and psychosocial risk factors were not the only barriers to employment in cancer survivors [49]. In other domains of rehabilitation, it has been suggested that successful return to work will be most likely achieved when intervention efforts can target risk factors that exist within the individual as well as risk factors that exist with the work environment [70].

Unsupportive work environments can present significant barriers to work re-entry for the cancer survivor [49]. Physical workload has also been shown to predict return to work in cancer survivors [50]. A number of research and policy reports have highlighted the role of discrimination on unemployment in individuals with or recovering from cancer [47, 105].

Early research in this area pointed to the importance of workplace factors that could either facilitate or impede successful work re-entry. One of the most robust findings in this area is that the availability of modified work greatly increased the probability of successful work re-entry and work retention [106, 107]. Modified work might take the form of reduced hours, modification of activities associated with the individual's occupation, and progressive or gradual resumption of occupational activities [107].

Recent research with individuals with musculoskeletal conditions suggests that brief interventions aimed at promoting communication between supervisors and work-disabled employees might impact positively on return to work outcomes [108, 109]. Interventions of this type might also be beneficial for work-disabled cancer survivors [26].

Effective return-to-work interventions for individuals with disabilities require the input of multiple stakeholders [110]. The impact of clinical approaches targeting symptoms or psychosocial risk factors can be augmented by intervention efforts designed to target workplace or organization barriers to work resumption [111]. In order to effectively target workplace or organization barriers to return to work, the intervention team must include not only the client and the treating professionals, but all relevant stakeholders such managers, supervisors, labor representatives and insurers [112].

Many countries around the globe have instituted legislation and incentive programs to facilitate return to work pathways for individuals with disabilities. Individuals with disabilities and employers are not always aware of these. Occupational rehabilitation programs must include an informational component that will familiarize both the individual with a disability and the employer with the policies and opportunities related to re-employment of cancer survivors [26, 113].

Conclusions

As cancer survivorship begins to increasingly characterize the life trajectory of individuals who have been diagnosed with cancer, there will be a corresponding increase in the need for effective rehabilitation services. Research shows that cancer survivors are likely to experience residual symptoms that might limit their ability to perform certain occupational activities. It follows that rehabilitation interventions that have been used with individuals with disabilities with similar debilitating symptoms might be usefully applied to cancer survivors. However, rehabilitation efforts for cancer survivors will need to consider the complexities of occupational disability and ensure that intervention efforts consider more than symptom-focused approaches.

Research to date clearly supports the use of exercise as an intervention that might impact on disease activity, symptom severity and physical function. These interventions might be usefully combined with pharmacological and psychotherapeutic approaches to minimize the physical and emotional distress of the cancer survivor. However, lessons learned from other domains of occupational rehabilitation clearly indicate that symptom-focused or function-focused interventions will not be sufficient to influence return to work outcomes in a meaningful manner.

One of the most important lessons learned from rehabilitation efforts with individuals with debilitating health conditions is that exclusive focus on symptom management will not impact in a meaningful way on return to work outcomes. Still numerous recent publications describing rehabilitation interventions for cancer survivors are almost entirely symptom-focused and return to work is not mentioned as an objective of treatment [1, 114, 115]. The medicalization of disability that has impeded rehabilitation progress in other domains also appears to have permeated cancer rehabilitation. It is not clear what strategies will be required to orient practitioners toward more functional and participatory objectives. The challenge of altering professional practice patterns might be particularly challenging in the case of cancer survivorship given that individuals might continue to receive disease-targeted medical interventions through the course of rehabilitation.

It is important to recognize that symptom management approaches to rehabilitation do not necessarily have to be at odds with disability reduction approaches. Within the educational component of rehabilitation, clients can be oriented to consider that symptom-management interventions will be used to facilitate participation in a disability reduction intervention.

Recent research has pointed to a number of psychosocial risk factors that might interfere with rehabilitation progress. Numerous investigations have shown that interventions that specifically target psychosocial risk factors for work disability can yield significant increases in life role participation and promote work resumption. It has also become clear that psychosocial risk factors for prolonged work disability exist not only within the person but within the work setting as well.

Work environments vary in their willingness and preparedness for accommodating the needs of the individual with a disability. Some of these barriers might emerge from discriminatory attitudes or practices. In other cases, barriers might emerge from misinformation about the occupational limitations of the cancer survivor. Employers might be concerned about the possibility of reduced productivity, absenteeism, and health care costs. Intervention approaches have been developed that can reduce these barriers to employment. Approaches that combine education and sensitivity training have been shown to increase employers' openness to accommodating employees' limitations or special needs. Education, direct contact and open communication have long been known to be useful tools for breaking down attitudinal barriers.

In other domains of work disability, research suggests that education, reassurance and encouragement to resume normal activities might be a key component of successful primary care interventions for return to work [56, 116]. This aspect of the management of work disability in cancer survivors appears to be lacking. Cancer survivors report that return to work is not a topic that is addressed by their treating physician [113]. Cancer survivors also note that they received little assistance about the benefits, drawbacks and time-frame for return to work [45].

Occupational rehabilitation for cancer survivors holds promise of becoming a model for rehabilitation in other domains of disability. By considering the distinct needs of cancer survivors and by reflecting on past rehabilitation errors, comprehensive rehabilitation programs can be built by design as opposed to successive approximation.

References

1. Franklin DJ. Cancer rehabilitation: challenges, approaches, and new directions. Phys Med Rehabil Clin N Am. 2007 Nov; 18(4): 899–924, viii.
2. Wolff SN. The burden of cancer survivorship: a pandemic of treatment success. In: Feuerstein M, (ed). Handbook of Cancer Survivorship. New York NY: Springer; 2007.
3. Jemal A, Murray T, Ward E. Annual report to the nation on the statistics of cancer, 1975–2001. Cancer. 2004; 101(1): 3–27.
4. Feuerstein M. Handbook of Cancer Survivorship. New York, NY: Springer; 2007.
5. Beck SL, Dudley WN, Barsevick A. Pain, sleep disturbance, and fatigue in patients with cancer: using a mediation model to test a symptom cluster. Oncol Nurs Forum. 2005 May; 32(3): 542.
6. Waddell G, Burton A, Main C. Screening to identify people at risk of long-term incapacity for work. London, UK: Royal Society of Medicine Press; 2003.
7. Von Korff M, Crane P, Lane M, Miglioretti DL, Simon G, Saunders K, et al. Chronic spinal pain and physical-mental comorbidity in the United States: results from the national comorbidity survey replication. Pain. 2005 Feb; 113 (3): 331–9.
8. Peters CM, Ghilardi JR, Keyser CP, Kubota K, Lindsay TH, Luger NM, et al. Tumor-induced injury of primary afferent sensory nerve fibers in bone cancer pain. Exp Neurol. 2005 May; 193 (1): 85–100.
9. Pronneke R, Jablonowski H. [Pain therapy in cancer patients]. MMW Fortschr Med. 2005 Jun 2; 147(22): 27–30.
10. Grond S, Zech D, Diefenbach C, Radbruch L, Lehmann KA. Assessment of cancer pain: a prospective evaluation in 2266 cancer patients referred to a pain service. Pain. 1996; 64: 107–14.
11. Caraceni A, Portenoy RK. An international survey of cancer pain characteristics and syndromes. IASP Task Force on cancer pain. Pain. 1999; 82: 263–74.
12. Berglund G, Bolund C, Fornander T, Rutqvist LE, Sjoden PO. Late effects of adjuvant chemotherapy and post-operative radiotherapy on quality of life among breast cancer patients. Eur J Cancer. 1991; 27: 1075–81.

13. Bjordal K, Mastekaasa A, Kaasa S. Self-reported satisfaction with life and physical health in long-term cancer survivors and a matched control group. Eur J Cancer. 1995; 31: 340–5.
14. Dow KH, Ferrell BR, Leigh S, Ly J, Gulasekaram P. An evaluation of the quality of life among long-term survivors of breast cancer. Breast Cancer Res Treat. 1996; 39: 261–73.
15. MacDonald L, Bruce J, Scott NW, Smith WC, Chambers WA. Long-term follow-up of breast cancer survivors with post-mastectomy pain syndrome. Br J Cancer. 2005; 92: 225–30.
16. Carpenter JS, Andrykowski MA, Sloan P, Cunningham L, Cordova MJ, Studts JL, et al. Post-mastectomy/post-lumpectomy pain in breast cancer survivors. J Clin Epidemiol. 1998; 51: 1285–92.
17. Portenoy RK. Cancer pain management. Clin Adv Hematol Oncol. 2005 Jan; 3 (1): 30–2.
18. Chaplin JM, Morton RP. A prospective, longitudinal study of pain in head and neck cancer patients. Head Neck. 1999; 21: 531–7.
19. Cleeland CS. The impact of pain on the patient with cancer. Cancer. 1984; 54: 2635–41.
20. Jung BF, Herrmann D, Griggs J, Oaklander AL, Dworkin RH. Neuropathic pain associated with non-surgical treatment of breast cancer. Pain. 2005 Nov; 118(1–2): 10–4.
21. Foley KM. Advances in cancer pain management in 2005. Gynecol Oncol. 2005 Dec; 99(3 Suppl 1): S126.
22. Cleeland CS, Bennett G, Dantzer R, Dougherty PM, al e. Are the symptoms of cancer and cancer treatment due to a shared biologic mechanism? Cancer. 2003; 97: 2919–25.
23. Curt GA. Fatigue in cancer. BMJ. 2001; 322: 1560.
24. Simmonds M. Physical functions in patients with cancer. Psychometric characteristics and clinical usefulness of a physical performance test battery. J Pain and Symptom Manage. 2002; 24: 404–14.
25. Lucia A, Earnest C, Perez M. Cancer-related fatigue: Can exercise physiology assist oncologists. Lancet Oncol. 2003; 4: 616–25.
26. Pryce J, Munir F, Haslam C. Cancer survivorship and work: Symptoms, supervisor response, co-worker disclosure and work adjustment. J Occ Rehab. 2007; 17: 83–92.
27. Fleishman SB. Treatment of symptom clusters: pain, depression and fatigue. J Natl Cancer Inst Monographs. 2004; 32: 119–23.
28. Meek PM, Nail LM, Barsevick A, Schwartz AL, Stephen S, Whitmer K. Psychometric testing for fatigue instruments for use with cancer patients. Nurs Res. 2000; 49: 181–90.
29. van Weert E, Hoekstra-Weebers JEHM, Otter R, Postema K, Sanderman R, van der Schans CP. Cancer-related fatigue: predictors and effects of rehabilitation. Oncologist. 2006; 11: 184–96.
30. Rodin G, Craven J, Littlefield C. Depression in the medically ill: an integrated approach. New York: Bruner Mazel; 1991.
31. Massie MJ. Prevalence of depression in patients with cancer. J Natl Cancer Inst Monographs. 2004; 32: 57–71.
32. Evans RL, Connis RT. Comparison of brief group therapies for depressed cancer patients receiving radiation treatment. Public Health Rep. 1995; 110: 306–11.
33. Recklitis C, O'Leary T, Diller L. Utility of a routine psychological screening in the childhood cancer survivor clinic. J Clin Oncol. 2003; 21: 787–92.
34. Kelsen DP, Portenoy RK, Thaler HT, Niedzwieki D, Passik SD, al e. Pain and depression in patients newly diagnosed pancreas cancer. J Clin Oncol. 1995; 13: 748–55.
35. Avis NE, Smikth KW, McGraw S, R.G. S, Petronis VM, Carver CS. Assessing quality of life in adult cancer survivors. Qual Life Res. 2005; 14: 1007–23.
36. Keefe FJ, Abernethy AP, Campbell LC. Psychological approaches to understanding and treating disease-related pain. Annu Rev Psychol. 2005; 56: 601–30.
37. Ganz PA, Desmond KA, Leedham B, al e. Quality of life in long-term, disease-free survivors of breast cancer: a follow-up study. J Natl Cancer Inst. 2002; 94: 39–49.
38. Glover J, Dibble SL, Dodd MJ, Miaskowski C. Mood states in oncology outpatients: does pain make a difference? J Pain Symptom Manage. 1995 120–128; 10.

39. McCorkle R, Tzuh Tang S, Greenwald H, Holcombe G, Lavery M. Factors related to depressive symptoms among long-term survivors of cervical cancer. Health Care Women Int. 2006; 27: 45–58.
40. Spiegel D, Sands S, Koopman C. Pain and depression in patients with cancer. Cancer. 1994; 74: 2570–8.
41. Zara C, Baine N. Cancer pain and psychological factors: A critical review of the litterature. J Pain Symptom Manage. [Review]. 2002; 24 (5): 526–42.
42. Karki A, Simonen R, Malkia E, et al. Impairments, activity limitations and participation restrictions 6 and 12 months after breast cancer operation. J Rehabil Med. 2005; 37: 180–8.
43. Rietman JS, Dijkstra PU, Debreczeni R, et al. Impairments, disabilities and health related quality of life after treatment of breast cancer: a follow-up study of 2.7 years after surgery. Disabil Rehabil. 2004; 26: 78–84.
44. Verbeek J, Spelten E. Work. In: Feuerstein M, (ed). Handbook of Cancer Survivorship. New York, NY: Springer; 2006.
45. Amir Z, Neary D, Luker K. Cancer survivors' views of work 3 years post diagnosis: A UK perspective. Eur J Oncol Nurs. 2008 Mar 12; 12(3): 190–7.
46. Feuerstein M. Cancer survivorship and work. J Occ Rehab. 2005; 15: 1–2.
47. Maunsell E, Drolet M, Brisson J, Brisson C, Masse B, Deschenes L. Work situation after breast cancer: results from a population-based study. J Natl Cancer Inst. 2004 Dec 15; 96(24): 1813–22.
48. Bishop SR, Warr D. Coping, catastrophizing and chronic pain in breast cancer. J Behav Med. 2003; 26: 265–81.
49. Spelten ER, Sprangers MA, Verbeek JH. Factors reported to influence the return to work of cancer survivors: a literature review. Psychooncology. 2002 Mar–Apr; 11 (2): 124–31.
50. Spelten ER, Verbeek JH, Uitterhoeve AL, Ansink AC, van der Lelie J, de Reijke TM, et al. Cancer, fatigue and the return of patients to work – a prospective cohort study. Eur J Cancer. 2003 Jul; 39(11): 1562–7.
51. Barofsky I. Work and Illness: The Cancer Patient. New York, NY: Praeger; 1989.
52. Hawkes M. Workers' Compensation in Western Australia Statistical Report. Stenton Park, WA: Workcover WA; 2007.
53. Corporation. AC. ACC Injury Statistics 2005. Section 14. Back Claims: First:http://www.acc.co.nz/wcm001/idcplg IdcService = SS_GET_PAGE&ssDocName = SS_WCM_115654&ssSourceNodeId = 8070. Accessed 5/09/2006 [updated 2006; cited]; Available from.
54. Wunderlich GS, Rice DP, Amado NL. The Dynamics of Disability: Measuring and Monitoring Disability for Social Security Programs. Washington, DC: National Academy Press; 2002.
55. SAAQ. La chronicite: Problematique biopsychosociale. Quebec: SAAQ; 2005.
56. Waddell G. The Back Pain Revolution. Second ed. Edinburgh: Churchill Livingstone; 2004.
57. WHO. International Classification of Impairments, Disabilities, and Handicaps. Geneva, Switzerland: World Health Organization; 1980 [cited].
58. WHO. International Classification of Functioning, Disability and Health: ICF. Geneva, Switzerland: World Health Organization; 2001.
59. Von Korff M, Katon W, Lin EH, Simon G, Ciechanowski P, Ludman E, et al. Work disability among individuals with diabetes. Diabetes Care. 2005 Jun; 28(6): 1326–32.
60. Sullivan MJ, Stanish W, Waite H, Sullivan M, Tripp DA. Catastrophizing, pain, and disability in patients with soft-tissue injuries. Pain. 1998 Sep; 77(3): 253–60.
61. Hogg M, Braithwaite M, Bailey M, Kotsimbos T, Wilson JW. Work disability in adults with cystic fibrosis and its relationship to quality of life. J Cyst Fibros. 2007 May; 6 (3): 223–7.
62. Yuval R, Halon DA, Lewis BS. Perceived disability and lifestyle modification following hospitalization for non-ST elevation versus ST elevation acute coronary syndromes: the patients' point of view. Eur J Cardiovasc Nurs. 2007 Dec; 6(4): 287–92.

63. Dionne CE. Psychological distress confirmed as predictor of long-term back-related functional limitations in primary care settings. J Clin Epidemiol. 2005 Jul; 58 (7): 714–8.
64. Waddell G, Aylward M, Sawney P. Back pain, incapacity for work and social security benefits: an international literature review and analysis. London: Royal Society of Medicine Press; 2002.
65. Von Korff M, Deyo RA. Potent opioids for chronic musculoskeletal pain: flying blind? Pain. 2004 Jun; 109 (3): 207–9.
66. Sullivan MJ, Adams A, Tripp D, Stanish W. Stage of chronicity and treatment response in patients with musculoskeletal injuries and concurrent symptoms of depression. Pain. 2007; 135: 151–9.
67. Seedat S, Lochner C, Vythilingum B, Stein DJ. Disability and quality of life in post-traumatic stress disorder: impact of drug treatment. Pharmacoeconomics. 2006; 24 (10): 989–98.
68. Pransky G, Gatchel R, Linton SJ, Loisel P. Improving return to work research. J Occup Rehabil. 2005 Dec; 15(4): 453–7.
69. Shaw W, Feuerstein M, Huang G. Secondary prevention and the workplace. In: Linton S, editor. New Avenues for the Prevention of Chronic Musculoskeletal Pain and Disability. Amsterdam: Elsevier; 2002.
70. Sullivan M, Feuerstein M, Gatchel RJ, Linton SJ, Pransky G. Integrating psychological and behavioral interventions to achieve optimal rehabilitation outcomes. J Occ Rehab. 2005; 15: 475–89.
71. Sullivan MJ. Toward a biospychomotor conceptualization of pain. Clin J Pain. 2008; 24: 281–90.
72. Stevenson C, Campbell KL, Sellar CM, Courneya KS. Physical activity for cancer survivors. In: Feuerstein M, (ed). Handbook of Cancer Survivorship. New York, NY: Springer; 2006.
73. Courneya KS. Exercise in cancer survivors: an overview of research. Med Sci Sports Excercise. 2003; 35: 1846–52.
74. Gordon S. Exercising and surviving: My cancer journey. Urol Oncol. 2008; 26: 215–6.
75. Ulman D. Exercise and rehabilitation of the cancer patient: Celebrating survivorship through "extreme exercise". Urol Oncol. 2008; 26: 213–4.
76. Meyerhardt JA, Giovannucci EL, Holmes MD, Chan AT, Chan JA, Colditz GA, et al. Physical activity and survival after colorectal cancer diagnosis. J Clin Oncol. 2006; 24: 3527–34.
77. Meyerhardt JA, Heseltine D, Niedzwiecki D, Hollis D, Saltz LB, Mayer RJ, et al. Impact of physical activity on cancer recurrence and survival in patients with stage III colon cancer: findings from CALGB 89803. J Clin Oncol. 2006; 24: 3535–41.
78. Friedenreich CM, Orenstein MR. Physical activity and cancer prevention: Etiologic evidence and biological mechanisms. J Nutr. 2002; 132: 3456S–63S.
79. Haydon AM, Macinnis RJ, English DR, Giles GG. Effect of physical activity and body size on survival after diagnosis with colorectal cancer. Gut. 2006 Jan; 55(1): 62–7.
80. Mock V, Dow KH, Meares CJ, Grimm PM, Dienemann JA, Haisfield-Wolfe ME, et al. Effects of exercise on fatigue, physical functioning, and emotional distress during radiation therapy for breast cancer. Oncol Nurs Forum. 1997 Jul; 24(6): 991–1000.
81. MacVicar MG, Winningham ML. Effects of aerobic interval training on cancer patients' functional capacity. Nursing Research. 1986; 38: 348–51.
82. Courneya KS, Friedenreich CM. Physical exercise and quality of life following cancer diagnosis: a literature review. Ann Behav Med. 1999 Spring; 21 (2): 171–9.
83. McNeely ML, Parliament M, Courneya KS, Seikaly H, Jha N, Scrimger R, et al. A pilot study of a randomized controlled trial to evaluate the effects of progressive resistance exercise training on shoulder dysfunction caused by spinal accessory neurapraxia/neurectomy in head and neck cancer survivors. Head Neck. 2004 Jun; 26(6): 518–30.

84. Monga U, Garber SL, Thornby J, Vallbona C, Kerrigan AJ, Monga TN, et al. Exercise prevents fatigue and improves quality of life in prostate cancer patients undergoing radiotherapy. Arch Phys Med Rehabil. 2007 Nov; 88(11): 1416–22.
85. Courneya KS, Mackey JR, Bell GJ, Jones LW, Field CJ, Fairey AS. Randomized controlled trial of exercise training in post-menopausal breast cancer survivors: Cardiopulmonary and quality of life outcomes. J Clin Oncol. 2003; 21: 1660–8.
86. Courneya KS, Friedenreich CM, Sela RA, Quinney HA, Rhodes RE, Handman M. The group psychotherapy and home-based physical exercise (group-home) trial in cancer survivors: Physical fitness and quality of life. Psycho-Oncology. 2003; 12: 357–74.
87. al Majid S, McCarthy DO. Cancer-induced fatigue and skeletal muscle wasting. Biol Res Nurs. 2001; 2: 186–97.
88. Segal RJ, Reid RD, Courneya KS, Malone SC, Parliament MB, Scott CG, et al. Resistance exercise in men receiving androgen deprivation therapy for prostate cancer. J Clin Oncol. 2003 May 1; 21(9): 1653–9.
89. Gordon LG, Battistutta D, Scuffham P, et al. The impact of rehabilitation support services on health-related quality of life for women with breast cancer. Breast Cancer Research and Treatment. 2005; 93: 217–26.
90. van Weert E, Hoekstra-Weebers JEHM, May AM, Korstjens I, Ros WJG, van der Schans CP. The development of an evidence-based physical self-management rehabilitation program for cancer survivors. Patient Educ Couns. 2008; 71(2): 169–90.
91. Schultz IZ, et al. Psychosocial factors predictive of occupational low back disability: Toward development of a return-to-work model. Pain. 2004; 107 (1): 77–85.
92. Gheldof E, et al. The differential role of pain, work characteristics and pain-related fear in explaining back pain and sick leave in occupational settings. Pain. 2005; 113(1): 71–81.
93. Picavet HS, Vlaeyen JW, Schouten JS. Pain catastrophizing and kinesiophobia: predictors of chronic low back pain. American Journal of Epidemiology. 2002 Dec 1; 156 (11): 1028–34.
94. Linton SJ. Do psychological factors increase the risk for back pain in the general population in both a cross-sectional and prospective analysis? Eur J Pain. 2005 Aug; 9(4): 355–61.
95. Kaivanto K, Estlander A, Moneta G. Isokinetic performance in low back pain patients: The predictive power of the Self-Efficacy Scale. J Occup Rehabil. 1995; 5: 87–99.
96. Lackner J, Carosella A, Feuerstein M. Pain expectancies, pain, and functional self-efficacy as determinants of disability in patients with chronic low back disorders. J Consult Clin Psychol. 1996; 64: 212–20.
97. Sullivan M, Ward LC, Tripp D, French D, Adams A, Stanish W. Secondary prevention of work disability: community-based psychosocial intervention for musculoskeletal disorders. J Occup Rehabil. 2005; 15: 377–92.
98. Sullivan M, Feuerstein M, Gatchel RJ, Linton SJ, Pransky G. Integrating psychological and behavioral interventions to achieve optimal rehabilitation outcomes. J Occup Rehabil. 2005; 15: 175–489.
99. Jacobsen P, Andrykowski MA, Thors CL. Relationship of catastrophizing to fatigue among women receiving treatment for breast cancer. J Consult Clin Psychol. 2004; 72: 355–61.
100. Sullivan M, Adams A, Rhodenizer T, Stanish W. A psychosocial risk factor targeted intervention for the prevention of chronic pain and disability following whiplash injury. Phys Ther. 2006; 86: 8–18.
101. Sullivan MJ, Stanish W, Sullivan ME, Tripp D. Differential predictors of pain and disability in patients with whiplash injuries. Pain Res Manag. 2002 Summer; 7 (2): 68–74.
102. Sullivan MJ, Stanish WD. Psychologically based occupational rehabilitation: the Pain-Disability Prevention Program. Clin J Pain. 2003 Mar–Apr; 19(2): 97–104.

103. Sullivan MJL, Thibault P, Savard A, Velly A. Pain and Function: A Psychosocial Perspective. In: Feuerstein M, (ed). Handbook of Cancer Survivorship. New York, NY: Springer; 2006.
104. Millward LJ, Lutte A, Purvis RG. Depression and the perpetuation of an incapacitated identity as an inhibitor of return to work. J Psychiatr Ment Health Nurs. 2005 Oct; 12(5): 565–73.
105. Feldman FL. Work and Cancer Health Histories: a study of Experiences of Recovered Blue Collar Workers. San Francisco, CA: American Cancer Society; 1978.
106. Baanders AN, Andries F, Rijken PM, Dekker J. Work adjustments among the chronically ill. Int J Rehabil Res. 2001; 24: 7–14.
107. Krause N, Dasinger LK, Neuhauser F. Modified work and return to work: a review of the literature. J Occ Rehab. 1998; 8: 113–9.
108. Shaw WS, Robertson MM, McLellan RK, Verma SK, Pransky G. A controlled case study of supervisor training to optimize response to injury in the food processing industry. Work. 2006; 26: 107–14.
109. Shaw WS, Linton SJ, Pransky G. Reducing sickness absence from work due to low back pain: How well do intervention strategies match modifiable risk factors? J Occ Rehab. 2006; 16: 591–605.
110. Franche RL, Baril R, Shaw WS, Nicholas MK, Loisel P. Workplace-based return-to-work interventions: Optimizing the role of stakeholders in implementation and research. J Occ Rehab. 2005; 15: 525–42.
111. Franche RL, Cullen K, Clarke J, Irvin E, Sinclair S, Frank JW. Workplace-based return-to-work interventions: a systematic review of the quantitative literature. J Occup Rehabil. 2005; 15:607–31.
112. Loisel P, Durand MJ, Baril R, Gervais J, Falardeau M. Interorganizational collaboration in occupational rehabilitation: Perceptions of an interdisciplinary rehabilitation team. J Occ Rehab. 2005; 15:581–90.
113. Main DS, Nowels CT, Cavender TA, Etschmaier M, Steiner FA. A qualitative study of work and return to work in cancer survivors. Psycho-Oncology. 2005; 14:992–1004.
114. Gerber LH. Cancer rehabilitation into the future. Cancer. 2001 Aug 15; 92 (4 Suppl):975–9.
115. Silver JK. Rehabilitation in women with breast cancer. Phys Med Rehabil Clin N Am. 2007 Aug; 18(3): 521–37, x.
116. Di Iorio D, Henley E, Doughty A. A survey of primary care physician practice patterns and adherence to acute low back pain problem guidelines. Arch Fam Med. 2000; 9:1015–21.

Chapter 11
Workplace Accommodations

Fong Chan, Elizabeth da Silva Cardoso, Jana Copeland, Robin Jones, and Robert T. Fraser

Introduction

Advances in cancer treatment in recent years have extended and enhanced the lives of millions of cancer survivors [1]. As pointed out in many of the earlier chapters in this book, the epidemiology indicates that cancer survivors are living longer and working longer than ever before. Returning to work and pursing one's career development has been identified as a critical part of enhancing the cancer survivorship experience [2].

Nevertheless, according to Short, Vasey, and Tunceli [3], about 20% of cancer survivors still report work limitations affected by cancer related problems five years post-diagnosis. Some of these cancer related problems affecting job performance include physical stamina/fatigue, pain, cognitive limitations (e.g., attention, concentration, and memory problems), depression, and social stigma that may require accommodations in the workplace. Bouknight, Bradley, and Luo [4] reported that perceived employer discrimination because of the cancer diagnosis was found to be a significant risk factor for unemployment, among participants in their study (odds ratio [OR] = 0.27; 95% CI: 0.10–0.71). They also indicated that accommodation was an important predictor of employment status for breast cancer survivors. In their study, women who perceived their employers as accommodating of their illness or cancer treatment were more likely to return to work than those who perceived their employers as not accommodating (OR = 2.2; 95% CI: 1.03–4.8).

With the passage of the Americans with Disabilities Act (ADA) in 1990 and since 1994, employers with 15 employees or more are legally obligated to provide reasonable accommodations for their employees with disabilities. Over the years, employers have learned to provide effective workplace accommodations for people with many types of high-incident physical disabilities such as persons with orthopedic injuries [5]. However, less is known about

---

F. Chan (✉)
Professor, Department of Rehabilitation Psychology and Special Education, University of Wisconsin-Madison, Madison, WI 53706, USA
e-mail: chan@education.wisc.edu

employer attitudes toward accommodating cancer survivors and types of accommodations that would best assist employees who are cancer survivors [6]. Conversely, there is evidence that cancer survivors face potential employment discrimination as supervisors frequently perceive cancer survivors as less productive and consider them poor candidates for promotion or advancement [7]. Since work resumption interventions for cancer survivors requires an interdisciplinary team approach, it is important for physicians, other health professionals, vocational rehabilitation professionals, and human resources managers to become familiar with accommodation needs of cancer survivors at home, in the community, and in the workplace. The purpose of this chapter is to provide an overview and discussion of the concept of reasonable accommodation under the ADA, the process for determining accommodation needs, specific accommodations for cancer survivors, general accommodations for people with other chronic illness and disability that may be applicable to cancer survivors, and resources for more information.

Reasonable Accommodations in the Workplace

The ADA provides protection to any qualified individual with a disability. An individual with a disability under the ADA is a person with a physical or mental impairment that substantially limits a major life activity (e.g., cognitive, social, emotional, and physical). The impairment must be severe, not temporary, and must have a permanent or long-term impact on the individual. A person may also be protected by ADA if he or she has a record of impairment or is regarded by others as a person with impairment. The "regarded as" standard applies to a person who is excluded from any basic life activity (e.g., employment), or is otherwise discriminated against, because of a covered entity's (e.g., an employer) negative attitudes toward that person's impairment...If the person's cancer is completely or substantially controlled through surgery, radiation, or chemotherapy with minimal or no residual symptoms or impairments, the person may not have a qualifying disability under the ADA because he or she would be unable to show a substantial impact on a major life function. However, the person diagnosed with and treated for cancer may be protected by one of the other definition prongs of the ADA; namely, he or she would have a history of impairment or the employer may be regarding him or her as having cancer-related impairments. If the employer discriminates against this person in the workplace because of his or her cancer history, this person will still be protected under the ADA even though the cancer no longer affected any major life function.

To be entitled to protection, the individual must also be qualified. A qualified individual with a disability is defined as

> An individual with a disability who satisfies the requisite skill, experience, education and other job related requirements of the employment position such individual holds or

desires and who with or without reasonable accommodation can perform the essential functions of such position (p.9) [8].

This definition implies that the individual must be able to perform the essential functions of the job. This requires a determination of essential versus marginal functions of the job. In general, essential functions are the basic job duties that an employee must be able to perform, with or without reasonable accommodation. Factors to consider in determining if a function is essential include

- whether the reason the position exists is to perform that function,
- the number of other employees available to perform the function or among whom the performance of the function can be distributed, and
- the degree of expertise or skill required to perform the function.

An employer must carefully examine each job to determine which functions or tasks are essential to performance. In general, cancer is a disability under the ADA when it or its residual or late effects (side effects) substantially limit one or more of a person's major life activities and because of these functional limitations, an employee who is a cancer survivor will likely need workplace accommodations.

The ADA Section 101(9) states that "reasonable accommodation" may include: (a) making existing facilities readily accessible to and usable by an individual with disabilities; and (b) job restructuring; part-time or modified work schedules; re-assignment to a vacant position; acquisition or modification of equipment or devices; appropriate adjustment or modification of examinations, training materials, or policies; the provision of qualified readers; and other similar accommodations for individuals with disabilities [9]. Employers are obligated to provide reasonable accommodations for persons with disabilities, unless the accommodation poses an undue hardship on the employer. Undue hardship is defined by the ADA as an accommodation that requires significant difficulty or expense and depends on factors such as cost; financial resources of the company; overall size of the employer; employer's operation including composition and structure of the workplace; and the nature and cost of the proposed accommodation [10]. Undue hardship is determined on a case-by-case basis. Where the facility making the accommodation is part of a larger entity, the structure and overall resources of the larger organization would be considered, as well as the financial and administrative relationship of the facility to the larger organization. In general, a larger employer with greater resources would be expected to make accommodations requiring greater effort or expense than would be required of a smaller employer with fewer resources.

Reasonable accommodation includes adjustments to assure that a qualified individual with a disability has rights and privileges in employment equal to those of employees without disabilities and should be provided to allow an individual to participate in the application process, perform the essential functions of the job, and to provide access to the benefits and privileges of employment. Importantly, accommodations must be made on an individual basis, because the nature and extent of a disabling condition and the requirements of a job will vary in each case. In selecting the particular type of reasonable accommodation to provide, the principal test is that of effectiveness, i.e., whether the accommodation will provide an opportunity for a person with a disability to achieve the same level of performance and to enjoy benefits equal to those of an average, similarly situated person without a disability.

A recent court case, Velente-Hook v. Eastern Plumas Healthcare, provides a concrete example of accommodations of cancer survivors in the workplace [11]. Ms. Velente-Hook, a licensed vocational nurse, was diagnosed with breast cancer. Her employer granted her four months medical leave for surgery, chemotherapy, and radiation treatment but refused to grant her additional medical leave time to complete her treatment because the company has a policy that no employee could have more than four months medical leave and would be terminated if he or she could not return to full duty after four months. The employer also refused to accommodate her to ease her transition back to work. Ms. Velente-Hook filed a disability discrimination lawsuit with the U.S. District Court for the Eastern District of California. The court ruled that there is no justification for not extending her medical leave for cancer treatment. (Under the ADA, an employer is required to make adjustments in leave policy as a reasonable accommodation. The employer is not obligated to provide additional paid leave, but accommodations may include leave flexibility and unpaid leave.) The court faulted the employer for not allowing this nurse to work part-time upon returning from her cancer treatments. (ADA explicitly stated that part-time and flexible work scheduling is considered a reasonable accommodation for people with disabilities.) The court also found that it is unreasonable for the employer to refuse this nurse's request to transfer to another facility owned by the company that would reduce her daily commute by 60 miles. (A transfer is considered a reasonable accommodation under ADA.) The nurse also requested her employer to create an office position for her because she no longer has the physical stamina to stand all day. In this situation, the court ruled that the company is not required to create a new position just to fulfill a disabled employee's need for reasonable accommodation. However, the court indicated that the employer should at least consider it under the obligation to communicate with an employee with a disability.

It should be noted that an employer can hold employees with disabilities to the same standards of production/performance as other similarly situated employees without disabilities for performing essential job functions, with or without reasonable accommodation. An employer also can hold employees with disabilities to the same standards of production/performance as other employees regarding marginal functions unless the disability affects the person's ability to perform those marginal functions.

If the ability to perform marginal functions is affected by the disability, the employer must provide some type of reasonable accommodation such as job restructuring but may not exclude an individual with a disability who is satisfactorily performing a job's essential functions. For example, for a receptionist, communicating with callers and visitors and providing information is an essential function, whereas caring for plants, arranging refreshments for meetings, ordering business cards for new employees may be considered marginal functions. The following is an example offered by the Equal Employment Opportunity Commission (EEOC) for a cancer patient:

> A receptionist with breast cancer is undergoing chemotherapy. As a consequence of the treatment, the employee is subject to fatigue and finds it difficult to keep up with her regular workload. So that she may focus her reduced energy on performing her essential functions, the employer transfers three of her marginal functions to another employee for the duration of the chemotherapy treatments. The second employee is unhappy at being given extra assignments, but the employer determines that the employee can absorb the new assignments with little effect on his ability to perform his own assignments in a timely manner. Since the employer cannot show significant disruption to its operation, there is no undue hardship.

The following is a job restructuring example related to a cancer survivor:

> MJ is a 42 year old accounts manager who has completed all cancer treatments including chemotherapy. However, she is still having difficulty focusing on complex reports and loses track of her work tasks when disrupted by telephone calls. By early afternoon she fatigues and becomes very anxious as she cannot get things done. MJ was advised to restructure her day by getting in at 7:30 am instead of 9:00 am in order not to be disrupted in her more complex tasks. All calls were held to two periods in the day, 10:00 am to 11:30 am and 2:00 pm to 3:00 pm. In this fashion she had more focus to her day. Her husband brought a mat bed into her office which she would lie on with her door closed over lunch. She left work at 3:15 pm. Both her early commute in and early departure saved her prolonged commute time and the fatigue involved therein. When she got home, before dinner she would work on bookkeeping duties that were less complex, such as corporate travel for an hour before dinner. This schedule and the midday rest period were invaluable in helping her to maintain her optimal cognitive functioning and be well rested. In addition, one home based work day during mid-week (Wednesday) was also offered to MJ.

Finally, an employer can consider health and safety when deciding whether to hire an applicant or retain an employee with a disability. The ADA permits employers to establish qualification standards that will exclude individuals who pose a direct threat—i.e., a significant risk of substantial harm—to the health or safety of the individual or of others, if that risk cannot be eliminated or reduced below the level of a "direct threat" by reasonable accommodation. However, an employer may not simply assume that a threat exists; the employer must establish through objective, medically supportable methods that there is significant risk that substantial harm could occur in the workplace. By requiring employers to make individualized judgments based on reliable medical or other objective evidence rather than on generalizations, ignorance, fear, patronizing attitudes, or stereotypes, the ADA recognizes the need to balance the interests of people with disabilities against the legitimate interests of employers in maintaining a safe workplace. A flow chart depicting the reasonable accommodation decision-making process is presented in Fig. 11.1.

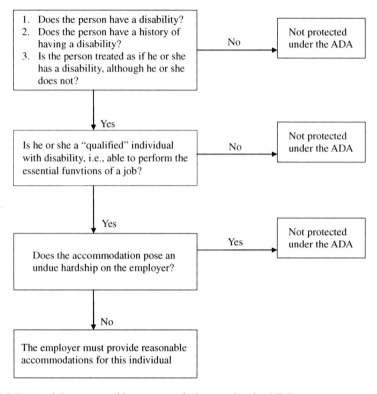

Fig. 11.1 Determining reasonable accommodations under the ADA

The Accommodation Process

The accommodation process begins with a request from the employee. In general, the applicant or employee with a disability is responsible for letting the employer know that an accommodation is needed to participate in the application process, to perform essential job functions, or to receive equal benefits and privileges of employment. Employers are not required to provide accommodations if they are not aware of the need.

According to the Equal Employment Opportunity Commission (EEOC), the federal agency charged with enforcing the ADA, an accommodation request does not have to be in writing. However, the EEOC suggests that individuals with disabilities might find it useful to document accommodation requests in the event there is a dispute about whether or when they requested accommodation. One way to document an accommodation request is to make a written request. Batiste [12] suggested that the following information should be included in the accommodation request letter:

- Identify yourself as a person with a disability
- State that you are requesting accommodations under the ADA (or the Rehabilitation Act)
- Identify your specific problematic job tasks
- Identify your accommodation ideas
- Request your employer's accommodation ideas
- Refer to attached medical documentation if appropriate
- Ask that your employer respond to your request in a reasonable amount of time

A Sample Accommodation Request Letter

Dear Mr. Smith:

I have worked as a receptionist for the company since July 2000. I am a breast cancer survivor. As a consequence of my cancer treatments, I still experience considerable pain from my surgery and I feel fatigue easily. To allow me to focus my energy on performing essential functions of my job, I am writing to request accommodations under the Americans with Disabilities Act. Specifically, I would like to request four extra 15-minute breaks each day. I will come in early and stay late to compensate for the break time. Since I still experience considerable pain when I type, I would need to purchase a copy of the *Dragon Naturally Speaking*, a speech recognition software, to help me with typing. These accommodations will help me to successfully perform my job. I am also open to any accommodation ideas that you may have.

For more information about my rights and your responsibilities under the Americans with Disabilities Act, I am enclosing a handout which explains this in more detail. You can also call either the Job Accommodation Network at 1-800-526-7234 or the Great Lakes Disability and Business Technical Assistance Center at 1-800-949-4232 for more information, free of charge.

If you have any questions about my request you can contact me in writing or by phone. However, I would appreciate a written response to this letter. Thank you very much.

Sincerely,
Jane Doe

For the employer, the first step in the accommodation process is to determine that the employee is a qualified individual with a disability. As mentioned in the previous section, an individual may qualify for an accommodations plan under ADA if (a) the individual has a diagnosed disability; (b) the individual has a record of the disability; and (c) the disability "substantially affects one or more major life activities." Therefore, these elements need to be addressed in the request. The term "substantial" is not clearly defined. However, it is suggested that employers should use "common sense" (e.g., a cancer survivor who has undergone brain surgery to remove the tumor will probably have a disability that substantially affects one or more major life activities) and a combination of diagnostic evidence. In considering accommodations, Brodwin et al. [10] suggested that it is more useful to conceptualize disability in functional terms. Functional limitation can be defined as "the inability to perform an action or a set of actions, either physical or mental, because of a physical or emotional restriction." (p. 167). Brodwin et al. [10] suggested that the vocational implications of disability may be better understood when medical conditions or disabilities are translated into functional terms. For example, the functional limitations of a person with below-the-knee amputation can be translated to maximum ambulation of one hour during an 8-hour workday, no ambulation on rough or uneven surfaces, and no climbing of stairs, etc. The functional limitations of a breast cancer survivor can be translated to difficulty reaching above shoulder height because of pain, lymphedema and problems concentrating for a long period of time.

The second step of the accommodation process is to perform an ADA functional job analysis. The purpose of the job analysis is to identify essential job functions, the extent an individual's medical condition (e.g., cancer) or disability affects his or her ability to perform essential job functions, and what kinds of accommodations will be needed. A functional job analysis will help the employer: (a) clarify the purpose of the position and why it exists in the organization in order to determine the criticalness of the position duties and tasks; (b) identify the functions (duties and tasks) in order to analyze the position; (c) identify and verify the position related qualifications (e.g., education, experience, skills/abilities, knowledge, and license/certification); (d) identify the physical demands related to the position (e.g., mobility [sitting, standing, walking], vertical work, horizontal work, strength [lifting, carrying, pushing, and pulling], and physical agilities [kneeling, bending, stooping, crouching, crawling, etc.]); (e) identify environmental and safety factors related to the position (e.g., indoors, outdoors, exposure to extreme hot or cold temperature, exposure to excessive noises, working with toxic chemicals, working with machinery, working with computers, working with people, working alone, etc.); and (f) identify machines, equipment, tools, and work aids used by the employee to perform his duties and tasks.

The third step of the accommodation process is to determine what functions are essential and what functions are marginal based on the functional job analysis. Thrush (1996) recommended the use of the following questions to verify if a function is essential.

Primary Considerations

1. **Does the employee actually perform the function?** If the function is not performed or performance of the function is not critical to the overall purpose of the position, then the function may not be essential.

2. **Would removing the function interrupt the flow or output of the required work, or deplete the reason for the position?** If removing the function would fundamentally change the position, then the function is likely to be essential.

Secondary Considerations

3. **Does the position exist to perform the function?**
4. **Are there a limited number of employees who can perform the function?**
5. **Is the function highly specialized?**

If the answer to question 3 is "Yes," and "Yes" or "No" to question 4 and question 5, then the function is likely to be essential. With job data for the specific position on hand, the employee with a disability should be consulted to find out how his or her physical or mental limitations impede job performance.

The fourth step in the accommodation process is to determine what accommodations are needed and whether such accommodation will pose undue hardship (i.e., too costly, too extensive, too substantial, and too disruptive, etc.). However, it should be noted that the cost of accommodations is rarely expensive. The Job Accommodation Network (JAN) reported that in their experience, more than half of all accommodations cost less than $500 [13]. Importantly, accommodations should be customized to the needs of the individual with disability and such accommodations must be effective in reducing barriers to employment [8]. Thrush [8] identified four common methods of reasonable accommodation:

- *Job restructuring*—this method involves eliminating, re-distributing, or replacing marginal duties from a position held by the employee with a disability. Activities can be eliminated or re-distributed if the activities are performed out of convenience or due to habits and not truly a position necessity. For example, an attorney with an emotional stress problem can be allowed to spend more time doing research, case presentation, legal briefs and less time litigating in court.
- *Job modification*—this method entails changing the methods and means (e.g., using specific adaptive tools and adaptive equipment) for performing essential job tasks, while maintaining the same job duties. Job site modifications are used to help a person with disability meets job performance standards and/or to eliminate aggravation to the existing medical condition. For example, an employer can change the work schedule of a secretary to come to work early so that she can leave early for physical therapy appointments.
- *On-the-job supports*— this method emphasizes helping the individual with the disability perform job requirements using natural supports in the job environment (e.g., co-worker assistance) or using job coaching, follow-up and follow-along, and job retention services. Workplace support such as the use of a job coach to teach the individual with disability job skills and

workplace socialization skills in the initial phase of employment is commonly used for people with developmental disabilities.
- *Barrier removal*—this method is concerned with removing architectural and institutional barriers. Architectural barriers restrict access to facilities and services of the company and institutional barriers related to organizational climate (e.g., negative attitudes and harassment) and practice toward hiring and retaining people with disabilities.

Accommodations for Cancer Survivors

The effective utilization of workplace accommodations, supportive workplace culture and good social climate at work are factors that have been positively associated with the effective return to work of cancer survivors [4]. Typical work limitations affected by cancer include physical stamina/fatigue, pain, cognitive limitations (e.g., attention, concentration, and memory problems), depression, and social stigma [3]. Loy [14] provided some field tested ideas from the Job Accommodation Network for accommodating cancer survivors in the workplace. Table 11.1 summarizes specific questions to consider in the accommodation process for cancer survivors. In addition, workplace accommodation ideas for employees with cancer are presented in Table 11.2.

The National Brain Tumor Foundation (NBTF) [15] provided specific suggestions to cancer survivors for accommodating cognitive limitations related to attention, concentration, memory and organization. For example, it may be helpful to keep a schedule to aid in remembering tasks and appointments by programming the computer to provide automatic calendar reminders; create checklists to keep track of the tasks that have been completed and those still in progress; use auditory or visual cues (e.g., tape-recorded messages, color-coded containers for specific items, and a pager or timer to remind about tasks); and use office products to help keep objects (e.g., rubber finger tips and electric staplers) in place and to improve work speed. The NBTF [14] also provided the

Table 11.1 Questions to consider in the accommodation process

1. What limitations is the employee with cancer experiencing?
2. How do these limitations affect the employee and the employee's job performance?
3. What specific job tasks are problematic as a result of these limitations?
4. What accommodations are available to reduce or eliminate these problems? Are all possible resources being used to determine possible accommodations?
5. Has the employee with cancer been consulted regarding possible accommodations?
6. Once accommodations are in place, would it be useful to meet with the employee with cancer to evaluate the effectiveness of the accommodations and to determine whether additional accommodations are needed?
7. Do supervisory personnel and employees need training regarding cancer?

Source: Job Accommodation Network.

Table 11.2 Workplace accommodations for cancer survivors

Fatigue/Weakness
- Reduce or eliminate physical exertion and workplace stress
- Schedule periodic rest breaks away from the workstation
- Allow a flexible work schedule and flexible use of leave time
- Allow work from home
- Implement ergonomic workstation design
- Provide a scooter or other mobility aid if walking cannot be reduced
- Provide parking close to the work-site
- Install automatic door openers
- Make sure materials and equipment are within reach range
- Move workstation close to other work areas, office equipment, and break rooms
- Reduce noise with sound absorbent baffles/partitions, environmental sound machines, and headsets
- Provide alternate work space to reduce visual and auditory distractions

Medical Treatment Allowances
- Provide flexible schedules
- Provide flexible leave
- Allow a self-paced workload with flexible hours
- Allow employee to work from home
- Provide part-time work schedules
- Respiratory Difficulties:
- Provide adjustable ventilation
- Keep work environment free from dust, smoke, odor, and fumes
- Implement a "fragrance-free" workplace policy and a "smoke free" building policy
- Avoid temperature extremes
- Use fan/air-conditioner or heater at the workstation
- Redirect air conditioning and heating vents

Skin Irritations
- Avoid infectious agents and chemicals
- Avoid invasive procedures (activities that could be harmful to a person's skin condition)
- Provide protective clothing

Stress
- Develop strategies to deal with work problems before they arise
- Provide sensitivity training to coworkers
- Allow telephone calls during work hours to doctors and others for support
- Provide information on counseling and employee assistance programs

Temperature Sensitivity
- Modify work-site temperature
- Modify dress code
- Use fan/air-conditioner or heater at the workstation
- Allow flexible scheduling and flexible use of leave time
- Allow work from home during extremely hot or cold weather
- Maintain the ventilation system
- Redirect air conditioning and heating vents
- Provide an office with separate temperature control

Source: Job Accommodation Network.

following practical solutions that have been used by employers to accommodate cognitive limitations of employees with cancer.

- Develop a job-sharing situation.
- Provide (minimal) assistance from a co-worker, supervisor or personal care attendant.
- Spread out work tasks.
- Modify work schedule to allow part-time hours, flexible hours, or doing strenuous work early in the day to accommodate the problem of fatigue due to cancer.
- Restructure meetings (e.g., one-on-one time with supervisor), schedule more frequent breaks, or use cue cards and other visual aids to help with inattentiveness.
- Reassign to a vacant position that is more suited to the employee's current abilities.
- Provide a temporary job coach to help train the employee.
- Provide additional unpaid leave for required medical treatment.

The American Cancer Society also provided similar suggestions for accommodations including the use of assistive devices, reassignment to a vacant position, modified work schedules, and job restructuring.

Job accommodations can enhance the employment success of cancer survivors. However, at present there is a paucity of research conducted to validate the efficacy of job accommodations for cancer survivors. Therefore, it may also be useful to consider job accommodations based on effective accommodations for persons with other chronic medical conditions or disability. The use of functional limitations (e.g., physical stamina/fatigue, pain, cognitive limitations, depression, and social stigma) to conceptualize accommodations for cancer survivors to improve their interaction with the work environment has significant merit, as occupational rehabilitation professionals and employers have extensive experience accommodating employees with functional limitations [10].

Limitations Related to Ability to Communicate

Cancer survivors may benefit from using alternative and augmentative communication (AAC) devices. For example, an individual may have low vocal volume or larynx damage due to cancer [16]. He or she can use a computer-based ACC device that will allow a range of input methods (e.g., the use of Morse code or scanning) and provide output in the form of voice, printed, visual, and tactile display. Some AAC systems provide a variety of synthesized voices in both genders and a range of ages that will match the client's personal characteristics. Other systems "listen" to the client's vocalization, electronically filter and manipulate it, and immediately "say" each spoken word more loudly and clearly. Conversely, a breast cancer survivor may still have upper body pain or functional limitations several months after surgery and may not be able to type and to use the computer at work as effectively as prior to the illness. The use of popular speech recognition software like *Dragon Naturally Speaking* and *IBM Via Voice* will allow the employee with cancer to talk into a microphone and the computer will type what he or she says [16; 17]. These approaches have improved considerably over the past few years.

Limitations Related to Vision

Childhood brain tumors present with visual symptoms about 50% of the time. Many more children will develop visual symptoms and or signs during and after treatment. Such signs may resolve over time or they can become long-term residual effects of the tumor or its treatment [18]. Many assistive technology resources are available for people with visual impairments that can be used by cancer survivors with visual symptoms. A variety of visual displays can maximize the utility of residual vision, and screen-reading software translates computer screen displays to spoken words. For individuals with more limited vision and a desire to return to work, devices to assist *Activities of Daily Living* (ADLs) may be helpful in some workplace situations. For example, sensors give an audible cue when a coffee cup is filled, talking clocks allow employees to manage time effectively, and a variety of optical and electronic magnifiers facilitate access to workplace paperwork. Mobility aids include canes and electronic sensors to detect a clear path. Following the military's development of the global positioning system (GPS), such units are now available as orientation aids. A GPS unit can locate one's position on the earth's surface to within a few inches, and indicate direction and distance to one's destination. These types of technologies assist employees with cancer-related vision loss and certain cognitive limitations effectively function in the workplace.

Limitations Related to Cognitive Abilities

As mentioned, many cancer survivors may have attention, concentration, memory, organization, and problem-solving limitations. Attention involves awareness of important stimuli in a person's environment. Concentration refers to a person's ability to focus and maintain attention and not be distracted by other stimuli for a period of time. Memory related to the ability to store and retrieve events or knowledge. Attention and concentration problems interact with memory deficits to significantly affect a person's ability to acquire and retain the knowledge and skills necessary for employment [19]. Many of these cognitive deficits manifested by some cancer survivors are similar to individuals with traumatic brain injuries (TBI) and learning disabilities (LD). Some of the accommodations used by people with TBI and LD may also be used to accommodate employees with cancer. A list of these suggested accommodations is presented in Table 11.3.

Table 11.3 Accommodations for concentration, organization, problem-solving, and memory problems

Cognitive Limitation	Accommodations
Concentration	
	• Reduce distractions in the work area
	• Provide space enclosures or a private office
	• Allow for use of white noise or environmental sound machines
	• Allow the employee to play soothing music using a cassette player and headset
	• Increase natural lighting or provide full spectrum lighting
	• Reduce clutter in the employee's work environment
	• Plan for uninterrupted work time
	• Divide large assignments into smaller tasks and steps
	• Restructure job to include only essential functions
Organization	
	• Make daily TO-DO lists and check items off as they are completed
	• Use several calendars to mark meetings and deadlines
	• Remind employee of important deadlines via memos or e-mail or weekly supervision
	• Use a watch or pager with timer capability
	• Use electronic organizers
	• Divide large assignments into smaller tasks and steps
	• Assign a mentor to assist employee determining goals and provide daily guidance
	• Schedule weekly meetings with supervisor, manager or mentor to determine if goals are being met
Problem Solving	
	• Provide picture diagrams of problem solving techniques, e.g. flow charts
	• Restructure the job to include only essential functions
	• Assign a supervisor, manager or mentor to be available when the employee has questions
Memory	
	• Allow the employee to tape record meetings
	Provide type written minutes of each meeting
	• Use notebooks, calendars, or sticky notes to record information for easy retrieval
	• Use a personal digital assistant (PDA) as a memory aid
	• Provide written as well as verbal instructions
	• Allow additional training time
	• Provide written checklists

Limitations Related to Physical Stamina

Fatigue and lack of stamina is a common problem among cancer survivors. It is also common among people with multiple sclerosis, chronic obstructive pulmonary disease, cardiac conditions, HIV/AIDS, and spinal cord injuries. Functional limitations may include shortness of breath, chronic, episodic or recurrent fatigue, and weakness. Accommodations may include flexible work schedule, part-time work, light or sedentary work, regular vs. rotating work shifts, and occasional leave during illness and exacerbation of symptoms [10]. In addition, modifying the work environment and the use of adaptive equipment (e.g., an electric wheelchair) to minimize bending, ambulation, reaching, lifting and carrying may be effective accommodation for employees with cancer who have variations in stamina.

Limitations Related to Pain Symptoms

The prevalence of pain at the time of cancer diagnosis and early in the course of disease is estimated to be 50%. Residual pain following primary treatment can be chronic or episodic. However, recent results from the European Pain in Cancer (EPIC) survey of 4,947 patients with breast cancer (n = 1427), prostate (n = 624), bowel/colorectal (n = 504), lung cancer (n = 417), gynecologic cancer (n = 411), head/neck cancer (n = 213), bone/muscle (n = 173), pancreatic (n = 142), brain tumor (n = 135), leukemia (n = 125), lymphomas (n = 102), blood borne (n = 90), and non-Hodgkins (n = 61) [20] indicated that pain in most cancer patients is frequent and often long-term (more than 12 months), with one in two patients suffering moderate to severe pain, 73% reporting pain which they attribute to their cancer, and almost one-third of cancer patients reporting that they have dealt with cancer-related pain for over a year. Chronic pain can contribute to a range of functional limitations and the severity and intensity of pain, Accommodations in the workplace may include change in work duties, modified scheduling, use of assistive technology, and time off to receive treatment.

Limitations Related to Stress and Depression

According to the Agency for Healthcare Quality and Research [21], the prevalence of major depression with rates varying from 10% to 25% for cancer patients is at least four times greater than the general population. Temporary changes in job requirements are effective accommodations for individuals experiencing social, emotional and intellectual limitations. Workplace support and employee education to provide supervisors and co-workers information on how to work, support, and interact effectively with employees with depression have been found to be appropriate accommodations. A company's employee assistance program is also a good resource for helping the employee with depression resulting from cancer diagnosis and treatment.

Accommodating the Cancer Survivor: Case Examples

As mentioned earlier, a cancer diagnosis and the related treatment can exacerbate several challenges for both employer and employee in the workplace. These include, but are not limited to, importance of maintaining health insurance benefits, fatigue and weakness, flexibility to receive medical treatments, temperature sensitivity, and mobility and sensory impairment. Fortunately, several low cost accommodations are available to address these workplace issues. The following are examples of actual cases and accommodation solutions for cancer survivors.

Case 1: Accommodations During Treatment
A doctor underwent chemotherapy and radiation treatment for lymphoma. She experienced periods of severe fatigue, pain, and dizziness during the treatments. To accommodate those limitations, her employer allowed her to work a modified schedule where she saw patients only during the mornings and processed paperwork and case files in the afternoons. She also worked three days a week during treatment periods. To accommodate immuno-deficiencies associated with her treatments, she only saw well patients, while other practitioners in her office saw her patients needing treatment for contagious conditions like cold and flu.

Case 2: Accommodation Following Treatment
A paralegal underwent chemotherapy following a diagnosis of breast cancer. She eventually underwent surgery for a mastectomy. Following her return to work, she experienced severe depression related to physical changes following surgery. Her employer allowed her to take periodic breaks throughout the workday for walks, personal calls, and other therapeutic activities. The attorneys also allowed her to play music in her workspace to help with her mood/depression. Finally, the law office provided a private, quiet space for the employee to take breaks during the day.

Case 3: Accommodation in a Physically Demanding Job
A truck driver was diagnosed with osteosarcoma that resulted in amputation of his foot. He was fitted with a prosthesis and returned to an average level of mobility. However, he did have some difficulties climbing on his truck to load materials onto the flatbed. His employer assigned additional personnel to assist him with loading and securing materials on his truck.

Case 4: Accommodations for Fatigue and Pain
A cashier for a home supply retailer returned to work following treatment for prostate cancer. Fatigue following treatment resulted in difficulty standing at the cash register for extended periods of time and pain in his lower extremities,

because of standing on concrete during his shift. After discussing the problems with his supervisor, the retailer modified company policy prohibiting sitting while at the register and allowed the employee to use a stool throughout his shift. They also purchased a padded mat to alleviate pain from the concrete flooring.

Case 5: Accommodations Related to Co-worker Relationships
The office manager of a construction firm returned to work following the removal of a cancerous growth on her cheek. The surgery resulted in significant scarring. Soon after her return, she overheard several co-workers making disparaging comments about her physical appearance. After discussing the incident with her supervisor, the company instituted mandatory disability etiquette training to increase awareness among all staff. The supervisor continued to monitor adherence to practice of appropriate interpersonal relationship strategies and met with the employee periodically to ensure that she did not encounter further stigma.

As these cases illustrate, return to work and the subsequent re-integration into the workplace of cancer survivors is feasible and appropriate through the use of effective accommodations. Frequently, low-tech or no-tech solutions are available to assist cancer survivors address functional limitations resulting from their diagnosis and treatment. Through the use of workplace accommodations, both employers and employees benefit from creativity, flexibility, and ongoing communication. While more research is needed to create an evidence-based approach to workplace accommodations for cancer survivors, we need continue to creatively apply universal accommodation concepts and techniques available to continue to effectively bring cancer survivors back to work. While studies show that cancer survivors are more likely to file ADA complaints related to job loss [7], these claims can alleviate through common sense strategies to re-integrate cancer survivors into the workplace following diagnosis and treatment.

Conclusion

With medical advances, many cancer survivors have a high prospect of living a long and productive life. Many adult cancer survivors will eventually go back to work. Although some cancer survivors will need accommodations, it is important to help employers recognize the abilities and potential of employees with cancers. It is also important to recognize that some cancer survivors may need help with their cancer-related limitations. Healthcare and rehabilitation professionals need to share with cancer survivors and employers information related to effective accommodation strategies and the relative low cost of accommodations. The high return on this investment in terms of enhancing productivity of employees who are cancer survivors should also be underscored. Employers need to be aware of ADA resources in the community and how to engage a variety of stakeholders (e.g., occupational therapists, physical therapists, doctors, nurses, rehabilitation counselors, mental health providers, and cancer survivors) to develop the most effective solution to accommodate functional limitations of employees with cancer. Importantly, we need to continue to explore additional cancer-specific accommodation solutions for a variety of job types and conduct research to validate their effectiveness to prevent the discrimination cited earlier [7] and improve the work productivity of those cancer survivors who are experiencing problems in the workplace [22].

Acknowledgments Preparation of this chapter was supported through the Virginia Commonwealth University's Coordination, Outreach and Research Center for the National Network of Americans with Disabilities Act (ADA) Resource Centers, National Institute on Disability and Rehabilitation Research, U.S. Department of Education (PR# H133A060087) and Southern University's Rehabilitation Research Institute for Underrepresented Populations, National Institute on Disability and Rehabilitation Research, U.S. Department of Education (PR#H133A031705).

Appendix: Resources for Job Accommodation Ideas and Technical Assistance

With the passage of the ADA, the federal government has provided funding to many entities to provide technical assistance and consultations to employers, rehabilitation and healthcare professionals, and persons with disabilities regarding the ADA and accommodations of people with disabilities in the workplace, including cancer survivors. The following is a list of selected technical assistance resources for reasonable accommodations:

Job Accommodation Network (JAN). It is a free service of the Office of Disability Employment Policy, U.S. Department of Labor, developed to employers with appropriate accommodations for employees under ADA.
800-526-7234 (V)
877-781-9403 (TTY)
http://www.jan.wvu.edu/

DBTAC National Network of ADA Centers. It is a free service funded by the National Institute on Disability and Rehabilitation Research, U.S. Department of Education to provide employers and people with disabilities with technical assistance related to the ADA.
(800) 949-4232 V/TTY
http://www.adata.org/

Region 1 (Connecticut, Maine, Massachusetts, New Hampshire, Rhode Island, Vermont)
DBTAC – New England ADA Center
Adaptive Environments Center, Inc.
180-200 Portland Street, First floor

Boston, Massachusetts 02114
Phone: (617) 695-1225 (V/TTY)
Fax: (617) 482-8099
E-mail: adainfo@newenglandada.org
Web site: http://adaptiveenvironments.org/neada/site/home

Region 2 (New Jersey, New York, Puerto Rico, Virgin Islands)
DBTAC – Northeast ADA Center
Cornell University
201 ILR Extension
Ithaca, New York 14853-3901
Phone: (607) 255-8660
Phone: (607) 255-6686 (TTY)
Fax: (607) 255-2763
E-mail: dbtacnortheast@cornell.edu
Web site: www.dbtacnortheast.org

Region 3 (Delaware, District of Columbia, Maryland, Pennsylvania, Virginia, West Virginia)
DBTAC – Mid-Atlantic ADA Center
TransCen, Inc.
451 Hungerford Drive, Suite 700
Rockville, Maryland 20850
Phone: (301) 217-0124 (V/TTY)
Fax: (301) 217-0754
E-mail: adainfo@transcen.org
Web site: www.adainfo.org

Region 4 (Alabama, Florida, Georgia, Kentucky, Mississippi, North Carolina, South Carolina, Tennessee)
DBTAC – Southeast ADA Center
Project of the Burton Blatt Institute – Syracuse University
1419 Mayson Street
Atlanta, Georgia 30324
Phone: (404) 541-9001 (V/TTY)
Fax: (404) 541-9002
E-mail: sedbtacproject@law.syr.edu
Web site: www.sedbtac.org

Region 5 (Illinois, Indiana, Michigan, Minnesota, Ohio, Wisconsin)
DBTAC – Great Lakes ADA Center
University of Illinois/Chicago
Department on Disability and Human Development
1640 West Roosevelt Road, Room 405
Chicago, Illinois 60608
Phone: (312) 413-1407 (V/TTY)
Fax: (312) 413-1856

E-mail: gldbtac@uic.edu
Web site: www.adagreatlakes.org

Region 6 (Arkansas, Louisiana, New Mexico, Oklahoma, Texas)
DBTAC – Southwest ADA Center
Independent Living Research Utilization
2323 South Shepherd Boulevard, Suite 1000
Houston, Texas 77019
Phone: (713) 520-0232 (V/TTY)
Fax: (713) 520-5785
E-mail: dlrp@ilru.org
Web site: www.dlrp.org

Region 7 (Iowa, Kansas, Missouri, Nebraska)
DBTAC – Great Plains ADA Center
University of Missouri/Columbia
100 Corporate Lake Drive
Columbia, Missouri 65203
Phone: (573) 882-3600 (V/TTY)
Fax: (573) 884-4925
E-mail: ada@missouri.edu
Web site: www.adaproject.org

Region 8 (Colorado, Montana, North Dakota, South Dakota, Utah, Wyoming)
DBTAC – Rocky Mountain ADA Center
Meeting the Challenge, Inc.
3630 Sinton Road, Suite 103
Colorado Springs, Colorado 80907
Phone: (719) 444-0268 (V/TTY)
Fax: (719) 444-0269
E-mail: technicalassistance@mtc-inc.com
Web site: www.adainformation.org

Region 9 (Arizona, California, Hawaii, Nevada, Pacific Basin)
DBTAC – Pacific ADA Center
555 12th Street, Suite 1030
Oakland, California 94607-4046
Phone: (510) 285-5600 (V/TTY)
Fax: (510) 285-5614
E-mail: adatech@adapacific.org
Web site: www.adapacific.org

Region 10 (Alaska, Idaho, Oregon, Washington)
DBTAC – Northwest ADA Center
Western Washington University
6912 220th Street SW, #105

Mountlake Terrace, Washington 98043
Phone: (425) 248-2480 (V)
Fax: (425) 771-7438
E-mail: dbtacnw@wwu.edu
Web site: www.dbtacnorthwest.org

References

1. Jemal A. Annual report to the nation on the status of cancer, 1975–2001, with a special feature regarding survival. Cancer. 2004; 101:3–27.
2. Hoffman B. Cancer survivors at work: a generation of progress. CA Cancer J Clin. 2005; 55:271–280.
3. Short P, Vasey J, Tunceli K. Employment pathways in a large cohort of adult cancer survivors. Psycho-Oncology. 2005; 10:259–63.
4. Bouknight RR, Bradley CJ, Luo Z. Correlates of return to work for breast cancer survivors. J Clin Oncol. 2006; 24:345–353.
5. Bruyere S. A Human Resource Perspective on Implementing the ADA. Program on Employment and Disability, Cornell University. www.ilr.cornell.edu/ped/ada
6. Bradley CJ, Bednarek HL. Employment patterns of long-term cancer survivors. Psycho-Oncology. 2002; 11:188–198.
7. Feuerstein M, Luff GM, Harrington CB, Olsen CH. Patterns of workplace dispute in cancer survivors: A population study of ADA claims. J Cancer Surviv. 2007; 1:185–192.
8. Thrush RA. ADA essential function identification: a definitive application of Title I. AccessAbility Press, El Cajon, California, 1993.
9. Habutzel N, McMahon BT. The Americans with Disabilities Act: Access and accommodations. Paul M Deutsch Press, 1992.
10. Brodwin M, Parker RM, DeLaGarza D. Disability and accommodation. In: Szymanski, E, Parker, RM, (eds). Work and disability. Pro-Ed; 1996. pp. 165–208.
11. Legal Eagle Eye Newsletter for the Nursing Profession. Breast cancer: US Court validates nurse's right to reasonable accommodation from her employer during and after treatment. Spring, 2005. p. 5.
12. Batistie L.C. Job Accommodation Network (JAN) ideas for writing an accommodation request letter. http://www.jan.wvu.edu/media/accommrequestltr.html; 2008.
13. Job Accommodation Network. JAN frequently asked questions. http://www.jan.wvu.edu/portals/faqs.html#request; 2008.
14. Loy B. Job Accommodation Network (JAN) accommodation and compliance series: Employees with cancer. Morgantown, WV: Job Accommodation Network; 2005.
15. National Brain Tumor Foundation. Return to work: Is it right for you. A guide for brain tumor patients. San Francisco, California; 2007.
16. Merbitz C, Merbitz N, Scherer M. Assistive technology for the rehabilitation case manager. In: Chan F, Leahy M, Saunders J, (eds). Case management for rehabilitation health professionals. 2005. pp. 200–230.
17. Merbitz C, Lam CS, Chan F, Thomas KR. Assistive technology for case managers. In: Chan F, Leahy M, (eds). Health care and disability case management. Vocational Consultants Press. 1999, pp. 379–414.
18. Packer RJ, Meadows AT, Rorke LB, Goldwein JL, D'Angio G. Long-term sequelae of cancer treatment on the central nervous system in childhood. Med Pediatr Oncol. 1987; 15: 241–53.
19. Warren CG. Use of assistive technology in vocational rehabilitation of persons with traumatic brain injury. In: Fraser RT, Clemmons DC (eds). Traumatic brain injury:

Practical vocational, neuropsychological, and psychotherapy interventions. CRC Press. 1996: 129–160.
20. European Pain in Cancer Survey. Media backgrounder: European Pain in Cancer survey, 2007. Downloaded on April 24, 2008. www.paineurope.com/files/EPIC%20survey%20backgrounder.doc
21. Agency for Healthcare Research and Quality. Management of cancer symptoms: Pain, depression, and fatigue. Summary, Evidence Report/Technology Assessment: Number 61. AHRQ Publication No. 02-E031, July 2002. http://www.ahrq.gov/clinic/epcsums/csympsum.htm
22. Feuerstein M, Hansen JA, Calvio LC, Johnson L, Ronquillo JG. Work productivity in brain tumor survivors. J Occup Environ Med. 2007; 49:803–811.

Chapter 12
Individuals with Cancer in the Workforce and Their Federal Rights

Peter Blanck, William N. Myhill, Janikke Solstad Vedeler, Joanna Morales, and Paula Pearlman

Introduction

It is not uncommon for employers and co-workers to have misperceptions about an individual's ability to work during and after undergoing treatment for cancer [1]. One in four individuals with cancer faces some form of discrimination in the workplace [2, 3]. In the United States, federal laws provide job protection from discrimination to individuals with cancer, such as the Americans with Disabilities Act of 1990 (ADA) and the Family and Medical Leave Act (FMLA). This chapter investigates the effectiveness of these laws in protecting the jobs, quality of life, and livelihoods of individuals in the workforce who are diagnosed with cancer.

In Part I, we review the work and home life of individuals with cancer, especially during illness, diagnosis, and on through the often extensive periods of treatment and recovery, collectively addressed as cancer survivorship in the present volume. These observations of work and home life that describe many situations among cancer survivors need to be considered as the backdrop for existing laws that are presumed to apply to many of the challenges that cancer survivors face. In Part II, we explain the applicable federal laws for the employee diagnosed with cancer. Then in Part III, through the experience of Patricia Garrett, a woman who survived breast cancer at the expense of her career, we present the challenges of invoking ADA and FMLA protections on the job and in the courtroom. Part IV reviews the larger picture of federal protections in light of the *Garrett* decision and emerging shifts in the law. Part V provides resources and best practices for employers and employees diagnosed with cancer, and future directions for the law. We close this chapter with recommendations for respecting and asserting ADA and FMLA protections.

P. Blanck (✉)
University Professor, Chairman, Burton Blatt Institute, Syracuse University, Syracuse, NY 13244-2130, USA
e-mail: pblanck@syr.edu

Key Issues Facing Persons with Cancer

The journey of an individual with cancer may be characterized as a roller coaster ride [4], impacting family and work relationships, and affecting a person's physical and psychological condition. A cancer diagnosis may also affect how others perceive the person, thereby impacting interpersonal arenas, like the family and the workplace. How these relationships play out in turn influences the social well-being of individuals with implications for quality of life [5].

Personal and Family Experiences

Cancer diagnosis impacts the whole family and in multiple ways [6]. Persons with cancer report their major concern is their family's well-being [5]. When a parent or child is diagnosed with cancer, family members experience fear of losing the loved one and of the suffering she/he likely will experience [7]. Adolescent children of a parent with cancer are in a particularly vulnerable phase in their development and often experience severe emotional distress and fear a parent will die. Changes in roles and expectations may require adolescents to take on extra household responsibilities and in the care of their siblings. Not knowing how to react to these new situations or a parent's depressed mood, children may develop behavioral problems [6].

In addition to coping with physical and psychological reactions to having cancer, parents experience additional stressors when they are limited or unable to maintain usual involvement in the lives of their children. Hospital and primary care staff, who gain awareness of how children and the individual with cancer respond to a cancer diagnosis, are well-positioned to guide the individual, spouses and children through an emotionally stressful time [8].

In one study of men diagnosed with prostate cancer, couples of working age (age 50–64) experienced more disappointment and anger of getting cancer than couples who had retired [9]. Potentially having much unaccomplished in life, people who were part of the workforce are more reluctant to accept the implications of having cancer than are people of an older age. Financial issues become stressful as the treatment of prostate cancer affected the husbands' ability to work and to carry out tasks he previously performed on a daily basis [9].

Financial issues may impact the dyadic relationship of couples in a variety of ways. In a study by Harden et al., [9] couples expressed that "Being in it together" was important, and working spouses were unhappy for not being able to accompany their partner to medical appointments and treatment:

> I couldn't be there for all his treatments because I had to work (...) because if I lose my work, I lose our insurance and possibly our house. So it was important for me to work, but it was hard. I just had to be strong and keep things going. [9, p. 372]

The need to work while at the same time wanting to be with her husband during treatment exemplifies the difficulty of balancing employment and care demands. Family caregivers often face this challenge and the result may be a need to reduce work hours. A reduction of work hours may impact family health insurance and retirement benefits [10].

Factors Related to Return to Work

Looking across the relatively few studies conducted focusing on work and return to work among individuals with cancer, Spelten, Sprangers, & Verbeek identified three main categories of factors motivating employment status: (1) work-related, (2) disease- and treatment-related, and (3) person-related. We discuss these in detail [11].

Work-Related Factors

There may be many reasons why people continue working during treatment, despite the fatigue, nausea, and other side effects of treatment. Fear of being fired or being repositioned to a lower status job are factors impacting one's decision to keep on working but work may also provide a source of social support facilitating recovery and long term adaptation to this life threatening experience. In one study by Main and colleagues [12], addressing patterns of work return and factors influencing post-cancer decisions among 28 persons with diverse cancer diagnoses, participants emphasized the importance of holding on to the job because it helped them take their mind off the cancer. One study participant explains the significance in these terms: "You forget about whatever else you're doing. It's not a support group. It's not acupuncture; it's not your appointments. It's something totally away from cancer" [12, p. 997]. To some, work represents an important social arena where the person with cancer meets people outside the family and treatment sphere [12].

> There's days when I want to go in there and just say you know 'I can't do this no more', but then I'm afraid of doing that because sometimes just being in there 1 or 2 days a week ... really helps with my mental ways of thinking and just not being stuck in the house .... It kind of lifts your spirit [12, p. 997].

These experiences corroborate the findings of Spelten and colleagues that a return to work may be associated with social support [11].

Two core factors are identified to impact work return—the nature of the job itself and the attitudes and culture in the organization. A supportive work environment or culture is found to facilitate a return to work, while manual work and work settings that require strong physical effort represent impediments [11]. In addition, the positive attitudes of employers and colleagues, and toward flexible or reduced working hours (i.e., workplace accommodations), are important elements of a supportive work environment [13, 14].

Study-participants in the Main study narrate on employers' flexibility during treatment [12]. One study-participant recounts: "[The employer] said 'Go on home if you don't feel good. Go home.' And they saved my job, like I said, for months so I could go back." [12, p. 1000] Others were reassigned tasks: "I had been traveling for 13 years. At least 9 months of the year I would be on the road Monday through Friday. When I came back, they said, 'No, you're not going to travel. You need to be close to your family'" [12, p. 1000]. In another study, one woman reports: "My employer was very understanding about the days missed each month when I had my chemo and the few days I took off because I was too nauseated to be there" [5, p. 661].

Disease and Treatment-Related Factors

The likelihood of returning to work increases with the time passed after the completion of treatment [11]. Nevertheless, some persons with cancer undergoing treatment keep on working [12]. Fatigue during and after treatment often is reported by individuals with cancer as explained by one study participant: "I was doing chemo and ... my energy wasn't good—you don't want to do anything. I was just really tired" [12, p. 997]. A profound feeling of fatigue is the most frequently reported manifestation of cancer treatment and often severely impacts everyday activities of the individual with cancer [7]. However, other common outcomes from treatment may include short or long-term lack of upper body strength, memory loss, and constant pain [15].

Person-Related Factors

Other motivational factors are not related to a work return [11]. Being diagnosed with a serious, sometimes life-threatening disease, may contribute to a scrupulous self-reflective period where existential questions are raised. Subsequently, a change in work attitude may emerge, such as feeling less inspired to work [11]. In a study by Edbril and Rieker [16], the significance of working after being diagnosed with testicular cancer decreased for some study participants because they realized that life is too short to be so involved only in work.

Studies show mixed results with respect to a positive or negative association between return to work and the type of cancer [11]. In one study on a heterogeneous group of individuals with cancer, those reporting the most problems on work return are individuals with head, neck and breast cancer [11, 17]. In another study, the problems experienced by persons with head and neck cancer of returning to work are also identified, while men with testicular cancer report few problems and have a high return to work rate [11, 18]. The findings of a recent study on work return among women with breast cancer identify a high return rate [19]. Compared to the study by Weis et al. [17], the recent study's findings may be explained by improvements in treatment and follow-up care, also experienced by a person with cancer: Brooks was first diagnosed with breast cancer in 1991 [4]. She recovered, but 14 years later another tumor was found. This time "the treatment I received was excellent, and I had much more support and information provided than in 1991. Because of better awareness on my part and prompt attention from the clinicians, this tumor was diagnosed earlier (grade I) and required no further treatment, other than drugs" [4, p. 33].

Overall, these accounts show the importance of supportive employers and flexible work schedules. Knowing employment is not only important as a realm where one makes use of one's competence, but also for a person's income, inclusiveness provided by the employer is significant for ensuring that more working age persons with cancer do not stop working. Moreover, as most people in the Unites States obtain their health insurance through employers, the loss of a job because of cancer impacts the person's health insurance coverage and income [7].

Some people with cancer experience non-inclusive work environments and face attitudinal discrimination. According to a recent study analyzing ADA claims among individuals with cancer and non-cancer related impairments, "job termination and terms of employment are more likely to be concerns for employees with cancer than employees with other types of impairments" [3, pp. 185–186].

Federal Protections for the Employee with Cancer

Persons who have or acquire a physical or mental impairment, a serious health condition, or a chronic illness enjoy protections from discrimination by employers and insurance companies, and in the workplace on the basis of these conditions. The Americans with Disabilities Act of 1990 (ADA) prohibits employers with 15 or more employees from discriminating against qualified employees with disabilities in "job application procedures, the hiring, advancement, or discharge of employees, employee compensation, job training, and other terms, conditions, and privileges of employment" [20]. The qualified employee is one who can perform the essential functions of the position with or without reasonable accommodations, and who has a substantial limitation in a major life activity [20].

While ADA Title I applies to the employment realm, the Family & Medical Leave Act (FMLA) provides for a person to take up to 12 weeks of unpaid medical leave per year for a serious medical condition [21]. It also allows for up to 12 weeks of unpaid leave to care for a seriously ill spouse, parent or child [21]. Although unpaid, the employee returns to the same or an equivalent position after the leave, and the employer is required to keep an employee's benefits intact [21].

Two additional federal laws provide health coverage security beneficial to an employee with cancer. The Health Insurance Portability and Accountability Act of 1996 (HIPAA) prohibits group health plans from excluding coverage based on pre-existing medical conditions covered under a previous creditable plan [22]. HIPAA also protects covered employees and their families from losing health insurance if the employee changes jobs [23]. The Consolidated Omnibus Budget Reconciliation Act of 1986 (COBRA) allows an employee to continue the same health insurance coverage the employee received through their former employer for a period of 18 months after leaving the position, being terminated, or reducing work hours [23]. We discuss these protections in detail below.

The ADA

The Americans with Disabilities Act of 1990 (ADA) passed with bipartisan support and was signed into law by President George H.W. Bush to provide people with disabilities the right to be judged with fairness and equality. President Bush hailed the ADA as "the world's first comprehensive declaration of equality for people with disabilities" [24]. This landmark civil rights law prohibits discrimination against persons with disabilities in the workplace, public accommodations, and by state and local government [25].

A cancer diagnosis, like any impairment or illness, is not per se a disability covered by the ADA. Cancer is considered a disability under the ADA when its effects, or the side effects of treatment, substantially limit one or more major life activities [20]. For instance, a person may experience depression as a result of cancer, thereby substantially limiting their sleeping or eating for an extended period [1]. Cancer also may be a disability if it substantially limited the employee in the past or if the employer incorrectly regards the employee as having a substantial limitation [20]. To determine if cancer is a disability as defined by the ADA, courts analyze each claim on case by case basis [1].

The ADA requires employers provide reasonable accommodations for employees with disabilities to assist them to perform essential job functions and ensure they have equal access to the facilities, programs, and benefits of the job [20]. Reasonable accommodations include making workplace facilities "readily accessible to and usable by individuals with disabilities," restructuring a job, modifying schedules, equipment and policies, acquiring assistive technologies, adapting training materials, providing qualified interpreters, and many other possibilities [20, 26]. Making a reasonable accommodation requires an individualized inquiry specific to the employee, the disability, job requirements, and other relevant factors [25]. Employers should be aware that not all individuals with cancer require accommodations, and two employees who have the same type of cancer may need different accommodations [1].

For instance, employees with cancer may request leave time for doctor's appointments or weekly treatments. They may ask for extra breaks during the work day to rest or to take medications. The employee with cancer may benefit from an adjustment in the work schedule while attending cancer treatments. Some employees may request to work from home for a temporary period. The employer and employee are encouraged to engage in an interactive process to make well-informed decisions about accommodations that will work best for both the employee and employer[1] [27].

Some employees feel shame, fear, uncertainty, or embarrassment when discussing their cancer diagnosis with an employer [28]. However, if an employee with cancer wishes to receive accommodations they need to let the employer know of the need, as only disabilities known by the employer require accommodations [20]. Requests for accommodation may come from friends, family members, or doctors. Some employees prefer a doctor to write a request for accommodation because it may carry more weight in the employer's mind [1].

Employers may request medical documentation after an employee has requested reasonable accommodations at work [27]. Employers only may view relevant medical documentation that will help formulate an accommodation plan [1]. Employers do not have to grant every accommodation request; they only must provide "reasonable" accommodations that do not impose an undue hardship [20]. Undue hardships are determined on an individual basis when an employee requests an accommodation, and requires a showing of "significant difficulty or expense" in light of the employer's overall resources [20].

In addition to protecting people with disabilities from discrimination, the ADA protects individuals, with and without disabilities, who are discriminated against because of their known association with an individual with a disability. The "associational discrimination" protection is not limited to those with a familial relationship with an individual with a disability, but also may include business, social, and care giving relationships. The protection means that, if an employer denies a job benefit (e.g., health insurance coverage) to an employee with a family member with cancer covered by the ADA, the entity may be liable for discrimination [25].

Other Federal Protections

The FMLA applies to employers with 50 or more employees [32]. Employees must have been employed at least a year and have worked a minimum of 1,250 hours in that year [32]. Sometimes, a person will need more than the 12 weeks of leave provided by the FMLA. In this event, a person may be able to take additional leave time as a reasonable accommodation under the ADA [32]. Alternatively, some states provide greater protections, such as requiring less employed hours in the year for initial FMLA leave eligibility and do not have a proviso for the number of employees within the specified radius of the

---

[1] Though the ADA encourages use of an interactive process, some courts have held it is required [29–31].

workplace.[2] Employment law attorney Loring Spolter provides a seven item "FMLA Checklist" to "minimize difficulties and preserve legal rights" under the FMLA [33]. The checklist addresses issues of documentation, requesting leave and extended leave, and quality of communications, among others.

Briefly mentioned above, COBRA allows an employee to continue the same health insurance coverage received through a former employer for up to 18 months after a reduction in work hours or leaving employment (including termination). However, the employee is responsible for paying the premiums [23]. COBRA applies to employers with at least 20 employees [22], though many states have similar laws covering employers with fewer than 20 employees[3] [34].

Under HIPAA, the employee receives "creditable coverage" for the period she previously had health insurance. Creditable coverage travels with them when they go to a new employer and is credited towards any pre-existing condition exclusions [22]. HIPAA limits the amount of time a pre-existing condition may be imposed (12 month maximum) and applies a 6-month limit on how far back an insurer can look at an applicant's health history for purposes of imposing a pre-existing condition exclusion [22]. HIPAA further permits a person to transfer from the group health plan to an individual health plan when meeting certain conditions, such as not having a break in health insurance coverage longer than 63 days [22]. State laws may provide greater protections [22].

Privacy and Confidentiality

Employers must keep all medical documentation and knowledge of an employee's diagnosis confidential. The only exceptions to the confidentiality rule are: (1) when employers need to inform the employee's supervisors to facilitate proper accommodations for the employee; (2) if worksite medical staff need to know of a possible disability-related emergency (e.g., fainting at work); and (3) if government officials require relevant information to investigate compliance [27].

The ADA strictly limits the circumstances under which employers may ask medical related questions of an employee with cancer. Employers are allowed to ask an employee to undergo medical testing if the employer has a reasonable concern that the employee's diagnosis is affecting the ability to perform the job [20]. For instance, an employer may ask an employee to have a medical evaluation when the employee seems to experience fatigue constantly at work, and the

---

[2] The U.S. Department of Labor offers a complete list of these states and their comparative protections [35].

[3] For example, Cal-COBRA in California covers employers of 2–19 employees and the Massachusetts Small Employer Health Reinsurance Plan covers employers of 1–50 employees [36, 37].

employer has a legitimate reason to believe they are unable to perform their job [27]. Employers must be careful not to request a medical exam if they only notice insufficient job performance, which may arise from a wide variety of non-health or disability related factors [1].

Furthermore, employers are permitted to ask an employee on medical leave for cancer treatment to submit medical documentation prior to returning to work [20] and clarifying their ability to return to work [32]. Employers are only entitled to medical documentation of an employee's present work ability and not their future work abilities [1].

The Story of Patricia Garrett

The story of Patricia Garrett, an experienced nurse working for the University of Alabama at Birmingham hospital ("University"), is a 13-year legal saga in which federal laws and courts failed an individual with cancer subject to discrimination on the basis of her illness. Ms. Garrett was a supervising nurse at the University when in August, 1994 she was diagnosed with breast cancer. She took time off for a series of treatments and returned to work full-time in September of that year. Due to her ongoing treatments, Ms. Garrett requested and received intermittent medical leave over the next year [38].

At work, Ms. Garrett was able to complete all of her duties with accommodation. Radiation therapy caused burns to her right arm that limited her lifting ability. She needed extra time and had to take frequent breaks due to fatigue. At home, she could not perform ordinary household tasks such as cleaning, laundry, and cooking, and it took her twice as long to complete her self-care tasks. In January 1995, she was hospitalized for an infection, and took medical leave again in March as an accommodation. She returned to work in July of that year. Two weeks later, she was transferred to a lower-paying position at a different University facility [39].

State Sovereign Immunity

Ms. Garrett originally brought suit in January, 1998 in the federal district court for the Northern District of Alabama under the ADA, the Rehabilitation Act of 1973, and the FMLA. The district court dismissed all three claims on the basis of state sovereign immunity [40]. The principle of sovereign immunity arises from the Eleventh Amendment to the U.S. Constitution, and protects state autonomy by immunizing states from suits in federal court by private citizens seeking money damages or other equitable relief [41].

Between 1998 and 2005, Ms. Garrett was embroiled in a dispute between the federal district court, the Eleventh Circuit Court of Appeals, and the U.S. Supreme Court over what conditions and under what federal laws a state affirmatively waives its sovereign immunity.[4] Two important decisions arose from the nine court decisions over the seven years. In 2001, the U.S. Supreme Court concluded the legislative record of the ADA failed to show Congress identified a pattern of state discrimination in employment against persons with disabilities. Hence the Supreme Court did not support abrogating the states' sovereign immunity under the ADA [41].

Then in 2003, the Eleventh Circuit concluded the University had waived its sovereign immunity under Section 504 of the Rehabilitation Act by accepting federal funds [42]. This ruling was important for plaintiffs for whom injunctive relief (e.g., the court ordering the University to give Ms. Garrett her job back) would not be effective. In Ms. Garrett's case, her previous job was no longer vacant, and she did not wish to return to a work environment she considered hostile [39]. Notably, twelve of the thirteen U.S. Circuit Courts of Appeals[5] agree that when a state voluntarily accepts federal funds, and is aware if it were to violate a federal statute that expressly waives state sovereign immunity, including Section 504, it will have waived its sovereign immunity to suit under that statute [46–57].

Qualified Individual with a Disability

The *Garrett* case was remanded once again to the federal district court and decided in January, 2005. The district court held that (a) Ms. Garrett's transfer to a lower-paying position was not an adverse employment action under the Rehabilitation Act; (b) Ms. Garrett was not a "qualified person with a disability"; and (c) Ms. Garrett's transfer did not constitute retaliation under the Rehabilitation Act [45]. She appealed to the Eleventh Circuit to determine whether because she requested and took medical leave for breast cancer treatments that limited her work performance (1) she was a qualified individual with a disability, and (2) the University made a retaliatory adverse employment

---

[4] To clarify, in 1999 on appeal, the Eleventh Circuit Court of Appeals reversed the district court decision holding the ADA and the Rehabilitation Act effectively abrogated state sovereign immunity [38]. On appeal in 2001, the U.S. Supreme Court overturned the Eleventh Circuit decision (discussed below) [41]. Later that year, the Eleventh Circuit ordered the district court to determine whether the State's receipt of federal funds waived its sovereign immunity for purpose of enforcing Section 504 of the Rehabilitation Act (providing substantially the same protections for an employee as the ADA) [43]. On remand, in 2002 the district court held state sovereign immunity was not waived under Section 504 [44]. In 2003 on appeal, the Eleventh Circuit reversed the district court's decision in this respect and ordered the court to determine whether the State had violated Section 504 [42]. The district court concluded Ms. Garrett was not a qualified individual with a disability and thus not entitled to Section 504 protections, and the Eleventh Circuit affirmed in 2007 [39, 45].

[5] The Court of Appeals for the Federal Circuit, which generally hears only specialized cases, has not addressed the issue.

action by transferring her to a lower-paying position in violation of the Rehabilitation Act [39].

Ms. Garrett argued she was a qualified individual with a disability. The parties did not dispute that she was qualified for her positions or that she had breast cancer. Ms. Garrett contended that she was substantially limited in the major life activities of caring for herself, ordinary household chores, lifting, and working because of the side effects from her cancer treatments. The court, however, determined her limitations (a) were temporary because they were simultaneous with her treatments, (b) were not present at the time of the alleged adverse employment action, and (c) were not sufficiently limiting in any major life activity to qualify as a disability [39].

Ms. Garrett argued the University retaliated against her because she requested and took intermittent medical leave for cancer treatments. To make this claim, Ms. Garrett had to demonstrate she (a) engaged in a protected activity, (b) suffered an adverse employment action, and (c) the protected activity was causally connected to the adverse employment action. The court assumed that making a medical leave request was a protected activity [39]. Ms. Garrett principally argued that the University demoted her on July 21, 1995 by transferring her to a lower-paying position in retaliation for her March 1, 1995 request for medical leave, which she took until July.

The University argued Ms. Garrett requested the transfer and, therefore, the lower pay, transfer, and approval of Ms. Garrett's request were legitimate, non-retaliatory, and non-discriminatory. There remains a genuine issue of material fact (i.e., disagreement) whether Ms. Garrett was demoted or voluntarily transferred to a lower-paying position. Nonetheless, the court determined that Ms. Garrett failed to show a causal connection between her request for leave and her transfer, because the timing of the leave request and the transfer were too far removed (over 4 months) "in the absence of other evidence tending to show causation" [45, p. 1251]. On November 15, 2007, the Eleventh Circuit affirmed this decision, and likely closed the book on the *Garrett* case.

Individuals with Cancer in Other Courts

Employment discrimination against qualified individuals with cancer takes a toll on society. Individuals with cancer report higher rates of employment discrimination including lost wages, unfair stereotyping, and unreasonable termination [3, 58]. Consequently, it is worth considering how the ADA has been interpreted by different courts to protect employees with cancer.

Individuals with cancer often claim their employer violated Title I of the ADA by failing to provide reasonable accommodations [59]. For individuals with cancer to succeed in a failure to accommodate claim under the ADA they must prove: (1) they are a qualified individual with a disability; (2) their employer is aware of the disability; and (3) their employer failed to reasonably accommodate their disability [20]. To satisfy the "qualified individual" prong, employees must show they have the proper training and skills to perform a certain job, and they can perform the essential job functions with reasonable accommodations if needed [20]. Attendance is considered an essential function for many jobs,[6] and people who need time off for cancer treatments may find difficulty attending work regularly.

A larger hurdle than acquiring an accommodation, however, often is showing the person with cancer has a covered disability. To invoke the ADA's basic protections, recall that a plaintiff must show he or she is substantially limited in a major life activity, has a record of this limitation, or is regarded by his/her employer as such (whether or not accurate) [25]. The Eleventh, Ninth, and Fifth Circuit Courts of Appeals have concluded plaintiffs with cancer were not substantially limited in the major life activity of working. These courts found cancer did not substantially limit the plaintiffs' "work activities" [60]. In *Gordon v. E.L. Hamm & Associates* [61], the Eleventh Circuit stated although the side effects of chemotherapy may constitute a disability under the ADA, they did not substantially limit the plaintiff in that particular case. The court reasoned the plaintiff's ability to work through the chemotherapy without requiring hospitalization, and the plaintiff's concession he carried on life in a normal manner, proved he was not substantially limited in the major life activity of working.

Similarly, the Fifth Circuit narrowly interpreted the ADA in *Ellison v. Software Spectrum* [62], and held a woman with breast cancer was not a qualified person with a disability because she was not substantially limited in the major life activity of working. The court reasoned her ability to continue working on a modified schedule, and to perform the essential functions of the job despite feeling sick, failed to demonstrate she was substantially limited. The court further concluded Ellison did not have a record of disability and was not regarded as having a disability by her employer.

In *Sanders v. Arneson Products., Inc.* [66], the Ninth Circuit concluded the plaintiff's psychological difficulties arising from cancer diagnosis and treatment did not qualify as a disability under the ADA. The court quoted the ADA's implementing regulations stating "temporary, non-chronic impairments of short duration, with little or no long term or permanent impact, are usually not disabilities" [66, p. 1354]. In each of these cases the courts focused on the individual's response to cancer and their ability to perform in spite of the disease and/or treatment.

Furthermore, some courts are inclined to view cancer as not typically substantially limiting any major life activities or otherwise constituting a disability for purposes of the ADA. In *Schwertfager v. City of Boynton Beach* [67], the federal district court for Southern Florida concluded a woman with breast

---

[6] For instance, insurance agent must be available to drive to accident sites [63]; Software Quality Engineer must have regular and reliable attendance at project, process, staff, and 1:1 bi-weekly meetings [64]; Dockworkers must be on site to perform basic duties [65].

cancer had no record of a disability, despite her diagnosis, hospitalizations, anatomical loss and treatments, because the record did not indicate she ever had been substantially limited by the cancer or treatments. Furthermore, the court concluded her employer did not regard the cancer to be "significant" [67, p. 1360–1361].

In *Hirsch v. National Mall & Service Co.* [68], the federal district court for Northern Illinois held a man was not a person with a disability under the ADA, despite being terminally ill with cancer. Mr. Hirsch was a 32-year veteran of National Mall & Service, a vending machine distributor. He was terminated to cut health care costs after informing his employer he had advanced lymphoma. His wife brought suit under the ADA on his behalf because he passed away shortly after losing his job. The court reasoned there was no evidence of impairment in Mr. Hirsch's daily work activities, and that his employer did not regard him as having a substantial limitation.

There is reluctance on the part of courts to find that cancer is a disability. The *Hirsch* and *Schwertfager* decisions demonstrate the uphill battle people with cancer have in proving a "record" of disability or that they are regarded as having a disability. This is in addition to the frequent challenge persons with cancer face demonstrating they are presently substantially limited because effective treatments can make cancer too temporary to qualify as a disability [15]. In contrast, research discussing prostate, breast and other cancers find that substantial limitations from surgery or treatments may continue for many years [15, 69–70].

Moreover, Farley-Short, Vasey, and Belue concluded because cancer treatments are so strenuous, cancer survivors "suffer from [disabilities] and/or work limitations at a higher rate than individuals with other chronic diseases" [69, p. 97]. Courts also may consider a limitation of greater severity to outweigh the absence of long-term effects [71]. Liu argued courts are given too much latitude to determine what "substantially limited" means, making it difficult for individuals with cancer to predict success in court under the ADA [60].

Best Practices and Future Initiatives

In the United States, there are 52 million people with disabilities and 11 million people with cancer [72]. As the treatment and survival rates for cancer improve, there are more people who decide to remain at work during treatment or who return to work after treatment is concluded [11]. A cancer diagnosis may carry a variety of potential legal issues, including employment discrimination, health care coverage, confidentiality, access to government benefits, and estate planning. These legal issues may cause unnecessary worry, confusion, and stress. When not addressed, people may find themselves surviving the disease yet losing their jobs and income, health coverage, and homes and families [58].

Model Programs and Services

There are a number of model programs and services in existence that educate employees about their legal rights in the workplace and teach employers about their legal responsibilities. In 2002, the Cosmetic Executive Women Foundation developed the Cancer and Careers program to change the face of cancer in the workplace by providing a comprehensive website, free publications, and a series of support groups and educational seminars for employees with cancer [73]. The Foundation sponsors the "Managing Through Cancer" program to provide employers, managers, and HR professionals with clear direction, resources, and concrete tools to maintain a fully productive workplace while proactively supporting their employees with cancer [74]. Tools include tips on what to say, templates for implementing flexible work arrangements, and a set of principles that may serve as a company's commitment to support employees with cancer, company-wide [75].

The Cancer Legal Resource Center (CLRC) provides information and resources on cancer-related legal issues to persons with cancer, their families, friends, caregivers, employers, health care professionals, and others coping with cancer [76]. The CLRC is a joint program of Loyola Law School and the Disability Rights Legal Center (DRLC) in Los Angeles, California. It was created to address the fact that while there were many cancer-related resources available for medical care and psychosocial support, there was nowhere to turn to get assistance with cancer-related legal issues [77]. Prior to contacting the CLRC, many people do not realize they qualify for protections under various laws because of their diagnosis [78].

The CLRC hosts a toll-free, national Telephone Assistance Line (866-THE-CLRC), staffed primarily by law students under staff attorney supervision. In 2007, the line received almost 4,000 calls addressing a variety of legal issues (for distribution of calls, see Fig. 12.1 below) [79]. The students educate the callers about cancer-related legal issues, while learning about the pertinent laws and dynamics of providing legal assistance to people with cancer [79]. The CLRC has received an increasing percentage of its calls from outside of California.[7] This increase may be attributed to the CLRC's partnerships with national cancer organizations, such as the American Cancer Society and the Lance Armstrong Foundation [79].

Over the last ten years, twenty percent of calls to the Telephone Assistance Line have addressed employment-related issues, such as (1) when persons are recently diagnosed and need information on working with their employer while they receive treatment; (2) receiving negative employment evaluations after disclosing their medical condition; (3) losing their job and requesting alternatives options; and (4) returning to the workforce and whether they should disclose to a potential employer [80]. In the last five years, the CLRC has

---

[7] In 2002, 40%; and in 2007, 56% [80].

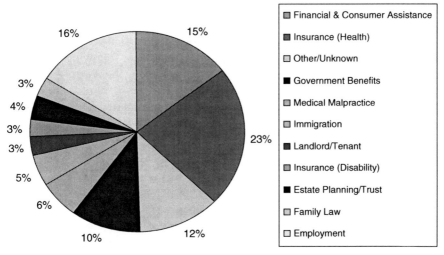

Fig. 12.1 2007 Telephone assistance line calls – legal issue

received over 1,000 calls from employees who believe they were terminated as a result of their cancer diagnosis [81].

The CLRC trains front-line oncology health care professionals to identify the presence of cancer-related legal issues for their patients, and to effectively advocate for people with cancer [77]. On April 19, 2007, the CLRC received its 20,000th call to its national Telephone Assistance Line [79]. Throughout its 11-year history, the CLRC has reached over 90,000 people through the Telephone Assistance Line, conferences, seminars, workshops, outreach programs, and other community activities [79]. When people need more than information about their legal rights, the CLRC refers individuals to an extensive national network of volunteer attorneys [79].

ADA Amendments Act of 2008 and the Future

Several decisions of the U.S. Supreme Court eroded protections the ADA provides to people with cancer, diabetes, epilepsy, and other chronic disabilities. [82–84] Courts have concluded people with cancer are too healthy to have a disability and, therefore, are not entitled to protections under the ADA. [62] After the U.S. Supreme Court decided *Sutton v. United Air Lines Inc.* in 1999, [85] a person's ability to mitigate the effects and limitations of a disability had to be considered when determining whether they have a substantial limitation. Consequently, individuals with cancer who mitigate or eliminate the limitations caused by cancer treatment often did not have a disability that meets the definition under the ADA.

When people with cancer undergo treatment, they often take medications that alleviate the side effects of treatment, such as nausea or fatigue. [86] In so doing, they may feel better, but they also may mitigate a substantial limitation to a major life activity. Without a substantial limitation, following the *Sutton* ruling, they were no longer entitled to protections under the ADA. An absurd "catch-22" was created where these individuals had no form of redress, even when told explicitly they were not hired or were terminated because of their disease. [58,62] For example:

- Mary is a 26-year old woman from California with a brain tumor. She worked for a small employer of 15 employees. Her employer terminated her after she requested time off to attend a doctor's appointment to address complications from her cancer treatment.
- In Utah, Trudy, age 39 working for a large national employer, was diagnosed with breast cancer. She wanted to continue working during her treatment, but her employer fired her after missing too may days of work.
- Robert, a 57-year old man from California and vice-president of a real estate company, was diagnosed with colon cancer. He took six weeks of medical leave to undergo surgery and treatment and was promptly terminated the day after he returned to work.
- Melanie, a 37-year old woman in Georgia diagnosed with lung cancer, was terminated from her job with a federal bankruptcy court after being told she was "difficult" when she asked for accommodations, such as turning down the heat in the office. [81][8]

There are thousands of people like Mary, Trudy, Robert, and Melanie, who are willing and able to work, yet are discriminated against on the basis of disability because of a serious health condition. These incidents are the kind of blatant, workplace discrimination and prejudice the ADA was intended to stop. [87] Yet these people-and many in their situation-have not been protected by the ADA, resulting in devastating consequences for people who are not only battling cancer (and for their families), but also struggling to stay afloat financially. They may have residual symptoms from their diagnosis or treatment and may find it difficult to search for a new job; they may face the loss of health insurance or foreclosure on their homes, and too often, personal bankruptcy. [58]

On July 26, 2007, House Majority Leader Steny Hoyer, Congressman Jim Sensenbrenner, and Senators Tom Harkin and Arlen Specter introduced draft bills to enact the ADA Restoration Act of 2007 (subsequently called the "ADA Amendments Act of 2008"), aiming to restore the ADA to its original intent and effectiveness. In a press conference introducing the original House bill, Congressman Hoyer noted, "the Supreme Court has improperly shifted the focus of the ADA from an employer's alleged misconduct, on to whether an individual

---

[8] Some names have been changed to protect the privacy of the individuals.

can first meet—in the Supreme Court's words—a 'demanding standard for qualifying as disabled.'" [88]

On, September 25, 2008, President George W. Bush signed Senate Bill 3406, the ADA Amendments Act of 2008, into law [89]. The Amendments assertively depart from Supreme Court decisions that severely limited the ADA's protected class, placing the focus on whether a person is qualified for the job, and minimizing the focus on the level or type of impairment. Specifically, the Act precludes courts from considering mitigating measures. Additionally, the Amendments will protect people episodic conditions or when in remission, if the condition does limit a major life activity when active [90].

There remains opposition from business entities and others who fear the Act will increase litigation. [91] There also is concern in the disability community that the Act will compromise existing protections in the law. On its face, the proposed Act does not seek to expand the rights guaranteed under the original landmark ADA. Instead, it seeks to clarify the law, restoring the scope of protection available under the ADA; it responds to court decisions that have restricted the class of people who may invoke protection under the law, and reinstates the Congressional intent behind the ADA. [90]

Recommendations and Closing Remarks

There are a number of steps to address the rights of employees with cancer in the workplace. First, and most importantly, it is crucial that people with cancer understand their rights under the ADA and other federal laws to navigate challenging workplace issues. This requires extensive consumer outreach and increasing consumer education programs and services, such as provided by the CLRC and the Cancer and Careers program.

Second, stakeholders such as business owners and the U.S. Small Business Administration require further training and technical assistance to improve compliance with the law. The EEOC and their state level counterparts are well-positioned to address this need. Funded research and technical assistance centers including the Job Accommodation Network and the Southeast ADA Center extensively engage in these education and outreach initiatives [26, 92]. These entities and others work with chambers of commerce and human resource staff and associations to create an effective educational campaign for employers and employees with cancer on their legal rights and responsibilities.

Third, there must be increased research and legislative advocacy to ensure that people with cancer and their family members are protected from discrimination. According to the National Organization on Disability [93], 70% of workplace accommodations may be made for less than $500. However, more research is needed on the costs and benefits of providing employer education programs and providing reasonable accommodations specifically to people with cancer [26]. At the federal level, the enactment of the ADA Amendments

Act will reverse Supreme Court decisions and restore the intent of the ADA, to better protect individuals with cancer. At the state level, legislatures may enact stronger protections from all discrimination "on the basis of disability," rather than against only persons with a substantial limitation in a major life activity. Together, these steps are important for educating employers and the public about the true capacities and needs of people with cancer.

Acknowledgment Peter Blanck, Ph.D, J.D., Chairman, Burton Blatt Institute (BBI), University Professor, Syracuse University (SU); William N. Myhill, M.Ed., J.D., Senior Research Associate, BBI, Adjunct Professor of Law (SU) (in loving memory of M.M., and with endearing love for E.A.M.); Janikke Solstad Vedeler, M.S., Visiting Pre-Doctoral Scholar, BBI, Research Associate, Norwegian Social Research (NOVA, Oslo); Joanna Morales, J.D., Director, Cancer Legal Resource Center, Adjunct Professor of Law, Loyola Law School (Los Angeles); Paula Pearlman, J.D., Executive Director, Disability Rights Legal Center, Associate Clinical Professor of Law, Loyola Law School. This research was funded, in part, by grants to Dr. Blanck from the U.S. Department of Education, National Institute on Disability and Rehabilitation Research (NIDRR) for (i) "Demand Side Employment Placement Models," Grant No. H133A060033; and (ii) "Southeast Disability & Business Technical Assistance Center," Grant No. H133A060094. The authors thank law students Lauren Chanatry, Janelle Frias and Ashleigh Hope, research assistant Aaron Gottlieb, and intern Erica Dolak for their research assistance.

References

1. Equal Employment Opportunity Commission ("EEOC"). Questions and Answers About Cancer in the Workplace and the Americans With Disabilities Act. August 3, 2005. Available from: http://www.eeoc.gov/facts/cancer.html Accessed March 31, 2008.
2. Touvell v. Ohio Department of Mental Retardation & Developmental Disabilities, 422 F. 3d 392 (6th Cir. 2005).
3. Feuerstein, M, Luff, GM, Harrington, CB, Olsen, CH. Pattern of workplace disputes in cancer survivors: a population study of ADA claims. Journal of Cancer Survivorship 2007; 1:185–192.
4. Brooks, JJ. A Patient' Journey: Living with Breast Cancer. BMJ 2006; 333:31–33.
5. Ferrell, BR, Smith, SL, Ervin, KS, Itano, J, Melancon, C. A Qualitative Analysis of Social Concerns of Women with Ovarian Cancer. Psycho-Oncology 2003; 12:647–663.
6. Grabiak, BR, Bender, CM, Puskar, KR. The impact of parental cancer on the adolescent: An analysis of the literature, Psycho-Oncology 2007; 16:127–137.
7. Adler, NE, Page, AEK. (Eds.) Cancer Care for the Whole Patient: Meeting Psychosocial Health Needs. 2008.
8. Forrest, G, Plumb, C, Ziebland, S, Stein, S. Breast cancer in the family—children's perceptions of their mother's cancer and its initial treatment: qualitative study. BMJ 2006; 332:998–1003.
9. Harden, JK, Northouse, LL, Mood, DW. Qualitative Analysis of Couples' Experience with Prostate Cancer by Age Cohort. Cancer Nursing 2006; 29(5):367–377.
10. Sherwood, PS, Donovan, HS, Given, CW, Lu, X, Given, BA, Hricik, A, et al. Predictors of employment and lost hours from work in cancer caregivers, Psycho-Oncology 2007. DOI: 10.1002/pon. Available from: http://www3.interscience.wiley.com/cgi-bin/fulltext/116833722/PDFSTART

11. Spelten, ER, Sprangers, MAG, & Verbeek, JHAM. Factors Reported to Influence the Return to Work of Cancer Survivors: A Literature Review. Psycho-Oncology 2002; 11:124–131.
12. Main, DS, Nowels, CT, Cavender, TA, Etschmaier, M, Steiner, JF. A Qualitative Study of Work and Work Return in Cancer Survivors. Psycho-Oncology 2005; 14:992–1004.
13. Schur, L, Kruse, D, Blanck, P. Corporate Culture and the Employment of Persons with Disabilities. Behavioral Sciences & the Law 2005; 23(1):3–20.
14. Schur, L, Kruse, D, Blasi, J, Blanck, P. Is Disability Disabling in All Workplaces? Disability, Workplace Disparities, and Corporate Culture. Industrial Relations. In press.
15. Bradley, C, Bednarek, H. Employment Patterns of Long-term Cancer Survivors. Psycho-Oncology 2002; 6(11):188–198.
16. Edbril, SD, Reiker, PP. The impact of testicular cancer on the work lives of survivors. Journal of Psychosocial Oncology 1989; 7:17–29.
17. Weis, J, Koch, U, Geldsetzer, M. Veränderung der beruflichen situation nach einer tumorkrankung: empirische studie zur beruflichen rehabilitation. Sozial Präventivmedizin 1992; 37:85–95.
18. van der Wouden, JC, Greaves-Otte, JG, Greaves, J, Kruty, PM, van Leeuwen, O, van der Does, E. Occupational reintegration of long-term cancer survivors. Journal of Occupational Medicine 1992; 34:1084–1089.
19. Bouknight, RR, Bradley, C J, Luo, Z. Correlates of Return to Work for Breast Cancer Survivors. Journal of Clinical Oncology 2006; 24(3):345–353.
20. Americans with Disabilities Act of 1990 (ADA), 42 U.S.C. §§ 12101 et seq. 2000.
21. Family and Medical Leave Act of 1993 (FMLA), Pub.L. 103-3, 107 Stat. 6 (Feb. 5, 1993).
22. Health Insurance Portability and Accountability Act of 1996 (HIPAA), 29 U.S.C. §§ 1181–1187 & scattered sections of Titles 18, 26 & 42. 2000.
23. Comprehensive Omnibus Budget Reconciliation Act of 1985 (Consolidated Omnibus Budget Reconciliation Act of 1985) (COBRA), 29 U.S.C §§ 1161–1168, scattered sections of Titles 7, 15, 42, & misc. others. 2000.
24. Woolley, JT, Peters, G. The American Presidency Project. 2008. Santa Barbara, CA: University of California (hosted), Gerhard Peters (database). Available from: http://www.presidency.ucsb.edu/ws/?pid = 18711
25. Blanck, P, Hill, E, Siegel, CH, Waterstone, M. Disability Civil Rights Law and Policy. 2004. St. Paul, MN: Thomson West.
26. Schartz, H, Hendricks, DJ, Blanck, P. Workplace accommodations: Evidence based Outcomes. Work 2006; 27:345–354.
27. C.F.R. Part 1630, Regulations to Implement the Equal Employment Provisions of the Americans with Disabilities. 2007.
28. Cancer and Careers. How to Tell. 2008. Available from: http://www.cancerandcareers.org/women/share_news/how_to_tell_people_you_have_cancer/ Accessed May 28, 2008.
29. Taylor v. Phoenixville School Dist., 194 F.3d 296, 314 (3rd Cir. 1999)
30. Barnett v. U.S. Air, Inc., 228 F.3d, 1105, 1114 (9th Cir. 2000).
31. Canny v. Dr. Pepper/Seven-Up Bottling Group, Inc., 439 F.3d 894, 902 (8th Cir. 2006).
32. 29 C.F.R. Part 825. The Family and Medical Leave Act of 1993. 2007
33. Spolter, L. Family and Medical Leave Act (FMLA): Protections for Parents. 2007. Available from: http://www.wrightslaw.com/advoc/articles/fmla.protect.spolter.htm Accessed June 3, 2008.
34. CobraHealth. State COBRA Law Directory. 2004. Available from: http://www.cobrahealth.com/statelawdirectory.htm Accessed May 28, 2008.
35. U.S. Department of Labor. Federal vs. State Family and Medical Leave Laws. Available from: http://www.dol.gov/esa/programs/whd/state/fmla/index.htm Accessed June 3, 2008.
36. Cal-COBRA ("California Continuation Benefits Replacement Act"). California Insurance Code §10128.50(b) (West 2008).

37. Massachusetts Small Employer Health Reinsurance Plan. Mass. Gen. Laws ch. 176 J §§ 1, 8–9 (West 2008).
38. Garrett v. University of Alabama at Birmingham Board of Trustees, 193 F.3d 1214 (11th Cir. 1999).
39. Garrett v. University of Alabama at Birmingham Board of Trustees, 507 F.3d 1306 (11th Cir. 2007).
40. Garrett v. University of Alabama at Birmingham Board of Trustees, 989 F.Supp. 1409 (N.D. Ala. 1998).
41. Board of Trustees of University of Alabama v. Garrett, 531 U.S. 356. 2001.
42. Garrett v. University of Alabama at Birmingham Board of Trustees, 344 F.3d 1288 (11th Cir. 2003).
43. Garrett v. University of Alabama at Birmingham Board of Trustees, 276 F.3d 1227 (11th Cir. 2001).
44. Garrett v. University of Alabama at Birmingham Board of Trustees, 223 F.Supp.2d 1244 (N.D. Ala. 2002).
45. Garrett v. Board of Trustees of Univ. of Ala. at Birmingham, 354 F.Supp.2d 1244 (N.D. Ala. 2005)
46. Barbour v. Washington Metropolitan Area Transit Authority, 374 F.3d 1161 (D.C. Cir. 2004).
47. Clark v. State of California, 123 F.3d 1267 (9th Cir. 1997).
48. Garcia v. S.U.N.Y. Health Sciences Center of Brooklyn, 280 F.3d 98 (2d Cir. 2001).
49. Jim C. v. United States, 235 F.3d 1079 (8th Cir. 2000).
50. Koslow v. Commonwealth of Pennsylvania, 302 F.3d 161 (3d Cir. 2002).
51. Litman v. George Mason University, 186 F.3d 544, 554 (4th Cir. 1999).
52. Nieves-Marquez v. Puerto Rico, 353 F.3d 108 (1st Cir. 2003).
53. Nihiser v. Ohio Environmental Protection Agency, 269 F.3d 626 (6th Cir. 2001).
54. Pederson v. Louisiana State University, 213 F.3d 858 (5th Cir. 2000).
55. Robinson v. Kansas, 295 F.3d 1183, 1189–90 (10th Cir. 2002).
56. Sandoval v. Hagan, 197 F.3d 484, 493–94 (11th Cir. 1999).
57. Stanley v. Litscher, 213 F.3d 340 (7th Cir. 2000).
58. Hoffman, B. Between a Disability and a Hard Place: The Cancer Survivor's Catch-22 of Proving Disability Status Under the Americans with Disabilities Act. Maryland Law Review 2000; 59: 352–439.
59. Liu, E. Bragdon v. Abbott: Extending the Americans with Disabilities Act To Asymptomatic Individuals. Journal of Health Care Law and Policy 2000; 3:382–408.
60. Gordon v. E.L. Hamm & Associates, Inc., 100 F.3d 907 (11th Cir. 1996).
61. Ellison v. Software Spectrum, Inc., 85 F.3d 187 (5th Cir. 1996).
62. Phillips v. Farmers Insurance Exchange, No. Civ. 3:04-CV-1113 N; 2006 WL 888095 (N.D. Tex., Feb. 9, 2006).
63. Knutson v. Medtronic, Inc., No. Civ. No. 05-180, 2006 WL 1851142 (D. Minn., Jul. 3, 2006)
64. EEOC v. Yellow Freight System, Inc., 253 F.3d 943 (7th Cir. 2001).
65. Sanders v. Arneson Products., Inc., 91 F.3d 1351 (9th Cir. 1996).
66. Schwertfager v. City of Boynton Beach, 42 F.Supp.2d 1347 (1999).
67. Hirsch *in re* Hirsch v. National Mall & Service, Inc., 989 F.Supp. 977 (N.D. Ill. 1997).
68. Hoffman, B. (Ed.). (2004). A Cancer Survivor's Almanac: Charting Your Journey. New Jersey: John Wiley & Sons, Inc.
69. Farley-Short, P, Vasey, JJ, Belue, R. Work Disability Associated with Cancer Survivorship and Other Chronic Illness. Psycho-Oncology. 2008; 17(1):91–97.
70. Farley-Short, P., Vasey, J.J., Moran, J.R. Long-Term Effects of Cancer Survivorship on the Employment of Older Workers. Health Services Research. 2008:43(1), pp. 193–210.

71. Leicht v. Hawaiian Airlines, Inc, 77 F. Supp. 2d 1134 (D. Hawaii 1999).
72. National Center for Technology Innovation. U.S. Census Bureau Disability Statistics. 2007. Available from: http://www.nationaltechcenter.org/index.php/2007/06/27/us-census-bureau-disability-statistics/ Accessed May 20, 2008.
73. Cosmetic Executive Women Foundation. CancerandCareers.org. 2008. Available from: http://www.cancerandcareers.org/ Accessed May 20, 2008.
74. Cosmetic Executive Women Foundation. Managing Through Cancer. 2008. Available from: http://www.cancerandcareers.org/employers/ Accessed May 20, 2008.
75. Cosmetic Executive Women Foundation. The Managing Through Cancer Principles. 2006. Available from: http://www.cancerandcareers.org/pioneers/managers/44002/ Accessed May 30, 2008.
76. Cancer Legal Resource Center ("CLRC"). About Our Programs and Projects. 2008. Available from: http://www.disabilityrightslegalcenter.org/about/about.cfm Accessed March 31, 2008.
77. Schwerin BU, Morales, JL. The Cancer Legal Resource Center-Assistance for Cancer-Related Legal Issues. Psycho-Oncology. 2005; 14:S9–S10.
78. Hewitt, M, Breen, N, Daveesa, S. Cancer prevalence and survivorship issues: Analyses of the 1992 National Health Interview Survey. Journal of National Cancer Institute 1999; 91(17):1480–1486.
79. CLRC. Cancer Legal Resource Center. 2008. Available from: http://www.disabilityrightslegalcenter.org/about/cancerlegalresource.cfm Accessed March 31, 2008.
80. CLRC. CLRC Telephone Assistance Line Statistics. 2008. Available from: http://www.disabilityrightslegalcenter.org/about/documents/CLRCStatistics2008.doc Accessed May 25, 2008.
81. Disability Rights Legal Center. Policy Advocacy. 2008. Available from: http://www.disabilityrightslegalcenter.org/about/documents/S1881SupportLetter.doc Accessed May 25, 2008.
82. National Council on Disability. Righting the ADA. 2004, December 1. Available from: http://www.ncd.gov/newsroom/publications/2004/pdf/righting_ada.pdf Accessed March 31, 2008.
83. ADA Restoration Act of 2007, H.R. 3195 and S. 1881, 110th Cong. (2007).
84. ADA Amendments Act of 2008, H.R. 3195 (2008).
85. Sutton v. United Air Lines Inc., 527 U.S. 471 (1999).
86. Perry, MC. Managing Side Effects of Cancer Treatment: Ask the Expert Live Chat (Transcript). 2005, July 25. Alexandria, VA: American Society of Clinical Oncology, Available from: http://www.ascocancerfoundation.org/patient/ASCO+Resources/Ask+the+ASCO+Expert+Series/2005+Transcripts/Managing+Side+Effects+of+Cancer+Treatment Accessed June 2, 2008.
87. Blanck, P. "The Right to Live in the World": Disability Yesterday, Today, and Tomorrow, 2008. Jacobus tenBroek Disability Law Symposium, Texas Journal on Civil Liberties and Civil Rights. In press.
88. Hoyer, S. Hoyer Introduces Americans with Disabilities Restoration Act of 2007. 2007, July 26. Available from: http://hoyer.house.gov/Newsroom/index.asp?ID=955&DocumentType=Press+Release Accessed May 25, 2008.
89. Administration News, President Bush signs legislation to expand protections under Americans with Disabilities Act. Kaiser Daily Health Policy Report (Sep. 26, 2008). Available from: http://www.kaisernetwork.org/daily_reports/rep_index.cfm?DR_ID=54684 Accessed Nov. 15, 2008.
90. ADA Amendments Act of 2008, S. 3406 (2008). Available from: http://frwebgate.access.gpo.gov/cgi-bin/getdoc.cgi?dbname=110_cong_bills&docid=f:s3406enr.txt.pdf Accessed Nov. 15, 2008.
91. Lorber, L. Statement of the U.S. Chamber of Commerce. 2007, October 4. Available from: http://www.uschamber.com/NR/rdonlyres/e7lkyi4xoc2jwlg7zxew7fekrk2pgrgv63mnbq

52xswaxoyvmbdtrso2rwqlwo5zobzpwjvsjta4mda4b6br25pptxa/LorberADATestimony 10304.pdf Accessed May 25, 2008.
92. Blanck, P, Adya, M, Myhill, WN, Samant, D, Chen, P. Employment of People with Disabilities – Twenty-Five Years Back and Ahead. Law & Inequality. 2007; 25:323–352.
93. National Organization on Disability. National EmployAbility Partnership. 2007. Available from: http://www.nod.org/index.cfm?fuseaction = Page.ViewPage&PageID = 1556 Accessed May 21, 2008.

Section V
Global View

Chapter 13
International Efforts: Perspectives, Policies, and Programs

Patricia Findley and Catherine P. Wilson

Introduction

With more people surviving cancer, it has become more likely that these cancer survivors can continue to work for many years following diagnosis and primary treatment. This chapter will provide a review of factors that are associated with work and the policies and programs in representative countries to address aspects of work in cancer survivors. Concepts of work, work disability following cancer, and optimization of function after primary cancer treatment in cancer survivors in various countries will be highlighted to identify some common themes and approaches across various nations, including an examination of the few programs that currently exist to support return to work efforts.

With the advent of cancer treatment enhancements and education of employers and employees, the notion of return to work following (or during) cancer treatment has become a relatively new phenomenon, therefore, return to work or maximizing work has not garnered much attention. Being able to quantify those with cancer has assumed much energy in the past decade for most of the European nations who have been able maintain cancer registries, with some contributing data to the EUROCARE project, the large international registry maintained by the International Agency for Research on Cancer (IARC). In 1989 the EUROCARE project was established by the European Community under Health Service Research to assess international variation in cancer survival. The individuals in EUROCARE are from 30 population-based cancer registries from twelve European countries that include Denmark, England, Estonia, Finland, France, Germany, Italy, The Netherlands, Poland, Scotland, Spain, and Switzerland. EUROCARE represents the first population-based collection and analysis of survival data on cancer patients using a common methodology so survivors can be followed over time to assess issues such as work and functional status [1].

P. Findley (✉)
Assistant Professor, Rutgers University, School of Social Work, New Brunswick, NJ 08901, USA
e-mail: pfindley@ssw.rutgers.edu

Factors Contributing to Return to Work

Developed Countries

Return to work and work in general over the long term for cancer survivors in the developed countries has become an increasing reality. In fact, it has been reported that 62–84% of cancer survivors across the European countries, Canada, and the United States do return to work [2]. Previous research indicates that cancer survivors may change jobs, reduce to part-time work, remain on sickness benefits for an extended period, retire, and even chose not to work [3–5]. However, some countries are reporting that cancer may not have the same level of impact on survivors as it did in even the recent past. The variations in the amount and type of labor force participation by survivors call attention to the differing needs of these individuals with respect to work and work optimization, pointing to the need for further study.

Developing Countries

Returning to work following cancer diagnosis and treatment is vastly different among the developing countries as compared to developed countries [6]. A search of the World Bank documents on their website and with posting for information on their listserv found no reports that looked at cancer survivors and work in developing countries; the bulk of the work reported from the World Bank focuses on prevention, detection, and treatment of cancer. This lack of emphasis from the World Bank points toward the role of cancer in society as it is still emerging with the priorities and needs of the developing countries being fairly rudimentary as they struggle with issues of poverty, AIDS, hunger, the rural nature of these countries, and the general decline of the world economy [6]. Individuals with cancer in these countries are just beginning to be included in registries. Many die due to lack of access to healthcare. Additionally, if they ever are diagnosed, equipment to treat is scarce [6]. Furthermore, with respect to work, in the poorer countries, formal work is not known in the same ways as it is known in the western world; a majority of individuals work in the informal sector or are self-employed, leaving the notion of measuring return-to-work as very challenging.

In many parts of the developing world, return to work for a cancer survivor is influenced more by the labor market and the economy in general. For example, in Argentina, Arossi and colleagues [7] demonstrate that the physical and emotional stress of cervical cancer is not restricted to just the woman, but it also impacts her family and neighbors. They report in a cross-sectional study of 120 women with cervical cancer that the socio-economic impacts on families are great, even though 96% of all medical care costs were covered. They found that for nearly half of the patients in their study that at least two households took part in the caregiving and assistance for the individual with cancer, so both families feel the economic impact. Additionally, when examining the issue of work absence, these researchers found for both the family members as well as the survivors that not showing up at work led to either a loss of wages or the loss of the job entirely because the employer could not hold a position for them since job tasks needed to be completed and others individuals were available to work, thus leaving no job for which the survivor could return.

Economics do play a significant role in the return to work efforts, but so do attitudes and perceptions, especially for some developing countries where timely treatment is gradually increasing the number of survivors. As a nation, Singapore recognizes its increased prevalence of individuals surviving cancer, particularly for cancers of the nasopharynx, breast, non-Hodgkin's lymphoma, leukemia, testis, cervix, ovaries, stomach, colon, and the rectum, all cancers that typically affect those younger than 34 years old [8]. However, reactions, attitudes, and awareness of cancer, its treatment, and how it affects return to work for both the survivor and his or her colleagues is not readily understood. Therefore, Chen and colleagues [8] conducted a small survey (32 cancer survivors and 30 members of the general public) during the "Cancer Vive" event in 2004 in Singapore (Cancer Vive was the inaugural event for the National Cancer Centre in Singapore in 2004. Cancer Vive is part of the National Cancer Survivors Day® program that is an international annual worldwide celebration of life that is held in hundreds of communities throughout the world [8]). These researchers found that the definition of "cancer survivor" is not readily used as people have not been surviving cancer to this point in Singapore; many misperceptions and negative beliefs based on limited knowledge of cancer exist including that one can develop cancer by having bad Karma, that cancer is a contagious disease, or that cancer survivors will not be as productive as other colleagues without cancer once they return to work. These researchers were particularly concerned that these misperceptions may reduce a cancer survivor's opportunities for work and other attempts at assimilation into the community. Table 13.1 presents the results of their

Table 13.1 Survey results on cancer survivors' and the public's misconception of cancer

Beliefs about cancer (% with misconception)	Cancer Survivors (n=32)	Public (n=30)
Everyone can have cancer	13.3	23.3
Cancer can spread to other parts of the body	80	80
Cancer might not have obvious symptoms	16.7	26.7
Cancer usually occurs with no known cause	36.7	55.2
Cancer can happen because of genetic malfunction	13.3	20
Cancer can be prevented	23.3	10
Cancer is contagious	23.4	6.7
Cancer happens due to bad "Karma"	13.3	6.7
Cancer can only be inherited from parents	20	16.7

Note: This table has been previously published in the Singapore Med J. 2006; 47(2):143–146 and is reproduced with the kind permission of the Editor.

survey addressing perceptions of cancer held by both cancer survivors as well as members of the general public. It is interesting to note that 13.3% of the survivors thought that cancer occurs from having bad Karma. While only 6.7% of the general public believed that cancer was contagious; both beliefs can potentially impact colleagues' attitudes when a survivor returns to work.

Chen and colleagues [8] also explored attitudes regarding survivors and employment. As shown in Table 13.2, with respect to cancer patients, 60.7% of the general public reported they felt that cancer patients are "always" dependent on their colleagues at work for assistance and support to complete job tasks. Most notably, 82.1% reported strongly disagreeing or disagreeing (and 17.9% with no opinion and 0% strongly agreeing or agreeing) with the statement "I would employ cancer patients if I am able to make employment decisions," meaning that they would not hire a cancer survivor if they had a position to fill. Furthermore, 82.6% strongly disagreed or disagreed with the statement "I would employ cancer patients in remission if I am able to make

Table 13.2 Public attitudes towards cancer patients (CPS) and cancer patients in remission (CPRS.)

	Strongly agree & Agree (%)	No Opinion	Strongly & Disagree (%)
Items for CPS			
I will consider working with a colleague who has cancer	89.7	6.9	3.4
Cancer patients tend to make use of their condition to gain benefits	3.6	28.6	67.8
I would feel nervous in the presence of cancer patients	3.6	3.6	92.8
Cancer patients should be given equal opportunities at work	10.7	10.7	78.6
I would employ cancer patients if I am able to make employment decisions	0.0	17.9	82.1
Cancer patients are less productive than other people	35.7	3.6	60.7
Cancer patients tend to frequently take medical leave	57.1	14.3	28.6
Cancer patients are always dependent on their colleagues at work	60.7	17.9	21.4
Cancer patients are fit to work	71.4	3.6	25.0
Cancer patients should work again	66.7	11.1	22.2
Cancer patients should be given a lighter workload/responsibility	55.6	18.5	25.9
Items for CPRS			
I will consider working with a colleague who has cancer	87.0	4.3	8.7

Table 13.2 (continued)

	Strongly agree & Agree (%)	No Opinion	Strongly & Disagree (%)
People with a history of cancer tend to make use of their condition to gain benefits	8.7	4.3	87.0
I would feel nervous in the presence of people with a history of cancer	4.3	0.0	95.7
People with a history of cancer should be given equal opportunities at work	8.7	0.0	91.3
I would employ cancer patients in remission if I am able to make employment decisions	4.4	13.0	82.6
People with a history of cancer are less productive than other people	21.7	0.0	78.3
People with a history of cancer tend to frequently take medical leave	21.7	21.7	56.6
Cancer patients in remission are always dependent on their colleagues at work	13.0	13.0	74.0
People with a history of cancer are fit to work	95.7	4.3	0
People with a history of cancer should work again	95.7	4.3	0
People with a history of cancer should be given a lighter workload/responsibility	36.4	18.2	45.4

Note: This table has been previously published in the Singapore Med J. 2006; 47(2):143–146 and is reproduced with the kind permission of the Editor.

employment decisions" while 91.3% strongly disagreed or disagreed with the statement, "People with a history of cancer should be given equal opportunities at work." These attitudes toward cancer survivors and work can impede return to work and work optimization efforts.

Finally, Chen and his associates [8] turned to those survivors who did work, as nearly 50% (n = 15) of the survivors in their study did work.[1] The majority continued to work for the same company (86.6%), in the same position (80.0%), with the same benefits (85.7%), and with eighty percent of their employers paying for treatment. Researchers found that 20% of those surveyed stated that those in treatment should never return to work again. While all of these results need to take into consideration the very small sample size, this study does provide an initial glimpse into the attitudes of the Singaporeans and their reactions to cancer survivors and work.

---

[1] Singapore's health insurance coverage is tied to employee contributions into a national health care plan using a co-payment and deductible plan with the government contributing as well, however, there are provisions for those who have exhausted their contribution pool or who are unable to work.

Socio-environmental Impacts on Cancer Survivors and Return to Work

Work Disabilities and the Role of Social Insurance

Physical and psychological symptoms of survivors do impact return to work, but so do socio-economic issues. For example, it has been noted that being able to take time off work during and after treatment with pay is not universal (i.e. being self-employed, not belonging to a union), and that time off work without pay may pose a financial burden [9]. Only a few countries offer any type of private disability insurance for purchase to extend the income period (e.g., U.S., Canada, and Germany). However, even the notion of considering a cancer survivor as an individual with a disability for eligibility for government programs, insurance schemes, and in service delivery is still evolving.

Cancer Survivors as Individuals with Disabilities

Disability is subjective by nature and often difficult to define. A disability has been defined as an impairment that restricts the ability to perform usual work or daily activities [10]. The effects of cancer or its treatment may or may not lead to functional limitations such as seeing, hearing, walking, or lifting, and it may or may not lead to limitations in the activities of daily living (ADLs) such as eating, dressing, bathing, and getting out of bed, and furthermore, these limitations of the ADLs for cancer survivors may or may not cause restrictions in instrumental activities of daily living (IADLs) such as grocery shopping, using a telephone, managing money, or meal preparation. Furthermore, even if the individual is experiencing some limitations, he or she may not consider themselves to be "disabled." How disability is viewed may vary by country.

As noted earlier, impairments or limitations in survivors caused by cancer and its treatment may lead to reduced work capacity. Up to this point, many individuals with cancer were not able to live long enough after diagnosis to warrant return to work efforts. Thus, it is not surprising that some countries, such as Sweden, do not yet make disability pension allowances for cancer survivors. (In Sweden's system, individuals with cancer would be covered under the sickness benefits that are not time limited.) Moreover, even if the individual was considered disabled, the variation in the types of health care benefits and eligibility requirements among nations contributes to a disparity in who actually receives disability benefits. For example, in England, Scotland, and Wales, the individual is considered disabled from the point of the cancer diagnosis, thus allowing the survivor access to all disability programs and protections, including allowances for work accommodations including reduced work time [11]. Whereas in other countries, such as Denmark and Norway, there is a stronger focus on individual assessment and demonstrating reduced work capacity to qualify for disability benefits.

Globally, and more pointedly in some countries over others, in the last few decades of the twentieth century, there was a shift in how people with disabilities in general were portrayed and supported. There was a "trend toward integration and normalization, to independence and self-determination" [12]. For example, the United Nations declared 1981 as the International Year of Disabled People, and announced 1983–1992 as the Decade of Disabled Persons. It was more recently that the European Union proclaimed 2003 as The European Year of People with Disabilities. This more inclusive view of individuals with disabilities has paved the way for cancer survivors on many fronts coinciding with the shift from viewing cancer as a terminal illness to seeing it as a chronic illness where individuals would be able to choose to return to work, despite limitations they may have. Fortunately for cancer survivors, the tide continues to shift in discussions of disability pensions or the return to work, with the focus now on partial disability programs that allow individuals to return to work in more limited capacities with accommodations. Such flexibility in job demands correlates well with the needs of cancer survivors who many need to shift or reduce work hours. Table 13.3 provides an overview of several developed countries' sickness and disability plans. Universal or national health care programs are a commonality across the countries, and all offer a short-term sickness benefit with coverage that ranges among countries from 6 months to 7 or 8 months until the individual might be eligible for long-term disability benefits [12]. Long-term (i.e., permanent) disability usually starts after a waiting period of 6–12 months to demonstrate the persistence of their disability, or after a vocational rehabilitation program has not helped the individual return to paid employment [12]. Several do offer partial disability programs including Germany, Italy, Spain, France, Austria, Canada, Denmark, and the Netherlands; however, it is Germany and Denmark that are leading the way for individuals to work part time while still receiving disability benefits to support a gradual return to work. More discussion on these two countries' programs can be found later in this chapter.

One key to keeping individuals with a reduced work capacity working is to avert any point of complete separation from the labor force [12]. Offering supports in current work situations could prevent this separation or, perhaps, a new job that is more appropriate given the work limitations or the opportunity to vary work hours. However, this type of optimization is not always a reality, particularly when dealing with a condition such as cancer that presents with an acute period when treatment is required and being at work is difficult, and then followed by a period or periods of time when accommodations may be necessary; this varies from the usual permanent disability perspective that is inherent in disability benefit programs.

In 1999, many of the European countries were forced to negotiate the pressures of a single European market as well as manage budget deficit restrictions that were required of the European Union members to be included in the European Monetary Union [13]; therefore, there has been much change for the financing of health care services in Europe. Most European nations have some form of health insurance that will cover cancer treatment and physician visits.

Table 13.3 Sickness and disability benefits and funding by country

Country	Funding			Sickness Benefit					Funding			Disability Programs		Disability Benefits
	Employer	Employee	Government	Available?	Coverage				Employer	Employee	Government	Partial	Permanent	
Germany	7%	7%	Subsidy to cover remaining need	Yes	Universal health care and cash benefits				7%	7%	A subsidy to compensate for the cost of benefits not covered by contributions.	Yes, step-wise reintegration	Yes	Cash benefits, universal health care, including rehabilitation programs.
Italy	0%	0%	100%	Yes	Universal health care				23.81%	8.89%	Full cost of income tested allowances and any overall deficit	Yes	Yes	Cash benefits, universal health care
Denmark	0%	0%	100%	Yes	Universal health care and cash benefits				0%	0%	100%	Yes, flex jobs	Yes	Cash benefits with partial compensation of additional expenses arising from the disability. Universal health care. Programs are income-tested.
Spain	23.60%	4.70%	Annual Subsidy	Yes	Universal health care and cash benefits				23.60%	4.70%	Annual Subsidy	Yes	Yes	Cash benefits with health care coverage
France	12.80%	6.80%	Variable percentage	Yes	Health care and cash benefits based on a reimbursement system				8.2% plus 1.6% of total payroll	6.55%	Variable Subsidies	Yes	Yes	Cash benefits with health care coverage
United Kingdom	13%	11.00%	Means tested, treasury grant	Yes	Universal health care and cash benefits				13%	11.00%	Means tested, treasury grant	No	Yes	Cash benefits with health care coverage

Table 13.3 (continued)

Country	Funding			Sickness Benefit		Funding			Disability Programs		Disability Benefits
	Employer	Employee	Government	Available?	Coverage	Employer	Employee	Government	Partial	Permanent	
Austria	There is no ceiling for contribution purposes for employers.	3.5% of payroll (wage earners) or 3.7% of payroll (salaried employees).	Income tested, subsidy	Yes	Health care and cash benefits	12.55%	10.25%	Any deficits and the cost of care benefit and income-tested allowance	Yes	Yes	Cash benefits with health care coverage
Canada	2.73%	1.95%	Most of the cost is met from federal, provincial, and territorial general revenues through block transfers, part of which are conditional on provinces and territories meeting federal program requirements as set out in the Canada Health Act.	Yes	Health care, cash benefits	0%	0%	100%	Yes	Yes	Cash benefits with health care coverage
Australia	0%	0%	Total cost of cash benefits	Yes	Health care, Cash Benefits, Rent assistance, Pharmaceutical allowance, Remote area supplement, Concession card	0%	0%	100%	No	Yes	Health Care, Cash allowances

Many have publicly financed (through taxes) health care systems (e.g., Austria, the Czech Republic, Denmark, England, Scotland, Sweden), and some are funded by a combination of citizen and employer contributions (e.g., France, Germany, The Netherlands) [13].

Supporting Return to Work Efforts

Coupled with the changes in the health care system, the European nations have also made tremendous strides in reforming their disability pension policies to focus on the active integration of workers with disabilities back into the labor force and to decrease the emphasis on passive compensation for disabilities. Several of the European Union countries (such as Denmark, Germany, the Netherlands, Greece, Luxembourg, Austria, Sweden, and the United Kingdom) are tightening how their disability pension schemes are granted, enhancing rehabilitation opportunities, and helping the individual locate reasonable alternative work rather than allocating disability benefits [14]. In fact, the Organization for Economic Cooperation and Development (OECD) [15] reported in 2007 that the major thrust of the movement specifically was to increase labor force participation by all people with health concerns with significant progress being made in how countries are addressing partial work capacity, particularly, as discussed earlier and shown in Table 13.1, for the countries that have disability systems that include partial disability benefit schemes.

Among countries that do support efforts of survivors who want to return to work, many have had strong traditions of working with those with disabilities already. For example, Germany has long supported rehabilitation for return to work over granting permanent disability pensions for individuals with disabilities [16]. This focus holds for cancer survivors as well, as Germany hosts specialized oncological rehabilitation programs for cancer survivors to facilitate improvement of functional deficits, health-related quality of life, and vocational re-entry through occupational therapy, physiotherapy, and psycho-oncological programming. The majority of cancer rehabilitation is still delivered as inpatient care with the usual length of stay being three weeks and costs approximately 2300–2500 Euros (or US $3,400–$3,700) with very few outpatient units [17]. Programming usually includes 2–3 inpatient and/or outpatient stays for the cancer survivor. The specialized rehabilitation centers employ social workers who are in contact with local and/or regional social services and organize support at home, or other types of services that they may need. Vocational counselors are also part of the overall program providing counseling as well as contact with German pension fund to consult with individuals regarding return to work, training needs, and job opportunities. Furthermore, if an individual needs to come back into the inpatient program for further rehabilitative therapies, they are allowed to after one year, and are allowed up to three inpatient rehabilitation program stays in the two years after diagnosis and initial rehabilitation.

Beyond the formal rehabilitation programs, Germany, as a nation, does support the return to work efforts of cancer survivors. The country supports a graduated return to work process called step-wise reintegration that allows the individual to return to work, for example, for two hours a day for the first four weeks, then four hours the next four weeks, or whatever pattern best suits the needs [16]. This type of reintegration process is well accepted by German rehabilitation professionals, and is used for a variety of rehabilitation diagnoses including burns and orthopedic conditions, and is implemented under the supervision of the individual's physician. The employee and employer determine the rate of return to work and establish a salary reflective of the time worked, specifying in a contract the start and stop dates of the stepwise process and the timing of the change in steps [16]. Currently, for cancer survivors making this transition back to work, the German pension fund (Deutsche Rentenversicherung) will pay for the returning employee's salary, so that the employer does not take the financial burden. This arrangement appeals to both the employee and the employer, particularly as there is no cost burden for the employer and as long as the employer is agreeable to allowing the worker to work less than an eight hour work schedule while in the reintegration process. There are no clearly defined research studies published on the step-wise process, but there are policy discussions that have reviewed the strengths and weaknesses of this approach as other countries seek reform to their own systems of disability management [16]; the role of the government and its funding is pivotal in the step-wise program. This program is unique to Germany. Overall, Germany hosts a very well-organized and comprehensive cancer rehabilitation program, with many supports to help the cancer survivor return to and remain at work.

Canada is another country that supports return to work efforts following cancer treatment, but also has the Canada Pension Plan (CPP) that contains a disability component if the individual has met the requirements of contributing into the system by working for and contributing to the benefit system in four of the last six years and are determined to be permanently disabled (i.e., cannot work in any job) and have been out of work for at least 12 months. The CPP Disability program does offer some allowances for work rehabilitation and Canada does provide for national health insurance covering medically necessary hospitalizations and physician services, including rehabilitation. (Supplemental health care coverage is also available for purchase; usually employer group-based insurance, to extend coverage for additional needs. However, self-employed individuals cannot buy into Canada's national insurance and the private insurance that is available for purchase is very expensive [18].) Canada's rehabilitation programs do include vocational counseling for return to work following the rehabilitation course, and currently offer cancer rehabilitation programs that include vocational counselors, social workers, and other therapists to help the individual return to work and optimize efforts. Canada has included cancer survivors into their rehabilitation programs as they would any disability; however, the National Cancer Institute of Canada (NCIC) Leadership Fund has recently included a five-year priority area for research project funding for Cancer Survivorship,

Supportive Care, and Symptom Control. This area is new and is posted on the NCIC website without much detail, encouraging researchers to check back for updates (http://www.ncic.cancer.ca/). Furthermore, across Canada's provinces there is not much variation in the types of programs offered to those with cancer. The focus is mainly on surveillance, treatment, and supporting the patient and his or her family psychosocially with no real clear linkage to vocational services or discussions of return to work [19]. It appears that the vocational work is remaining with the rehabilitation centers at this point in Canada.

Along with the change in perspective of how disability is conceptualized, there is also a shift in how work capacity is assessed across counties for individuals with all types of medical conditions and limitations, including cancer. For example, in Denmark, local disability authorities (i.e., the municipality) do not assess whether the occupational ability of someone with a limitation in function is reduced. Instead they assess the client's work ability, and they relate the work ability to the client's potential labor market attachment [20]. In other words, Denmark attempts to find ways to keep individuals working at any capacity rather than placing them onto disability benefits. Furthermore, eligibility determination demands that the municipality assess that the applicant is unable to work in an ordinary job or in a "flex job." A flex job is a wage subsidized job on special conditions (e.g., reduced working hours and reduced job demands). These flex jobs were developed for individuals with classic disabilities, but now include cancer survivors who may also have some work limitations. The flex jobs are permanent jobs. Eligibility for a flex job requires that the applicant's work ability is permanently reduced by at least 50%. Eligibility for permanent disability benefits demands that the applicant's work ability is permanently reduced and that it cannot be improved through medical or vocational rehabilitation. The possibility for improvement of the work ability through medical or vocational rehabilitation should be exhausted and employment on usual conditions should be impossible.

Norway, as do many countries, offers its citizens, as well as foreign citizens, insurance under the National Insurance Scheme as long as the individual is a resident or is employed in Norway. The system is financed jointly by employer and employee contributions. In 2008, the employee contributes 7.8% of gross wage income (11% if self-employed); employers pay out a contribution based on wages paid out and geographic regional zones within a range of 0–14.1% [21]. The benefit under this plan includes medical and disability benefits as well as an allowance for "attendance" benefits or services for supervision or extra attention for special care or nursing services, covering individuals from one to four years based on reassessments. Cancer is a covered diagnosis under the Norwegian disability scheme. Individuals may receive, through the medical benefit portion, up to 100% of the annual leave income for one year, after that point, if the individual is aged 17–67 years a disability pension may be awarded if the individual's work capacity is permanently reduced by at least 50% [22]. Although, as with the other European nations, Norway has also restricted eligibility for permanent disability programs by encouraging quick return to work after illness and a focus on rehabilitation programs to further increase the pace at which a worker can rejoin the labor force [23]. However, Norway has struggled with implementing some of its plans to reduce the amount given in benefits and to tighten its eligibility criteria as a way to encourage return to work in general [23], and this may affect how cancer survivors are considered for benefits within their system.

Legislation

As discussed above, Canada, and many of the European countries, particularly those in the United Kingdom, have begun to recognize the more chronic nature of cancer and have modified their disability pension programs to account for this shift in perspective [24]. Legislative efforts have helped to change programming for survivors as well. For example, in Canada, anyone who has cancer is protected by human rights legislation of their province or territory. A significant catalyst in this movement for the UK came in December 2005 by the Disability Rights Commission (DRC), when the Disability Discrimination Act (DDA) of 1995 was extended to include individuals with HIV, cancer, and multiple sclerosis throughout the United Kingdom [24]. (Note: policy makers felt the inclusion of these individuals under this act was important even if the individuals did not consider themselves "disabled." This is important as this designation allows cancer survivors to participate in established disability programs including flexible work scheduling and vocational rehabilitation.) The DRC became part of the Equality and Human Rights Commission on October 1, 2007. The act protects anyone with HIV, cancer, multiple sclerosis, and other disabilities from unfair treatment in the workplace, educational settings, managing, renting, or buying land or property, and in accessing services for the point of diagnosis. These changes were made in response to perceived stigma that these specific diagnoses were thought to engender. Such as, in earlier versions of the proposed extension of the act, it was proposed to exclude certain types of cancers as some cancers do not require as intense treatment as others, but given the heterogeneity of treatment protocols, the policy makers felt that it would be discriminatory to separate out protection based on specific diagnosis. Therefore, all cancers are covered under this revision.

Discrimination

Despite legislation in several countries that protects workers from discrimination due to disability or health condition, many cancer survivors experience discrimination [25, 26]. For example, a Swedish study on breast cancer survivors found that women with breast cancer were likely to lose their jobs, be demoted, faced unwanted changes in their jobs, developed problems with their co-workers and their employers, found themselves making personal changes regarding attitudes with respect to work, and felt less physically strong [27]. Some survivors perceived such actions as discrimination, thus highlighting the need for social support, both emotional and practical (i.e., an accommodation) especially within the work place [28, 29]. On the other hand, a Canadian study of 646 breast cancer survivors three years post-diagnosis from the Quebec Tumor Registry matched with 890 aged matched community cancer-free controls (both groups of women were employed at the time of the study) found little evidence of discrimination in the work environment being any different than it was prior to diagnosis [30]. Furthermore, these researchers noted that a change in job was not necessarily always on the prompting of the employer, most job change decisions were the survivor's own; if a survivor was terminated by the employer it was usually a result of a change in the need for the number or type of workers. (Also, note Quebec is a very pro-worker province.) This finding was similar to another study where the breast cancer survivors acknowledged that some jobs just do not have security and to be absent from work for several months might be a hardship on the employer as well, so survivors did not see losing that position as a discriminatory act [27]. In the end, the women in the Quebec study who did change jobs reported being able to find new positions with wages at the same level as the position they had left during the three years since the time of diagnosis [30].

Despite the inclusive intentions of the DDA, a report based on an analysis of calls placed to the helpline of the DRC during an eight-month period, found that nearly 15% of cancer survivors who are employed are laid off from the work force or chose ill-health retirement [31]. Even with the change in the Disability Discrimination Act made in 2005, the DRC reported that it received an average of two calls per week from breast cancer survivors complaining that they were being treated unfairly in their workplace. The complaints took several forms. Some women reported feeling unduly pressed to return to full work immediately following major surgery rather than being given the opportunity to incrementally return to work. Other women stated that they have had job offers rescinded after disclosing their health conditions, while still others were given lower paying or lower status jobs after their medical care. Table 13.4 illustrates the cancer-related complaints that were made to the DRC. The majority of the calls (82%) reported a failure on the behalf of the employer to make the reasonable accommodations; eighteen percent lost their jobs because of disability and other medically related concerns despite these practices being illegal. The DRC voiced concern that the unfair treatment suggests that employers have not yet understood the DDA, leaving the work environment not conducive to supporting return to work efforts. Interestingly, many of these attitudes and the actual discriminatory actions are not very different than what Chen et al. [8] found in their study, discussed earlier, of attitudes among workers and colleagues in Singapore.

Cultural Perceptions

The reactions or attitudes of society and the survivors themselves regarding cancer, its treatment, and the acceptance of cancer survivors are other important factors in return to work for cancer survivors. Dein [32] reports that

Table 13.4 Cancer-related complaints to the DRC

Nature of complaint	Percentage of all calls relating to cancer
Employers not making reasonable adjustments	82.0
Dismissed because of disability; capability concerns; sickness absence; dismissed after informing employer of medical condition	18.0
Forced into redundancy/ill-health retirement	14.5
Threatened with dismissal/redundancy	13.5
Disability-related absence has led to	7.5
Job relocated due to disability	5.8
Issued with formal warning due to taking time off to attend treatment	5.8

Based on 103 calls to the DRC helpline between December 2005 and August 2006.
Source: Disability Rights Commission.
Source: Attendance and Absence, IRS Employ Rev. (2006); 858:17–18.

attitudes do vary by culture and that attitudes may hinder return to work efforts; societal attitudes held by employers and colleagues have been reported to be deterrent as well for return to work for individuals with disabilities [33]. In the earlier section of this chapter, researchers from Singapore, Chen and associates [8], reported attitudinal barriers limited survivors' desire and ability to return to work. However, those authors admit that their sample size is very small (n = 30) and that the sample may be potentially biased, but it was the first study to document attitudes towards cancer survivors in Singapore.

In a study conducted in Israel [34], adult survivors of childhood cancer reported that their condition did negatively impact their ability to achieve both academically and within the labor force in terms of the educational level they could achieve and the types of positions they could hold. However, with a control group matched on age, sex, and parent's education level, no significant differences existed. Eight percent of survivors and 14% of controls had university degrees, 36% of survivors and 34% of controls were in school at the time of the study, and 74% of both had plans to return to school in the future. Despite the similarity in the percentages, 45% of the cancer survivors felt that having had cancer influenced their educational achievements "to a great extent" or "to a very great extent." Likewise with employment, as with educational achievement, 46% of the survivors felt that having cancer negatively affected their employment histories "to a great extent" or "to a very great extent" in terms of having low earning potential and likelihood for being let go from the job itself. Forty-five percent of the survivors had been let go from a job, compared with 19% of the controls ($p < 0.01$). Nearly 50% of the survivors felt the job loss was because of their cancer history. However, again, as with the educational pursuits, there were no statistical differences between the two groups with 67% of the survivors and 61% of control group with employment. It appears that perceptions play a large role for survivors in the work place, despite the actual differences in achievement being insignificant. It is interesting to observe that similar issues that have been noted in the United States cancer survivor population as well, particularly concerns around issues related to job termination among cancer survivors over employees with other types of illness [35].

Attitudes impact perceptions as well as interactions; therefore, these attitudes represent another area where cancer survivors need support and some type of accommodation in returning to and remaining at work. In a study conducted by Abrahamsen and associates [36], 495 patients in a single institution, treated for Hodgkin's Disease (HD) between 1971–1991 in Norway, were followed to see if they returned to their former jobs or educational pursuits within 6, 12, and 18 months from the initiation of treatment. Ninety-seven percent of their subjects answered the questions regarding whether they felt that their education or professional plans or career had changed because of cancer. Thirty-two percent responded that, yes, their plans had changed, 54% said no, and 15% were unsure. Among those who did report a change, 9% lost their job and had problems getting a new job, 44% reported less ambition to pursue further education or a job, and 17% had more ambition for continuing their education. Among all respondents, after a one-year follow-up in 1994, 19% were permanently disabled, which is twice the rate that would be found in the general population in Norway [36]; nearly half of those reporting permanent disability felt that cancer and issues related to treatment was the greatest reason for their disability. In Norway, individuals with severe and/or permanent disabilities are entitled to a disability pension. The researchers found that the rate of patients reporting to be permanently disabled in their study was higher than in other studies of long-term survivors of HD [37-40]. They felt that the high rate of unemployment in Norway, as well as the fact that being able to receive a pension at all, may have contributed to this higher reported frequency. However, in the current study, the employment status was, for the majority of the patients, the same at the point of diagnosis to follow-up in 1994, with nearly 50% of patients having the same job at diagnosis and at follow-up, with these results being similar as reported in other studies for survivors of HD [36]. With only 50% able to maintain the same job, it presents a challenge to understand the remaining 50% who were unable to maintain their job and to understand how to facilitate job retention, if that is something the survivors desired.

In sum, it is apparent that supporting efforts of cancer survivors to return to work requires attention to attitudes on the part of the survivors as well as colleagues and employers, awareness of the potential for discriminatory acts, and an understanding of survivor's rights covered under disability policies. More specific data are needed on the types of cultural perceptions to see how they truly differ across the different countries and the idiosyncratic benefit structures in order to develop evidence-based policies and interventions within the workplace. This is critically important as much of the focus is moving from addressing issues of quality of life and turning toward active reintegration into work-focused lifestyles.

Return to Work Programs to Support Cancer Survivors

Negotiating the maze of the employment systems is not an easy task, and can be compounded for survivors trying to manage their physical, medical, emotional, and financial needs as they face return to work. Only a handful of countries have begun to focus programs specifically on cancer survivors to help them return to work as well as reintegrate in other aspects of their lives. Most often such programs are operated within the scope of physical rehabilitation programs. Mainly, such programs are found in Canada, the UK, the Netherlands, Germany, Italy, France, and Australia. The following section describes some of the leading programs within the various nations. The programs themselves vary in scope and breadth, with many of them being fairly new and all still evolving to meet the needs of survivors and employers.

Association of European Cancer Leagues

The Association of European Cancer Leagues (ECL) is a non-profit organization that seeks to enhance communication and collaboration between European Leagues/societies to promote programming between European Cancer Leagues and other health and social service organizations to support the growing number of individuals with cancer in Europe. They are an information source as well as a legislative advocate for a variety of issues and projects related to cancer and return to work for cancer survivors. They also facilitate dialogue of best practices to promote an exchange of learning.

In 2004–2005, the ECL Working Group on Patients' Rights and Duties turned its focus to cancer patients and their working environment by reviewing various issues related to return to work, including, the right to keep a job, searching for a new job, and the social and financial supports related to these issues. The "European Framework for Protecting Cancer Patients at Work" was adopted by ECL members in November 2005 (Fig. 13.1) and was presented to 20 Members of the European Parliament in January 2006. Figure 13.1 highlights and details important points in the seven key areas of: (1) Protection of employees; (2) Maintaining employment; (3) Looking for a new job; (4) Pensions and insurance; (5) The work; (6) Vulnerable groups; and (7) Carers and family members. This framework is unique as it offers guidance to survivors as well as employers and policy makers to create a supportive work environment for the cancer survivor; ongoing debate continues in Parliament on how to best adopt these recommendations across policies as well as ways to look into discrimination related to them. Future work should focus on the outcomes of the recommendations as they relate to work optimization to allow for an evaluation and ongoing refinement of the recommendations.

The Association of European Cancer Leagues (ECL) is fully aware of the very different legal and cultural conditions for employees affected by cancer in Europe. Nevertheless, ECL considers the following seven areas to be of common interest and recommends these areas to constitute a European framework to be considered when developing legislation, policies, and other tools intended to offer basic protection for workers who are also cancer patients.

1. Protection of employees

    - dismissal of seriously ill employees
    - privacy and confidentiality of employee's personal health information retained by employers
    - employees' right to be absent from work because of treatment
    - employees' right to be absent because of rehabilitation and related compensation systems
    - anti-discrimination acts and laws, on grounds of health status or disability

2. Maintaining employment

These policies enable the employee either to go back to the same job or to be redeployed to a different position in the same company, by introducing the following elements:

    - flexible working conditions during treatment and rehabilitation, i.e.,
    - time off for treatment, flexible working hours etc.
    - adjust duties and tasks to suit employees health condition and
    - abilities
    - offers to be trained for a different position
    - support of further job training
    - ensuring the physical work place is safe and comfortable

    - financial compensation in keeping with the disability of the
    - employee
    - where possible, securing a number of positions for the disabled
    - and other persons with reduced working capacity
    - gradual return to work
    - adequate social protection and support for employees who leave
    - employment because of their illness
    - arrangements allowing employees to choose to leave their job
    - indefinitely without losing their social security rights

3. Looking for a new job

    - special support from employment authorities
    - access to training and re-training schemes

4. Pensions and insurance

    - a basic social security system ensuring a combination of sick pay
    - for time-off, social security benefits for longer-term absences, and
    - partial or full permanent disability pension where it applies
    - a collective workplace insurance securing a reasonable amount
    - of money for employees who are diagnosed with cancer or
    - another life threatening disease
    - the cancer patient who returns to work should see his/her social
    - benefits adjusted to his/her specific case

Fig. 13.1 European framework for protecting cancer patients at work Adopted in Prague, 5th of November 2005

5. The work

- company policy containing recommendations or regulations about communication, contact during absence, returning to work etc

- specific company schemes for employees who develop a life threatening disease, i.e. low interest loans, psychological counseling or company emergency funds to be used in specific cases for the employees' benefit

- establishing a company Occupational Health Service available to both the employer and the employee, to act as a source of information, advice and assessment, as well as an objective party in evaluating the situation and recommending necessary adjustments on both sides

- offering education to company managers and union representatives

- offering information and support to colleagues

6. Vulnerable groups

Special efforts would be beneficial for cancer patients who have an especially high risk of losing their job. This may be due to limited skills and qualifications, a vulnerable economical situation or to social/family isolation. Groups with a possibly high risk are:

- unskilled workers
- single parents
- patients with special diagnoses, for instance cancer of the larynx
- older patients
- ethnic minorities
- self-employed
- employees with short contracts

7. Carers and family members

When a person is diagnosed with cancer the whole family is affected. Therefore it is important that policies support the family members, for instance through:

- special leave during the cancer patient's treatment
- possible financial support
- practical arrangements offering flexibility at work

ECL consists of 31 members coming from Belgium, Croatia, Cyprus, Czech Republic, Denmark, Finland, France, Germany, Greece, Hungary, Iceland, Ireland, Italy, Luxembourg, The Netherlands, Poland, Portugal, Slovakia, Slovenia, Switzerland, Turkey and United Kingdom.

www.europeancancerleagues.org

Fig. 13.1 (continued)

Cancerbackup (British Association of Cancer United Patients – and Their Families and Friends)

Cancerbackup (British Association of Cancer United Patients – and their families and friends) is Europe's leading cancer information service as a national charity. Established in 1985, the website's founder, Dr. Vicky Clement-Jones, a cancer survivor herself, acknowledged the need for current, high quality information, as well as the need for practical advice and support, and now includes information on return to work [41]. Their website (www.cancerbackup.org.uk) is staffed by experienced cancer nurses and offers publications written to benefit patients, survivors, and their families at no cost. The database for the website attests to having the most comprehensive list of resources, community organizations, and support groups listings for cancer patients and their families in the UK. Its website hosts a page (Work and Cancer) dedicated to those working while in treatment and return to work, as well as targeting employers to help them support employees who have cancer. The website provides information on employment rights, primarily directed at those who work for a company, but they also have information for those who are self-employed.

Table 13.5 below illustrates the topics included on their webpage, specifically: Work & cancer; What is cancer?; Cancer treatments; Working during treatment; Symptoms & side effects; Time off; Talking to colleagues; and Talking to employers. For employers: How employers can help; For employers—Discrimination; Financial issues; Going back to work; Self-employed;

Table 13.5 Cancerbackup.org.uk Website Overview

Topic	Information provided
For Cancer Survivors	
Talking to colleagues	Tips on how to respond to people who might avoid the worker in fear of not being able to say the right thing. It suggests that the worker bring up the topic to demonstrate a willingness to talk about the cancer. It also suggests that disclosing the condition may actually be helpful so colleagues have a better idea of what to expect and gives them an opportunity to support the survivor.
Talking to employers	Tips on talking to employers and disclosing the cancer diagnosis. It provides information about the Disability Discrimination Act, and how the Act provides employees and employers the guidelines needed to accommodate the worker with cancer. Also, it also provides information about talking to employers about diagnosis, treatment, and accommodations that the employee may need.
How employers can help	This topic includes subject guidelines about the employee's rights, flexible working schedule, support and privacy, and confidentiality. Workers are given information on how to talk to their human resources managers about sick leave and on how to talk to employers about changes in duties and hours to accommodate a flexible working schedule. It also provides information on the employee's privacy and the legal right to confidentiality.
For Employers	
Discrimination	This section provides information about the Disability Discrimination Act, which defines an employee with cancer as disabled. Therefore, it is illegal for an employer to discriminate against a person with cancer in the workplace. Topics include reasonable adjustments the employer must make, such as time off, light duties, working from home, etc. This section also reviews ways in which an employer may discriminate and victimize the employee (when an employee with cancer is treated less favorably as a result

Table 13.5 (continued)

Topic	Information provided
	of trying to claim their rights). Also included: what to do when an employee is being discriminated, victimized, how to deal with unresolved problems and seeking help with legal costs. The most important topics: know the employee's rights, legal deadlines, contact a lawyer, contact the Citizens Advice Bureau, find a union representative and contact the employment rights organizations.
Giving up work for good	Tips about how choosing not to work can impact the individual's financial future. It suggests meeting with an independent financial advisor, and if retiring early, speaking to the pension administrator at the place of employment. Other issues to consider: the time involved in claiming benefits (13–26 weeks), state, occupational, private pensions, savings, shares, and benefits. Also, it suggests considering the rights the employee may be giving up if leaving work early, such as sick pay and statutory sick pay, pension rights, death-in-service benefits, occupation-linked private medical insurance, and other occupational benefits.
Financial issues	This topic includes information about taking sick time, and stresses the importance of contacting an independent financial advisor, and any insurance companies the employee may have policies with. Also covered: sick pay, which is paid through the employee's contributions to the Statutory Sick Pay (SSP), for a maximum of 28 weeks. Some companies also may pay occupational sick leave. An employee must also return to work for eight weeks before claiming SSP again. Also covered: Sick certificates, Benefits, Disability/Life assurance, and occupational pensions. Employees can get more information on these topics from the Department for Work and Pensions website at www.dwp.gov.uk.
Going back to work	Topics include meeting with your employer, job flexibility, financial considerations when going back, claiming a benefit, benefits not affected, benefits affected, welfare to work, and permitted to work. All topics include information for the employee when returning to work. The first recommendation is to meet with the employer and the human resources department to discuss any changes to the work place that may benefit the employee, which can include a return to work plan. This includes possible schedule changes for flexibility. An important part of this topic for the employee is the financial considerations which include the benefits—both private insurance and public and tax credits. The employee is encouraged to contact the Department for Work and Pensions to discuss any questions regarding the public benefits and tax credits.
Self-employed	If the cancer patient is self-employed, the patient is entitled to the Incapacity Benefit, as long as they have paid the correct National Insurance contributions. Benefits may include Housing/Council Tax Benefit, Working/Child Tax Credits, NHS Benefits, Incapacity Benefit, Disability Living Allowance, and Attendance Allowance. Also, it suggests that the patient contact the benefits advisor at the Citizens Advice Bureau or a Law Centre to find out about possible benefits. Also, a reminder that if the patient's financial or working circumstances change, changes in benefits may occur.

Table 13.5 (continued)

Topic	Information provided
Disability	The Department of Work and Pensions has a program called *Access to Work* that provides employers 80% to 100% of the costs of adjustments or help a disabled person may need to work. The program supports part-time, full-time, and self-employed employees. This money can be used to adapt the premises (wheel chair ramps, etc.), the cost of an interpreter, items of support, a personal reader for the blind, special aids and equipment, a support worker, and travel to work. Special attention needs to be paid to the time limits of this program in terms of when the employee was hired and when the employer files to participate in the program. PACTS (Placement Assessment and Counseling Teams) based at Jobcentre Plus offices also provides information and financial support for those employers who hire disabled persons.
Careers or family members	This topic includes the three legal areas in which family members, including parents of a sick child, are able to take leave from work. There is compassionate leave, dependency leave, or unpaid leave for family members who may have to care for a cancer patient. Flexible working was enacted in April 2007, and provides for the employee, who must either be a spouse or civil partner and living at the same address, for flexible work time. Dependency leave provides for an employee to take time off in caring for a dependent, such as a child or elderly parent. This is usually unpaid leave, however; some employers allow paid leave. Parents may have up to 18 weeks of unpaid parental leave. It also suggests that caregivers may also experience employment discrimination, and it is important for the employee to contact employment rights organizations.
After treatment	This topic covers what employees may feel after they return to work from having cancer treatment. Some are more productive, feeling that the cancer is behind them. Others are depressed; however these feelings will go away after time. It suggests searching the Life After Cancer section of this website.
Organizations	Provides the employee with six web links to organizations that provide information regarding cancer and the workplace: the Advisory, Conciliation and Arbitration Service (employment relations); Citizens Advice (network that helps people with money, legal, and other issues); Disability Rights Commission (advice and information on rights and equality for disabled persons); GMB (Britain's General Union); Health and Safety Executive (ensures that peoples' health and safety from work are properly monitored); the Learning Disability Helpline (free, confidential, independent information on disabilities).

Disability; Giving up work for good; Carers or family members; After treatment; Organizations; and References. Details of what each section covers are also included in the table.

Cancerbackup has also produced a publication entitled, *Cancer and Working Guidelines for Employers, HR and Line Managers* [42]. These guidelines were a result of a collaborative effort between Cancerbackup, the Chartered Institute of Personnel and Development (CIPD), United Kingdom's leading professional body for those involved in the management and development and training of personnel, and Working with Cancer (WwC) group, a group started in 1985 by four women who recently had cancer with a mission of providing information to employers about how they should work with employees affected by cancer, as well as providing advice for employees. The guidelines outline what is considered best practices at this point in time recommending ways to manage the continuum of needs that survivors face at various times in the treatment and recovery process. However, while very thoughtful, these programs have not yet been evaluated to establish them as evidence-based practices. The guidelines can be accessed at the following website: http://www.cipd.co.uk/.

The guidelines were the outgrowth of results of a survey conducted by the authors of the guidelines. The *Working with Cancer Survey* [43] was conducted to examine how work environments were managing individuals with cancer. Conducted in May and June of 2006, 219 organizations responded to the online survey. Respondents ranged from organizations with less than 250 employees to six with more than 10,000 employees, reaching manufacturing and production, the private sector (e.g., finance, media, and transport), voluntary, and community and not-for-profit organizations. The CIPD found that 73% of employers did not have a formal policy in place to manage employees with cancer, and less than half of the organizations surveyed made sure that key staff had a working understanding of cancer and how having cancer may impact the work place. Less than 50% of the organizations in the survey volunteered that they provide support to their employees who are affected by cancer, and that, despite 80% of employers having heard that the DDA includes cancer in their classifications of disabilities, the CIPD was very concerned that 20% of employers had not understood the extension in coverage (with the majority of those lacking awareness being in the manufacturing and production organizations). In fact, they found that more than 40% of those surveyed stated that their organization provided no information or support for their colleagues with cancer. However, if they did provide information and support, employees most wanted the information in PDF files, printed materials, and CDs, in that order, over website downloads, information sent via the company intranet or via the Internet in general. Whereas it is important to understand some of the issues related to the program, the above observations reported on the CIPD program document the problems, but what is needed is an outcome study on the program itself. Again, if the effectiveness of the program is demonstrated, it would provide support how the use of the guidelines might support evidence-based practice.

One of the salient features of the *Cancer and Working Guidelines for Employers, HR and Line Managers* is the Cancer Policy Template that is provided within their document that they encourage employers to adapt to their particular organization, as well as, being useful for employees to use in working with their employers to create policies to support transitions that the survivor may go through, and how they relate to the work environment so as to accommodate needs at those transition points [43]. The policy template structure is presented in Fig. 13.2. The guidelines elaborate on each section to help organizations

Introduction	• what the policy is and about and who is covered by it • why the company has such a policy—its commitment to the employees
Employee Diagnosed with Cancer	
1. Scope of the policy	• who is covered
2. On diagnosis	• outline of company private medical care scheme (as applicable in your organization) • telling your line manager and HR • telling your work colleagues and clients • payment of salary during sickness absence • counseling and support (as applicable in your organization) • planning how and where this will take place • time off during work for treatment
3. Working during treatment	
4. Time off during treatment	• extended period of absence • staying in touch
5. After treatment	• extended period of absence • staying in touch
6. Disability caused by cancer	• impact on return to work • reasonable adjustments to work schedule and place
7. Giving up work	• whether early retirement is an options
8. Unfair treatment	
Careers or Family Members Affected by Cancer	
1. Scope of the policy	• who is covered
2. On diagnosis	• outline of company private medical care scheme (as applicable in your organization) • telling your line manager and HR
3. Impact on work	• family and parental leave

Fig. 13.2 Cancer policy template
Source: CIPD. *Cancer and Working Guidelines for Employers, HR and Line Managers*. London: CIPT Publishing, 2006. Reprinted with permission from CIPD Publishing.

create a policy that is indicative of the goals and missions of an individual organization. The template focuses organizations to create policy around prominent time points and key areas that need to be addressed from diagnoses to return to work, and even the need to consider retiring or leaving work: On diagnosis; Working during treatment; Time off during treatment; After treatment; Disability caused by cancer; Giving up work; and Unfair treatment. Each section contains bullet points to guide employers in their thinking about what each policy section should address. At this point, as with other elements, there has been no formal evaluation of this template. It is important to recognize that the template has only been in use for just nearly a year.

Danish Cancer Society

Denmark has also created a handbook entitled, *When an Employee Develops Cancer*. The booklet was first published in 2002. This handbook covers nearly the same areas as those identified in the CIPD publication in the UK. The foreward of the handbook attests to the need for such a publication in Denmark today, and would pertain to many countries around the world. The foreward states the following:

> An employee gets cancer: it may happen in any business. Every year over 11,000 Danes of working age develop cancer. Nowadays, many are cured and many live a long time with their illness.
>
> Over the past few years, the Danish Cancer Society has received an increasing number of enquiries from managers, colleagues and cancer patients experiencing problems at work during or after the illness. These enquiries show a great deal of uncertainty about how the problems can best be tackled.
>
> Typical examples would be that managers and colleagues take too little account of the situation of the person who is sick, or that on the other hand, they worry too much about it, so that the sick person is isolated both at work and socially. Another problem may be the difficulty of making the necessary changes in the work tasks of a sick employee who wants to continue working during treatment. Or that a long absence from work followed by a period with reduced work capacity after treatment, means that the employee may lose contact with the labour market.
>
> With these points in mind, the Danish Cancer Society has carried out the project 'Cancer and Work' with financial support from the Social Affairs Ministry. The project has resulted in practical solutions to problems of dealing with workers who have cancer, taking into account both the individual resources of the cancer patient and the working conditions of the business in question.
>
> This handbook is based on our experience with this project, and has been written for managers and others with responsibility for human resources in workplaces in Denmark.
>
> In addition to offer practical solutions one of the aims has been to improve employers' knowledge of cancer and of the special situation of cancer patients in order to reduce the risk of their exclusion from the labour market [44].

The key chapters in the handbook are depicted in Fig. 13.3. The use of this handbook has not been tracked or evaluated, however, in 2007 it was translated into English facilitating a more wide spread use and is an important start.

The first few months
- The further course of the disease
- An early meeting
- If the employee is off sick throughout his illness
- If he is off sick for part of the time
- What can be done if the sick person's work is not good enough?

Going back to work
- A meeting before the employee returns to work
- Late effects
- If it is necessary to change the sick employee's jobs
- Keeping colleagues informed

Possible financial and practical support
- Support during the illness – when the patient is temporarily less fit for work
- Support after the illness – when the patient is permanently less fit for work
- Working together with the local authorities

Colleagues of cancer-sufferers
- Reactions among colleagues
- How colleagues behave towards their sick fellow worker
- Taking care of the sick employee's tasks
- Useful information for the colleagues of someone with cancer

A personnel policy on serious illness
- How do you draw up a personnel policy on serious illness?
- Three case studies of employees with cancer
- An example of personnel policy on serious illness

Fig. 13.3 *When an employee develops cancer*, danish cancer society handbook Original summary of Olgod J., Engelbrekt P. *When an Employee Develops Cancer*, Danish Cancer Society, 2002.

United Kingdom's Breast Cancer Care (BCC)

Breast Cancer Care (BCC) [45], UK's foremost provider of information, practical assistance, and emotional support for anyone who has been impacted by breast cancer through a helpline, peer support, and other direct services, launched a campaign around employment and breast cancer in May 2008. Breast Cancer Care recognizes that despite the DDA and the legal protections it brings for cancer survivors in the work place, many survivors are not aware of what they are entitled to under this new law, likewise, many employers are also unaware and unknowingly discriminate against both current employees as well as job applicants. Breast Cancer Care is concerned as this lack of awareness on both sides may lead to breast cancer survivors not being able to maintain employment. Thus, they have been conducting a survey to facilitate the development of a policy briefing, charter, charter booklet and website that form part of their EMPLOY Charter campaign. This charter uses each letter of the word EMPLOY to provide best practice guidance on how employers can support members of staff who have had a diagnosis of breast cancer. The charter also points out the legal employment rights of people with cancer and employers' corresponding responsibilities under disability discrimination law in the UK.

Cancer Council Australia

Australia has a program similar to the BCC's that is administered through Cancer Council Australia (CCA) [46], the leading national non-government cancer organization. It draws its members from both state and territory cancer councils to collaborate on cancer research, prevention, and control, and to provide a variety of information for all individuals who are affected by cancer. They also work as a fund raising organization to support themselves. The CCA developed a workshop and manual entitled: *Working with Cancer* [47]. The publication was a joint effort between the CCA, employers, and individuals who had been diagnosed with cancer. The manual can be downloaded from their website (http://www.cancer.org.au/cancersmartlifestyle/workingwithcancer.htm) and is designed for use by any size of company, providing case studies, handouts, and workshop materials to facilitate return to work. Topics include: Supporting Patients and Carers in the Workplace; Talking to Workmates about Cancer; Developing Supportive Policies; Employer Responsibilities; Helping Everyone Cope with Cancer at Work; and Balancing Company and Individual Needs.

Working with Cancer was developed to support employees dealing with cancer, their managers, and employers by: (1) Increasing awareness, knowledge and understanding of cancer; (2) Correcting myths and misconceptions about cancer; (3) Helping employees empathize with those living with cancer or caring for a person living with cancer; (4) Improving attitudes and reducing stigma; (5) Increasing knowledge of appropriate behavior and management practices around cancer; and (6) Increasing the willingness to engage and assist people to access appropriate help [47]. The curriculum for the program includes the materials necessary for running the program, the PowerPoint© slides for the program, and case studies and other information to be shared with attendees. The program is also available in a downloadable version for web-based instruction.

The manuals for the program are laid out to assist both individuals with cancer as well as trainers and employers. The authors of the manual direct individuals (survivors and co-workers) to sections titled *In Short* to help point readers to the most pertinent information, referring the readers to electronic resources and references and providing the contact information for The Cancer Council Hotline for more immediate questions. [The Cancer Council is national non-government cancer organization (NGO) comprised of state and territory cancer councils throughout Australia.] The workshop materials are provided free of charge.

The Cancer Council has conducted a brief preliminary program evaluation of the participants who attended a training session for Working with Cancer. The presenters had 10 individuals in their session. Overall, the participants reported agreement ($n=3$) or strong agreement ($n=5$) with gaining an overall basic understanding of Working with Cancer. Overall, participants agreed (n = 5) or strongly agreed (n = 3) that the overall presentation of the session was satisfactory. Anecdotal comments reflected that the participants liked the interactive nature of the training and found that case studies helped to aid discussion. This was the first evaluation and the program will be conducting further evaluations to refine the process. At this point, no specific outcomes study is planned on the effect of the program on organizations, but the Cancer Council may want to consider such an option as they gain more experience in presenting the material and as employers apply the information to their individual organizations.

Canada

Willow Breast Cancer Support Canada

Willow Breast Cancer Support Canada (http://www.willow.org/), established in 1996, after the UICC (the International Union Against Cancer) held their first annual Reach to Recovery International Breast Cancer Support Conference, is a breast cancer support agency that is currently funded predominantly with private funds (i.e., donations), but they received 1/8 of their funding from the Ontario Ministry of Health.

Willow offers support to breast cancer survivors, their families, and more recently, employers helping to support return to work efforts for survivors. Their primary intervention is via a toll-free support call-in line that serves all of Canada. The call-in line is staffed by breast cancer survivors who are available to answer questions and to help callers negotiate the health care system. Their key program for helping breast cancer survivors return to work is called the Corporate Education Program (CEP). The goal of the CEP is to inform and raise the awareness of employers on work issues for those in treatment and/or returning to work following cancer treatment. The program, delivered as a "lunch and learn" presentation, is provided by a breast cancer survivor who is currently the president of their board. Topics covered include body image, changes in fatigue and stamina, effects of treatment, issues of fertility, and general awareness of the emotional journey a survivor may encounter and help the audience retool reactions to the survivor/employee based on their new learning from the CEP. They have presented nearly 24 sessions to date.

Materials supplementing their CEP suggest the notion that the survivor needs to design a *business plan* for how you manage your breast cancer and return to work. The materials offer guidance on how to speak with employers and colleagues, specifically offering ways to provide support while respecting the employee's right to privacy. The box (Fig. 13.4) below lists the helpful suggestions from Willow's *Working with Breast Cancer: A Guide for Employees and Employers Dealing with Breast Cancer in the Workplace* pamphlet. Although several of the tips on their pamphlet may seem common sense, the individuals who run the program report many employers and workers do need

Here is what you CAN do:

1. Be sympathetic. Think about how you would feel if you were told you had a life-threatening disease that was going to require surgery and/or prolonged treatment.

2. Listen to what your co-worker is saying how she is say it. Take your cues from her.

3. As if your co-worker would like you to tell others or would she prefer that you keep the matter confidential. Respect her wishes in this regard.

4. Offer support. There is no need for a grand gesture. Simply bringing a cup of tea to her desk shows that you care. If you know she is concerned about some work-related aspect of her life, you could offer to assist, but only if this is realistic and within the rules of the workplace.

5. Ask how you can help. Are there any tasks you could take on to make it easier for her, either immediately, or upon her return to work? If appropriate, make sure to clear this adjustment of responsibilities with your employer.

Fig. 13.4 Excerpt from working with breast cancer: a guide for employees and employers dealing with breast cancer in the workplace (Willow Breast Cancer Support and Resource Services) Source: Willow Breast Cancer Support Canada. Reprinted with the permission of Willow Breast Cancer Support Canada.

pointers on how best to interact with survivors. Currently there are no formal program evaluation efforts regarding the CEP, however, an informal evaluation caused Willow to shift their focus of the programs to train occupational nurses working in larger organizations, who, in turn, can carry the message back to people at various levels within their organizations.

Germany

As covered earlier in this chapter, the German pension fund finances inpatient and outpatient rehabilitation to enhance patient's functional capacities and health-related quality of life, with laws guaranteeing patients' access to these rehabilitation programs. One very specialized rehabilitation program called the "inpatient step-by-step rehabilitation program" [44] recognizes the value of a conventional inpatient rehabilitation program for breast cancer patients, but found that results of those programs did not persist. Therefore, Hartmann and her colleagues [44] created a pilot program that brought the patients back to inpatient rehabilitation for two additional one-week stays at four months and eight months after the conventional rehabilitation program. The step-by-step program resulted in greater improvement in cognitive function, emotional function, and quality of life over those who only participated in the conventional rehabilitation program. Currently, the researchers have plans to expand the step-by-step program to help prolong the efforts of step-wise reintegration. Furthermore, they would like to recommend a continuous outpatient "stabilizing program" that could follow patients for about six months after inpatient discharge. However, as with the other programs discussed in this chapter, these researchers also note that modifications and extension of services require much greater levels of communication between payers, the health care providers, and legislators. In this case of the stabilizing program, the researchers report that the costs would be covered by the German pension fund.

Internationally, countries have not yet become very active in pursuing research regarding programming for return to work and cancer survivors. Germany has and is using the strength of their government's support in funding an innovative gradual rehabilitation program that does have a research component to assess the effectiveness of the programming. This governmental support through a national health care program with supplemental funding to subsidize the employee's gradual return to work is not possible in many countries due to economic or policy constraints. Many countries have taken a different tact by providing educational programs to facilitate transition to work and to optimize work supports. Evaluation of these programs with an eye to outcomes, particularly regarding sustainability of the work effort would be critical. Furthermore, the evaluation of the policies that support the linkages to community resources and supports by country could shed light on how these linkages are made and maintained.

Future Directions

Although work, especially, return to work, work retention, and work optimization for cancer survivors are recent concerns, some strides have been made across the globe to accommodate the complex needs of these individuals. Much more work is needed given the rapidly increasing number of survivors, survivors who are both young and old and are surviving a variety of cancers—all with different issues and needs, and their increasing desire to return to work for a variety of financial and psychosocial reasons; targeted return to work programs need to be developed and evaluated.

A broader sweep needs to be spearheaded globally to address this important issue of facilitating and maintaining return to employment. The focus of the World Health Organization and the International Cancer Union has been rightly placed on prevention and treatment of cancers and at present both direct, very little attention on those who survive treatment, for return to work support. While prevention and treatment remain the most salient focus for these organizations, in many parts of both the developed and developing world, greater attention should be directed at least in those countries where people are surviving the diagnosis. Unfortunately though, little NGO support was found any where in working with cancer survivors at this point. The support is directed at those diagnosed with cancer and requiring treatment.

Some countries have developed important efforts to support return to work. As expected, in countries where the role of individuals with disabilities was more evolved and more clearly defined in terms of legislation for their rights and protections against discrimination, such as the UK and Canada, the greater opportunity there was that cancer survivors also found better defined roles and supports, with most cancer survivors being brought more explicitly into service and benefit coverage as would any individual with disability. Therefore, several nations are offering small specialty programs that help to bolster support for the survivor by educating the employer on his/her legal responsibilities, but also on the types of issues to expect to help ease accommodations for the survivor.

Despite the shifts in legislation in the European countries, attitudes seem to be slower to adjust and to accommodate. There has been a substantial amount of research examining attitudes and working with individuals with disabilities. Some of the issues in the disabled population, such as needs for accommodations and the irregular cycle of ability to work due to problems with fatigue, depression, need for medical care, and the need for support from and education of both the corporate employers as well as colleagues [48, 49] are also present in the cancer survivor population. There may be some opportunity for the transfer of learning between the two areas. There is a need to enhance employment outcomes through education of employee and employer, symptom management, organization climate change, and accommodations, but only a handful of programs exist to address these areas in a few countries with solidly conducted research. Although, Hartmann and colleagues [50] presented a well-designed randomized study, it was not specifically focused on return to work, even though it had implications for return to work. Much more work needs to be undertaken to establish additional programs that build on the notion of supporting the survivor and educating both the survivor and his/her employer and colleagues. Furthermore, there needs to be a systematic evaluation of the programs that are currently in existence to highlight areas that are working, and to attempt to adjust or modify the areas that are not quite as successful. The evaluation needs to include both the employer as well as the employee examining adjustment, transition, maintenance, and optimization of employment, and the needs and supports of colleagues to explore their awareness and understanding of the needs of cancer survivors to facilitate work for the survivors.

There is also a need for longitudinal studies to better understand the natural history at various points in their relationship with their work environment including the point of initial return, the early phases of returning with attention paid to work place responses to potential irregular work schedules, both supportive and not supportive, and at points after longer periods of time that address the issues of sustaining and optimizing the work experience. This includes studies to clear up some of the discrepancies and misperceptions in our understanding of how cancer survivors, employers, and coworkers are impacted by their return to and ongoing participation in the work force. Additionally, it would be important to address the role of universal healthcare coverage and the other supports offered by the various countries to understand the differential impact of these supports on cancer survivors and their employers, including the role of creative and flexible work schedules and environments. Germany has initiated step-wise reintegration to work [50], but such innovation might not be possible without the support of the German government that subsidizes the employees' salaries; the exploration of other ways to manage the economics of partial work for cancer survivors needs to be untaken to broaden this type of flexible work to other countries. Studies on the cost-effectiveness of this approach are also needed.

Given the WHO's current primary stance on prevention and detection of cancer and treatment of cancer, it seems that a greater role of NGOs should be explored to assist in work efforts of cancer survivors. The NGOs do play a role in prevention, detection, and treatment of cancer internationally [6]; therefore, there is precedence for a potential role in the work aspect through the partnering with private and public employers. This effort would need to be supported through enhanced use of work-related policies for cancer survivors, much the same as the CIPD has set forth and as was discussed earlier in this chapter.

Work is an essential component of life regardless of the environment in which it is carried out. For cancer survivors, as for individuals with disabilities, work can be made easier through planning, open communication, and the use of necessary accommodations and the establishment of work place policies to outline what to expect in terms of commitment from the employer. For others, paid work may not be what they chose to pursue. Whether the cancer survivor chooses to return to work or not, internationally there needs to be a greater emphasis placed on the role of the cancer survivor in work and work optimization to ensure these individuals are able to return to roles that bring them fulfillment, and where they are treated with respect and are free from discrimination.

While many countries around the world are creating educational materials and some specific interventions, it is important to monitor the social environment and workplace climate to maximize the outcomes of such processes and evaluate the cost effectiveness of many types of efforts. It's time for international occupational settings to be aware that individuals with cancer are surviving and are able to return to work, but they may need some supports to do that, but there needs to be a better understanding gained through well-designed studies to examine needs by type of cancer, by age of the survivor, as well as the type of employment to continue to highlight the needs of cancer survivors in the work place to devise work environments that can support the varying physical and emotional health needs of those surviving cancer.

References

1. Berrino F, Gatta G, Chessa E, Valente F, Capocaccia R. The EUROCARE II study. Eur J Cancer. 1998 Dec 1; 34(14):2139–53.
2. Pryce J, Munir F, Haslam C. Cancer survivorship and work: symptoms, supervisor response, co-worker disclosure and work adjustment. J Occup Rehabil. 2007 Mar; 17(1):83–92.
3. van der Wouden JC, Greaves-Otte JG, Greaves J, Kruyt PM, van Leeuwen O, van der Does E. Occupational reintegration of long-term cancer survivors. J Occup Med. 1992; 34:1084–9.
4. Bradley CJ, Bednarek HL. Employment patterns of long-term cancer survivors. Psychooncology. 2002 May–Jun; 11(3):188–98.
5. Bradley CJ, Bednarek HL, Neumark D. Breast cancer survival, work, and earnings. J Health Econ. 2002 Sep; 21(5):757–79.
6. Feuerstein M, ed. Handbook of Cancer Survivorship. New York: Springer 2006.
7. Arrossi S, Matos E, Zengarini N, Roth B, Sankaranayananan R, Parkin M. The socioeconomic impact of cervical cancer on patients and their families in Argentina, and its influence on radiotherapy compliance. Results from a cross-sectional study. Gynecol Oncol. 2007 May; 105(2):335–40.
8. Chen HM, Tan WH, Tan WC, Yu CK, Lim TH, Tay MH, et al. Attitudes toward cancer survivors: a small survey. Singapore Med J. 2006 Feb; 47(2):143–6.
9. Drolet M, Maunsell E, Mondor M, Brisson C, Brisson J, Masse B, et al. Work absence after breast cancer diagnosis: a population-based study. CMAJ. 2005 Sep 27; 173(7):765–71.
10. World Health Organization. International Classification of Functioning, Disability, and Health. Geneva: World Health Organization. 2001.
11. Citizens Advice Bureau. Advice guide. [cited 2008 February 21]; Available from: http://www.adviceguide.org.uk/
12. Prinz C, ed. European Disability Pension Policies. Brookfield, VT: Ashgate Publishing Company. 2003.
13. Micheli A, Coebergh JW, Mugno E, Massimiliani E, Sant M, Oberaigner W, et al. European health systems and cancer care. Ann Oncol. 2003; 14(Suppl 5):v41–60.
14. Current trends in disability pensions in Europe. Seminar; 2003 April 8, 2003; Helsinki, Finland: Finnish Centre for Pensions. 2003.
15. Office of Economic and Co-operation Development. New ways of addressing partial work capacity OECD thematic review on sickness, disability and work issues paper and progress report. 2007.
16. US General Accounting Office. SSA disability return to work strategies from other systems may improve federal programs. 1996:GAO/HEHS-96-133.
17. Bartsch J. What is the benefit of oncological rehabilitation programs for cancer patients in palliative care? Therapeutische Umschau. 2001; 58:453–8.
18. Lauzier S, Maunsell E, Drolet M, Coyle D, Hebert-Croteau N, Brisson J, et al. Wage losses in the year after breast cancer: extent and determinants among Canadian women. J Natl Cancer Inst. 2008 Mar 5; 100(5):321–32.
19. Ministry of Health and Long-Term care. Targeting cancer: An action plan for cancer prevention and detection (Cancer 2020). [cited 2008 March 11]; Available from: http://www.cancercare.on.ca/index_cancer2020.htm
20. Office of Economic and Co-operation Development. OECD Ecomonic Surveys: Denmark. 2006.
21. Ministry of Labour and Social Inclusion. Norwegian Social Insurance Scheme. [cited 2008 February 19]; Available from: http://regjeringen.no/
22. Johannesen TB, Langmark F, Wesenberg F, Lote K. Prevalence of Norwegian patients diagnosed with childhood cancer, their working ability and need of health insurance benefits. Acta Oncol. 2007; 46(1):60–6.

23. Economic and Development Review Committee. Policy brief: Economic survey of Norway, 2005. In: Office of Economic and Co-operation Development, ed. 2005.
24. Disability Rights Commission. A guide to the disability discrimination act for peole with HIV, cancer, and MS. 2006.
25. Canadian Human Rights Commisssion. Canadian Human Rights Act. [cited 2007 December 23]; Available from: http://laws.justice.gc.ca/en/ShowFullDoc/cs/h-6///en
26. Office of Public Sector Information. Disability Rights Act of 2005. [cited 2007 December 8]; Available from: http://www.opsi.gov.uk/acts/acts2005/ukpga_20050013_en_1
27. Maunsell E, Brisson C, Dubois L, Lauzier S, Fraser A. Work problems after breast cancer: an exploratory qualitative study. Psychooncology. 1999 Nov–Dec; 8(6):467–73.
28. Bouknight RR, Bradley CJ, Luo Z. Correlates of return to work for breast cancer survivors. J Clin Oncol. 2006; 24:345–53.
29. Taskila T, Lindbohm ML, Marikainen R, Lehto US, Hakanen J, Hietanen P. Cancer survivors' received and needed social support from their work place and the occupational health services. Support Care Cancer. 2006; 14:427–35.
30. Maunsell E, Drolet M, Brisson J, Brisson C, Masse B, Deschenes L. Work situation after breast cancer: Results from a population-based study. J Natl Cancer Inst. 2004; 96: 1813–22.
31. Anonymous. Attendance and absence. IRS Employment Review. 2006; 848:17.
32. Dein S. Explanatory models of and attitudes toward cancer in different cultures. Lancet Oncol. 2004 Feb; 5(2):119–24.
33. Tataryn M. Attitudes that don't work: Women with disabilities and employment. Women and Environments International Magazine. 2005; 21–4.
34. Dolgin MJ, Somer E, Buchvald E, Zaizov R. Quality of life in adult survivors of childhood cancer. Soc Work Health Care. 1999; 28(4):31–43.
35. Feuerstein M, Luff GM, Harrington CB, Olsen CH. Patterns of workplace disputes in cancer survivors: A population study of ADA claims. J Cancer Surviv. 2007; 1:185–92.
36. Abrahamsen AF, Loge JH, Hannisdal E, Holte H, Kvaloy S. Socio-medical situation for long-term survivors of Hodgkin's disease: a survey of 459 patients treated at one institution. Eur J Cancer. 1998 Nov; 34(12):1865–70.
37. Fobair P, Hoppe RT, Bloom J, Cox R, Varghese A, Spiegel D. Psychosocial problems among survivors of Hodgkin's disease. J Clin Oncol. 1986 May; 4(5):805–14.
38. Joly F, Henry-Amar M, Arveux P, Reman O, Tanguy A, Peny AM, et al. Late psychosocial sequelae in Hodgkin's disease survivors: a French population-based case-control study. J Clin Oncol. 1996 Sep; 14(9):2444–53.
39. Kornblith AB, Herndon JE, 2nd, Zuckerman E, Cella DF, Cherin E, Wolchok S, et al. Comparison of psychosocial adaptation of advanced stage Hodgkin's disease and acute leukemia survivors. Cancer and Leukemia Group B. Ann Oncol. 1998 Mar; 9(3): 297–306.
40. van Tulder MW, Aaronson NK, Bruning PF. The quality of life of long-term survivors of Hodgkins disease. Ann Oncol. 1994 Feb; 5(2):153–8.
41. Clement-Jones V. Cancer and beyond: the formation of BACUP. Br Med J (Clin Res Ed). 1985 Oct 12; 291(6501):1021–3.
42. Cancerbackup, CIPD, Working with Cancer (WwC) group. Cancer and working guidelines for employers, HR and line managers. [cited 2007 November 12]; Available from: http://www.cipd.co.uk/
43. Chartered Institute of Personnel and Development. Working with cancer. [cited 2007 November 12]; Available from: http://www.cipd.co.uk/
44. Olgod J, Engelbrekt P. When an Employee Develops Cancer: Danish Cancer Survivor 2002.
45. Breast Cancer Care. [cited 2002 December 8]; Available from: http://www.breastcancer-care.org.uk//
46. The Cancer Care Council Australia. [cited 2007 December 8]; Available from: http://www.cancer.org.au/Home.htm

47. The Cancer Council Australia. Working with Cancer: A Workplace Resource for Leaders, Managers, Trainers and Employees: NSW: The Cancer Council Australia 2007.
48. Pransky G, Shaw W, McLellan R. Employer attitudes, training, and return-to-work outcomes: a pilot study. Assist Technol. 2001; 13(2):131–8.
49. Schur L, Kruse D, Blanck P. Corporate culture and the employment of persons with disabilities. Behav Sci Law. 2005; 23(1):3–20.
50. Hartmann U, Muche R, Reuss-Borst M. Effects of a step-by-step inpatient rehabilitation program on quality of life in breast cancer patients. A prospective randomized study. Onkologie. 2007 Apr; 30(4):177–82.

Section VI
Future Directions

Chapter 14
Future Research, Practice, and Policy

Michael Feuerstein

The financial burden of surviving cancer as it relates to work is a costly public health problem. Research described in Chapter 2, based on data from the US and a recent study from Norway [1], provides confirmation that the challenges related to cancer survivorship and work present an economic burden to society, one that has been rarely discussed. Although more countries must weigh in on the economic impact of cancer survivors as it relates to employment, there is no reason to assume the problem is specific to a few nations.

At the level of the individual cancer survivor, the impact can be major as well. Income can be significantly reduced following diagnosis and treatment [2]. Family members who worked in the past may no longer be employed because the demands of caregiving forced them to choose family over job. Survivors may no longer work because of functional limitations that preclude work or make it difficult to complete certain work tasks without necessary accommodations [3]. Three to four years post-diagnosis, some cancer survivors leave the workforce for reasons related to persistent cancer-related challenges at work [3] or employer and employee friction [4]. Loss of income has been reported [5] and despite some improvements in levels of distress, fatigue and cognitive limitations over time [6], these symptoms may continue to impact work and recovery of income to pre-cancer levels is never realized. Survivors may decide to pursue other opportunities besides work [7]. Since many cancer survivors are close to retirement age [8], surviving this life threatening illness motivates some to make the decision to leave the workforce earlier than anticipated. What about those who must work to support themselves and their family and/or maintain health benefits at least in the US? What do we know about them, their challenges, and options to remain at work and optimize their work abilities?

The authors of the various chapters provided a window into many of the issues facing cancer survivors. We have provided a perspective on work in

M. Feuerstein (✉)
Professor, Departments of Medical and Clinical Psychology, and Preventive Medicine and Biometrics, Uniformed Services University of the Health Sciences, Bethesda MD 20814-4799, USA
e-mail: mfeuerstein@usuhs.edu

cancer survivors that should help maximize function. We look at this problem as it can impact work outcomes (return to work, work retention, and work optimization), however, as each chapter highlighted, we have barely scratched the surface in terms of knowledge that truly informs practice and policy related to work. This disconnect between knowledge and practice can impact the day-to-day work lives and future ability of a number of cancer survivors to remain productive at and obtain satisfaction from work over the long term. It does not need to.

Recently, I was asked to review a case of a breast cancer survivor who experienced prolonged fatigue that interfered with her work productivity. Following her treatment which included surgery, radiation, and chemotherapy this survivor could not perform at the level her employer expected given her high level position. She was placed in a position that had no potential to generate the income she desperately needed for her family. Both fatigue and cognitive limitations influenced completing certain elements of her new position as well. Not receiving any accommodations or assistance for the symptoms she was experiencing her performance waxed and waned and she eventually lost her job, despite over 15 years of highly productive income generation. The employer's rationale was simply that those who are treated for breast cancer and are now "recovered" should not have any residual symptoms that are related to the treatment such as fatigue or cognitive limitations. The employee was three years post-diagnosis, no longer receiving any treatment for the cancer and, as such, should be back to "normal." Their position was that the fatigue she continued to experience was related to "stress at home she now experienced with her children and husband" and the memory problems were "simply related to age that we all experience".

A few years ago I read a newspaper article about a secretary at the National Cancer Institute in Bethesda, Maryland who had filed an ADA claim because her employer, a cancer researcher, fired her. The fatigue and organizational problems she experienced "reportedly" related to the cancer treatment contributed to problems in her ability to optimally complete her work [9]. We need to create new approaches to help cancer survivors maximize their abilities at work. However, we also must recognize the needs of employers as well. Employers are major stakeholders. In order to improve this situation for all, we must include employers in future research, practice, and policy.

Some Questions that Await Answers

What are some of the research areas we need to pursue in order to develop a sound evidence base that will help us optimize outcomes related to work in cancer survivors who desire or need to work but just find it to challenging? I will organize these gaps in knowledge using the topics addressed in this book. Areas that appear to be particularly important given the state of the literature to date are provided in a working list below.

As we think about a research agenda related to cancer survivorship and work it is important that we are sensitive to cultural differences both within and between countries and, as always, the "so what" and "why not" question for all of these suggestions need to be considered. The diversity perspective both across and within nations not only needs to be recognized and studied, but must be attended to when implementing specific health care, workplace intervention, and policy reform. It is also critical to recognize that there are many stakeholders when it comes to work: the cancer survivor, their family, health care providers, employers, coworkers, insurers of various types (private and public disability, long-term care insurers, private and public health insurance), unions (when applicable), and cancer organizations including generic and cancer specific groups.

I had the opportunity to finalize these topics after carefully considering the contributions of each chapter. Equally important, as someone who is a cancer survivor, I have a very personal interest in this effort. I have tried to be inclusive in my suggestions but I am certain I left out some area. If I have left out your interest area, please accept my apologies. On first principles I am assuming that those with this illness, even if they experience challenges that may impact work, who desire or need to work should have the right to do so. The other point I wish to make is that we currently do not know how to efficiently and effectively achieve such an outcome. We must move aggressively toward efforts to identify, eliminate, or mitigate barriers (i.e., health care system, individual workplace, worker function, psychosocial, system burden related, policy related, or lack of adherence to existing policies) that prevent us from achieving this goal.

The list presented below represents a cross section of issues related to work and cancer survivorship. Information generated from efforts to address these areas should help develop a more informed approach to this global public health problem.

Models of Work Disability

1. There is a need to develop cancer specific work disability models based on the natural history of work disability in various types of cancer survivors. We can learn from work available in other chronic illnesses.
2. Cancer survivor specific models should be as parsimonious as possible. These models should allow us to better understand the processes involved in specific work outcomes of interest and address the perspectives of multiple stakeholders.
3. We may need to consider separate models for return to work, work retention, and work optimization or for various types of cancer survivors with cancer specific challenges.

Optimal Work

1. What does optimization mean in the context of the cancer survivor or in relation to specific types of work?
2. Should cancer survivors be expected to produce the same level of output as non-cancer workers?
3. If so, how best can it be measured?
4. If so, how best can it be achieved from an individual medically oriented approach, public health approach, or combination of the two?
5. How can we integrate approaches in 3 and 4?
6. How can we integrate research and practice from human factors as well as information and methodologies from research in other chronic illnesses and work such as musculoskeletal disorders, where there is a long history of such research?

The Economic Burden

1. What other economic information can we capture? For example, what is the added economic burden related to various types of residual symptoms?
2. What about economic burden on caregivers?
3. What are the economic costs (i.e., health care, indemnity, productivity) of medical co-morbidities and measurable changes in residual function in relation to work?
4. Can we measure the economic impact of job stress that can be triggered by friction at work (caused either by an inability to complete work efficiently or the economic impact of strained relationships with supervisors and/or coworkers)?
5. Is it possible to develop dynamic models of long term patterns of the economic burden of work disability among different types of cancer survivors, types of pre-cancer employment history, and types of work?

Employer's and Survivor's Perspectives

1. How do cancer survivors and their employers really address cancer, return to work, and work retention both following the first occurrence and recurrence?
2. What about perspectives from other stakeholders such as family, insurance companies, and labor unions?
3. What do employees and employers perceive as specific, persistent barriers to work retention?
4. What can both employers and employees do to facilitate work retention over the long term?

14 Future Research, Practice, and Policy

5. What about employees with co-morbid health problems? What do they indicate as being their problems or challenges? Do they differ from those who have cancer without such comorbidities?

The Meaning of Work in Cancer Survivors

1. How can we better understand the significance of work in the lives of cancer survivors?
2. What does well-conceived and controlled research, in addition to anecdotal observation, tell us are the psychological and social benefits that cancer survivors receive from work?
3. How might work be related to physical health and adjustment during long-term survivorship?
4. Can we efficiently and effectively address the meaning of work in our large-scale interventions?

Fatigue, Pain, and Functional Impairment

1. What are the specific mechanisms that relate symptom burden to work outcomes? Are there biobehavioral mechanisms that impact long-term fatigue, stress, cognitive limitations, and work?
2. What is the link between fatigue and/or pain and optimization of work tasks in cancer survivors? Is fatigue at work influenced by central and/or peripheral processes in cancer survivors? Can we impact this with pharmacological and non-pharmacological approaches? What role does depression play?
3. There needs to be valid and reliable measures of function for use with various cancer survivors in order to predict residual physical ability and the ability to perform certain work tasks.
4. What are the limitations in actual physical capabilities associated with certain cancers and treatment exposures? Can we create a taxonomy of limitations and relate them to work outcomes?
5. Can research in human factors and ergonomics better inform us how to design work for cancer survivors? Can it help us develop innovative and effective return to work and work optimization strategies?
6. What measurement strategies do we need to develop (or adapt) from human factors and ergonomics for research on work, rehabilitation, and occupational health to validly and reliably evaluate residual function and predict ability to perform certain work tasks over time?

Cognitive Limitations

1. What is the impact of specific residual cognitive impairments, however subtle, on work task completion, efficiency, and/or productivity?

2. Are there differences, either qualitative or quantitative, across different types of cancers, exposure histories, and time from end of primary treatments that contribute to variation in cognitive function and its relationship to work?
3. Can we develop cost effective and survivor efficient ways to reduce the impact of these cognitive limitations related to the work?
4. Can we develop more sensitive and efficient measures of cognitive deficits related to work?
5. Can we develop pharmacological aids that are less susceptible to side effects and/or more cognitive deficit specific?

Survivors of Childhood Cancer

1. How can we develop programs that effectively include survivors of childhood cancer in the competitive workforce?
2. Are there certain jobs that are less sensitive to some of the residual challenges experienced by this group of survivors?
3. In the U.S. and when available in other countries, can we utilize the vocational rehabilitation services that exist at the state and federal levels to mobilize efforts to help this group?
4. What can we learn by studying this group to develop effective job accommodations once at work and over the long term?

Primary and Occupational Health Care

1. What approaches do we need to take to facilitate greater attention by providers health system wide to work and cancer survivorship?
2. Can we apply what has been developed for occupational physicians to other primary care providers and oncologists who are willing to address this aspect of adaptation during and following treatment?
3. What specific steps do providers need to take to really provide assistance in regard to return to work and work retention?
4. What research needs to be done to better understand the relationship between symptom burden, late effects, recurrence, and work?

Work–Related Rehabilitation

1. There is a need to determine cost effective approaches to facilitate work reentry post-cancer diagnosis and post-treatment.
2. We need to evaluate the use of public supported vocational rehabilitation services including career counseling for cancer survivors, especially high risk cases.

3. What are effective components of rehabilitation for return to work and more importantly work retention in cancer survivors?
4. We need to determine what type of health professionals can provide what type of services to cancer survivors in order to achieve specific outcomes.
5. How can cancer survivors increase awareness of these options in number 4 and how best to access these services?

Workplace Accommodations

1. There is a need to identify specific work accommodations for well-defined work limitations in specific types of cancer.
2. What evidence-based strategies are practical, unobtrusive, and inexpensive that address the concerns of both workers and employers?
3. There is a need for the development and testing of new approaches for accommodation that take advantage at evolving technologies.

International Activities

1. We need to document that return to work and work retention is a challenge for many countries across the globe despite varying social security nets and the impact on the world economy.
2. There is a need to share approaches or specific programs developed across the world so we do not waste resources of money, talent, and time re-creating programs. Global knowledge transfer is very manageable and such transfer could be facilitated by a central repository, perhaps linked with a journal managed by a major journal publisher.
3. Create an international collaboratory on cancer survivorship and work to facilitate innovative research, program development, and evaluation around the world. This group of researchers, clinicians, employers, cancer survivors, and policymakers can communicate and meet regularly over the Internet using an effective collaborative system available for such an activity.
4. Utilize knowledge about cancer survivorship at work within various social systems to educate us as to what are some country specific problems and solutions and place these in a more global perspective. As our world economy continues to evolve this will become an even greater concern.

Legal, Regulatory, and Policy Matters

1. There is a need for system changes to better comply with the spirit of existing laws, potentially through more consistent training of human relations staff.
2. We need to rework laws developed to address disabled workers that will truly include current challenges that cancer survivors and others with chronic

illness face. New efforts to facilitate appropriate recognition that certain employees with work-related disabilities fall within the protected class. There is a need for better documentation processes, protections, and surveillance for cancer survivors at work.
3. There is a need for improved corporate/employer/employee cooperation as it relates to retention, insurance, promotion or raises among cancer survivors at work.
4. Innovative policies should be created recognizing the nature of work now and in the future and what is needed to facilitate employment of cancer survivors in such future work.

Evidence-Based Policy

While some research gets translated into practical solutions, the problems related to cancer survivorship and work can't be solved in the clinic alone. This requires many stakeholders and steadfast attention. Most of us are familiar with the concept of evidence-based medicine [10] and how, in principle, it can impact practice, improve outcomes, and reduce variability in care. While adherence to these types of guidelines vary [11] despite major efforts to facilitate implementation [12], they do influence the fundamental practices related to treatment. What about research that informs our approaches to problems outside the clinic?

How Is Evidence Translated into Policy?

There have been several descriptions of evidence-based policy [13]. The cancer-related problem most widely considered in the context of policy is cancer screening. Dobrow et al. [14] provide information on an evidence-based policy making process that was based on interviews of expert group members and investigation of documents generated during meetings where policy was actually created related to cancer screening. Since cancer screening can be a contentious public health concern because of various stakeholders and certain options with very different health and economic implications, this example is similar in many ways to work and cancer survivorship where different stakeholders with varying concerns are involved. Dobrow was able to modify an original model of this process [15]. The revision of his original model is presented in Fig. 14.1.

The revised model indicates the need to specifically define all policy objectives rather than simply provide an overall goal. There is also an explicit need to identify different sources and types of evidence that need to be considered in order to achieve each of the specific objectives specified. It is important to highlight that scientific data is not the only "evidence" considered throughout the process. More specifically, as the objectives of policy development shift

14 Future Research, Practice, and Policy

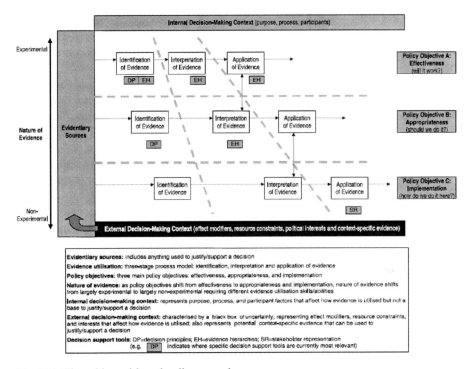

Fig. 14.1 The evidenced-based policy procedure
Note. From "The impact of context on evidence utilization: a framework for expert groups developing health policy recommendations," by Dobrow, Goel, Lemieux-Charles & Black, 2006, *Social Science & Medicine*, 63, p. 1821. Adapted with permission.

from "effectiveness" to "appropriateness" to actual "implementation," the type of evidence used to make decisions change from experimental to non-experimental. It is crucial that one recognizes that the level of evidence that is brought into this process will vary and that different forms of evidence are more or less prominent at different levels of development. The scientist who stays "close" to the data and the advocate who is zealously committed to "change regardless of the data or cost" throughout policy development need to recognize that policy development is a process that involves consideration of diverse types of information.

The model proposes that the evidence-based policy process explicitly consider three major policy objectives (effectiveness, appropriateness, and implementation) in the context of three major decision support tools (decision principles, evidence hierarchies, and stakeholder representation). This 3 x 3 matrix can help identify and define major elements of the policy process and the types of proof that should be considered when developing responsive evidence-based policy.

The potential utility of such a framework for structuring policy related to work among cancer survivors is illustrated in the example below. Let's take the problem of vocational re-entry or initial employment in young cancer survivors (either childhood cancer survivors or survivors of cancer diagnosed in young adulthood). The difficulty young adult cancer survivors experience finding paid employment is clearly a problem. Let us go through the process and see if it helps structure this problem in a way that can facilitate action.

Let us first consider policy objective A – determining the "effectiveness" of the assumption that unemployment in young adult cancer survivors represents a prevalent and significant problem for this group of cancer survivors. There are data that inform us that at a population health level, educated young adult cancer survivors are unemployed and find jobs at a lower rate than their non-cancer counterparts [16]. We also know from longitudinal studies that young cancer survivors experience residual cognitive limitations associated with the disease and treatment [17]. These cognitive limitations may help explain some of the unemployment. Qualitative studies also inform us that these cancer survivors desire work but often run up against problems when trying to return to work [7] and many of them lack vocational or career goals [18].

In relation to policy objective B – "appropriateness", many stakeholder groups and reports of young survivors inform us that survivors remain relatively healthy for years, desire to work, and want to begin families but need some help achieving these goals. These observations further justify the need to go forward with some type of policy to address this problem. Evidence from a population-based study using national data on vocational services informs us that, young cancer survivors who use vocational services offered at the state level are more likely to be employed than those who do not use these services [18]. It looks as though efforts to assist are needed and current practices seem to help

Objective C – "implementation" represents the final step in this process. Discussion and debate related to actual implementation raises the need for very specific cost data on the burden to society because if policy proposes expanding simple vocational services to young adult cancer survivors there needs to be some cost justification. These additional services have a dollar value. These data can be brought back into the discussion. Also concerns from employers are raised in terms of expectation for lower productivity and the rise in cost of the company's health insurance and impact on the company's bottom line. The economic and social costs of providing such services would then be debated by key stakeholders including potential funding sources, employers, insurers, survivors, and related advocates. Based on public opinion, a decision to go forward with a specific policy or not is made. As scientists, it is important that we remember this process does not consider scientific "data" in a societal vacuum. The process is typically lengthy, complex, and contentious. The process depends upon resources and the "appetite for change" in relation to other social or health priorities at the time. The model illustrated below depicts the key elements and specific processes involved in such evidence-based policy development. Figure 14.1 provides a helpful framework that the reader can refer to when considering policy development. It can remind us of the challenges we face in effectively addressing this problem.

An Interactive Process that Requires Patience and Persistence

While evidence based policy appears to involve a logical and stepwise process, in reality, specific research findings only rarely translate into specific heath services or governance policies in a linear fashion. Why? Black, a British health services researcher with many years of experience in studying the research to policy translation process, provided a very thoughtful discussion of the evidence based policy process and places it in perspective [19]. Black describes the effort as an "interactive process" where funding sources, researchers, and policymakers work in concert. All stakeholders are jointly involved in the conceptualization and conduct of research that can truly inform policy. However, he also discusses the need for a "policy community" [20] that includes: (1) government (to translate research into policy considerations), (2) stakeholders, (3) journalists (to educate and interest the public in the issues and proposed solutions), and (4) practitioners (to translate the new information into practice). Rather than simply having researchers create new information in the hopes that someday this research will be incorporated into policy, the approach of Black describes the need for policy concerns to be well articulated. This is very similar to Dobrow's emphasis [15]. Following this clear delineation of just what needs to be addressed, all parties then play an integrative role taking full advantage of "windows of opportunity" where the implications of research findings (from many sources, not simply one investigation) coincide with policymakers' values. This alignment is both rare and brief and stakeholders need to be prepared to "seize the moment." The need for those interested in policy change must always stay vigilant for these opportune times.

Conclusions

While many who survive cancer simply "go about their lives," there are some who experience problems at the individual level, the workplace or societal level, or some combination. For them, cancer impacts aspects of their lives that can have adverse effects on work. Cancer and its residual consequences tear at the very fabric of adjustment. Work is an important dimension of adaptation to this life threatening illness. As we have seen in this volume, work is often related to a survivor's well-being as well as an essential element of a productive, vibrant society [21]. It is prudent that we attend to the societal implications of work and cancer survivorship as it is also clear that this problem is associated with an economic burden on society. It is associated with major personal and financial loss when one is unable to work because of difficulty finding employment related to the illness or is restricted either because of symptoms or reactions by the workplace. This economic burden and personal loss creates a strain on the person and the "system." This strain will increase as the prevalence of cancer survivorship grows in our global population unless effective proactive action is initiated.

It is now more important than ever that our incentives for studying work and cancer survivorship are motivated by the need for effective approaches at both the primary and secondary prevention levels. Many individuals who survived cancer are your colleagues, co-workers, or family members. They wish to continue to be long-term contributors to our work communities. Those involved in revising existing policies or creating new ones need to consider the challenges discussed in this book. Those involved in evaluating existing policies and operations to enforce such efforts and/or in creating new interventions have your work cut out for you. This is no simple task.

Let us not forget that this is a global matter. Many are involved in research, practice, and policy related to cancer survivorship and work. We can learn form each other. The goals, financial incentives, and specific operations of various stakeholders need to be better aligned. The information presented in this book should facilitate a more serious international dialogue among the various stakeholders in order to achieve improved outcomes for all involved. Meaningful progress depends on this.

References

1. Syse A, Steinar T, Kravdal O. Cancer's impact on employment and earnings – A population-based study from Norway. Journal of Cancer Survivorship. 2008.
2. Chirikos TN, Russell-Jacobs A, Jacobsen PB. Functional impairment and the economic consequences of female breast cancer. Women Health. 2007;36(1): 1–20.
3. Short PF, Vasey JJ, Tunceli K. Employment pathways in a large cohort of adult cancer survivors. Cancer. 2005; 103(6): 1292–301.
4. Feuerstein M, Luff GM, Harrington CB, Olsen C. Pattern of workplace disputes in cancer survivors: A population study of ADA claims. Journal of Cancer Survivorship. 2007; 1(3):185–92.
5. Hoffman B. Cancer survivors at work: A generation of progress. CA: A Cancer Journal for Clinicians. 2005;55:271–80.
6. Bower JE. Behavioral symptoms in patients with breast cancer and survivors. Journal of Clinical Oncology. 2008; 26:768–777.
7. Main DS, Nowels CT, Cavender TA, Etschmaier M, Steiner JF. A qualitative study of work and work return in cancer survivors. Psychooncology. 2005;14:992–1004.
8. Edwards BK, Howe HL, Ries LA, Thun MJ, Rosenberg HM, Yancik R, et al. Annual report to the nation on the status of caner, 1973–1999, featuring implications of age and aging on U.S. cancer burden. Cancer. 2002; 94(10): 29766–2792.
9. Williams C. Cancer survivor in dispute with NCI in Bethesda. Bethesda Gazette. 2005 June 1, 2005.
10. Sackett DL, Rosenberg WMC, Gray JAM, Haynes RB, Richardson WS. Evidence based medicine: What it is and what it isn't. BMJ. 1996; 312:71–2.
11. Feuerstein M, Hartzell M, Rogers HL, Marcus SC. Evidence-based practice for acute low back pain in primary care: Primary outcomes and cost of care. Pain. 2006; 124:140–9.
12. Cretin S, Farley DO, Dolter KJ, Nicholas W. Evaluating an integrated approach to clinical quality improvement: Clinical guidelines, quality measurement, and supportive system design. Medical Care. 2001; 29:II70–II84.

13. Elliott H, Popay J. How are policy makers using evidence? Models of research utilization and local NHS policy Making. Journal of Epidemiology and Community Health. 2000; 54:461–8.
14. Dobrow MJ, Goel V, Lemieux-Charles L, Black NA. The impact of context on evidence utilization: A framework for expert groups developing health policy recommendations. Social Science and Medicine. 2006; 63:1811–24.
15. Dobrow MJ, Goel V, Upshur REG. Evidence based health policy: Context and utilization. Social Science and Medicine. 2004;58:207–17.
16. de Boer AG, Verbeek JH, van Dijk FJ. Adult survivors of childhood cancer and unemployment: A meta-analysis. Cancer. 2006;107:1–11.
17. Nathan P, Patel SK, Dilley K, Goldsby R, Harvey J, Jacobsen C, et al. Guidelines for identification of, advocacy for, and intervention in neurocognitive problems in survivors of childhood cancer. Archives of Pediatrics and Adolescent Medicine. 2007;161(8): 798–806.
18. Strauser D, Feuerstein M, Chan F, Arango J, da Silva Cardoso E, Chiu C. Vocational services associated with employment in young cancer survivors. Journal of Cancer Survivorship. 2008; 2(3):169–78.
19. Black N. Evidence based policy: Proceed with care. BMJ. 2001;323:275–9.
20. Detmer D. Clinician-managers: The "boundary spanners" of health services. Journal of Health Services Research and Policy. 2000;5:197–8.
21. Morin EM. The meaning of work in modern times. *10th World Congress on Human Resources Management*. Rio de Janeiro, Brazil 2004.

Index

A
Aaronson, N. K., 294
Abbruzzese, J. L., 149
Abenhaim, L., 94, 99
Abernethy, A. P., 213
Abraham, L., 148
Abrahamsen, A. F., 294
Activities of Daily Living (ADLs), 284
Adams, A., 215, 220, 222
Adde, M. A., 169
Adler, N. E., 256, 258–259
Adya, M., 271
Ahles, T. A., 115
Ahmed, F., 25
Akechi, T., 116
Albitar, M., 147
Alexander, B., 100, 183, 195
Alfano, C. M., 116
Alici Evcimen, Y., 158
Allan, S., 148, 151
al Majid, S., 220
Amado, N. L., 214
American Congress of Rehabilitation Medicine, 155
Americans with Disabilities Act of 1990 (ADA), 73, 233–237, 239–240, 255, 260–261, 272
Amir, Z., 82–86, 152, 195, 213
Anasetti, C., 151
Anderson, S. W., 149
Andrews, P. L., 125
Andries, F., 225
Andrykowski, M. A., 106, 116, 126, 212, 220
Ansink, A. C., 8, 10–11, 83, 110, 130–131, 181, 193, 199, 203, 213
Arango, J., 326
Armbruster, W., 99
Armstrong, K., 123, 126
Arnetz, B. B., 132

Arrossi, S., 280
Arveux, P., 294
Association of European Cancer Leagues (ECL), 295–297
Augustine, E., 129, 173
Autier, P., 4, 6
Avis, N. E., 213
Aylward, M., 215

B
Baanders, A. N., 225
Baas, P., 123, 127
Back Pain Limiting Activities, 95–96
Badell, I., 165
Bailey, M., 215
Baine, N., 213
Baker, B., 100, 183, 195
Baker, K. S., 123
Bakitas, M. A., 123, 127–128
Barenberg, P. D., 170
Baril, R., 95–96, 225
Barlow, W. E., 25
Barnett, R. C., 108
Barnett, V., 261
Barofsky, I., 213
Barrera, M., 175
Barsevick, A., 123–126, 212–213
Bartsch, J., 287
Baruch, G. K., 108
Batistie, L. C., 238
Battistutta, D., 123, 127, 129, 130, 220
Bauerfeind, I., 151
Beasley, R. D., 123–124
Beaton, D., 99
Beaty, B. L., 110
Beck, S. L., 123–126, 212–213
Beck, T., 151

Bednarek, H., 8–9, 19, 25, 69, 131, 152, 234, 258, 267, 280
Bell, G. J., 220
BeLue, R., 15, 83, 110, 267
Bender, C. M., 256
Bendz, I., 129
Benner, D., 132
Bennett, G., 125–127, 212
Bergeron, J. A., 170
Berglund, G., 126, 212
Bergquist, T. F., 154
Bernaards, C., 123, 125–126
Bernad, M., 129, 173
Bernard, T. E., 133, 138
Bernien, J., 99
Berrino, F., 279
Berthelette, D., 95–96
Beschenes, L., 25
Bhat, A., 128
Bhatia, S., 123
Bianchi, M., 169–171
Binns, M. A., 158
Biopsychosocial Models, 97–98
Bishop, C., 127, 130
Bishop, J. K., 127
Bishop, S. R., 213
Bjordal, K., 123, 126, 212
Blaauwbroek, R., 192
Blacklay, A., 176
Black, N., 324, 327
Blanck, P., 257, 260, 270, 271, 309
Blank, L., 131
Blasi, J., 257
Bleijenberg, G., 123, 125
Block, S., 115, 117
Bloomfield, D., 148, 151
Bloom, J., 294
Boake, C., 153–154
Bodegard, G., 111, 168–169, 176
Boeren, R. G., 96, 98
Bogduk, N., 96
Bolund, C., 126, 212
Boman, K. K., 111, 168–169, 176
Bombardier, C., 99
Boniol, M., 4, 6
Boogerd, W., 148
Booker, H. E., 132
Booth-Jones, M., 151
Borgatta, E. F., 8, 131, 138
Borgeraas, E., 10, 16
Bos, E. H., 132
Bos-Ransdorp, B., 19, 201

Bouknight, R., 10, 14, 18, 84, 131, 179–180, 198, 233, 258, 292
Bouma, M., 192
Bower, J., 123–125, 148, 318
Bowman, M. A., 123, 126
Boyle, P., 4, 6
Bradford, C. R., 127
Bradley, C., 7–9, 10, 12, 14, 15, 18, 19, 21, 25, 69, 48, 114, 124, 130, 131, 152, 179–180, 198, 233, 258, 267, 280, 292
Bradley, S., 153
Brain Cancer
  brain tumor progress review, 155
  and relative employment probability, 58
  surgery and, 197
  survivors of, 153
Brain Injury Interdisciplinary Special Interest Group (BI-ISIG), 155
Braithwaite, M., 215
Braun, I. M., 115
Bray, F., 4
Breast Cancer
  Breast Cancer Care (BCC), 304–305
  employment pattern, validity of, 50
  surgery and, 197
  survivors, 10, 194
    average sickness absence of, 12
    case of, 318
    employment outcomes, 50
  work and
    body strength and fatigue, 11
    education, 14
Breen, N., 268
Breitbart, W., 116, 125, 158
Brentnall, S., 155
Bretschneider, W., 171
Briand, C., 99
Brisson, C., 10, 18, 25, 85, 183, 192–193, 195, 196, 198, 213, 283, 291–292
Brisson, J., 10, 25, 192–193, 195, 198, 213, 283, 288, 292
British Study, 86–87
Brodwin, M., 235, 240, 244, 247
Bromberg, C., 165, 168
Brooker, A. S., 138
Brooks, J. J., 256, 258
Brown, D. J., 129
Brown, J. B., 191
Brown, M. L., 15, 25–26, 69, 130, 136
Brown, P., 151
Bruce, J., 123, 126, 212
Bruning, P. F., 294

Index

Bruyere, S., 233
Bubela, N., 125
Buchbinder, R., 98, 136
Bucher, B., 171
Buchvald, E., 169, 293
Buckwalter, A. E., 127, 130
Buick, D., 181
Buist, D. S., 25
Bureo, E., 165
Burton, A., 96, 212, 214, 221
Burton, W., 123–124, 126, 131
Butler, L. D., 116
Butler, R. J., 67
Butow, P., 82
Buzdar, A., 147
Byrne, J., 169–170, 171
Byrne, K. S., 147

C

Callan-Harris, S., 99
Calvio, L. C., 88, 130, 152, 153, 203, 250
Cameron, L. D., 181
Campbell, K. L., 218, 220
Campbell, L. C., 213
Canada Pension Plan (CPP), 289
Cancer, 282–283
    Cancer Council Australia (CCA), 305–306
    cancer-free age-matched individuals, 110
    Cancer Legal Resource Center (CLRC), 268–269
    Cancer Patients in Remission (CPRS), 282–283
    changes in employment trends for, 51
    cognitive behavioral approaches, 116
    cognitive work limitations and, 16
    consumer and family focus groups, 109
    cost of cancer-related productivity in colon cancer, 65, 67, 69–70
    duration's impact on employment rate, 53–54
    employees' rights, 271–272
    employment changes post diagnosis, 58–59
    and employment rates, impact of mortality and morbidity, 62
    factors influencing individual decisions to work after cancer diagnosis, 81
        demographic characteristics, 82
        financial circumstances, 82–83
        individual accomplishment, 83–84
        physical conditions, 83
    fatigue
        and depression, 197
        management, 12
    Federal protections for, 256–260
        Americans with Disabilities Act of 1990 (ADA), 260–261
        privacy and confidentiality, 262–263
    Finland survivors study, 18
    health care and social security, 193
    health status study of survivors diagnosed from less than two to more twenty years ago, 14–15
    individuals with, 255
        counseling and psychotherapy, 116
        personal and family experiences, 256–257
        person-related factors, 258–259
        treatment-related factors, 258
        work-related factors, 75–76, 257–258
    legal issues, 267
        ADA Amendments Act of 2008, 269–271
    metaphors and cultural meanings of, 106–108
    model programs and services, 268–269
    morbidity and employment, 26
        cancer types and, 58
        drop in employment, 61
        logistic regressions, 55–57
        post diagnosis, 58–59
        work limitations and anability, 58
    morbidity by years since diagnosis, 63
    National Health Interview Survey in USA, 15
    net fraction working, combining morality and morbidity trends, 64
    in Norway, survivors and employment rate, 16
    nurse experiences, 263
        qualified individual with, 264–265
        state sovereign immunity, 263–264
    occupational
        health physician, 191
        and primary care physicians, 196
    paid work, impact of
        American pioneers, 6–7
        studies, literature reviews of, 7–8
    pain, 126–127
    physical functions, 127–130
    productivity losses by types, 68–69
    psychiatric complications of, 115
    qualified individuals, employment discrimination, 265–267

Cancer (cont.)
  quality of life and work outcomes, 9–10
  registries for working status of patients, 7
  rehabilitation
    majority of, 288
    programs of, 289
    related fatigue, 125–126
    return to work, 202
      cancer site and, 10–11
      duration's impact on employment rate, 53–54
      educational attainment and occupational status, 12–14
      health status and extent of work limitations, 14–17
      multiple cancer types after one to five year follow-up, 198
      multivariate analyses after one to three years follow-up, 199
      occupational physician recommendation for, 201
      physician/health care provider role, 85–86
      psycho-social factors at work, 17–18
      qualitative study from United Kingdom, 18
      rate for survivors and, 10
      retirement from, 19–20
      returning to paid work after treatment, 84–85
      role of medical profession, 18–19
      supervisors and co-workers role, 18
      treatment and symptom, impact of, 11–12
  status
    demographic characteristics by, 27–32
    outcomes by, 34–49
  studies costs of, 25–26
  survivors
    cancer-related fatigue, 125–126
    changes in employment trends for, 51
    developmental stages of, 111–113
    factors associated with work ability, employment, and social support of, 101
    factors influencing individual decisions to work after, 81–84
    grip strength, 128–129
    items to assess for risk of unemployment in, 200
    pain syndrome, 126–127
    physical function and, 127–128
    quality of life, 110
    real world tasks, 156–157
    relationship with employer, 86–87
    study in Pennsylvania and Maryland, 15
    symptom burden in, 124–125
    work-related factors and employment outcomes, 131
    work trends and no cancer population, 60–61
  survivorship, 3–4
    average age of, 33
    employment outcomes, 33
    global incidence and mortality by gender, 5
    health interview survey, 52–53
    registry data across Europe and USA, 6
    scale of, 4
    situation in USA, 17
    and treatment-related impairments, 128
    and working guidelines for employers, 301–303
Cancerbackup (British Association of Cancer United Patients), 297–303
Cancer Survivors
  accommodation, 238–239
    case examples, 248–249
    primary considerations, 240–241
    request letter, 239–240
    secondary considerations, 241–242
  accommodation, workplace
    international collaboratory on, 323
    legal, regulatory, and, 323–324
  Alternative and Augmentative Communication (AAC) devices, 244–245
  attitudes of, 282–283
  childhood cancer of, 322
  cognitive limitations, 321–322
  compensatory and accommodative interventions
    targeting risk factors for, 222–224
    in workplace, 224–225
  cultural perceptions, 291–294
  disability nature of, 214–215
  disability programs and, 284–288
  discrimination, 291–292
  employer's perspectives and, 320–321
  evidence-based policy
    stakeholders and, 324–327
  future directions, 308–310
  future research, practice, and, 317–319
  legislation, 291

Index   335

optimization and economic burden, 320
perspectives, policies and, 279
physical and psychological symptoms
    of, 284
rehabilitation of, 211, 322–323
    exercise and, 218–221
    nature of, 216
    orientations, 217–218
residual symptoms and, 212–214
return to work
    factors contributing in, 280–284
    programs, 295–308
significance of work in, 321
work disability models of, 319
workplace accommodations, 233–238
    Activities of Daily living (ADLs), 247
    effective utilization of, 242–244
    limitations related
        ability to communicate, 244–245
        cognitive abilities, 245–246
        physical stamina and pain
            symptoms, 247
        stress and depression, 247–248
        vision, 245
world bank role of, 280
Cancer Vive, 281–282
    See also National Cancer Survivors
        Day®
Capocaccia, R., 279
Caraceni, A., 126, 212
Carayon, P., 137
Cardoso, E. d. S., 73
Cardous-Ubbink, M. C., 164
Carlsen, K., 20
Caroll, J. K., 158
Carosella, A., 99, 220
Carpenter, J. S., 126, 212
Carr, D., 115
Carroll, J. K., 125
Carter, A., 123
Carter, S. R., 171
Carver, C. S., 213
Cash, D. K., 174
Cashy, J., 125
Castellon, S., 148
Castillo, E. M., 128
Cavender, T., 7, 17–18, 21, 82, 84, 85, 110,
    123, 124, 183, 200–201, 225,
    227, 257–258, 318
Cecchi, F., 128
Cella, D., 125, 294
Cervical Cancer
    cross-sectional study of, 280–281

Chambers, W. A., 123, 126, 212
Champagne, F., 99
Chan, A. S., 158
Chan, A. T., 219
Chan, F., 73, 76, 80, 177, 245, 326
Chan, J. A., 219
Chan, J. H., 158
Chan, J. Y. C., 73, 177
Chaplin, J. M., 126, 212
Chaudhry, U., 129, 173
Cheing, G., 73
Chemo Brain, 115, 147
Chemo-Induced Peripheral Neuropathy, 128
Chen, E., 168–169
Chengalur, S. N., 133, 138
Cheng, C., 168
Cheng, T., 203
Chen, H. M., 281–283, 292–293
Chen, P., 271
Cherin, E., 294
Chessa, E., 279
Cheung, A. M., 203
Cheung, M., 158
Childhood Cancer, young survivors, 163
    blood cancers
        unemployment in, 168–169
    bone cancers, 170–171
    CNS and brain tumors, 169–170
    educational achievements and, 174–176
    Emma's Children's Hospital of
        Academic Medical Center
        (AMC), 177
    Hayashi's Late Effects Program at St. Louis
        Children's Hospital, 177
    interventions on employment, 176,
        178–180
    leukemia and Hodgkin's disease, 172
    long-term medical and psychological
        effects, 164
    model of illness representations, 180
    outcomes of employment and
        functioning at work, 181–182
    prognostic factors on employment,
        173–174
    program for adolescents with juvenile
        arthritis, 181
    survivor study, 172
    Swedish study on young adult
        survivors, 176
    Texas Children's Cancer Center in
        Houston, 177
    unemployment in, 165–166
        meta-analysis and, 166–168

Childhood Cancer (*cont.*)
    U.S. Childhood Cancer Survivor Study
        (CCSS), 163–164
    WHO model, 177–178
    Wilm's tumor, 171
    work importance of, 164–165
Chirikos, T. N., 318
Chiu, C., 326
Choi, K. S., 14
Chou, C., 124–125
Christensen, A. J., 127, 130
Chronic Illnesses, 131–132
Chronister, J. A., 73
Cicerone, K., 154, 156
Ciechanowski, P., 215
CINAHL Electronic Databases, 166
    See also Childhood Cancer, young
        survivors
Clarke, J., 132, 225
Clark, J. C., 195
Classen, C., 116
Clauser, S., 15, 25–26, 69, 130, 136
Clay, C. A., 123, 127, 129
Cleeland, C. S., 123, 125–126, 132, 212
Clement-Jones, V., 298
ClinPSYCH Electronic Databases, 166
    See also Childhood Cancer, young
        survivors
Clohisy, D. R., 170
Coderre, T. J., 96
Coebergh, J. W., 26, 163, 285, 288
Cognitive symptoms
    impact on work, 149–154
    management of, 154
    neuropsychological evaluation and,
        148–149
    non-pharmacologic strategies, 154–157
    pharmacologic management of, 157–158
    vitamin E, 158
Cohen, L., 176
Cokkinides, V., 25
Colditz, G. A., 219
Cole, D. C., 132, 138
Cole, M. P., 158
Cole, P. D., 178
Cole, S. W., 125
Collado-Hidalgo, A., 125
Colombet, M., 4, 6
Colon Cancer, average employment rate
        after diagnosis with, 67
Colorectal Cancer Survivors, 12
Conceptual Model and Work Disability, 132
Connelly, R. R., 169–170

Connis, R. T., 213
Conrad, C. A., 149
Consolidated Omnibus Budget
        Reconciliation Act of 1986
        (COBRA), 260–261
Cool, P., 171
Cooper, A., 157
Cooper, J. E., 191
Cordova, M. J., 126, 212
Corporate Education Program (CEP),
        306–307
Correll, J., 111, 173, 175
Cosmetic Executive Women
        Foundation, 268
Cote, P., 132
Cotter, I. M., 171
Courneya, K. S., 218, 219, 220
Coutu, M., 100
Cox, R., 294
Coyle, D., 288
Crandall, J., 158
Crane, P., 212
Craven, B., 200
Craven, J., 213
Cretin, S., 324
Crevenna, R., 123, 127–128
Crom, D. B., 174
Crossen, J. R., 149
Cruickshank, S., 147
Crusio, W. E., 158
Cruz, J., 200
Cubells, J., 165
Cull, A., 148
Cullen, K., 132, 225
Cunningham, L., 126, 212
Curt, G. A., 123–125, 129, 212

D

Dagher, C. R., 183
Dagher, R. K., 100, 195
Dahl, A. A., 10, 16, 127–128
Dahlberg, C., 154
Damasio, H., 149
D'Angio, G., 245
Danish Cancer Society, 303–304
Danjoux, C., 170
Dantzer, R., 125–126, 212
da Silva Cardoso, E., 326
Dasinger, L. K., 99, 225
Daveesa, S., 268
Davis, R. N., 153
Davis, W. W., 15, 25–26, 69, 130, 136

de Boer, A. G., 127–128, 165–167, 181, 199, 326
Debreczeni, R., 123, 128, 213
de Croon, E. M., 132
de Haan, R. J., 171
de Haes, H. C., 116
Dein, S., 292
Dekker, J., 225
DeLa Garza, D., 235, 240, 244, 247
Dell Orto, A. E., 108
DeLorenze, G. N., 8, 11, 131
Del Po, M. C., 167
Demand-Side Employment Models, 74
de Reijke, T., 8, 10–11, 83, 112, 130–131, 181, 193, 199, 203, 213
Deschenes, L., 10, 192–193, 195, 198, 213, 292
Desmond, K. A., 123, 125–126, 213
Detmer, D., 327
Deutsch, G., 148, 151
DeVine, D., 115
de Vries, J., 123, 127, 128
Dexmethylphenidate (d-MPH), 157
Deyo, R. A., 215
Dibble, S. L., 213
DiClemente, C. C., 97
Dideriksen, F., 20
Diefenbach, C., 126, 212
Dienemann, J. A., 219
Dietrich, J., 158
Di Iorio, D., 227
Dijkmans, B. A., 132
Dijkstra, P. U., 123, 128, 213
Diller, L., 213
Dilley, K., 326
Dima, F., 128
DiMiceli, S., 118
Dionne, C. E., 215
Dirks, S. J., 8, 131, 138
Disability Discrimination Act (DDA) of 1995, 291–292
Disability Rights Commission (DRC), 291–292
    cancer-related complaints, 293
Disability Rights Legal Center (DRLC), 268
Dixon, M., 111, 173, 175
Dobrow, M. J., 324
Dodd, M., 125, 129, 213
Dodier, F., 95
Dolgin, M. J., 169, 293
Dolsma, W. V., 123, 127
Dolter, K. J., 324
Donaghy, S., 156

Donovan, H. S., 153, 257
Dougherty, P. M., 125–126, 212
Doughty, A., 227
Dow, K. H., 126, 212, 219
Drolet, M., 10, 25, 192–193, 195, 198, 213, 283, 288, 292
Dubois, L., 18, 85, 183, 196, 291–292
Dudley, W. N., 123–126, 212–213
Duff, S., 203
Duivenvoorden, H. J., 116
Dunn, A. J., 125–126
Dupuis, M., 94, 95, 100
Durand, M., 95–96, 99, 100, 225
Durand, P., 94, 99
Dworkin, R. H., 126, 212
Dyer, D., 99

E
Earnest, C., 212
Ecological Case Management Models, 98–99
    See also Cancer
Edbril, S. D., 258
Edwards, A. G., 116
Edwards, B. K., 26, 318
Eiser, C., 164, 171, 175, 176
Elad, P., 176
Elliott, H., 324
Ellis, A., 171, 176
Ellis, C. J., 181
EMBASE Electronic Databases, 166
    See also Childhood Cancer, young survivors
Employers' Attitudes Regarding People with Chronic Illness and Disability, 75–76
    actions and, 86
    attitudes and actions, 86
    cancer survivors' relationship with, 86–87
    factors influencing individual decisions to work after cancer diagnosis, 81
    hiring and retention, 78
    productivity concerns, 77
    strategies, 78–81
Engelbrekt, P., 303, 307
Engel, G. L., 97
English, D. R., 219
Equal Employment Opportunity Commission (EEOC), 237–239
Erikcson, E., 111
Ervin, K. S., 256, 258
Esclamado, R. M., 127
Esdaile, J. M., 94, 99
Estey, E., 147

Estlander, A., 220
Etschmaier, M., 17–18, 82, 85, 110, 123,
    183, 200–201, 225, 227,
    257–258, 318
EUROCARE project, 279
European Monetary Union, 285–288
European Pain in Cancer (EPIC) Survey, 247
European Union Countries
    disability pension schemes, 288
    European Year of People with
        Disabilities, 285
Evans, J. J., 155
Evans, R. L., 213
Evans, S. E., 165
Exercise
    disease activity and, 219–220
    rehabilitation and, 218–219
    strength and function, 220
    training in occupational rehabilitation of
        cancer survivor, 220–221

F
Fagevik Olsen, M., 129
Fahy, J., 156
Fairclough, D. L., 110, 167
Fairey, A. S., 220
Falardeau, M., 225
Faleck, H., 157
Family and Medical Leave Act (FMLA),
    255, 259
    federal protections, 261–262
Fanciullo, G. J., 123–124
Farley, D. O., 324
Farley Short, P., 83, 267
Farrar, J. T., 123, 126
Fears, T. R., 170, 171
Felder-Puig, R., 169, 171
Feldman, F. L., 6, 10, 225
Feldman, F. R., 165
Felicetti, T., 154
Felsberger, C., 169
Ferlay, J., 4, 6
Ferrell, B. R., 126, 212, 256, 258
Ferrucci, L., 128
Fesko, S. L., 108–109
Feuer, E. J., 163
Feuerstein, M., 3, 17, 88, 95, 97, 99, 100,
    102, 130, 132, 136, 152, 153,
    167–168, 177, 203, 212, 213,
    215, 220, 234, 249–250, 255,
    280, 294, 310, 318, 324, 326
Fialka-Moser, V., 123, 127–128

Field, C. J., 220
Fiscella, K., 125
Fischer, E. G., 169–170
Fisch, M. J., 123–124
Fleischman, S., 157
Fleishman, S. B., 213
Fobair, P., 153, 294
Focalin, *see* Dexmethylphenidate (d-MPH)
Foley, K. M., 126, 212
Folstein, M. F., 148
Folstein, S. E., 148
Fordyce, W. E., 96
Forensic Model of Disability, 95
Formann, A. K., 171
Forman, S. J., 123
Fornander, T., 126, 198, 212
Fossa, S. D., 10, 16, 127–128
Fowler, K. E., 127, 130
Franche, R. L., 132, 225
Francisco, L., 123
Frank, J., 99, 132, 138, 225
Franklin, D. J., 211
Frazer, A., 18, 85, 196, 183, 291–292
Frazer, M. B., 132
Frederiksen, F., 20
Freedman, R. I., 108–109
French, D., 220
Friedenreich, C. M., 219, 220
Fried, L. P., 128
Friedman, D. L., 172–174
Frings-Dresen, M. H., 132
Funk, G. F., 127, 130
Funk, M., 99
Furukawa, T., 116

G
Gadner, H., 169
Gagnon, D., 95–96
Gajjar, A., 175
Ganz, P., 115, 123, 125–126, 148, 213
Garber, S. L., 220
Garssen, B., 116
Garwood, D., 149
Gatchel, R., 95, 97, 215, 220
Gatta, G., 279
Gattamaneni, H. R., 170
Gauthier, N., 100
Geenen, M. M., 164
Geertzen, J. H., 123, 127, 128
Geldsetzer, M., 258
Gelke, C. K., 149
Gerberich, S., 100, 183, 195
Gerber, L. H., 129, 173, 226

Index

Gerhardt, C. A., 111, 173, 175
German Pension Fund, 307–308
Gerstein, M., 108
Gervais, J., 225
Gheldof, E., 220
Ghilardi, J. R., 126, 212
Giampaoli, S., 128
Gibbs, I. C., 175, 180
Gielissen, M. F., 123, 125
Giese-Davis, J., 116
Giles, G. G., 219
Giovagnoli, A. R., 154
Giovannucci, E. L., 219
Girgis, A., 82
Given, B. A., 129, 257
Given, C. W., 129, 257
Glatstein, E., 149
Global Positioning System (GPS), 245
GLOBOCAN Series of International Agency for Research on Cancer, 4
Glomstein, A., 169
Glover, D. A., 165, 169
Glover, J., 213
Goel, V., 324
Goldberg, R., 132
Goldner, G. U., 132
Goldsby, R., 326
Goldwein, J. L., 245
Goldwein, J. W., 169–170
Gomez, P., 165
Goodman-Gruen, D., 128
Gordon, L. G., 220
Gordon, S., 218
Gosselin, L., 94, 99
Goudas, L., 115
Goulet, C., 100
Grabiak, B. R., 256
Graydon, J. E., 125
Gray, J. A. M., 324
Greaves, J., 258, 280
Greaves-Otte, J. G., 258, 280
Greenberg, D. B., 115
Greenberg, M., 170
Greenberg, P. E., 130
Greendale, G., 148
Green, D. M., 167, 169, 173
Greenfield, S., 19, 105
Greenspan, S. L., 123, 127, 129
Greenwald, H., 8, 131, 138, 213
Greider, W., 76
Griggs, J., 126, 212
Grimer, R. J., 171

Grimm, P. M., 219
Grizzard, W. R., 74
Groll, D. L., 126
Grond, S., 126, 212
Groopman, J. E., 125
Grootenhuis, M. A., 164, 171
Groothoff, J. W., 132
Grove, W., 149
Gudbergsson, S. B., 10, 16
Gulasekaram, P., 126, 212
Guo, M. D., 168–169
Guralnik, J. M., 128
Gurney, J. G., 124, 127, 174
Gutstein, H. B., 125
Guzman, J., 191

H
Haafkens, J., 201
Habutzel, N., 235
Hadar, N., 129
Haddy, T. B., 169
Hailey, S., 116
Haisfield-Wolfe, M. E., 219
Hakanen, J., 18, 84, 114, 206, 292
Hall, B., 167, 173
Halon, D. A., 215
Hamilton, R., 153
Handman, M., 220
Hankinson, S. E., 204
Hannisdal, E., 294
Han, R., 158
Hansen, J. A., 88, 130, 152, 153, 203, 250
Hao, Y., 4, 6
Harden, J. K., 256
Harila-Saari, A. H., 176
Harle, M. T., 124–125
Harrington, C. B., 17, 167–168, 234, 249–250, 255, 294, 318
Hartmann, U., 309
Hartzell, M., 324
Harvey, J., 326
Haslam, C., 18, 82–83, 85, 116, 125, 183, 193, 195, 202, 203, 212, 280
Hawkes, M., 214
Hayashi, R. J., 174
Hay, C., 148
Haydon, A. M., 219
Hayes, S., 123, 127, 129, 130
Haynes, R. B., 324
Hays, D. M., 164, 167, 169, 171, 174
Hazard, R., 98, 136
Head and Neck Quality of Life Pain Scale, 127
  See also Cancer

Health and Retirement Survey, 83
Health Insurance Portability and
    Accountability Act of 1996
    (HIPAA), 259–261
Heanue, M., 4, 6
Hebert-Croteau, N., 288
Heinen, R. C., 164
Hellebostad, M., 169
Hendricks, D. J., 260, 271
Henley, E., 227
Henrichs, M. H., 165
Henriques, J. A., 158
Henry-Amar, M., 294
Hermelink, K., 151
Herndon, J. E., 294
Herrmann, D., 126, 212
Heseltine, D., 219
Hewett, K. D., 167, 169, 171
Hewitt, M., 14, 19, 26, 69, 105, 124, 130, 148, 268
Hickey, P., 99
Hickok, J. T., 125
Hietanen, P., 10, 12, 16–19, 84, 114, 192, 196–197, 200, 206, 292
Hill, E., 260
Hill, J., 164, 171
Hirst, C., 129
Hladiuk, M., 128
Hobbs, M., 130
Hodgkin's Disease (HD), 294
Hoekstra, H. J., 123, 127
Hoekstra-Weebers, J., 125, 213, 220
Hoffman, B., 17, 131, 233, 267, 318
Hoffman, K., 129, 173
Hoffman, S., 200
Hogg-Johnson, S., 99, 132, 138
Hogg, M., 215
Holcombe, G., 213
Holen, A., 169
Hollis, D., 219
Holmes, M. D., 219
Holohan, C. J., 108
Holohan, C. K., 108
Holte, H., 294
Holzner, B., 125
Hoppe, R. T., 294
Horning, S. J., 125
Horowitz, M. E., 170
Hotopf, M., 117
Hou, P., 176
Howe, H. L., 25, 26, 318
Hoyer, S., 271
Hricik, A., 257

Hrywna, M., 116
Huang, G., 97, 99, 215
Huchcroft, S., 128
Hudes, M., 132
Hudson, M., 163, 164, 170, 174
Hulshof, C., 132, 193
Hyatt, R. H., 128

I
Ibrahim, S., 132
Iddenten, R., 82–83
Igual, L., 165
Ilmarinen, J., 100, 199
Instrumental Activities of Daily Living
    (IADLs), 284
International Agency for Research on
    Cancer (IARC), 279
International Classification of Functioning,
    Disability and Health (ICF),
    214–215
International Classification of Impairments,
    Disabilities and Handicaps
    (ICIDH), 214–215
Irvin, E., 132, 225
Irvine, D., 125
Irwin, M. R., 125
Itano, J., 256, 258
Itri, L. M., 125

J
Jablonowski, H., 126, 212
Jacobsen, C., 326
Jacobsen, P., 125, 151, 220, 318
Jacobs, S. R., 151
Jahansen, C., 20
Jahkola, A., 100, 199
Janss, A. J., 169–170
Janssen-Heijnen, M. L. G., 26
Jemal, A., 4, 6, 25, 233
Jenkin, D., 170
Jenkins, V., 148, 151
Jereb, B., 164, 169–170, 174
Jha, N., 220
Job Accommodation Network (JAN), 241
Johannesen, T. B., 173, 290
Johansson, H., 198
Johnson, L., 88, 130, 153, 203, 250
Johnsson, A., 198
Joly, F., 294
Jones, L. W., 220
Joshi, G., 158
Jung, B. F., 126, 212

Index

K

Kaasa, S., 123, 126, 212
Kaatsch, P., 163
Kadakia, R., 123, 126
Kaivanto, K., 220
Kalmar, K., 154
Kalso, E., 128
Kamen, B. A., 178
Kammeijer, M., 85, 100, 180, 203, 205–206
Kamps, W., 192
Kaplan, S., 176
Karjalainen, A., 10, 19
Karki, A., 213
Karnell, L. H., 127, 130
Kasl, S. V., 167
Katajarinne, L., 100, 199
Katon, W., 215
Katz, J., 96
Kawashima, T., 164
Kayl, A. E., 147, 155
Kazak, A. E., 171
Keefe, F. J., 213
Keller, R., 98, 136
Kelsen, D. P., 213
Kennedy, F., 18, 82–83, 85, 183, 193, 202
Kerrigan, A. J., 220
Kerr, L., 158
Kerr, M. S., 132
Kessler, R. C., 130
Keyser, C. P., 126, 212
Khokhar, J., 191
Kievit, J., 198
Kiltie, A. E., 170
Kim, E. J., 14
Kim, S. G., 14
Kingma, A., 175
Kleihues, P., 4
Kleinberg, L., 153
Kneipp, S., 154
Koch, U., 258
Kohli, S., 158
Kolenda, K. D., 99
Kole-Snijders, A. M., 96, 98
Kolstad, H. A., 195
Komaki, R., 147
Kondryn, H., 171
Koocher, G. P., 165
Koopman, C., 116, 213
Kornblith, A. B., 294
Korpan, M., 123, 127–128
Korstjens, I., 220
Kotsimbos, T., 215
Koul, O., 158
Krapcho, M., 163
Krause, N., 99, 132, 225
Kravdal, O., 58, 69, 318
Kreienberg, R., 151
Kremer, L. C., 164
Kricik, A., 153
Kritz-Silverstein, D., 128
Kroenke, C. H., 204
Krol, B., 132
Kruse, D., 257, 309
Kruty, P. M., 258
Kruyt, P. M., 280
Kubota, K., 126, 212
Kudelka, A. P., 149
Kumar, S., 137–138
Kvaloy, S., 294
Kyyrönen, P., 176

L

Lackner, J., 220
Laden, F., 204
Lahiri, S., 132
Lambert, M. T., 127, 130
Lamche, M., 169
Lam, C. S., 245
Lamdan, R. M., 116
Landis, L., 195
Landsverk, J., 167, 169, 171
Lane, M., 212
Langenbahn, D. M., 154
Langeveld, N. E., 164, 171
Langmark, F., 173, 290
Lankhorst, G. J., 132
Lannering, B., 170
Lanning, M., 176
Lapuerta, P., 128
Lashford, L. S., 170
Last, B. F., 164, 171
Late Effects Program, 177
Lau, J., 115
Laurent, D., 130
Lauzier, S., 18, 85, 183, 196, 288, 291–292
Lavery, M., 213
Lawrence, D., 115
Lawrence, W. F., 15, 25–26, 69, 130, 136
Law, S. C., 158
Learning Disabilities (LD), 246
LeBlanc, F. E., 94, 95, 100
Leedham, B., 213
Lee, H., 132
Lehmann, K. A., 126, 212

Lehto, U., 18, 84, 114, 206, 292
Leigh, S., 126, 212
Lemaire, J., 99
Lemaire, R., 95
Lemieux-Charles, L., 324
Lensing, S. Y., 174
Lenzi, R., 147, 153
Lepor, H., 198
Leung, W., 168
Levenstein, C., 132
Leventhal, H., 181
Levin, V. A., 157
Levitt, G., 179
Levy, M. E., 123, 129
Lewis, B. S., 215
Likert-Scaled Variables Measuring Health and General Mental State of Cancer Patients, 33
Lim, J. H., 14
Lim, M. K., 14
Lim, T. H., 281–283, 292–293
Limoges, J., 95
Lin, E. H., 215
Lindbohm, M., 12, 16–17, 18, 84, 114, 130, 153, 154, 183, 192, 196–197, 200, 206, 292
Lindsay, T. H., 126, 212
Linton, S. J., 215, 220, 225
Little, M., 106
Littlefield, C., 213
Liu, Y., 174
Lochner, C., 215
Loge, J. H., 294
Loisel, P., 94–96, 98–100, 136, 215, 225
Lombardo, E. R., 170
Long, C., 156
Lo Noce, C., 128
Lorber, L., 271
Lorig, K. R., 130
Lote, K., 173, 290
Love, S., 148
Lower, E., 157
Loy, B., 242
Lu, X., 257
Lucia, A., 212
Luctkar-Flude, M. F., 126
Ludman, E., 215
Luebke, A., 158
Luff, G. M., 17, 167–168, 234, 249–250, 255, 294, 318
Luger, N. M., 126, 212
Luker, K., 82–83–86, 152, 195, 213
Lundberg, A., 170

Luo, Z., 10, 14, 15, 18, 25, 69, 84, 130, 131, 179–180, 198, 233, 258, 292
Lutte, A., 222
Lux, M. P., 151
Luzzatto, L., 169–171
Ly, J., 126, 212

M
McCabe, M. S., 198, 206
McCarthy, D. O., 220
McCorkle, R., 8, 131, 138, 213
MacDonald, E., 131
McDonald, J., 67
McDonald, N. K., 170
Macedoni-Luksic, M., 164, 169–170, 174
McGovern, P., 100, 183, 195
McGrath, K. A., 181
McGraw, S., 213
McHugh, P. R., 148
MacInnis, R. J., 219
McKee, L., 171
Mackey, J. R., 220
Mackie, E., 171
Mackie, M., 148
Mackworth, N., 153
Maclean, R., 126, 131
McLellan, R., 225, 309
McMahon, B. T., 235
McMillan, D. C., 129
McNally, R., 171
McNeely, M. L., 220
McQuellon, R. P., 200
McQuestion, M., 203
MacVicar, M. G., 219
Maddrey, A. M., 170
Madsen, B., 169
Magnani, C., 169–171
Magrath, I. T., 169
Main, C., 96, 97, 212, 214, 221
Main, D., 7, 17–18, 21, 82, 84, 85, 110, 123, 124, 183, 200–201, 225, 227, 257–258, 318
Malec, J., 154, 156
Malkia, E., 213
Malkin, M. G., 154
Mallinson, T., 125
Malone, S. C., 220
Manning, D., 157
Mao, J. J., 123, 126
Marcus, S. C., 324
Marijnen, C. A., 198
Marikainen, R., 292

Mariotto, A., 163
Markkanen, P., 132
Marky, I., 170
Martikainen, R., 10, 12, 16–17, 18, 19, 84, 114, 192, 196–197, 200, 206
Maruff, P., 151
Mason, H. R., 10, 12
Masse, B., 10, 25, 192–193, 195, 198, 213, 283, 292
Masseling, H. G. M. B., 26
Massie, M. J., 213
Massimiliani, E., 285, 288
Mastekaasa, A., 123, 126, 212
Mateer, C. A., 155, 156
Matos, E., 280
Matteson, S., 125
Matthes-Martin, S., 169
Maunsell, E., 10, 18, 25, 175, 183, 192–193, 195, 196, 198, 213, 283, 288, 291–292
Maunsell, M., 85
Maurischat, C., 99
Maxwell, J. D., 128
Maxwell, M., 116
May, A. M., 220
Mayer, R. J., 219
Mayer-Proschel, M., 158
Meadows, A. T., 164, 165, 168–169, 171, 245
Meares, C. J., 219
Medline Electronic Databases, 166
    See also Childhood Cancer, young survivors
Meek, P. M., 213
Mehnert, A., 151
Meigs, J. W., 167
Meisel, R., 132
Melancon, C., 256, 258
Melbert, D., 163
Meller, I., 176
Melzack, R., 96
Mendoza, T. R., 124–125
Meneades, L. M., 130
Mental Health Disorders (MHDs), 95–96
Merbitz, C., 244–245
Merbitz, N., 244–245
Merskey, H., 96
Mertens, A. C., 164, 172–174
Methylphenidate Hydrochloride, 157
Meyboom-de Jong, B., 192
Meyerhardt, J. A., 219
Meyerowitz, B. E., 123, 125–126
Meyers, C., 125–126, 147–149, 151, 153–155, 157

Miaskowski, C., 129, 213
Micheli, A., 285, 288
Mickelson, K. D., 130
Miglioretti, D. L., 212
Mildner, A., 171
Miller, B. A., 163
Miller, E., 116
Miller, K., 173
Miller, M. E., 123, 127
Miller, V. I., 97, 99
Mills, J. L., 165, 169
Millward, L. J., 222
Milroy, R., 129
Mineur, Y., 158
Mini-Mental Status Examination (MMSE), 148
Minton, M., 117
Minton, O., 125
Miovic, M., 117
Mitby, P. A., 175, 180
Mittag, O., 99
Mock, V., 219
Modafinil Cancer-Related Fatigue, 157–158
Moe, P. J., 169
Mondor, M., 283
Moneta, G., 220
Monga, T. N., 220
Monga, U., 220
Mood, D. W., 256
Morales, J. L., 268–269
Moran, A., 82–83
Moran-Klimi, K., 116
Morin, E. M., 327
Morris, R., 148, 151
Morrison, A., 126, 131
Morrissey, M., 124–125
Morrow, G. R., 125, 158
Morton, D. J., 128
Morton, R. P., 126, 212
Mosso, M. L., 169–171
Mostow, E. N., 169–170
Muche, R., 309
Mugno, E., 285, 288
Muller, M., 148
Mulne, A. F., 170
Mulvihill, J. J., 167, 169–170
Munir, F., 18, 82–83, 85, 114, 125, 183, 193, 195, 202, 203, 212, 280
Murray, T., 4, 6
Murry, M., 76
Musculoskeletal Disorders (MSDs), 95–96
Mustian, K., 125, 158

Myers, M. H., 167
Myhill, W. N., 271

N
Nachemson, A., 94, 99
Nachreiner, N. M., 100, 183, 195
Nagarajan, R., 170
Nail, L. M., 213
Nanavati, K. A., 127
Nasir, S., 157
Nasopharyngeal Carcinoma Survivors, 158
Nathan, P., 326
National Brain Tumor Foundation (NBTF), 153, 242
National Cancer Institute and National Institute of Neurological Disorders and Stroke, 155
National Cancer Institute of Canada (NCIC) Leadership Fund, 290
National Cancer Survivors Day®, 281–282
National Council on Disability Report, 73
National Institute on Disability and Rehabilitation Research (NIDRR), 73–74
Neary, D., 83–86, 152, 195, 213
Needham, P., 155
Neglia, J. P., 170
Nelson, J. B., 123, 127, 129
Nerenz, D. R., 181
Ness, K. K., 123, 124, 127, 164, 174
Neubauer, N. A., 169
Neuhauser, F., 99, 225
Neumark, D., 15, 25, 69, 130, 280
Neuwalt, E. A., 149
Nevitt, M. C., 8, 131, 138
Newman, B., 123, 127, 129, 130
Nicholas, M. K., 225
Nicholas, W., 324
Nicholson, H. S., 165, 169, 170
Niedzwieki, D., 213, 219
Nieuwenhuijsen, K., 19, 201
Nijssen, T. F., 132
Nilstun, T., 193, 204
Noble, M., 158
Norcross, J. C., 97
Nordman, K. J., 99
Northouse, L. L., 256
Norway National Insurance Scheme, 290–291
Norwegian Disability Scheme, 290
Novakovic, B., 170
Novy, D., 126–127

Nowels, C., 17–18, 82, 85, 110, 123, 183, 200–201, 225, 227, 257–258, 318
Nystedt, M., 198

O
Oakes, J. M., 124, 127
Oaklander, A. L., 126, 212
Oberaigner, W., 285, 288
Oberst, K., 12, 130
Occupational Physician, 200
  fatigue and treatment-related symptoms, 203
  occupational cancer, 203–204
  occupational injuries and, 132
  quality indicators and, 205
  questionnaire regarding diseases, 205
  recommendation for return to work, 201–202
  supervisors and colleagues, 203
  work accommodations, 202
ODEP's Employer Assistance Recruiting Network (EARN) Group Studies, 74
Oeffinger, K. C., 164, 176, 198, 206
Oksbjerg-Dalton, S., 20
Okuyama, T., 116
Oldenburg, J., 127–128
O'Leary, T., 213
Olgod, J., 303, 307
Olsen, C., 17, 88, 130, 152, 167–168, 234, 249–250, 255, 294, 318
Olsson, E., 170
Olsson, M., 198
Onder, G., 128
O'Neill, M. J., 132
Onishi, J., 116
Orenstein, M. R., 219
Organization for Economic Cooperation and Development (OECD), 288
Ortega, J. J., 165
Ortiz, J. M., 97, 99
OSHROM Electronic Databases, 166
  See also Childhood Cancer, young survivors
Ostir, G. V., 128
Otter, R., 125, 213
Ovretveit, J., 193, 204

P
Packer, R. J., 169–170, 245
Page, A. E. K., 256, 258–259

Pain Syndrome, 126–127
    See also Cancer
Palmer, S. L., 175
Pang, J. W., 172–174
Papadatou, D., 111, 173
Papen-Daniel, M., 108
Park, A., 151
Park, J. G., 14
Parker, A. W., 129
Parker, R. M., 235, 240, 244, 247
Parkin, D. M., 4
Parkin, M., 280
Parks, R., 129, 173
Parliament, M., 220
Parry, D. M., 171
Passik, S. D., 213
Pastore, G., 169–171
Patel, S. K., 326
Patenaude, A. F., 167, 169, 171
Patterson, H., 153
Paul, S. M., 129
Pazdur, R., 149
Pendlebury, S., 82
Penninx, B. W., 128
Peny, A. M., 294
Perera, S., 123, 127, 129
Perez, M., 212
Perry, M. C., 270
Peteet, J. R., 123
Peteet, J. T., 113, 116
Peters, C., 126, 169, 212
Peters, G., 260
Peters, J., 131
Petersen, C., 151
Petersen, L., 148
Petrie, K. J., 181
Petronis, V. M., 213
Phillips, P., 169–170
Picavet, H. S., 220
Pickvance, S., 131
Piedmonte, M., 165, 168
Pirl, W., 115
Pisani, P., 4
Poce, A., 128
Pogany, L., 175
Poirier, P., 197
Poitras, S., 99
Popay, J., 324
Portenoy, R. K., 126, 212, 213
Postema, K., 125, 213
Postma, A., 175, 192
Postone, N., 116
Prados, M., 153

Pransky, G., 215, 220, 225, 309
Preissler, T., 158
Prinz, C., 285
Pritchard-Jones, K., 163
Prochaska, J. O., 97
Prochaska's Readiness for Change Model, 97–98
Progressive Goal Attainment Program (PGAP), 222
    components of, 223
    goal of demonstration, 224
Pronneke, R., 126, 212
Prostate Cancer Survivors, 12
Pryce, J., 18, 82–83, 85, 114, 125, 183, 193, 195, 203, 212, 280
PsycINFO Electronic Databases, 166
    See also Childhood Cancer, young survivors
Pui, C. H., 168
Pukkala, E., 10, 12, 19, 176, 192, 196–197, 200
Punyko, J. A., 174
Purvis, R. G., 222
Puskar, K. R., 256
Putter, H., 198

Q
Quebec Task Force Report, 94
Quinney, H. A., 220
Quittan, M., 123, 127–128

R
Radbruch, L., 126, 212
Radcliffe, J., 169–170
Radford, M., 165
Rai, S. N., 168, 174
Rammeloo, L. A., 175
Razenberg, P. P. A., 26
Recklitis, C., 213
Rectal Cancer Survivors Study, 198
Reddick, W. E., 175
Rehabilitation Interventions, 211
    cancer survivorship and, 216
    orientations, 217–218
Reid, R. D., 220
Reiker, P. P., 258
Reiriz, A. B., 158
Rekers-Mombarg, L., 175
Reman, O., 294
Rempel, D. M., 132
Reolon, G. K., 158
Reuss-Borst, M., 309

Rhabdomyosarcoma Survivors Study, 172
Rhodenizer, T., 222
Rhodes, R. E., 220
Rice, D. P., 214
Richardson, A., 117
Richardson, J. L., 10, 12
Richardson, W. S., 324
Riemens, L., 201
Ries, L. A., 25, 26, 163, 318
Rietman, J. S., 123, 127, 128, 213
Rijken, P. M., 225
Ritter, P. L., 130
Rivera, G. K., 168
Rivilis, I., 132
Robertson, M. M., 132, 225
Robinson, D. P., 123, 128
Robison, L. L., 124, 127, 163, 165, 168–169, 172–174, 175, 180
Rodgers, S. H., 133, 138
Rodin, G., 213
Roesler, R., 158
Rogers, H. L., 324
Ronis, D. L., 127, 130
Ronquillo, J., 88, 130, 153, 203, 250, 255, 260–261, 263
Ronson, A., 116
Rorke, L. B., 245
Rosado, J. O., 158
Roscoe, J., 125, 158
Rosenberg, H. M., 26, 318
Rosenberg, W. M. C., 324
Rosenthal, D. A., 73
Rosenzweig, M., 153
Ros, W. J. G., 220
Roth, B., 280
Rourke, S., 115
Rowland, J., 14, 26, 69, 116, 123, 125–126, 130, 148
Ruderman, E., 126, 131
Russell, G., 200
Russell-Jacobs, A., 318
Rutqvist, L. E., 126, 198, 212
Ryan, E. P., 125
Ryan, J. L., 125
Rydehn, B., 132

S
Sackett, D. L., 324
Sakai, Y., 158
Sallan, S. E., 167, 169, 171
Saltz, L. B., 219
Samant, D., 271

Sanchez, K. M., 10, 12
Sanderman, R., 125, 213
Sandlund, J. T., 168
Sandoval, R., 126–127
Sands, S., 213
San Francisco, CA, 193
Sankaranayananan, R., 280
Sankila, R., 176
Sant, M., 285, 288
Satariano, W. A., 8, 11, 131
Saunders, K., 212
Savard, A., 222
Sawney, P., 215
Sayers, E. J., 106
Schagen, S., 148
Schartz, H., 260, 271
Scheel, I., 98, 136
Schenk, M., 12, 15, 25, 69, 130
Scherer, M., 244–245
Schernhammer, E. S., 204
Scherwath, A., 151
Schirmer, L., 151
Schleimer, B., 151
Schmitter-Edgecombe, M., 156
Schnurr, B. E., 128
Schoonover, D., 167, 169, 171
Schouten, J. S., 220
Schultz, I. Z., 95, 97, 220
Schulz-Kindermann, F., 151
Schur, L., 257, 309
Schwartz, A. L., 213
Schwerin, B. U., 268–269
Scott, C. G., 220
Scott, N. W., 123, 126, 212
Scott, S., 128
Scott Baker, K., 174
Scrimger, R., 220
Scuffham, P., 220
Seedat, S., 215
Segal, R. J., 220
Seger, D., 25
Seikaly, H., 220
Seitzman, R. L., 165, 169
Sela, R. A., 220
Sellar, C. M., 218, 220
Sengers, M. J., 201
Servaes, P., 123, 125
Servitzoglou, M., 111, 173
Severin, C. N., 132
Shafranske, E. P., 116
Shannon, H., 99
Sharpe, M., 117
Shaw, A. K., 175

Shaw, W., 97, 99, 215, 225, 309
Shear, E. S., 181
Shelby, R., 116
Shelke, A. R., 125
Sherbrooke Model, 94
Sherwood, P. R., 153
Sherwood, P. S., 257
Shilling, V., 148, 151
Shillito, J., 169–170
Short, P., 6, 9, 14–15, 25–26, 58, 69, 110, 127, 130, 197, 233, 318
Siegel, C. H., 260
Siegel, J. E., 116
Siegel, R., 4, 6
Sikorskii, A., 129
Silver, J. K., 226
Simmonds, M., 126–127, 212
Simonen, R., 213
Simon, G., 212, 215
Sinclair, S., 99, 132, 225
Sisler, J. J., 191
Sjoden, P. O., 126, 212
Sjogren, B., 132
Skinner, R., 179
Sklar, C. A., 164
Sloan, P., 126, 212
Slova, D., 198
Sluiter, J. K., 132
Smikth, K. W., 213
Smith, J., 138
Smith, M. J., 137
Smith, R. B., 127, 130
Smith, R. G., 82
Smith, S. L., 256, 258
Smith, W. C., 123, 126, 212
Snider, M. A., 174
Sobel, D. S., 130
Sohlberg, M. M., 155, 156
Somer, E., 169, 293
Sontag, S., 107
Speechley, K. N., 175
Speigel, D., 116
Spelten, E., 6–8, 10–11, 83, 85, 100, 110, 130–131, 165, 180–181, 183, 193, 197, 199, 203, 205–206, 213, 257–258, 267
Sperry, L., 116
Spiegel, D., 213, 294
Spitzer, W. O., 94, 95, 99
Spolter, L., 259, 262
Sprangers, M., 7, 19, 85, 100, 110, 180, 183, 197, 201, 203, 205–206, 213, 257–258, 267

Stam, H., 164
Stanish, W., 215, 220, 222
Stanton, A. L., 116, 201
Steele, D. J., 181
Steinar, T., 318
Stein, D. J., 215
Steiner, F. A., 225, 227
Steiner, J., 7, 17–18, 21, 82, 84, 85, 110, 123, 124, 183, 200–201, 257–258, 318
Steliarova-Foucher, E., 163
Stensrud, R., 76
Stephen, S., 213
Step-Wise Reintegration Process, 289
Stevenson, C., 218, 220
Stewart, B. W., 4
Stewart, D. E., 203
Stewart, M., 148, 191
Stiller, C. A., 163
Stock, S., 99
Stokland, T., 169
Stone, P., 117, 125
Stovall, E., 19, 105
Stovall, M., 172–174
Stowell, A. W., 95, 97
Strauser, D., 73, 76, 80, 177, 326
Stubblefield, M. D., 148
Studts, J. L., 126, 212
Suissa, S., 94, 99
Sullivan, M., 215, 220, 222
Sultan, R., 158, 198
Sutton, L. N., 169–170
Swedborg, I., 128
Syse, A., 58, 69, 318

T
Tangpong, J., 158
Tanguy, A., 294
Tannock, I., 115, 158
Tan, W. C., 281–283, 292–293
Tan, W. H., 281–283, 292–293
Taplin, S. H., 25
Tarbell, N. J., 169–170
Taskila, T., 12, 16–17, 18, 84, 100, 114, 130, 153, 154, 183, 206, 292
Taskila-Abrandt, T., 10, 19, 192, 196–197, 200
Taskila-Brandt, T., 12
Tasmuth, T., 128
Tataryn, M., 293
Tay, M. H., 281–283, 292–293
Taylor, J. C., 127, 130
Taylor, K. L., 116
Taylor, V., 261

Tebbi, C. K., 165, 168
Temple, W., 128
Terracini, B., 169–171
Terrell, J. E., 127, 130
Tersak, J. M., 175, 180
Testicular Cancer Survivors, 194
Teta, M. J., 167
Thaler, H. T., 213
Theriault, R., 147, 153
Thewes, B., 82
Thibault, P., 222
Thiel, B., 198
Thomas, C. S., 95
Thomas, K. R., 245
Thompson, E. I., 167
Thompson, L., 125
Thornby, J., 220
Thors, C. L., 220
Thrush, R. A., 235, 241
Thun, M. J., 26, 318
Todorovski, L., 164, 169–170, 174
Touvell, v., 255
Tranel, D., 151
Tranmer, J. E., 126
Traumatic Brain Injuries (TBI), 246
Tretli, S., 58, 69
Tripp, D., 215, 220, 215, 222
Truesdell, S. C., 181
Tse, V. K., 158
Tsiantis, I., 111, 173
Tucker, M. A., 170
Tuinier, W., 192
Tulkki, A., 100, 199
Tunceli, K., 6, 9, 14–15, 25–26, 58, 69, 110, 127, 130, 197, 233, 318
Tuomi, K., 100
Tuomi, L., 199
Tzuh Tang, S., 213

U
Ubbink, M. C., 171
Uitterhoeve, A., 8, 10–11, 83, 110, 130–131, 181, 193, 199, 201, 203, 213
Uitterhoeve, L. L., 19
United Nations International Year of Disabled People, 285
United States Department of Labor's Office of Disability Employment Policy (ODEP), 74
Untch, M., 151
Upshur, R. E. G., 324
Upton, P., 175

V
Vaccarino, A. L., 96
Valente, F., 279
Valentine, A. D., 125, 157
Valerius, K. S., 111, 173, 175
Vallbona, C., 220
Vance, Y. H., 164
van Dam, F., 115, 148
vand der Lelie, J., 83
van den Bos, C., 164
van den Brink, M., 198
van den Hout, W. B., 198
van der Does, E., 258, 280
Vanderheiden, G., 139
van der Heijnen, L. H., 26
van der Lelie, J., 8, 10–11, 110, 130–131, 193, 203, 213
Van der Molen, H. F., 132
van der Pal, H. J., 164
van der Schans, C., 125, 213, 220
Van Der Star, A., 132
van der Wouden, J. C., 258, 280
van de Velde, C. J., 198
van Dijk, F., 127–128, 165–167, 202, 205, 326
van Eek, H., 96, 98
van Leeuwen, O., 258, 280
van Londen, G. J., 123, 129
Vannatta, K., 111, 173, 175
van Tulder, M., 98, 136, 294
van Weert, E., 125, 213, 220
Vardy, J., 115, 151, 158
Varekamp, I., 202
Varghese, A., 153, 294
Vargo, M. M., 148
Vasey, J., 6, 9, 14–15, 25–26, 58, 69, 83, 110, 127, 130, 197, 233, 267, 318
Vasilatou-Kosmidis, H., 111, 173
Velly, A., 222
Verbeek, J., 6–8, 10–11, 19, 83, 85, 100, 110, 127–128, 130–131, 165–167, 180–181, 183, 192, 193, 197, 199, 201–203, 205–206, 213, 257–258, 267, 326
Verhagen, S., 123, 125
Verma, S. K., 225
Vézina, N., 95–96
Vicious Cycle, 98
  See also Cancer
Vidmar, M., 132
Vincent, L., 125
Vink, P., 132
Virtanen, S. V., 12, 192, 196–197, 200
Visser, A. P., 116

Vlaeyen, J. W., 96, 98, 220
Vogelzang, N. J., 125
Von Korff, M., 212, 215
von Smitten, K., 128
vore, M., 158
Vos, P. J., 116
Voute, P. A., 171
Vrijhof, B. J., 192
Vythilingum, B., 215

W
Waddell, G., 96, 97, 212, 214, 215, 221
Wagner, J. M., 123, 127
Wagner, L., 151
Waite, H., 215
Wall, M. M., 124, 127
Wallace, W. H., 179
Wallgren, A., 128
Wallner, K., 153
Walsh, L., 82–83
Wang, P. S., 130
Wang, X. S., 124–125
Ward, E., 4, 6
Ward, L. C., 220
Warr, D., 213
Warren, C. G., 245
Wasserman, A. L., 167
Waterstone, M., 260
Wefel, J., 147, 148, 153, 155
Weinman, J., 181
Weis, J., 258
Weiss, R., 168–169
Weitzner, M. A., 157
Welch, K., 169–170
Wells, M., 200
Wells, R. P., 132
Wesenberg, F., 173, 290
Westerholm, P., 193, 204
Wexler, L. H., 170
Whelan, J., 156
Whiplash Syndrome, 95
White, P. H., 181
Whitelaw, M. N., 128
Whitmer, K., 213
Whitney, C., 171
Whitton, J. A., 172–174, 175, 180
Wilford, J., 131
Wilimas, J. A., 167
Williams, C., 319
Williams, W., 156
Willow Breast Cancer Support, 306–307
Wilson, B. A., 155

Wilson, J. W., 215
Windhager, R., 171
Wingard, D. L., 128
Winningham, M. L., 219
Winocur, G., 158
Winston, K. R., 169–170
Wolchok, S., 294
Wolf, G. T., 127
Wonacott, N. L., 108
Wong, F., 203
Wong, K., 151
Wood, P. M., 97, 99
Woodend, K., 126
Woolley, J. T., 260
Work
  cancer
    large-scale survey study to examine hiring managers' attitudes, 80
    mortality effect of, 26
    obstacles to returning to paid work, 84–85
    physician/health care provider input on matters related to work, 85–86
    risk factors by body part, 133–134
    sites and, 10
  compensatory and accommodative interventions in workplace, 224–225
  disability, 93–94
    Americans with Disabilities Act, 17
    arena in prevention, 98
    diseases and, 99
    low back pain, 99
    mental health disorders, 99
    models for, 97–99
    recent qualitative study, 99–100
    as specific paradigm, 95–97
    study of survivors in age range of 55–65 years old, 15
  disease-specific work problems, 115–116
  ergonomic and work system interventions, 139
  impact of cognitive symptoms on, 149–154
  medical professional and patients intervention study in the Netherlands, 19
  paid work
    employment rate of male survivors, 16
    impact of cancer on, 6–7
    methodological criteria for evaluation of impact of cancer on, 7–8

Work (cont.)
	practical work-related interventions, 8
	short-and long-term impact of cancer on, 8
	physician and fitness for dilemmas, 204–205
	problems and, 113–114
	psycho-social work-related factors, 17–18
	relationship of work system and work capacity, 137
	self-esteem and the self-concept, 108
	system interventions, 136–139
	work ability index, 100
	working age cancer survivors in Finland study, 19
	working with cancer survey, 301
	Working with Cancer (WwC) group, 301
Workplace
	accommodations in, 234–238
		ability to communicate, 244–245
		cancer survivors, 242–244
		cognitive abilities, 245–246
		limitations related to vision, 245–246
		pain symptoms, 247
		physical stamina, 247
		process, 238
		request letter, 239–240
		stress and depression, 247–248
	job accommodation ideas and technical assistance, 250–253
World Health Organisation's Disability Model for Cancer Survivors, 7
Wunderlich, G. S., 214
Wu, X., 25

X
Xie, S. X., 123, 126
Xu, J., 4, 6

Y
Yabroff, K. R., 15, 25–26, 69, 130, 136
Yagil, Y., 176
Yancik, R., 14, 26, 69, 130, 318
Yang, Y., 158
Yassi, A., 191
Yasui, Y., 170
Yelin, E. H., 131, 138
Yi, Q. L., 151
Yoshida, C. K., 25
Yu, C. K., 281–283, 292–293
Yuval, R., 215

Z
Zaizov, R., 169, 293
Zara, C., 213
Zebrack, B. J., 176
Zech, D., 126, 212
Zeldis, J., 157
Zeltzer, L. K., 168–169
Zengarini, N., 280
Zevon, M. A., 167, 169, 173, 175, 180
Zhang, J., 158
Zheng, L. X., 73, 177
Zuckerman, E., 294
Zwart, N., 192

CPSIA information can be obtained at www.ICGtesting.com
Printed in the USA
LVOW070303200412

278415LV00003B/14/P

9 781441 981554